SO-BIJ-710

APOSTLES
OF
CULTURE

APOSTLES
OF
CULTURE

The Public Librarian
and American Society, 1876–1920

Dee Garrison

THE FREE PRESS
A Division of Macmillan Publishing Co., Inc.
NEW YORK

Collier Macmillan Publishers
LONDON

59541

Copyright © 1979 by The Free Press
A Division of Macmillan Publishing Co., Inc.

All rights reserved. No part of this book may be reproduced or transmitted in any form
or by any means, electronic or mechanical, including photocopying, recording, or by any
information storage and retrieval system, without permission in writing from the Publisher.

The Free Press
A Division of Macmillan Publishing Co., Inc.
866 Third Avenue, New York, N.Y. 10022

Collier Macmillan Canada, Ltd.

Library of Congress Catalog Card Number: 78-66979

Printed in the United States of America

printing number

1 2 3 4 5 6 7 8 9 10

Library of Congress Cataloging in Publication Data

Garrison, Dee.
    Apostles of culture.

    Includes bibliographical references.
    1.   Public libraries--United States--History.
2.   Libraries and society--United States.   I.   Title.
Z731.G38   027.4'73   78-66979
ISBN 0-02-693850-2

027.473
G193a

59541

For Tray and Marty

59541

Contents

Part 4   The Tender Technicians

Acknowledgments

My COLLEAGUES AT Livingston College encourage scholarship by the supportive interest they take in each member's professional development. I am grateful to all of them, as well as to the Rutgers University history department as a whole, which provided a steady state of intellectual stimulation. The criticism of Phyllis Crew, Michael Gasster, Philip Greven, Gerald Grob, Mary Hartman, Norman Markowitz, William O'Neill, David Oshinsky, James Reed, and Richard Schlatter greatly improved the manuscript. Samuel Haber, Michael Harris, Daniel Howe, Alan Lawson, John Leggett, and Robert Wiebe gave generously to me of their time and knowledge. To those archivists and librarians who assisted me I owe the historian's eternal debt, with special thanks to the staff at the University of Illinois, Urbana, and Columbia University, New York City. This study was guided by the counsel and acumen of John P. Diggins. Financial aid to permit travel, research, and leave from teaching duties was provided by the Rutgers University Research Council.

Introduction

THIS ANALYSIS OF THE American public library system, during the crucial years of its formation from 1876 to 1920, has two related purposes. The first is to examine the origins, functions, and evolution of the public library as one of the institutions for urban reform designed to cope with the problems of an industrializing society. The second is to consider the relation of librarianship to the larger professionalization movement that transformed American society during this period. I am especially interested in librarianship as one of the emerging feminized service professions of the late nineteenth century. Prior to this study there has been no substantial historical analysis of the natural linkage in a sex-biased culture between protoprofessionalism and feminization.

My concern with library history derives in part from a widespread misconception. The development of the public library has generally been considered as evidence of the humanitarian and democratic ethos of American society and history. This uniquely American institution, established by liberal, idealistic, middle-class leaders, is thus viewed by some as the counterpart to the public school in bringing educational and economic opportunity to the common people. This first and oldest interpretation of library history might be described as the "progressive interpretation," with the public library being regarded as one aspect of the general movement for social reform and moral uplift in the late nineteenth century.

My research suggests that the progressive viewpoint is deficient for several reasons. First, and perhaps most important, those writing it lacked the benefit of the volume of material that has recently been published on the nature and achievement of American reform activity, research that makes the older categories of liberal and conservative more complex than we had once assumed. Moreover, the progressive interpretation failed to define accurately the social philosophy of those responsible for the establishment of the American public library system and of the library leaders who initially influenced its development. Even more seriously, the progressive analysis, for all its merits, was marred by an inadequate awareness of the effects on institutional development of sex, class, and generational conflict. The older interpretation of the development of the public library, while certainly valuable and not entirely false, suffers from the virtues of its own innocence. A simple story of democratic idealism does not reveal the complexities that give library history its real human dimensions.

To point out that problems associated with sex and class played a dominant part in the formation of the public library and the ideology of library leadership is not, hopefully, to suggest a conspiracy view of history. My analysis is not meant to negate the sincerity of democratic ideals and aspirations in the early library movement but rather to bring some balance to the story of public library development. My concern is to make clear the opposing arguments that support alternative views of library history and to discuss the partial validity of these formulations. Conflicting interpretations of library history are based upon a variety of considerations, among which there are four that have a particular importance.[1]

The first might be termed the multiple social forces argument. According to this view, well argued in the two classical works on library history by Jesse Shera and Sidney Ditzion, the intellectual origins of the public library in the United States were dependent upon several developments: the growth of sufficient community resources and a population dense enough to support a public library; the urge to conserve historical records; the existence of civic pride that led to rivalry among communities to establish themselves as cultural centers; the desire of workers for vocational instruction; and the influence of the Jacksonian period, which created a widespread belief in the value of universal education.[2] Certainly all these forces contributed to library development. The orthodox progressive interpretation, however, tends to deemphasize or ignore the patrician source of much of the library's activities and to greatly exaggerate the support given the public library by the working class. All studies indicate that library patrons were predominantly middle class and that library boards of trustees were overwhelmingly composed of wealthy, white, Protestant business and professional men. While it is true that a measure of altruism influenced library founders, other considerations, less noble but no less pronounced, were also uppermost in their minds. The behavior of library sponsors must be understood in its full historical context. One undeniable reality of that context was the precarious position in which members of the older gentry class found themselves as a result of growing labor unrest and mass discontent during this period. The formation of the public library was one response to that troubling situation. How its patrons conceived the potential uses of the library as a means of arresting lower-class alienation from traditional culture represents the neglected story of library history in America.

The second point of view recognizes that all institutions practice social control and that the upper-class orientation and administration of the public library should come as no surprise to anyone. It is the purpose of ruling elites, after all, to perpetuate their power by disseminating their own cultural values, and this is true even in political democracies. This point of view has the virtue of reminding us that there were no clear alternatives to the formation of the American public library as it took its shape and character historically. Given the lack of leisure and money among the masses of people, it is difficult to imagine any other group in America but a cultured elite establishing public libraries. Nor is it amazing that librarians—bookish, educated persons—reflected values consistent with their upper- and middle-class origins. Moreover, as neophyte professionals, it is understandable that librarians were eager to establish their authority within the province of literature. Nonetheless, if we are to overcome library mythology, it is important to consider that the building of public libraries was motivated by a fear of egalitarianism and upheaval from below as much as by a desire for democratic extension of education.

These considerations lead to the third point: There is considerable evidence to suggest that a significant segment of library leadership during this period held a favorable view of mass culture and welcomed the dissolution of Victorian morality. Librarians like John Dana led a successful attempt to democratize the electoral machinery of the American Library Association, fought against institutional paternalism, and challeged the genteel ethic. However, Dana, the leader of the library mavericks, was a sexual and religious radical who remained uncritical of the economic order. Despite occasional heresies, the liberal element within library leadership accepted and affirmed the middle-class service mission of the public library.

The fourth argument concerns the undeniable contribution made by the public library to a free society. The public library, in the period 1876–1920 under consideration here, was chiefly concerned with arresting change in literary and moral standards. Except during the brief period of World War I, it did not practice stringent censorship of political and economic ideas. Despite its conservative origins, the public library developed as a less intellectually restrictive institution than the public school. Because it was a marginal institution, the public library was able to establish a more flexible, less coercive attitude toward its users. Certainly use of the public library increased social mobility for a few and opened educational opportunity for many. That workingmen did not use the library in the numbers for which the elite had hoped cannot be attributed entirely to the sanitized, feminized, middle-class atmosphere within the library. Working-class reading was limited by the ten-to-twelve-hour workday and six-day week typical of this period. Many workers found alternative sources of literature in dime novels, newspapers, and material published by ethnic, labor, religious, or political organizations. We must not confuse the stated goals of library leadership with either the conservative latent function of the library or with the practical reality of library development.

The librarians whom I am considering looked forward as well as backward. They were simply men and women of their time, shaped by an educational and social background to respond in a similar way to the confusing industrialized world not of their making. With a cultural arrogance limited only by their moral sincerity, they upheld their mission to serve the masses who supposedly sought material and moral advancement through education. As social critics, they shared a faith in progress and looked forward to moderate reform as the answer to the country's problems. Their drive toward professionalism combined romantic ideas of reform, democratic principles, genteel liberalism, and the missionary impulse with their own frustrated desires for greater status and standing. The most prominent characteristic of their social thought is its ambivalence. They maintained conflicting desires — to elevate public thought and to meet public demand. It was not authoritarianism which dominated their thought. It was, rather, the tensions within their code — between the censorship and the consumership models of the library.

It was the elitist nature of public library leadership that interacted with the predominance of women in the profession to produce the "library hostess" of the late 1800s. And it is this respectable middle-class lady who does indeed demonstrate some of the stereotypical traits of that grim, prim, spinster librarian who has become a commonplace figure in American popular thought. The majority of early women librarians are best understood as true believers in that sexual ideology, essentially antifeminist in tone, which so thoroughly dominated public thought at the turn of the century. They were not seriously or openly critical of the belief that the goals and capacities of women were inherently limited in the working world. Their influence upon the library was not always favorable either to social reform or to access to diverse popular literature — or to the advancement of professionalization. A natural extension of the nineteenth-century library heritage was the self-image of the second and third generations of the library woman: the idealistic servant, the militant maid, the "modern librarian" of the Progressive period who "is more hostess than scholar, and [to whom] skill in social leadership is as necessary . . . as to the society queen. She welcomes men and women, boys and girls, all ages, all classes, under the library's hospitable roof."[3]

I am aware that the problems faced by these emerging women were not so different from those encountered by women professionals today. The ways in which they coped with their environment resemble some of my own responses

and were no doubt as unsatisfactory to them as they are to me. I have a sympathetic understanding of their choices. As Ann Douglas, a scholar committed to feminism, has noted in a similar vein:

> It is undeniable that the oppressed preserved, and were intended to preserve,
> crucial values threatened in the larger culture. . . . Nineteenth-century
> American women were oppressed and damaged; inevitably, the influence they ex-
> erted in turn on their society was not altogether beneficial. The cruelest aspect of
> the process of oppression is the logic by which it forces its objects to be oppressive
> in turn, to do the dirty work of their society in several senses.[4]

Still, the most striking point to be made about women's adaptation to
library work between 1876 and 1920 is the extent to which they supported the
traditional female concern for altruism and high-mindedness. They invoked
the Victorian definition of proper female endeavors at the same time as they
struggled to widen it. Librarianship, when defined as self-denying and
spiritual, offered women the opportunity not to change their status but to
confirm it, not to fulfill their self but to perpetuate their limited self-image.
When women's advance became justified in terms of the good they could do,
rather than of their human right to equality, it became conditional in
nature.

My analysis is based upon an examination of social ideals held by the
library leadership. These leaders were chosen because they headed large urban public libraries, were active in the American Library Association, or had
a major effect upon public library development. My primary sources are
published and unpublished statements by and about these men and women,
library reports, and printed library journals of the period. The articulate national leadership may or may not have expressed the sentiments or even the
problems of librarians in small towns or have influenced the hundreds of
librarians who had little contact with it. Library leaders were chiefly heads of
institutions in the East, and most were shaped by their New England
heritage. The prejudices of Boston may not have been typical of the country
as a whole. I am confident, however, that I have correctly represented the
social attitudes of the library leadership and have accurately traced some of
the effects of feminization upon the development of the library profession
during the period 1876–1920. The conclusions I draw are obviously confined
by the borders of my study. Certainly more research is needed upon the way
in which feminization and establishment ideals affected the library history of
small communities in the West and South. I am hopeful that the emphasis I
place upon the importance of social class and sex roles in public library
development will interest others in exploring the use of these models and in
testing these hypotheses.

A modified chronological approach has been selected for the presentation of this study. Part 1 presents a profile of the selected leaders and discusses the "missionary phase" of librarianship and the "gentry stage" of professionalism. Part 2 describes how the library's attempt to dilute the influence of "immoral" literature was slowly replaced by a less paternalistic approach. Part 3 discusses the psychological structure, amazing career, and profound influence of Melvil Dewey, who is representative of the "new professional." The final section, Part 4, assesses the impact of feminization upon the public library and the profession of librarianship; it also briefly deals with post-1920 library history and the development of libraries abroad.

In the development of the public library, as it was shaped into its distinct American profile, one can see how early library leaders were caught between the demand of their social ideals and the demand that public institutions serve social needs. As a group, public librarians were among the first educated Americans to feel deeply the tensions between the preindustrial past and modern society. Behind all their squabbles, their primness, their innovations and restorations, their stated and unstated hopes and fears, stand the ordinary men and women who sought to bring knowledge and recreation to the average citizen. Their story embodies all the paradoxes of America itself, its flawed realities and its high ideals, or, as Langston Hughes once phrased the contradiction, "the land that never was, but yet must be."

PART 1

The Missionary Phase

Such was the failure of my generation in respect to the time in which it was cast—a time of new and aggressive intellectual demands, of unfinished moral tasks, of widespread changes in the social order . . . it was not a time through which one could find his way clearly, either the way of knowledge or the way of duty. But it was from first to last, as I have said, a period of incentive and challenge. One felt all the while that he was living in the region of undiscovered truth. . . .[T]he times which I have described seem orderly and undisturbed; but when at last the true perspective of history is reached, I doubt not they will regain their natural place in the opening era of the modern world.

—William Jewett Tucker, *My Generation*

1

The Genteel Setting

THE AMERICAN LIBRARY ASSOCIATION was born on a warm October morning in 1876 at the centennial celebration in Philadelphia, in the heavily draped and book-lined rooms of the Historical Society. The commissioner of education had reported in 1870 that there were 209 librarians in the United States, with 99 of these in Massachusetts and New York. Therefore, the 103 persons present at Philadelphia who were interested in library development actually represented a significant portion of the whole. So pressing was the devotion of these library pioneers that they claimed to have neglected the wonders of the Centennial Exposition, for "no one desired to go . . . so long as this valuable opportunity to meet was before them, and so the conference drove, drove, drove for three days."[1] Having enjoyed this opportunity to excitedly exchange information and ideas, they were received on the last evening by the "other literary gentlemen and ladies of Philadelphia for informal social intercourse" and "an elegant collation."[2] The 90 men and 13 women who met in Philadelphia had created a lasting movement. When Justin Winsor, the first president of the ALA, died in 1897, the association claimed 434 members; when Melvil Dewey, the designer of the Dewey Decimal System, died in 1931, there were 3,225.

Perhaps accelerated by the communications revolution, attempts to organize the library profession were far in advance of the cohesive efforts of most occupational groups in the United States. The first convention of library enthusiasts had been held in 1853 in New York. This earlier meeting of 82 men had been instigated by publisher Charles B. Norton and dominated by the librarian at the Smithsonian Institution, Charles C. Jewett.

3

The participants seconded Jewett's plan to establish a national library and discussed the merits of a central printing agency to provide catalogues of library holdings. Neither of these hopes, nor a third plan to meet again the next year in Washington, was ever realized.

Between 1853 and 1876, despite the intervention of hard times and the Civil War, American libraries grew apace. Five hundred and fifty-one libraries had been formed between 1825 and 1850, while 2,040 were opened from 1850 to 1875. By 1876 there were 188 public libraries—free municipal institutions supported by general taxation—in eleven states, ranging from Massachusetts with 127 to Iowa and Texas with one each.

A summation of the knowledge and experience gained in libraries during the period since 1853 was issued by the U.S. Bureau of Education in preparation for the Centennial Exposition. The first bound copies of this report, weighing five pounds and listing all libraries in the nation holding more than 300 volumes, were carried to the librarians in Philadelphia by the editor himself, on the second day of the convention. Containing statistical compilations and expert advice on the major aspects of library science, this publication was to become an indispensable library manual for several years to come. Although the government report mainly addressed itself to the librarian's moral responsibilities, there was also much practical advice given regarding library construction and appliances, the mechanics of record keeping, and systems of indexing and cataloguing.

Perhaps no mechanical problem so perplexed the young profession as that of devising an efficient and usable catalogue. Since the public was not generally admitted to the shelves to examine the books directly, a detailed printed catalogue was necessary so that readers might direct the library attendant to the exact information they desired, with a minimum number of false starts. The advocates of this system of intervention between reader and book argued that open stacks in public libraries would not only lead to disorder and theft but would also encourage aimless reading. Accordingly, librarians spent much ink upon the elucidation of exhaustive systems of catalogue organization that attempted to list under a few references all the pertinent material on any topic—an increasingly impossible task as the volume of printed knowledge expanded. Cataloguing problems were hopelessly complicated by the then-current system of assigning each book a fixed location on the shelf, generally according to the date it was received by the library. Thus books on closely related subjects were widely separated in space, and fixed location of books made constant recataloguing and reclassifying necessary when new books were acquired. Before the library leaders in 1876 lay the major task of developing a system that would provide access to the sudden accumulation of printed material. By trial and error they were to slowly develop and standardize a library science and to publicize adequate index systems, central card catalogues, open shelves, periodical indexes, children's rooms, bibliographies, branch libraries, and special collections.

No man's mind was more fired in 1876 with visions of the library's destiny and mission than that of a recent graduate of Amherst College. Melvil Dewey was twenty-five years old when he entered the New York office of *Publishers Weekly* in 1875 and set into motion the organizational machinery that would create the American Library Association and a whole new sense of librarianship as a scientific, yet sacred, endeavor. Pushed along by Dewey's frenetic energy, the editor and the publisher of the book-trade journal appointed Dewey managing editor of the new *American Library Journal* and issued a call for a convention to the most prominent librarians in the country. After their initial suspicions about the real motives of young Dewey and the publishers were allayed, most of the major librarians gave their active support to a library conference to promote "efficiency and economy" and to "afford opportunity for mutual consultation and practical co-operation."[3]

Dewey, whose library experience was limited, was careful not to antagonize the older, more conservative library leaders. As unobtrusively as possible, he worked to mold the agenda of the 1876 convention. The papers presented led to animated discussions of the technical problems involved in library economy, cataloguing, indexing, and binding, as well as mutilation and theft of books. The most earnest remarks were brought out by the higher moral questions — the personal qualifications of a librarian and the value and selection of fiction.

Dewey deliberately took a back seat during the conference proceedings, ostensibly out of modest deference to the older chiefs but surely also because he felt ill at ease and insecure with male coworkers. In 1876 Dewey had not yet assembled around him his idolatrous corps of female lieutenants who would serve as the instruments to fulfill his dreams. Almost thirty years later his natural affinity for women would prove to be one of the causes of his retreat from the library world. But in 1876 he had made few enemies and was free to play the part of "frank, mirthful Dewey,"[4] youngest member of the convention, whose behind-the-scenes energy had brought them together, smoothed over small difficulties, and overcome the inertia of librarians more influential than himself.

Only after long coaxing would Dewey arise to describe the new method of classification he had applied to the Amherst Library. His solution to end library chaos was to divide printed knowledge into ten areas, subdivided into indefinitely more minute classes, expressed by means of arabic numerals. The Dewey Decimal System, which allowed for cooperative cataloguing ventures and provided the capability for indefinite, accurate growth, seemed amazingly useful. Probably many librarians agreed with Lloyd P. Smith of Philadelphia that the system devised by Dewey, and printed in the government report, was the most valuable idea they carried home from the convention of 1876. By 1927, 96 per cent of public libraries in the United States had adopted Dewey's classification; in a real way the esoteric knowledge it represented helped to bring solidarity to the newly emerging profession.

The most conspicuous among the library leaders at the conference was forty-five-year-old Justin Winsor from the Boston Public Library. Winsor's presence lent the greatest legitimacy and prestige to the convention. Peering soberly through his heavy eyeglasses, which periodically fell from his nose with a great deal of clatter, he was a gracious speaker, confident in his quiet good manners and proven scholarship. It was unthinkable that anyone but Winsor should preside or that anyone else should serve as the first president of the librarians' national association formed at Philadelphia. A year later he would become the librarian at Harvard, and from that post would continue for the next nine years as the president of the ALA. During that decade, as the national political and economic crisis deepened, the librarians' national leader was a perplexed but aloof observer in the haven at Cambridge.

When Winsor finally stepped down from the presidency in 1886, William Frederick Poole, the acknowledged elder statesman of the profession, followed him as a matter of course. Poole was fifty-five years old at the time of the meeting in Philadelphia. He had recently taken charge of the Chicago Public Library, hired at the grandiose salary of $4,000 a year. When Winsor moved to Harvard, Poole reigned as the chief public librarian of the country. Tall and commanding in appearance, with walrus-like side whiskers that reached past his collar, he was thoroughly at ease as a speaker.

Poole had originally distinguished himself as the librarian of the Boston Athenaeum, where he became well acquainted with the New England intelligentsia. Despite the innovative push he gave to indexing and to more functional library architecture, Poole was reluctant to give up old methods of administration and was usually suspicious of new ideas. In the years ahead, Poole would resist Dewey's attempts to standardize library practice. Both Poole and Winsor were urbane, ceremonial, and scholarly, sensitive to the proprieties and careful to observe them. As joint chieftains of the ALA in its formative years, they and their cautious gentility would have inevitable effects upon the profession as a whole.

In 1877, Charles Cutter, the librarian at the Boston Athenaeum who was to succeed Poole as ALA president in 1887, assured the readers of *The Nation* that the founders of the ALA were guided by moral, not bureaucratic goals.

> As soon as the friends of education, the believers in culture, the lovers of books can be made to feel that the Society [of the ALA] is not devoted to the dry details of management, but intends to take in hand the objects in which they are most interested, we fancy they will be ready to join and assist with purse and influence.[5]

Cutter's appeal was successful. Two years later such noteworthy representatives of genteel New England as Thomas Wentworth Higginson, James Freeman Clark, and Charles Francis Adams attended the yearly ALA conference and gave the newly organized profession their active support.

⋄ ⋄ ⋄

The professionalizaton process that librarians began in Philadelphia was part of a national movement toward occupational cohesion. Also meeting at Philadelphia in 1876 were societies of dentists, dairymen, photographers, and lawyers. The patterns of professionalization manifested themselves everywhere in the 1870s and 80s — in literature and journalism, in sports, in charity work and schoolteaching; among undertakers, spiritualists, and veterinarians; in the university and in business.[6] The American Association for the Advancement of Science, founded in 1848, spun off between 1876 and 1889 no less than eleven specialized national groupings, from chemists to mathematicians. This process was similar to the American Social Science Association's spawning of six professional associations between 1884 and 1889. By 1891, a plumber, speaking before the American Public Health Association, used metaphors that were coming to sound familiar: "Plumbing is no longer merely a trade. Its importance and value in relation to health, and its requirements regarding scientific knowledge, have elevated it to a profession."[7] Even the chore of housekeeping would become "domestic science," as the mid-Victorian woman cultivated her own public symbols of professional authority and scientific expertise. Between 1880 and World War I thousands of new organizations emerged at the national level as aspiring professionals, businessmen, farmers, and laborers sought greater power and prestige through occupational activity.

Sociologists have paid the most direct attention to this process of professionalization. In their attempt to make sense of the characteristics and rate of development of the professions, they have devised literally scores of categories, sets, and subsets from which the historian can choose. Indeed, to a less orderly-minded historian, some sociologists' concerns with paradigms, types, models, graphs, measures, charts, and tables seems in itself to be illustrative of at least one type of professionalization.[8]

Historians, in their study of the professions, tend toward a concentration on analysis of specifics and toward a descriptive narrative, sometimes reaching cautious conclusions informed by a sociological perspective. Louis Galambos, substituting the organization for the American frontier as a framework to explain historical change, argues that the emergence of the organizational society, spanning the last decades of the nineteenth century and the first decades of the twentieth, is the single most decisive influence on modern America. Seen from this perspective, professional groupings are one segment of the organized society. A response to urban and industrial development, the organized society is characterized by highly specialized work-roles, functional rather than geographical connections, cosmopolitan rather than local relationships, and an upward flow of decision making.[9] The impact of organizational activity upon American society is self-evident to historians, who employ several general approaches to an analysis of this phenomenon.

Robert Wiebe, utilizing what Galambos has called a brand of the social equilibrium model, suggests that Americans in the late nineteenth century turned to organization as a way of bringing order to a new technical, industrial, and urban society. The disintegrating "island communities" of the rural past were replaced with organizational ties and bureaucratic values more appropriate to a pluralized and rationalized society. Wiebe's "new middle class"—businessmen, farmers, professionals, labor leaders, and others who identified with their occupational roles rather than with their geographical, familial, or social status—directed the "search for order" and profited from the restoration of stability.[10] Samuel Hays is representative of another group of historians which emphasizes that the organizational revolution should be understood not so much as an irresistible and inevitable concomitant of modernization, but as a strengthening of the control of the business and professional elite and a tightening of the national commitment to a capitalist economy and a corporate value system.[11] A third group of historians, more loosely defined, stresses the accidental and unconscious factors influencing the nature of professional development. They point out the attitudinal differences between and within professions and the selective support given to bureaucratization and capitalistic values by professionals, at different times for different reasons. Sharing either a distant or a tragic view of history, this third group sees human behavior as most often inconsistent and confused and human achievements as usually falling far short of the intentions and aspirations of individuals in the past.[12] Despite their differences, however, most historians agree that the "new professional" class described by Wiebe did emerge in the late nineteenth century.

There is general agreement, too, that the new professionals came together in functional associations partly in response to the disintegration of rural localism. In the older America, fine gradations of wealth or obvious family, ethnic, or political distinctions were sufficient to establish personal identity or to structure loyalties within semiisolated communities. There was still a feeling of homogeneity in many small American towns in the 1870s. At the top of the social order stood the successful merchants and farmers, who almost invariably had Anglo-Saxon names. In provincial America, adherence to the Protestant code had assured a widespread allegiance to certain precepts of behavior and morality believed to be universally valid. But as the pace of industrialization, mechanization, and urbanization quickened, the social order grew more complex and less comprehensible to many middle-class Americans. The transportation and communication revolutions penetrated the local communities and fostered a social interdependence that had previously been unknown. Each person's life was increasingly influenced by strangers in remote places; operative social realities seemed to lie far beyond the surface of events. As Wiebe noted, the loss of an ordered traditional community brought a sense of disorder and drift to many Americans late in the nineteenth century:

> In a manner that eludes precise explanation, countless citizens in towns and cities across the land sensed that something fundamental was happening to their lives, something they had not willed and did not want, and they responded by striking out at whatever enemies their view of the world allowed them to see. They fought, in other words, to preserve the society that had given their lives meaning. But it had already slipped beyond their grasp.[13]

Within their associations, the new professionals could find some small segment of society where they felt comfortably secure, in communication with like-minded others.

Members of the new professional class sought to extend the influence of technocratic principles. They increasingly defined themselves in terms of their occupation and of its importance to a growing scientific-industrial society. Once organized, the new professionals claimed adherence to scientific objectivity and neutrality; this enabled them to make an expedient accommodation to economic and political realities, although their conformity was often to a liberal rather than a conservative consensus.

Their shared consciousness was a revolution in values that accompanied the steady social transformation from *Gemeinschaft* to *Gesellschaft,* from an organic community to an urban-industrial life. In the distended society of the late nineteenth century, the new professionals, committed to expertise and to what they believed to be a scientific mode of thought, attempted to weigh, measure, and count their world as a way of imposing order upon it. Their bold visions were sometimes little more than attempts to make the world over in accordance with their private needs. But the militant spirit of those with professional aspirations did serve to reorient training, increase technical knowledge, integrate a seemingly fragmented cosmos, organize a secular vision, and chart a path to the modern world.

However, the social attitudes of the earliest library leaders, men like Justin Winsor, William Poole, and Charles Cutter, do not fit this model of the "new professional." Within librarianship, the new professional ideology, represented by the forces of Melvil Dewey, did not come to dominate the ALA until the mid-1890s, and only then after a protracted battle with older elements in the national association. Librarianship first passed through a kind of preprofessional, missionary phase, through what I have termed the "gentry stage" of professionalism. The attitudes characteristic of this stage were anchored in a more provincial past, when family, education, and righteous behavior were the marks of a gentleman or lady within the local community. The social ideals of Winsor, Poole, and Cutter were formed in a time when a more clearly defined group exercised unspecialized authority within a more deferential and cohesive society. The trio who led the ALA from 1876 to 1889 are representative members of that segment of American bourgeois culture that has been variously described by historians, but often termed the "gentry" or the "genteel."

Stow Persons is one of the historians who have discussed the emergence of this group in nineteenth-century America—a group he calls the "new gentry elite." By the Jacksonian period, Persons argues, the old colonial gentry class had disappeared, and its powers and functions were distributed to several functional elites: "Two of these elites derived directly from fragments of the old colonial gentry class: the social-economic elite, and a new gentry elite."[14]

The new gentry elite were not merely an extension of the colonial gentry. They were a new urban, middle-class group of professionals, literary gentlemen, and some businessmen whose commitment was to genteel standards as prescribed in the printed media.[15] They placed great emphasis upon moral norms, as a way of governing themselves and of shaping the moral values of a society in which they felt disoriented and bypassed. Whereas ladies and gentlemen had once been defined at birth, the American mode of gentility was not dependent upon ancestry or wealth, but could be achieved through education and adherence to a properly conceived value system.

Active in educational, charitable, municipal, and civil service reform, this recognizable group of civic leaders and literary figures was of native, usually New England, stock and often had graduated from eastern colleges. In cities across the nation, they embarked in the late nineteenth century upon an effort to educate and uplift the unfortunate. Responding to a mixture of class fear, self-interest, and humanitarianism, alternating between excited optimism and gloomy foreboding, they attempted to alleviate the problems of political corruption, urban poverty, and labor unrest that challenged their familiar way of life. They never doubted the validity of imposing upon others their middle-class values: thrift, self-reliance, industriousness, and sensual control. Never comfortable in industrial America, they viewed themselves as saviors of society. "Reformers in search of yesterday," they envisioned a perfect society of "clean, pleasant homes efficiently managed by devoted wives and mothers; attractive schools attended by attentive, well-scrubbed children; factories whose workers were industrious, disciplined and contented; and a city where intelligent voters elected qualified officials and enjoyed the cultural advantages generously provided for them" by the elite.[16] By the end of the century many of them had lost control of economic and political affairs in their communities, while retaining, for a while, preeminence in the cultural sphere.

The distinction between the social-economic elite—composed of wealthy business and financial leaders—and this new gentry elite—a loosely defined group of literati, professionals, educators, and scholars—is made graphic by the perennial concern of the genteel in the late nineteenth century with the difference between "fine" and "fashionable" manners. The true gentleman's and lady's "fine" manners were based on personal characteristics of simplicity, benevolence, integrity, and honor; these were "morals in bloom." "Fashionable" manners, on the other hand, were conventionalized, superficial attempts to ape the traditions of European aristocracy. Mere fashionable manners marked the social-economic elite, which had been created by an artificial social order based on economic standards alone. The natural social order, in which the American gentry believed, was founded on a "natural aristocracy" of those whose fine manners, refined tastes, virtues, and talents would win for them the deference and respect of their society. In a natural, egalitarian society, so went the gentry rhetoric, the ranks of the gentleman and lady would be open to all, regardless of birth and wealth. Repeatedly, in genteel writings, one encounters the story of the poor boy who, either through self-culture or a hard-won liberal education, acquires the interests and manners that admit him to the world of the respectable few. Gentility, in short, could be taught, and the genteel circle most zealously sought to do so.

The genteel were closely associated with a New England–based culture. Moral elitism had a long tradition in New England, where the interpretation of God's purpose for humanity had once been given over almost entirely to the clergy. As early as the 1830s, however, the privileged class had learned to accept the disestablishment of religion in a pluralized, secular society. Daniel Howe has described how academics, clergy, and merchant families in Massachusetts struck a mutually satisfying bargain before the Civil War to protect their common interests: "The implicit bargain . . . came down to this; the moralists would provide a rationale for capitalism and the protection of property, if the merchants would grant them the positions of cultural and moral leadership."[17] By the Civil War the long decline in the influence of the clergy was well along. Yet the tradition of an educated elite providing moral direction to an integrated society still seemed a viable hope to the cultural establishment of New England. For the Puritan faith in a theocracy of sober men, the New England moralists had substituted, by the 1870s, a faith in moral suasion and a proper education for the masses as the best instruments of social control. At a time when the institutions of a modern mass society—the educational establishment, the corporate entities, the welfare-oriented state—had not yet stabilized, and at a time when the once-dominant religious institutions were declining in influence, genteel leaders also placed a heavy reliance upon the mid-Victorian concept of the family as a guarantor of tradition.

Thus the separation of the gentry elite from the social-economic elite gave a new importance to the lady, no more simply a foil for the gentleman but a person of consequence in her own right. Her support of the genteel code was necessary for its survival. George Santayana, in his well-known indictment of the genteel tradition, pointed to its feminine sensibilities as the malady of American intellectual life.

> America . . . is a country with two mentalities, one a survival of the beliefs and standards of the fathers, the other an expression of the instincts, practice and discoveries of the younger generations. In all the higher things of the mind—in religion, in literature, in the moral emotions—it is the hereditary spirit that still prevails. . . . The truth is that one-half of the American mind, that not occupied intensely in practical affairs, . . . has floated gently in the backwater, while, alongside, in invention and industry and social organization, the other half of the mind was leaping down a sort of Niagara Rapids. . . . The one is the sphere of the American man; the other, at least predominantly, of the American woman. The one is all aggressive enterprise; the other is all genteel tradition.[18]

The division of labor produced by industrialism assured the feminization of American culture. Women, who had formed the majority of the reading audience since the mid-nineteenth century, became the standard bearers of the genteel value system. Publishers and magazinists—the term used to describe the genteel journalists—shaped the cultural products entering American homes in the late nineteenth century so as not to offend the pristine unmarried girl. Indeed, it is not too much to say, as Daniel Howe does, that "the genteel tradition became, especially toward the end of its life, primarily a woman's value system."[19]

At the same time as the lady upheld the genteel endeavor, she also served as a model for emancipated womanhood. Although her base of operation was still the home, the lady's newly defined responsibilities ranged far afield, embracing ethics, culture, education, and the state of societal morality itself. The genteel doctrine of woman's superior sensitivity and spirituality was, of course, a rationalization of her secondary status, but it also had a quite different effect, for the crusading woman of the late nineteenth and early twentieth centuries assumed a new public role in many reform causes of the day. This middle-class lady became a new social type—a curious transitional blend of feminist and domestic queen.

A recognition of the dominant position of the lady as custodian of culture and morality helps us to better understand the appeal of gentility to the early women librarians. Since the genteel tradition was dependent upon the support of the lady, the male librarians formed an alliance with the educated women drawn to library work. These women quickly came to dominate the emerging profession, at least numerically. The genteel male, however, was caught in a paradox. Catering to the feminine increased his identification with what many regarded as the weaker sex. On the other hand, since women were his chief allies, to exalt womanhood was to enhance his own declining status and authority.

The decline of the gentry elite, which most commentators agree was complete by World War I, came about because of various counteracting factors.

Prime among them was the growing dominance of the new social-economic elite. The economic elite itself was changing as new fortunes were made in industrial and financial endeavors. As business and politics became more openly aligned after the Civil War, the gentry were displaced from political power and privilege. Even within their local communities, the gentry met resistance in their claim to public leadership, especially among the recent immigrant groups, for whom local patricians held little appeal. Gentry rebellion against the regular party structure, as among the Liberal Republicans in 1872 and the Mugwumps in 1884, eventually reduced them to political impotence. Caught between the growing economic elite of wealthy businessmen and financiers on the one hand and the common masses on the other, many gentry withdrew from the rough and tumble of politics. During the last decades of gentry decline, they tended to concentrate their activities in nonpartisan crusades for reform of municipal government, the civil service system, or educational and charitable structures.

The shift in the late nineteenth century from a classical curriculum to a form of college education that included instruction in science, technology, and the social sciences also served to lessen the influence of the gentry. Without a distinctive brand of learning to mark the gentleman, as traditional education's emphasis upon Greek and other classical studies had once done, there no longer existed a select group trained in the lofty impracticalities of the intellect. As the average college student's education became more specialized and technical in nature, the gentry lost control of their center of recruitment in the liberal arts colleges.

Additionally, the gentry suffered because they unwisely clung to literary idealism under conditions of widespread intellectual liberation from religiosity. The genteel tradition relied upon the concept of a stable, ordered cosmos in which fixed principles were established for all time. Unable to adjust this essentially theologically-based view to the new scientific world of flux and relativity, the genteel could only fall back upon an attempt to find in culture some basis for traditional religious values. But culture was no substitute for theology, and theology itself was fast losing intellectual respectability. In the long run it was the gentry's defense of principles that were religious in nature rather than their lack of accommodation to science which pushed them farther into the backwater of modern thought. Their final loss of cultural dominance was a consequence of their fatal evasion of the painful questions raised by the decline of religious faith. Their secularized value system was still basically a defense of the world God had made before the Industrial Revolution. Their unreal sexual primness left them men and women devoid of flesh and blood, of sweat and pain. Their world of art seemed unconnected to human realities; "their creed thinned down their experience, their representation, and their understanding of too much of life."[20]

The rise of mass culture was a final blow to the genteel endeavor. In late Victorian America the rise of literacy, the decline of religion, economic shifts, the processes of specialization and consolidation—all the awesomely complex developments in the process loosely termed "modernization"—diluted the deference once paid to the educated class of New England. The genteel had responded with a claim that esthetics was a branch of ethics, and that as products of a refined education for a leisure class they alone had the ability to interpret for a literate middle class the proper artistic standards. In New England "it was still possible to conceive of a secular priesthood, a conservative intellectual class based on learning and culture,"[21] which would become stand-ins, in a sense, for the Puritan preachers who had at one time served as moral guards for society. Aesthetic judgments, like moral ones, were to be based on the expert's vision of virtue and beauty. But by 1920 the near-hegemony of the staid old nineteenth-century publishing houses like G. P. Putnam's and Sons and Harper & Brothers had crumbled, as a fresh group of book-publishing firms emerged to bring into print the authors who reflected the values of the newer America.[22] Under the pressure of mass consumption, the genteel tradition tottered and collapsed in the second decade of the new century.

The decline of the gentry was also partially a result of the professionalization process itself—a social movement that permeated so many areas of American intellectual life. The specialization of skills inevitably narrowed the interests of the scholars, doctors, lawyers, and teachers from whom the gentry had traditionally drawn much of their support. Those who clung to the older view of the gentleman as a man of varied concerns and talents began to seem like mere amateurs; they became isolated within the associations that served as a base of power for the new professionals in the new organizational society.

As their real economic and political power steadily declined, members of the cultural establishment of New England took a kind of last-bastion stand in their long battle to arbitrate public morality. After the Civil War, as social change assumed threatening proportions, they took as their purpose the guardianship of conservative literary ideals and sought to shape and control institutions of culture—the library, the school, philanthropic agencies, the republic of letters. Affiliated with the artistic, charitable, and educational elements, the cultural elite relied upon the printed word both to provide a social identity for themselves and to shape the moral values of the reading masses. Quite naturally, the cultural guardians turned to the institution of the public library as one means of broadening the base of refined and right-thinking citizens.

As agents of the cultured class, Winsor, Poole, and Cutter chose to work through the institutional structure just being developed—the "people's university" in the free public library system. They expected that the equality of educational opportunity offered by the public library would encourage social mobility and ameliorate the estrangement of capital from labor. Like other custodians of culture in this period, they sought not so much to aid in the assimilation of moral, social, or economic change as to keep the challenge at arm's length. The library triumvirate held to an essentially untenable intellectual position that sought to retain the traditional comforts of literary idealism while seeming to accept the undeniably explanatory power of science. They hoped that mass taste would flood along behind their own, that the public would follow their informed leadership. As we shall see, the story of the early missionary phase of the public library movement is in large part a history of this erroneous assumption.

2

Profile of the Library Elite

NINETEENTH-CENTURY MEMBERS OF the profession often spoke scornfully of the popular conception of librarians as former teachers who had failed in discipline, sickly preachers who could not hold a congregation, lawyers who never won a case, or women who could not find a husband. They frequently reminded each other that the "days are gone by when any broken-down editor or clergyman, or any unoccupied woman, was considered entirely competent to be a librarian."[1] Indeed, the librarians did protest too much. Their preoccupation with the public's derogatory stereotype indicates the strength of the popular image.

How accurate was the public view of the librarian? What were the social origins, levels of education, rates of occupational stability, and other personal characteristics of public library leaders? To answer this question, a socioeconomic profile of thirty-six librarians who held influential positions in 1885 will be presented.* Following this analysis, a discussion of the early library triumverate—Winsor, Poole, and Cutter—will elaborate the distinctive features of library leadership during the gentry stage of professionalism.

One would expect most of the public librarians in this period to be of

*These men and women were selected because of their prominence in the national association or because their views were influential on public library development. The list was completed by the addition of all public librarians who in 1893 presided over collections of more than 50,000 books. See the Appendix for capsule descriptions of the selected leaders.

New England heritage because New England was so advanced in the number and importance of its libraries. Less predictable, however, is the degree of dominance New Englanders enjoyed in the highest levels of library leadership. Sixty-four per cent of the selected library leaders of 1885 were of New England birth, 34 per cent from Massachusetts alone. A little over half of these men and women migrated from New England to develop libraries in the eastern and midwestern states. By contrast, less than one-third of the librarians born in the midwestern or northeastern states performed library service outside their native sections. In fact, only two of the thirty-six library leaders traveled east for work. Chief librarians, then, came from the East, moving westward, and although they eulogized the opportunities of the West they were supremely self-conscious of the superiority of the cultural heritage they brought with them.

Their roots in eastern culture were deep—44 per cent of the librarians came from prominent New England families of the colonial period. Their ancestors were described as the merchants, ministers, lawyers, and social leaders who had enjoyed status and long tenure in their community. Families like the Danas, Winsors, Perkinses, Beans, Cutters, Bretts, Greens, Noyes, Rices, and Capens, for example, held the firmest claim to the oldest and best in colonial ancestry.

An analysis of fathers' occupations confirms the upper- and upper-middle-class origins of the library leaders. If categorized as having professional, agricultural, business, or manual occupations, only 10 per cent of the librarians' fathers can be classified as manual laborers.* Eleven per cent of the fathers were farmers. The largest proportion of librarians, 39 per cent, had businessmen fathers. The majority of these businessmen were merchants or owners of small stores, and several were associated in some way with the book world—as publishers, booksellers, or printers. Twenty-eight per cent of the fathers were in the professional category. Of the fathers in this highest-status class, most were members of the older professions: medicine, law, and the ministry.

Librarians James Hosmer and Edward Capen were sons of professional men. Both Hosmer and Capen left their Unitarian ministries in Massachusetts because their liberal theological views did not suit their more traditionally oriented parishioners. Hosmer, whose father and grandfather were ministers, also had a great-grandfather on his mother's side who was the minister at Plymouth for fifty-nine years. A graduate of Harvard, Hosmer continued for a while in the family tradition. He was ordained in 1860 but left his church in 1866 because of "unorthodox ideas." He began teaching at Antioch College, where his father was then president, and continued his career as a professor of German and English literature at the University of Massachusetts and at Washington University in St. Louis for the next twenty-six years. Unlike most library leaders, Hosmer did not enter the profession

*The father's occupation is not known for 12 per cent of the librarians.

until he was well into his middle years. Edward Capen, also a graduate of Harvard, lasted less than two years in his pulpit. For the next four years Capen was a private secretary to a physician while he read in preparation for a medical career. Apparently he lost interest in that endeavor, for after a year abroad he returned to Massachusetts, where he remained in library work for forty-two years.

A similar pattern of initial vocational instability is apparent in the careers of Bernard Steiner and Stephen Noyes, whose fathers were also professional men. The son of a physician, Steiner graduated from Yale in 1881 and received his doctorate from Johns Hopkins in 1891. He was a practicing lawyer for several years before he became a librarian. Stephen Noyes was the son of Professor George Noyes of the Divinity School at Cambridge. Noyes spent two years as a law clerk in a relative's firm, then became a librarian at the Boston Athenaeum in 1857.

The remaining two librarian sons of professional fathers graduated from Yale in the 1850s and for a time were involved in the literary world. Frederick Beecher Perkins, a grandson of the Reverend Lyman Beecher, was the editor of *Saturday Magazine;* James Lyman Whitney was in the book trade. Perkins went west in 1879 to become the fighting, irascible librarian at the San Francisco Public Library, while the singularly gentle Whitney began his life of quiet gentility at the Boston Public Library in 1869.[2]

In the middle-class category of businessmen fathers, the same pattern of shifting occupational status holds true for their librarian sons. Of the sixteen librarians in this category, seven were qualified to enter the ministry or practice law. Only one of the seven became a librarian before his thirty-third birthday. The most common progression of these men was to enter the library field only after many years at other occupations. Samuel Green preached just one sermon and then became a bank teller.[3] Henry Carr, John Cheney, and John Dana became qualified lawyers but were never in active practice. Carr worked as an accountant; Cheney was a struggling poet for nineteen years, "unsettled as to vocation or residence"; Dana tried his hand at engineering, teaching, surveying, and reporting. Only George Putman and William Rice worked in their respective fields of law and the ministry for a significant period of time.

As a whole, then, the librarians did demonstrate a remarkable inability to settle down into their life work. Only one-fourth of library leaders entered library service as their first career field. Although there is no evidence to indicate that librarians were incompetent in their work as teachers, lawyers, or ministers, it is apparent that they were dissatisfied in those fields. Among the thirty-six librarians surveyed, there were seven who could have become lawyers, five who were trained as ministers, and six who were former teachers. Thus 50 per cent of the library leaders must have felt sensitive about the public's image of librarians as people who had been ineffectual in their discarded occupational fields.[4]

As a result of their initial occupational instability, librarians entered their profession at the relatively high average age of thirty-four. Among the women the average age of entry, forty-two, was significantly later. Ages of entry vary from William Fletcher and Frederick Hild at seventeen to James Hosmer at fifty-eight. Comparing the age of entry with previous professions reveals no unusual patterns. A comparison of the age of entry with the father's profession, however, shows a striking pattern: Those librarians whose fathers were at the highest and lowest status levels — either professional men or manual laborers — entered library service at an average age of twenty-three. This denotes a considerably earlier age of entry than for librarians whose fathers were farmers or small businessmen. Perhaps the librarians who came from practical, striving, middle-class homes were more reluctant to confess their lack of interest in entrepreneurial activity. At any rate, many of them toyed with moneymaking occupations before they finally opted for the literary surroundings and relative penury of the public library. On the other hand, the bookish sons of professional or working-class fathers may have received less direction at home toward a profit-oriented career.

Most of the library leaders of this period were as well educated as they were well bred. At a time when a small proportion of the population was college-educated, 50 per cent of the public library elite had earned college degrees and another 20 per cent had partial college training. Only 10 per cent of the library leaders had not graduated from high school. Among the college graduates, Harvard and Yale claimed ten of the eighteen men. Eleven of the eighteen also held M.A. degrees, mostly from Harvard, Yale, and Dartmouth. Even the librarians who did not hold college degrees were acknowledged to be men of intellectual distinction; four of the ten were awarded honorary M.A.'s. Moreover, 24 per cent of the selected male librarians held one or more doctoral degrees from major universities. None of the eight women library leaders had graduated from college, although four had partial college training. The remaining four women held high school degrees. At a time when less than 2 per cent of American women were enrolled in institutions of higher learning, these women leaders were highly atypical in their attainment of formal education.*

Another measure of the high educational level of the library leaders is their production of printed material. From the pens of these thirty-six men and women have come thirty-nine books and hundreds of published articles and pamphlets. The major portion of this literary output is, of course, related to the library field, but several of the men were well-known authors outside the library profession. John Cheney published several volumes of poetry and a well-received book on esthetics. James Hosmer's fiction was nationally popular and he was renowned for his writing in the fields of history

*The percentage of all women in the United States between eighteen and twenty-one years of age attending institutions of higher learning varied from 0.7 in 1870 to 1.9 in 1880. These eight librarians received their education in the years between 1855 and 1878.

and philosophy. William Foster and Charles Cutter published over ninety articles in *The Nation* alone between 1874 and 1902. William Poole and Justin Winsor were widely respected historians. J. N. Larned was especially talented; his social criticism and comments on current affairs were noted for their wit and intellectual power.

An analysis of religious affiliation supports the other evidence of the generally high cultural level of library leadership in this period. Of the nineteen librarians for whom religious association can be determined, there were eight Unitarians, two Congregationalists, four Episcopalians, two Presbyterians, and three Quakers. With the possible exception of the Quakers, their churches tended to have a more educated ministry and less appeal to the common man than the aggressive revivalism of denominations like the Baptists or the Methodists.

The selected librarians tended to follow normally accepted patterns in their domestic life. Seventy per cent were married and among these there were only two divorces. John Cheney and Frederick Perkins, the two divorced men, both migrated from New England to the Far West before 1880, and both present the most avant-garde patterns among the otherwise relatively traditional life styles of the sample librarians. Cheney was an impecunious poet and Perkins an ill-tempered rebel who had once thrashed his Yale professor because of a fancied "insult." Seventeen per cent of the male librarians were widowed and had remarried; one man, Homer Bassett, outlived three wives. Five of the eight women librarians never married.

These five spinster librarians were remarkably similar in their family backgrounds and intellectual ambitions. Mary Plummer had attended Wellesley in 1881 and Caroline Hewins had been enrolled at Boston University and the Massachusetts Institute of Technology. Plummer, whose father was a merchant, taught school for about five years and then became a student at the first library school in the country, which was opened at Columbia University in 1887. Caroline Hewins's father was also a prosperous merchant. She, too, taught for a short period of time before she changed professions, becoming an assistant at the Boston Athenaeum in 1866. Eliza Browning's merchant father died when she was five years old; her mother died when Browning was nineteen. Evidently she was adequately provided for after her mother's death, because she began her work at the Indianapolis Public Library in 1880 by serving for a year without salary. The father of Hannah James was a lawyer and state legislator in Massachusetts. Educated in a private school, James was active in the Sanitary Commission during the Civil War and moved into library work at Newton, Massachusetts, in 1870. The family background of Mary Bean is obscure. She graduated from the Boston public schools and apparently went directly into library work at the Boston Athenaeum in 1860.

With the possible exception of Mary Bean it is unlikely that these women were driven to outside work because of financial need. Yet all found occupations outside the home when they were in their early twenties. The two earlier librarians, Mary Bean and Hannah James, perhaps because of the lesser opportunities open to women before 1900, were influential primarily in their local communities and in the library profession. The three spinsters who were productive workers in the first decades of the twentieth century, however, won public renown within their states as well as within the library profession. It is evident that these five women were unusually capable, ambitious, and articulate leaders. One can safely assume that they chose an active life of work because their intellectual power and advanced education alienated them from the traditional feminine role of domesticity.

Among the three women librarians who married, two did so quite late in life. Theresa Elmendorff, married at age forty-one, continued library work as assistant to her librarian husband. After her husband's death she became, in 1911, the first woman president of the American Library Association. She had entered librarianship at age twenty-four, five years after her graduation from a seminary in Milwaukee. Before her marriage she had been one of the most highly paid women librarians in the country. Mary Salome Cutler Fairchild was forty-two when she married a Congregational minister. A graduate of Mt. Holyoke Seminary, she had been a teacher there for four years, entering library work when she was twenty-nine. Cutler was chairwoman of the American Library Association's exhibit at the Columbian Exposition of 1893 and the director of the New York State Library School. Minerva Sanders, unlike the other two women, was married at an early age. Widowed when she was twenty-six, she also taught for a while before she became a librarian, in 1877.

All but one of this first generation of public library leaders experienced the upheaval of the Civil War years. Of the eight women, four were children during the war, two were teachers, one was a librarian, and one worked with the Sanitary Commission. Half of the men were either too young or too old to serve as soldiers. Only 28 per cent of the eligible men, however, elected to enlist in the Union army. The rest, all northerners, chose to stay at home as students, librarians, or newspapermen.

Many of the inactive pleaded illness as a reason for their noninvolvement. Indeed, physical weakness is a common complaint among the total sample of male librarians.* Their frequent references to ill health are often used as an explanation for their early inability to settle down to one career. Their physical frailties, real or imagined, may have been one factor motivating them toward library work, with its relative seclusion and low demand for physical exertion. Nevertheless, it is interesting to note that the library elite are a long lived group. The average age of death among these men and women, most of whom were born before 1850, reaches the high figure of seventy-five years.

---

*Interestingly, the reverse is true of the women librarians, who often spoke of how physically hardy they felt themselves to be.

The sense of displacement from the world their parents had known is reflected in the occupational groping of the selected librarians. Some of their vocational instability stemmed from the nagging recognition that as cultivated products of New England they did not mesh easily into the raw, new urban-industrial society. Seeking an acceptable outlet for their active faculties, they drifted for years, aware of social maladjustment but uneasy about their relationship to the nation's problems. Finding it difficult to adjust to new social conditions, most of them tended to exaggerate the defects of the age and to overrate the achievements of the past. That such a group should support most of the prevailing notions about race, the working class, the status of women, popular culture, and the functions of government is not surprising. Like most of their educated contemporaries, their mild, safe reform objectives reflected little criticism of the economic basis of political corruption and social injustice.

A design of ideas, however, does not emerge from the walls of an institution but from the personal imperatives of real people. The acknowledged library chieftain of 1876 was the many-faced Justin Winsor — Boston patrician, man of the world, and sulking rebel. When he died at age sixty-six, Winsor was universally hailed as the country's foremost librarian and one of America's greatest historical scholars. Curiously, he began neither of these careers until his late thirties.

Even to a Bostonian, Winsor's family line was impressive.* His merchant father had secured the family fortune when he won an exclusive contract during the Mexican War to provide transportation for troops and supplies from Boston to the Gulf on his line of packet ships. By the 1850s the elder Winsor had extended his shipping business to San Francisco. Justin's commitment to an intellectual life perhaps was motivated by his resentment of his father's single-minded attention to money-making. "He . . . sits and thinks, thinks and thinks of his business, without relaxation, and allows it even to disturb his nights; 'tis business, business, business," Justin said of his stern Whig father.[5] Apparently his father felt just as little empathy for his unruly only son. When Justin was ten he was sent away to the Spring Hill School. It was the elder Winsor's hope that the headmaster might prevail where he had failed. Within a few days, however, Justin had wrestled the school's matron to the ground, because she had unwisely sought to confiscate a letter from his mother. Four years later, at the insistence of his father, Winsor entered the Boston Latin School. Considerably older than the other pupils, he kept to himself while suffering through the mind-deadening routine of recitation and moral discipline.

His entrance into Harvard, in 1849, was equally unsatisfying to the

*Winsor's mother was a Howland and his father was tied to the Soules, Delanos, and Lorings.

rebellious and withdrawn Winsor. Having already authored a reasonably well received volume on the history of Duxbury, Massachusetts, Winsor had discovered that his happiest moments were spent in the sole company of books. Although few undergraduates were allowed free access to the Harvard Library shelves, Winsor gained admission through his friendship with the librarian and spent most of his Harvard years in scholarly seclusion. Perhaps because he habitually skipped attendance at chapel and recitations, he was dismissed from Harvard in his junior year.* During the next two years Winsor reached a kind of intellectual stability and peace of mind while working from 4:00 A.M. to 7:00 P.M. on his studies at the University of Heidelberg. Deciding to spend his life as a man of letters, Winsor returned to the United States in 1854 and ensconced himself in his family's fabulously appointed new home, dubbed "Winsor's Castle" by their less favored neighbors in Boston.

In his new abode the young Winsor planned the construction of a special study for his muse. Corinthian columns at each corner of the room supported an arched panelled ceiling that spanned fresco walls and carved walnut bookcases. A white marble mantlepiece, morocco leather armchair, and bronze chandelier were added. In the center of the room Winsor placed his specially designed desk from which protruded carved heads of Washington, Franklin, Webster, and Shakespeare; these represented the soldier, the philosopher, the statesman, and the poet. Significantly, he could find no American bard to honor.

In these surroundings, Winsor sat down to begin his new artistic career as literary critic and poet. Unhappily, for the next fourteen years he produced no poetry or prose that was worthy of the setting. Even his sympathetic biographer concedes that Winsor's writing style veered toward "uninspiring" and "ploddish," while Edward Channing, in his eulogy written after Winsor's death, was forced to admit that he created sentences in which "frequently the phrases chosen were not the most fortunate that could have been selected."[6] Winsor earned a small income during the years before the war as editor of America's first art journal and as literary correspondent for the Boston *Post* and the *New York World*. Despite his lack of literary success, as the wealthy scion of one of Boston's best families he was able to mingle with the cultural elite at the Art Club, and later at the Thursday and Saturday Evening Club. Here he encountered men like Theodore Parker, Edward E. Hale, Richard Henry Dana, Sr., Oliver Wendell Holmes, and Francis Parkman. Excused from army service in 1862 for "myopia," Winsor continued until 1867 to publish book reviews and translations of German authors and to lecture occasionally on literary subjects. Although he was disturbed by his failure to win

*He was later granted an honorary B.A. from Harvard, but in 1893 he still had not lost his distaste for pedagogic structure. In that year he gave a course at Harvard in cartography but refused to give an exam. Pressed, he issued his students all A's, an action that greatly agitated the school authorities. The next time he was allowed to give the course, it was not for credit.

literary recognition, he began a biography of David Garrick, a project that became hopelessly bogged down in minutiae.

It was in this stage of midlife depression that Winsor met Thomas Bailey Aldrich. Thus began the chain of events that led Winsor to a library career. In that first winter after Aldrich returned to Boston to edit *Every Saturday,* he sent an appreciative letter to a local critic, the thirty-five-year-old Winsor, who had given public praise to one of his poems. Later Aldrich and his wife welcomed Winsor to their home. "Evidently a recluse, shut away from the world of men and women: seeing life only through other eyes and written pages," Winsor, with his shiny seams and shabby coat, impressed them as a man in need of money. With reluctance, they accepted Winsor's offer to drive them about the city on a sightseeing tour, "the two unwilling beneficiaries powerless to avert the unnecessary expenditure." The Aldrichs, dressed simply so as not to embarrass their seemingly needy host, were astonished to see Winsor arrive at the appointed hour with "a handsome span of horses, coachmen in livery and a carriage perfect in its appointments," from which he alighted "with the nonchalant air of possession."

During the next months Winsor visited the young Mrs. Aldrich "nearly every day through that first winter." While sipping tea and toasting bread over the fire, he expressed his doubt and frustration about his writing career. In the spring of 1867 the meetings ended when Mrs. Aldrich, feeling compassion for this lonely, learned man who seemed to find so little joy in life and work, learned of a vacancy on the Boston Public Library Board of Trustees and suggested to Winsor that he fill the position. Later Winsor spoke gratefully of the "young woman friend [who] had given him entrance to a new world" — his career as a librarian and historian. Yet when he accepted the job as trustee, he also broke off their friendship. Puzzled at his distancing, she, like others, found Winsor had become a difficult friend, "silent and *distrait"* during the few occasions in which she later saw him.[7]

When Justin Winsor was appointed superintendent of the Boston Public Library in 1868 he moved with extraordinary energy to increase the circulation and to improve the service. Unable to succeed as a creative artist, he came at last into his own through library work, which gave free expression to his great administrative and bibliographical skill. Winsor's model annual reports to the trustees contained "detailed statistics upon every conceivable subject concerning the library's books, their nature, growth, use and abuse."[8] He defended the circulation of fiction on the grounds that mass taste would improve with time. In the meanwhile, prepared annotated lists of fiction for the public would "instigate a study by comparison, and lead the mind to history and biography by the inciting of the critical faculties."[9] During his nine years as superintendent, Winsor opened library branches and delivery stations and installed a public card catalogue. Through the use of a continuous inventory of the books by an expanded library staff, a pioneer innovation in 1869, and through Sunday openings, in 1873, he reduced the normal number of days of closing of the library during the year from the previous eighty-six to the five legal holidays. The president of Harvard, Charles Eliot, commented that Winsor was the first librarian he had ever seen whose purpose was to get books used, even if they should be used up. Under Winsor's direction the use of the Boston Public Library increased from 175,727 books borrowed in 1868 to 1,140,572 in 1877.

The library's improved circulation and service also cost money. The panic of 1873 led to the election of a new mayor of Boston in 1876 who promised to reduce municipal expenses. In the winter of that year the City Council abruptly cut Winsor's salary from $3,600 to $3,000. At just this time President Eliot offered Winsor the post of Harvard librarian at $4,000 a year. Winsor hesitated, but after a public statement by a Boston alderman that "hundreds of citizens . . . could fill that place [of librarian] after a few weeks experience with just as much ability as Mr. Winsor,"[10] Winsor decided to move to Harvard, where the political climate was more agreeable to patrician scholars.

At Harvard, Winsor's leadership also led to a great increase in the use of books—by 1893 he could report that only 41 of the 1,449 undergraduates had made no apparent use of the library. As an American apostle of German scholarship, Winsor was instrumental in the development of the seminar method of teaching. The "reserve" system in the university library, as first developed at Harvard by Winsor, was designed to provide a working collection on a narrow topic for the use of students and professors investigating a seminar subject. In the last two decades of the nineteenth century, Winsor, along with Melvil Dewey at Columbia University, led a revolution in library practice that transformed the university library from a repository of knowledge to a workshop for scholars. As early as 1877 Winsor issued shelf passes to selected faculty and students and introduced the modern call-slip delivery system. He developed the inter-library-loan system, reclassified the Harvard collection, revised the card catalogue with guide-cards and an index, and installed a new accounting system.[11]

Yet from about 1880 onward Winsor's library interests were clearly secondary to his absorption in historical research. However, the library continued to prosper despite his lack of attention to library administration. He chose capable assistants to direct the library and then "seldom interfered in their labors."[12] As a scholar-librarian who spoke six languages, Winsor was respected by the Harvard faculty. Increasingly the time in his library office was spent in research or in conversation with visitors like Parkman, Holmes, or Woodrow Wilson. In 1879 he edited *The Memorial History of Boston* and then immediately began work on a *Narrative and Critical History of America,* a study which "dominated for some forty years the realm of American historical scholarship."[13] The latter work, completed in 1889, consisted of chapter essays by various historians and dealt with American history from 1763 to 1850, with a critical bibliography of primary and secondary sources appended by Winsor.[14]

Although Winsor served as president of the American Library Association from its founding in 1876 to 1885, he in fact soon tired of the endless discussions of library technicalities that were so encouraged by Melvil Dewey. In 1885 he wrote to Dewey that a new president "could take a more active agency in looking after the success of our meetings."[15] After 1889 Winsor did not even attend the annual conventions.[16]

Nor did Winsor feel at ease at the ALA gatherings, which by 1890 were more and more dominated in number by serious ladies, many of whom were not even New Englanders.* The descriptions of Winsor by his library co-workers convey an unmistakable sense of his personal stiffness and exaggerated attention to manners. "He was born to command and no one disputed his right . . . his most impressive personal traits were strength and dignity." Josephine Rathbone recalled that "one would *address* him rather than *talk with* him."[17]

As his interest waned in librarianship, Winsor became a pivotal figure in the professionalization of historians. The professional organization of librarians and historians is integrally related, not merely because there is overlapping of leadership but because both are part of a larger movement "for the establishment of authority in American intellectual life" characterized during the 1870s and 1880s by the founding of over 200 learned societies—"an organizational revolution comparable to the trust movement in American business."[18] The American Historical Association sprang in 1884 from the American Social Science Association, of which Winsor was a member. The ASSA was a New England gentry group of patrician reformers, cultivated scholars, and men of affairs who felt a common need to uplift the masses and to counteract the class conflict building between labor and the nouveaux riches.

Founded in Boston in 1865, the ASSA sought to "conquer every social evil from crime to pauperism." Generalists in an age that would demand specialization, its members tended to treat complex and interdependent social, political, and economic questions as though they were chiefly ethical ones and to locate social causation in the conscious wills of individuals, rather than in external factors. But it was as the "mother of associations" that the ASSA best served the development of a professional spirit among the emerging groups of experts. As a seedbed of professionalism, the ASSA's fertility was slowly depleted, its original impulse spun off into the formation of the National Conference of Charities and Corrections in 1874, the American Historical Association in 1884, the American Economics Association in 1885, the American Political Science Association in 1903, and, indirectly, the American Sociological Society in 1905.[19]

*After 1891, there were always more female than male librarians at the ALA conventions.

When the American Historical Association became the first of the professional social science organizations to emerge from the ASSA in 1884, it seemed hardly more specialized than its parent group. Of the original forty-one members of the AHA, only nine were professors of history. For nearly two decades the AHA selected for its presidents nonacademic historians whose sympathy with genteel idealism often made them spokesmen for the past. Their community was at first primarily organized by social and familial, rather than by functional, criteria.[20] Winsor served as temporary chairman at the first meeting of the AHA, where he was selected vice-president, and in 1887 he was elevated to the presidency.[21]

Winsor was a transitional figure in the shift of historical leadership from the gentleman scholar to the academic professional. Like Herbert Baxter Adams and John W. Burgess, he helped to pioneer the movement for modern graduate education. But Winsor was also representative of the men whom John Franklin Jameson called the "elderly swells who dabble in history."[22] Winsor frequently made errors in citing names and dates, mostly because he carried so much information in his head. He had little sense of historical interconnections and boasted that he wrote history in "shreds and patches."

Winsor's influence upon the library profession was also transitional. During the first stage of library professionalization his leadership of the ALA helped to win prestige and the favorable attention of the New England "best men" for the new organization. As the forces of the irrepressible Melvil Dewey threatened control of the ALA in the mid-eighties, Winsor retired graciously, perhaps gratefully, into the cloistered environment of the Harvard library. Although he was a pioneer in the expansion of library use and a convincing voice urging the provision of fiction demanded by the public, he could never understand the bustling adoration of Dewey for technical solutions. Winsor's death in 1897 symbolizes the dissolution of the genteel missionary phase of library work. By the turn of the century librarians no longer felt so bound to the cultural ideals upheld by the moral guardian class centered in Boston.

William Frederick Poole, along with Winsor and Charles Cutter, was a member of the reigning triumvirate of library leaders during the first thirteen years of the ALA's existence. Poole was ten years older than Winsor and always lagged somewhat behind him in reputation, yet he rarely voiced his resentment of his secondary position. In 1873, when Poole was fifty-two, he was appointed head of the Chicago Public Library. Although he was then at the height of his reputation, he was offered the position at Chicago only after Winsor had refused it. In 1885 Poole followed Winsor as a matter of course into the ALA presidency, and three years later Poole replaced him as president of the American Historical Association.

Unlike Winsor, Poole was not born into the New England elite. Although his ancestors had been in Massachusetts for generations, his father was a tanner, and it was only after several years of teaching to finance his education that Poole was able to complete Yale in 1849. Yet entry into the cultural aristocracy of Boston was dependent upon education, attitude, and manners, not wealth or family standing. The Brahmin role could be learned. Poole was admitted to the company of the Boston patricians when he served as librarian at that prestigious citadel of learning, the Boston Athenaeum, from 1858 to 1868.[23]

Poole was hearty and forthright, often even brash. Apparently he never felt comfortable in Boston. When he moved to Ohio and later, in the early 1870s, to Illinois, he quickly identified himself with the robust West. Get out from under "the shadow of Winsor, and Cutter," he advised librarian Charles Evans in 1872, and come West since "nobody can make a mark in a library in the vicinity of Boston." In order "to be independent, and to be a man" an ambitious librarian would do well to leave the East. In Boston there were "too many tape-rolls of respectability running down through seven or eight generations," whereas in the West, Poole believed, "we all stand on an equal footing."[24] (This was written at a time, it must be remembered, when many eastern notables would have considered a trip as far west as Chicago a risky expedition to visit the outlanders.) Poole enjoyed the easier social mobility in Cincinnati and Chicago. In the Literary Club of both cities, he mixed socially with business and political leaders, with no need to assume the apprentice Brahmin role he had played in Boston. It seemed particularly fitting, then, that it was Poole, the adopted westerner whose comments about his New England birthplace sometimes had the flavor of sour grapes, who arranged for the presentation of Frederick Jackson Turner's famed paper, "The Significance of the Frontier in American History," at the World's Congress of Historians held in Chicago in 1893.

Poole finished his library career as head of Chicago's Newberry Library, founded in 1887. The trustees of the Newberry were, like Poole, college-educated descendents of colonial New England families and proponents of gentility. Paul Finkelman has described the organization of the Newberry Library as motivated by a curious blend of patrician snobbery and democratic ideals, reflecting "the reaction against urbanization then taking root among America's social elite." The Newberry was to be "an institution for gentlemen," and "like the gentleman's study, the Newberry would be, by its own self-conception and the comments of its critics, a reflection of upper class values. . . . The Library was still open to the public, but the beauty and value of the collection made it impossible for a mass audience to either use or appreciate them."[25] Poole, whose greatest expertise lay in the area of bibliography, carefully built a substantial collection of books on history, music, and art, as well as rare books, at the new research library in Chicago.

Living in the shadow of Winsor could not have been easy. But Poole's natural tendency to self-confidence strengthened during his years in Chicago, and as his years advanced, often expanded into arrogance. Melvil Dewey remarked in 1894 that Poole "thought he knew all that was worth knowing about librarianship." Although Dewey is hardly the most unbiased of reporters, this comment about Poole rings true. As the Nestor of the library profession, Poole was jealous of his rank and authority and relished any opportunity to state his views.

Poole's selective support of a modern conception of library service was important in spreading awareness of new thought. Like Winsor, he defended the provision of approved popular fiction and sought to increase the circulation figures. Poole was one of the first heads of a major public library to provide large numbers of foreign-language books to immigrant readers, to give formal instruction to schoolchildren in the use of the library, and to establish a separate reference department. His greatest achievement, *Poole's Index to Periodical Literature*, was the consuming interest of his life and made his name a familiar one to scholars on both sides of the Atlantic. Apparently Poole was the first librarian to index a catalogue so that author, title, and subject were arranged in alphabetical order.

Perhaps Poole's most original contribution to library thought, however, was his crusade to reform library architecture. Beginning in the 1870s Poole advocated a secular approach to construction that emphasized practical, rather than traditional, design. "In libraries," he argued, "abundant light is more essential than facilities for fortification."[26] Poole did not oppose the erection of magnificent cathedral facades; he only insisted that the interior of the library be functionally designed. At the time he began his reform efforts most new library buildings were patterned after European palaces, fortified manors, or most commonly, Gothic churches, with a vast, vaulted, open hall surrounded by alcoves and galleries above. Such a design not only wasted space but made it necessary for attendants to climb up and down stairs many times a day, while the heat rising to the galleries above slowly cooked and consumed the stored books. Poole favored a series of small rooms, each with an attendant and a collection of books on a specific subject. Each room was carefully planned to allow the entrance of light and the dissipation of heat. Throughout his life Poole continued to urge the construction of small rooms housing special subject collections. Yet it was Winsor's book-stack plan, incorporated into Harvard's Gore Hall, which became the most popular form of library construction in the United States.[27]

But if Poole was frequently innovative in his approach to library service, he was also capable of stubborn adherence to methods of the past. He refused throughout his career to use one of the newer, more practical systems of classification devised by Dewey, Cutter, and others. Instead he clung to the plan of a fixed location for books, a solution that was no longer workable after the midcentury increase in printed materials. Poole did not assign distinctive numbers to individual books but rather numbered them according to their location on particular shelves. Thus, as new books were added, it was necessary for the library staff to periodically relocate and renumber the volumes, as well as to change the call numbers printed in the catalogue. Poole also obstinately refused to develop a public card catalogue. He relied instead on the preparation of the traditional and expensive printed catalogue, frequently supplemented by lists of new books. Nor did Poole ever accept the new concept of open shelves. In fact, Poole had serious inadequacies as an administrator. He did not provide careful supervision for his staff and eschewed formal plans of organization. He thought of himself as primarily a scholar and bibliographer. Predictably, Poole saw little value in library school training, believing that "persons of scholarly and linguistic attainments" could be better trained as apprentices. Before his death Poole appeared a reactionary figure of the past to many of the young graduates of the Dewey-inspired library schools.[28]

Conflict over the wisdom of library school training was only one of the disputes between Poole and Melvil Dewey, the apostle of standardization and order. As Poole's biographer correctly points out, Dewey exaggerated the extent to which Poole had initially opposed the formation of the ALA[29] so as to discredit whatever resistance Poole might be showing to his current ideas. In the long run, Dewey's influence prevailed. But the running battle the two men fought between 1876 and 1894 was as much over personal differences as over philosophical ones. Poole's dislike of Dewey's egotistical personality was deep and real, and by the early 1890s they were openly hostile. Poole, the cautious, staid scholar, was unconcerned with mechanical details. Dewey, thirty years his junior, was the messianic, technical-minded entrepreneur.*

Tension between Dewey and the older leadership of the ALA grew stronger in the spring of 1892. Poole had not openly objected to Dewey's selection as ALA president in 1890 but he was greatly agitated when Dewey was chosen again in 1892, for this meant that Dewey would preside over the international librarians' conference to be held in Chicago during the Columbian Exposition of 1893. Dewey had set himself up as "the great bibliographer and librarian of the land," Poole sputtered to Winsor in protest against the increased domination of ALA meetings by Dewey's disciples — the library school crowd.[30]

A major point of contention in 1893 was the appointment of Mary Salome Cutler, who directed Dewey's library school at Albany, New York, as the director of the library exhibit to be displayed at the exposition in Chicago. Opposition to a woman as chief came from the Chicago faction of librarians. Poole wished Charles Cutter to assume direction of the exhibit. Dewey led a successful campaign to assure that Cutler would remain in charge. Frank Hill dismissed the opposition to Cutler as "nothing but a Chi[cago] growl . . . [which] should not be listened to."[31] Frederick Crunden said, "When the cheeky Chicagoans present a formal request (prac-

*See pt. 3 for a full discussion of the Poole-Dewey conflict and of the 1889 ALA debate.

tically demand) it raises my combativeness." It was absurd, Crunden thought, for Frederick Hild, who replaced Poole as chief of the Chicago Public Library in 1887, to object to work under a woman "so much his superior in intellect, character and professional attainments as Miss Cutler. . . . It would be exceedingly unjust — indecent, to expect Miss C. to do the work and let some man have the honor. No sir! . . . Glad Poole isn't pres[ident] or Hild or Winsor."[32] A few months later the trustees at the Newberry, frustrated by Poole's inattention to library administration, offered Crunden the position of director, apparently intending to allow Poole to remain as a figurehead. Relationships were thus considerably strained between the Deweyites and the Poole-Hild camp at the 1893 ALA convention. "It was a shame the way things were botched at Chicago," Dewey later apologized to one of the six foreign librarians at the "international" conference. "We decided to grin and bear it because Poole and his associates there are the most touchy people we have and . . . would have made a dreadful fuss" if criticized openly.[33]

Just prior to the convention the head cataloger at the Newberry, Edith Clarke, had written confidentially to Dewey about Poole's problems. She had predicted that the trustees would not keep the seventy-two-year-old Poole even as a figurehead and that there was "no hope for any efficient work unless they retire him."[34] Despite the warnings he was given, Poole made no real effort to reform. Poole had long been more involved in scholarly activities than in the daily affairs of the library. In November 1893 the Newberry trustees abruptly demoted Poole to consulting librarian and cut his salary in half. He was stunned by this sudden end to his career and quickly weakened physically. He suffered several serious falls, finally went into a coma, and died in March 1894. With the death of Winsor three years later, Dewey was then secure in his position of acknowledged influence.

Charles Ammi Cutter was the third member of the ALA ruling trio of 1876. He was sixty years old when Winsor died and was Dewey's elder by fourteen years. Cutter effectively withdrew from the struggle for leadership of the ALA at the time of Poole's death in 1894; after that year he almost entirely restricted his library work to local organizations. Before 1893, however, Cutter held a dominant position within the national association, serving as Poole's successor to the presidency from 1887 to 1889 and as editor of the *Library Journal* (formerly the *American Library Journal*) from 1881 to 1893.

Like Winsor, Cutter enjoyed a proud New England heritage. Since 1640 the Cutter family had produced in Massachusetts a group of scholar and merchant sons from solid commercial-class stock. Following the death of Charles's mother, when he was three years old, his merchant father handed him over to the care of his grandfather and three maiden aunts. An extremely shy and myopic boy, Charles grew up in Cambridge. He attended the Hopkins Classical School, where he was prepared for his future as a Unitarian minister, and entered Harvard in 1851, at fourteen years of age. Upon graduating third in his class in 1855, he first considered a scientific career and then entered Harvard Divinity School in 1856 under the direction of Frederick Henry Hedge.

For nine months after his graduation from divinity school Cutter studied and preached, then in 1860 began his library career as assistant librarian at the Harvard College Library. Charles Eliot, one of the library committee that appointed Cutter to the new position, boasted that Cutter was no "mere clerk" but an educated gentleman who spoke four languages. Cutter redirected his religious zeal into his new "parish church of literature and education." During his eight years at the Harvard Library he married a young library assistant, probably the first woman to be employed in the Harvard cataloging section, and quickly sired three children. By 1868, Cutter, at thirty-one, an established and respected librarian in the Boston area, seemed the natural replacement for Poole when Poole left the Boston Athenaeum for his new career in Chicago.[35]

As chief of the genteel stronghold of the Athenaeum for the next twenty-six years, Cutter reached his apex of fame and prestige.[36] While there he introduced more efficient administrative measures and developed a classification scheme that became a partial model for the later Library of Congress classification system. In 1878 Cutter originated the book-charging system still in use in many public libraries—the use of signed loan cards placed in a pocket pasted to the book cover. Thanks to this new system it was no longer necessary to close libraries for several weeks each year in order to inventory the holdings.

In the 1880s Cutter increasingly came into conflict with the Athenaeum trustees, as they sought to limit his authority and to curtail his attempts to institute a more liberal extension of loan privileges. In 1893 Cutter resigned his post at the Athenaeum, perhaps at the request of some on the board of trustees. The *Library Journal* commented that Cutter's exit from the Athenaeum "emphasizes a weakness which the library shares with the ministerial calling—a willingness to let tried servants go after long years of service, because of what is commonly known as 'differences in the congregation.' "[37] After a few months abroad, Cutter accepted a much-reduced salary at the Forbes Library in Northampton, where he worked from 1894 until his death in 1903, at age sixty-six.[38]

Soft-spoken and businesslike in his relations with others, Charles Cutter was an easier man to know than Winsor or Poole. Although Cutter consistently aligned himself with Poole and Winsor on most questions, often in opposition to Dewey, Dewey felt Cutter to be the most sympathetic of the older trio. The unfailingly gentle Cutter, Dewey said, was "the one man who from the first . . . has always had faith. . . . The other older librarians were often in doubt, but Mr. Cutter never failed to join heartily in every advance movement."[39] Cutter's early defense of the value of popular fiction, his simple joy in a feeling of communal oneness among librarians at their national conventions, his sincere belief in the important contribution of the librarian to public welfare — all indicate a man of unusual warmth and charm. Perhaps partly because he was raised in a home with three surrogate mothers, he also held an advanced view of women's capabilities. As early as 1878 Cutter gave his support to women's suffrage, an attitude that may have endeared him to some in his rapidly feminizing profession.

Admitted to the Boston patriciate by way of education and birth, Cutter was a cautious conservative who adhered, in the main, to genteel conventions and to the Brahmin world-view. He was allied with that group of New England community leaders whom Daniel Howe has called both "religious liberals and social conservatives, at once optimistic and apprehensive, . . . elitists in a land dedicated to equality, proponents of freedom of conscience who supported a religious establishment."[40]

Cutter's commitment to the preservation of traditional class values is demonstrated in his projection of the "Buffalo Public Library in 1983." Led by a tireless informant friend, Cutter took a fantasy tour over the seven floors of the well-lighted, fireproofed building and marveled at its efficiently mechanized system of book distribution that united patron to volume in a matter of seconds. Able reference librarians stood at the ready on every floor, with "on the one hand their knowledge of the shelves, volume by volume, on the other, their personal intercourse with the students," which enabled them "to give every book to that reader to whom it will do most good, . . . to answer every inquiry with the best work the library has on that matter." Yet, in his model library, Cutter rejoiced that the installation of "listening rooms" about the city — where workers could relax in the evenings while they listened to books being read to them on phonograph records — would enable librarians to censor fiction for the benefit of the masses. Here, fiction choice would be "more in our control" than in the main library. But even in the main collection, Cutter fantasized, by 1983 careful missionary vigilance would drive the fiction circulation figure down from 75 per cent to a mere 40 per cent.[41]

Cutter's ambivalence toward the value of fiction was shared by most of the older generation of library leadership, reflected in their attempts to establish some standard by which to determine "immoral" reading — a standard that was, in fact, determined by the class prejudice of the genteel. Cutter often spoke eloquently of the need for the public library to provide the books the people wanted if it was to survive as an institution: "The library should be a practical thing to be used, not an ideal to be admired. . . . They *were* the libraries of the one fit reader; they *are* the libraries of the million unfit as well as the one fit. . . . Here, as in all *pastoral* work, success comes from sympathy." And he seemed genuinely eager to increase public access to new political, economic, and scientific ideas: "Soundness or unsoundness of doctrine, whether in theology or philosophy, in the social or the natural sciences, is not to be considered by the buyer [of books for the library], even if he thinks himself competent to decide. The ability with which the views are maintained, the fame which they have gained, are the points for him to regard. For the book which will mislead the reader there is an antidote in the book written on the other side."[42] Yet, in regard to fiction that questioned the traditional male and female sex roles played out within the family, Cutter believed that reading should be censored, and he bowed to no one in the responsibility he felt to maintain moral order.

Fiction of a frivolous sort was only admissible, Cutter taught, as a kind of temporary practical device, as a means through which the librarian could lead the misguided reader to better novels. Suspect fiction, it seemed, did bring the masses pleasure, "and being suited to them brings them a certain amount of intellectual profit and a kind of moral instruction." Most importantly, fiction attracted the masses to the library, "where there is a chance that something better may get hold of them."[43] No matter that this pastoral work seemed painfully slow in producing the desired results; as Cutter wrote, the library "missionaries think all their labor is repaid by the saving of a single soul."[44]

In 1881, in a response to a demand that the Boston Public Library exclude *all* fiction from its holdings, Cutter wrote a defense of novel reading in *The Nation*. He argued that "adulterous literature," whether on library shelves or in the newspaper accounts of the Henry Ward Beecher trial in real life, did not lead directly to imitative sin. The "real evil" lay in the public's long-term exposure to popular fiction that contaminated lesser minds with the assumption that "passion is rightly lord of all."[45] While agreeing that the fiction distributed by the Boston Public Library was corrupting public morals, Cutter also argued that the library must democratically serve the demands of the taxpaying public. Yet while defending this democratic faith, Cutter nervously recommended that any list of "immoral books" should be kept "locked up in the trustee's desk . . . an *index expurgatorius* too apt to be used by certain tastes to guide their reading in the way it should not go."[46]

Amidst the contradictions in his thought, one point seems certain. Cutter clearly had two groups of readers in mind: the fit and the unfit, the readers of *The Nation* and the hordes in the factories and the tenements. Like Winsor and Poole, Cutter was unwavering in his belief that the public library should enforce moral orthodoxy. Freedom of thought in political and economic areas, even when heretical, might be tolerated in the library. But at a time when the family, the basic institution of socialization, was threatened by feminism, economic change, and an increasing denial by the young of the need for sexual repression, the defenders of social order responded with an intensified concern for habits of self-control and obedience. Library collections could not be allowed to threaten the hierarchy of the family, the domesticity of women, and the sanctity of monogamous lifelong marriage. In the public library, fiction that questioned these values was to be judged, not by esthetic standards, nor by any independent criteria of reality, but primarily by its expected social consequences.

As successive presidents of the ALA from 1876 to 1889, Winsor, Poole, and Cutter set the early tone of gentry professionalism. Professional activity or technical expertise was not the primary source of their identity. For them, authority rested in their own character and in the support of the cultured few. Their central attraction was to a generalist, scholarly role for the gentleman-librarian. They found the basis of their prestige in family or local connections. The center of their world was New England, especially Boston — even if, like Poole, or to a lesser extent Cutter, they defined themselves by rebelling against it. These leaders abhorred the notion that society was composed of groups struggling for power and privilege. They shared a faith in an aristocracy of intellect that would alleviate class conflict and the wretched conditions of the urban poor by educating "the public" and shaping its intelligence as a whole. They were not attracted to Dewey's image of the new professional in the library — a person trained in details of management and technique whose primary allegiance was to expertise and organization, rather than to any abstract mission to reform society. Unlike the new professionals who would replace them, Winsor, Poole, and Cutter were chiefly concerned with moral leadership. They needed no warrant for their authority more compelling than proper attitudes, generous intentions, and a genteel upbringing.

3

The Social Ideals of
Early Library Leaders

WHEN PUBLIC LIBRARIANS FIRST came together in 1876, they met to better organize their service to a modern society, certain that through their efforts a moral resurrection was in the making. Intellectually oriented as a group, the librarians were both facilitators and products of that process of consolidation when "American culture shifted significantly from diffusion to concentration, from spontaneity to order."[1] Reformers who feared change, librarians sought to restore past verities and to create a new profession. Librarianship offered a ready-made role outside politics, school, and church and opened a new career with which they could become completely identified.

In speech after speech the newly organized librarians extolled their mission and set forth their professional credo. Although the prime purpose of the library was clearly educational, the function of the library as a social stabilizer—a motive that had played so large a part in British library development—was also present in American minds.[2] The public library would serve as a direct rival to the saloon and would help to prevent crime and social rebellion. With such possibilities at hand, it is little wonder that the public librarians, who felt themselves responsible for the direction of a mighty force, held exalted opinions of their functions and their future.

One of the most promising institutions yet born into the world must be bequeathed to our successors as an instrument always working in the direction of moral and social development. . . . To the . . . [free library] we may hopefully look for the gradual deliverance of the people from the wiles of the rhetorician and stump orator, with their distorted fancies and one-sided collection of facts. As the varied intelligence which books can supply shall be more and more wisely assimilated, the essential elements of every political and social question may be confidently submitted to that instructed common sense upon which the founders of our Government relied. Let us . . . perfect the workings of this crowning department in our apparatus for popular education.[3]

Librarians couched their desire to serve in broadly religious terms. The town librarian should be the literary pastor of the town; "he must be able to become familiar with his flock, . . . to select their reading, and gradually to elevate their taste." Like ministers, librarians would be satisfied with meager results, with the slowly ripening fruits of their success, as the townspeople responded to their literary sermons and ministerial visits.[4] In 1876 the concept "of the Library as a moving force in the world, of the Librarian as a missionary of literature, was one which a few men only had grasped; but with which those few had already begun the doing of a revolutionary work."[5] Justin Winsor remarked how librarians came together in 1876 largely motivated by the idea that a library was "in essentials a missionary influence," a philanthropic profession.[6] The modern librarian would serve not as a "bookwatchman," but as a "professor of bibliograpfy [sic], or better still, a teacher of reading . . . an intellectual adviser, a mental doctor for his town."[7] As a disseminator of ideas, the library profession, "devoted heart and soul to all the interests of . . . social reform,"[8] defined itself as a field of exalted ethical significance.

In part, librarians were responding to the religious uncertainty of their age. The ante-bellum years brought with them a theological confusion unknown to most lettered Americans in the first decades of the century. As the editor of *Scribner's Monthly* knew, society was "honeycombed with infidelity. Men stagger in their pulpits with their burden of difficulties and doubts. The theological seminaries have become shaky places, and faith has taken its flight from an uncounted number of soul. . . . [A]ll this is true . . . so true that tears may well mingle in one's ink as he writes it."[9] Materialistic science threatened religious orthodoxy in new and startling ways. Knowledge of evolutionary theory and an increased awareness of the relativity of social mores worked to dissolve old religious imperatives, leaving many better-educated Americans to work out their ethical beliefs according to individual standards. Even shorn of its Calvinistic form, traditional Christian dogma had ceased to be functional for large numbers of people.[10]

The chief librarians, almost as a whole, were painfully conscious that their religious beliefs were out of joint with traditional Protestant theology. Of the four selected librarians who were trained for the ministry and did not continue in that profession, three voiced their grave religious doubts. John Dana and Melvil Dewey, easily the most robust of the library leaders, often expressed their common concern about the conservative nature of organized religion. Dana, a descendant of the minister John Cotton, believed that societal advance would come not through the church but through secular institutions of education. Dana spent a lifetime tilting with the status quo.

Once a Unitarian, he judged himself an agnostic by 1887. Dewey, like Dana, looked to education and science, not the church, to fight the injustices of the world. And library literature abounds with the comments of other librarians who contrasted the limited outlook and influence of the ministry with the wider ideals and opportunities of the public librarian.

To these public librarians, most descendants of New England families, the spiritual crisis of the age was made more poignant by the visible decline of New England itself. Scientific development challenged their spiritual heritage; immigration and industrialization were transforming their social position. But the missionary spirit of the library leaders was more than just the product of a "status revolution" or the result of the "alienation" of New England intellectuals. Their identification with the ministry was partly a rhetorical technique designed to strengthen their drive toward professionalization.[11] Certainly, though, the librarians inherited a sense of personal responsibility, a sense of mission to do something about social disorders, from their Calvinistic upbringing. Abandoning religious dogma, they were still optimists at heart, preaching an expanded religious ethic that had been freed from its theological moorings but in its secular form was still designed as a system of moral control. The public library movement, like the social-settlement activities later, came partially into being because it was an endeavor which enabled doubters to restructure the Christian impulse and because it helped to create a secularized ethical system.

Alongside their claim to a ministerial function, the librarians also demanded recognition as educators. The library was to be a superstructure upon the public school system. It was to provide a means of continuing education and personal development for the mass of citizens who had acquired only the rudimentary skills of learning in the school. Librarians continually emphasized their "high privileges and responsibilities as teachers," just as they believed their minister-like qualities gave them authority as moral guides. In the minds of the early library leaders, the library patron was transformed into an eager pupil.

Until the 1890s most librarians were openly disdainful of the public school curriculum and the public school teacher. Unqualified instructors, the large number of children not in school, the boredom induced by the rote process and other aspects of traditional education — all seemed to the librarian to alienate more readers than they created. Dewey was "convinced that our present system of educational institutions . . . are more than half failures." Larned felt that school was "well-nigh barren of true educational results." Most librarians agreed that the school's "rigid conformity to fixed standards" was "at war with vitality and independence of thought." Here the library supposedly had the advantage: "It appeals to and nurtures every idiosyncrasy."[12] The social conservatives in the library imagined themselves to be guardians of the process of free inquiry. They expected that a free-thinking people would not challenge, but would rather uphold, the traditional standards that governed morality and political and economic organization. As teachers and pastors of the public library—the "people's university"—the librarian could "soon largely shape the reading, and through it, the thought of his whole community."[13]

But the emerging profession demanded much more than simple moral fervor from its ideal recruit. At least a knowledge of Greek and Latin was expected of a librarian candidate, and a mastery of French and German was even more welcome. It was well if the examination of a prospective library assistant "went back of the candidate himself, to his ancestors, to see what of intellectual as well as physical quality he has inherited from them." Patrician blood in library leadership would keep out those who took up the work "merely as a means of making a living."[14] A librarian "should belong to the Brahmin caste," Lloyd Smith stated unequivocally, and "should present his diploma as a graduate of some college of respectable standing."[15] The library profession established itself very early, then, as a career in which an education and a display of proper breeding were the most desired prerequisites.

The cultivated gentleman librarian, added Samuel Green, had "no right, however, dealing as he does with persons many of whom had not had the opportunity to develop fine manners, to be fastidious or sensitive."[16] Green admonished:

> It is important to have a democratic spirit in dealing with readers in popular libraries. The librarian is not, of course, to overlook the neglect of deference which is due him, or to countenance in any way the error which prevails to a considerable extent in this country, that because artificial distinctions of rank have been abolished here, there need be no recognition of the real differences among men in respect to taste, intellect and character.[17]

A librarian of proper dignity ran "little risk in placing readers on a footing of equality with himself." His superior culture would enable him to secure the respectable treatment he merited.[18] The librarian was expected to be a person of tolerance and depth, able to "address the ignorant without mortifying them, the indolent without discouraging them, and the restive without alarming their pride."[19]

Especially in the urban setting of the late nineteenth century, the class differences between librarians and their clientele—sometimes composed of shabby immigrants, ill-educated workers, and giggling factory girls—were clearly apparent to all. Even middle-class housewives, who already were heavy users of the library and were close in social standing to the librarian, were met by the librarian with some disdain, for too many of these women seemed to be interested in little else but popular fiction and to lack intellectual ambition and cultivated taste. Facing such a horde of the uncultured, librarians struggled to uplift the taste, manners, and knowledge of their patrons.

The tutelary attitude of the well bred toward the less educated must have frightened—or angered—many potential readers. In 1891 the *Library Jour-*

nal printed a letter from a librarian who chided the magazine for ridiculing in print the limited knowledge of some library clientele. Many newspapers reprinted the journal's "Humors and Blunders" column, which was a recitation of readers' errors in calling for book titles. Surely the average reader is shy enough, the librarian said, without airing his mistakes in public. A librarian and his patrons should have the same confidential relationship as a minister and his congregation.[20]

This felt cultural superiority of librarians led them to a concept of the library as a sort of benevolent school of social ethics. The library, "while not expressly a school of manners and morals," was "much and closely concerned in maintaining a high standard in both," Frederick Perkins believed.[21] One might as well let children into an empty school, with only janitors and no teachers, as let them pour into the library with no guidance from the librarian, who should take the client "by the hand and lead him from book to book, so long as he needed help." Library patrons were "often like children, learning to walk; they must be led awhile, but they soon cater for themselves."[22] Ethical guidance was extended even to the space between the stacks. The librarians of the Boston Athenaeum foiled the love life of a couple who met in the dark German Literature alcove. The librarians constantly withdrew German books and turned on the lights until the two left.[23] The early public library, then, was designed to operate as more than just an educational institution; it had the "function of [a] positively civilizing influence . . . by counseling and protesting against the 'ephemeral'—in thought as well as literature."[24]

To function as an elite corps with a spirit of democratic equality was essentially an impossible goal. But during the years before public librarians relinquished their position as moral guides they attempted to outline the traits of the librarian who could lead without appearing to control. This model librarian

> must be of an unbounded hopefulness, but not in the least impatient. . . . He must . . . have a quick discernment of character, mental and moral, to know how far he can go and what to say to each of his patients; for he is to be, in a literary way, the city physician, and must be able to administer from the bibliothecal dispensary just that strengthening draught that will suit each case.[25]

In a time of rising social discontent, it seemed important to librarians that the common people should understand that persons of culture and learning were eager to assist, in any reasonable way, in the upward progression to middle-class respectability.

The problems created by the unwashed poor in the library were frequently mentioned by librarians in the 1880s. Most worrisome was the presence in the reading room of unemployed or homeless men who used the library as a temporary haven from the elements, a situation still common today in our large city libraries. An attendant at the Boston Public Library said in 1887 that he was proud that there had never been a fight in his library.

This was "very remarkable" in consideration of the fact that the doors were open to "every man, woman, and child who is not positively dirty or ragged."[26] Charles Cutter speculated that in the enlightened years ahead, the "great unwashed" might either be segregated in special reading rooms or kept out of the library completely.[27]

The emphasis upon cleaning up one's patrons did not stem from a concern for library sanitation so much as it did from a desire to elevate the social habits of the poor or to altogether exclude the hopelessly dirty. During Poole's first year at the Cincinnati Public Library he made "ample arrangements" for washing and instructed his assistants "to deliver no periodical or book into unclean hands."[28] The socializing of the reader seemed an endless task. Thirteen years later, Poole was still concerned with the large number of unkempt persons who frequented the reading room of the Chicago Public Library. The stench of the working class, especially in winter, was "sickening even after every known principle of ventilation" had been applied and despite the exclusion of those of unusually forbidding aspect. Poole admitted the difficulty of maintaining and enforcing a standard of judgment as to how untidy a person should be before he was refused entry to a public reading room. Perhaps the only satisfactory solution was to employ a sanitary expert for the purpose of decontaminating the air or to introduce "such elegance and refinement of taste in the furniture and appointments of . . . reading-rooms that unclean persons will not frequent them."[29]

The felt necessity for some moral control over library users is apparent in the first annual report of the Bridgeport, Connecticut, public library in 1882. The trustees were pleased to report that the library circulation had been high in the first six months of operation, even though 23,350 of the 36,547 books circulated had been novels. The city council had passed several regulations to aid the librarian's work. A $200 fine was levied upon any patron who mutilated or destroyed books or other library property. Disorderly conduct in the library or the loss of a book, pamphlet, or paper was punishable by a fine of $10. Periodically, a city policeman was detailed to the library to assure that a borrower's references were valid, to collect fines, to assist in the recovery of stolen books, or, at the librarian's request, to supervise the patrons in the reading room. Users of the library were pledged to abstain "from all avoidable noise and unbecoming conduct" and instructed that it was not considered proper there "to wear a hat, to chew tobacco, to smoke, nor, most of all, to spit on the floors."[30]

Of course the librarian's desire for deference surely had some realistic basis. A crowd of unwashed inside a warm building *is* a problem, and the unwashed were often distressed by the situation, too, as witness the many efforts they supported to get better sanitary conditions in their tenements and to have public baths built. When some patrons had to be restrained from spitting tobacco juice on the floor, it is obvious that there were some problems of decorum to be solved. In any case, authoritarianism by institutions was prevalent in this period. Strict rules and regulations were probably taken for granted by the public. The concern over library etiquette is best understood not as an example of an entirely elitist measure, but as an illustration of the cultural gap between the librarians and a portion of the public they sought to instruct.

Almost all of this first generation of public library leaders who were bent upon education of the masses came of age during the years 1840 to 1860. They were reared in that period of optimism when the humanitarian and the liberal were given almost universal hearing in America, when many Americans were filled with faith in the perfectibility of men and institutions. The future, they believed, would be whatever they and their children wished to make it. If the modern assumption is correct that a child's life script is formed by the time of puberty, and that the script generally conforms to parental and societal value systems, then we can perceive this group of librarians as that generation of men and women who were imbued with the spirit of what one historian has called the Sentimental Years—that period when privileged Americans were most confident of their ability to raise the downtrodden and saw no limits to the material and intellectual advancement of the individual and the nation.

That education was the key to illimitable progress was an opinion that underlay all the social ferment of the two decades before the Civil War. Educators, lecturers, revivalists, utopians, transcendentalists, philanthropists, reformers—perfectionists of all types—worked for continued progress of American society with an unalterable faith in the panacea of individual self-improvement. When education was diffused throughout the nation, reformers knew, Americans would automatically solve any existing social problems. As the great equalizer, education would dissolve class conflict and regenerate society. Service to education was a high cause, worthy of the best efforts of cultural leaders who scorned political involvement. Before the Civil War the religious impulse and perfectionist ideal met most securely in the educational crusade that became a missionary-like enterprise. After the Civil War education retained its place among genteel reformers as the best hope for the preservation of democratic institutions.[31]

Like their perfectionist precursors in reform, public librarians were convinced that to advance the education of the people was the highest of worthwhile endeavors. They shared a driving determination to "restore" good government, economic equality, and moral strength to the nation by extending self-culture to the lowliest and poorest of Americans. As public librarians they found their mission—to help solve the problems of urban and industrial America by a proper instruction of the masses.

During these early years of genteel influence upon the development of the public library, American society was shaken by frequent economic conflict. An unprecedented number of immigrants in the work force often led social observers to associate this disorder with ethnic strife. Worker discontent was expressed in violent strikes and attempts at unionization. Between 1880 and 1894 alone there were approximately 14,000 strikes and lockouts involving about 4 million workers in the United States. From the protest of the railroad workers in 1877, to the final repression of the Industrial Workers of the World in 1917, businessmen and politicians were continually forced to take the defensive against labor's demand for an alteration in the distribution of privilege. To compound their insecurities, the position of the more established was threatened by the Populist agitation of the 1890s and by the existence of a radical and socialist movement.

Thus, in the eyes of many refined men and women of culture and breeding, post–Civil War America seemed to have gone badly awry. The nation that emerged from the war was not the democratic utopia of their wishes. America, rather than becoming through some mysterious alchemy a harmonious society of the good and prosperous, was rent instead with discord and corruption. Business control, political bosses, and mindless materialism were the enemies on the right; wild-eyed radicals and the easily deceived and ignorant masses threatened on the left. Those who stood warily in the middle, the "respectable" educated few, with whom the librarians identified, were caught between what seemed to them the two extremes of American society.

Most library leaders frankly feared the rebellious rabble that challenged established patterns of distribution. Labor leaders, union members, agrarian radicals, alien agitators, anarchists, and socialists — all seemingly threatened American individualism and conventional morality. The great railroad strikes of 1877 were an example of how mob rule undermined all that was decent and desirable in American society, said an editorial in the *Library Journal:* "The voice which insists that intelligence is worth no more than ignorance and that every man must be ranked on an equality with the lowest" seemed "to be growing in volume throughout the country . . . the friends of public libraries . . . furnish the most effective weapons against the demagogic ignorance that glorifies ignorance and challenges civilization . . . every book that the public library circulates helps to make . . . railroad rioters impossible."[32]

The disorder fomented by the working class could only be the result of ignorance, most chief librarians insisted. If protestors understood the basic identity of interests between capitalists and labor and the immutability of "natural" economic laws, then class hatreds would end. A properly educated people would understand that the operation of supply and demand, not violence and strikes, dictated wages and profits. It was the librarian's job to provide the quality literature that would counteract the dangerous ignorance of the workers. "When suddenly a communist mob lifts its bloody head all over the land . . . setting at defiance all correct ideas of ownership . . . and of government, we are made painfully to reflect that . . . only the direst ignorance could engender such anarchy."[33]

Plainly, the books of the public library had to be judged by quality, not quantity. At a public meeting held on behalf of a free library in New York City, a few months before the 1886 Haymarket Square bombing, one speaker charged the libraries of the country with the chief responsibility for preventing unrest. Although the church and school were "safety valves," the speaker said, still the masses "hunger for knowledge." It was the uneducated to whom could be ascribed the "growth of wild theories that assail the church, the community, property and all established and organized institutions." A second speaker said with prophetic force: "Is it possible that the rich men . . . do not see the cloud? . . . Is it possible that they do not see that for the first time in the history of the world labor is organized, perhaps better organized than capital?" With men dying of hunger and women working for twenty-one cents a day, only the magnanimity of "those who call themselves the ruling classes" could save society. The philanthropists who would finance a public library would teach the poor that

> the millionaire of today is the pauper of tomorrow, and that the pauper of today is the millionaire or the president of the future. You may teach them that there is a prospect, if not for them, at least for their children . . . They will discover that the interests of labor and capital are not antagonistic.[34]

Library literature never went so far as to celebrate, with Andrew Carnegie, the moral fiber that the experience of poverty built into a man. It did support the concept that if men were to escape poverty and ignorance in "these times when heartless demagogues try to array labor against capital, when Georgism, Socialism and Anarchism excite the minds of the masses and threaten to shake the world in its foundations of religion, law and order," it would be only if the library could educate the masses "to good judgement and moral principles."[35] It was "absolutely necessary" that the workers "learn to discriminate between their own real interests and such sham reforms as are brought before them by so-called labor leaders. The fortunes of the nation depend largely upon the intelligence of the laboring classes . . . for they control the ballot."[36]

J. N. Larned, a prominent library chief at the turn of the century, is a representative spokesman for the economic and political ideals expressed by the majority of library leadership in the late 1800s. Larned presented his presidential address to the American Library Association in the same year as the Pullman Palace Car strike, which had been settled by a massive use of federal military and judicial power. Coming as it had after the Homestead battle and the march of Coxey's Army, all amid Populist agitation, the Pullman protest of 1894 thoroughly frightened the "best men" in the library.[37] Larned reacted to the national crisis by speaking at length of his fear of radical change.

Larned emphasized a commonly expressed concern of library leaders that the growth of newspapers was a grave threat to social order. The communications revolution had given an "appalling facility of alliance and organization . . . to men and women of every class and character, for every kind of aim and purpose." An irresponsible press had invested "popular ignorance with terrors which had never appeared in it before." Nor could Larned look to the schools for help; unsupplemented, the public education system was practically useless. The public library was the only institution that seemed to give promises for the future which were "safer and surer than any others that society can build hopes upon."[38]

Larned maintained his faith in the democratic system only by believing that the "knowledge of the learned, the wisdom of the thoughtful, the conscience of the upright, will someday be common enough to prevail . . . over every factious folly and every mischievous movement that evil minds or ignorance can set astir." When the traditional morality of Americans was again enshrined in its place of dominance, when sanity returned to all segments of the working class and the farmers, "none will rank rightly before those who have led and inspired the work of the public libraries." Two years later Larned still bemoaned the "continual eruption of modern social theories . . . and the widening acceptance of more innocent and more dangerous dreams." He continued to believe that democracy depended upon the distribution by the library of the proper books "far more than upon any other agency that is working in the world."[39]

The violence of the Pullman strike was also a concern to William Brett in his address to the 1894 national library convention. In a time, he said, of "political and social dissatisfaction leading to visionary political projects and the earnest advocacy of various social panaceas," the greatest danger lay in the "corruption of the ballot due to ignorance and vice." Obviously the church and school had failed in some major way to provide the populace with the proper instruction. One solution to social problems was a more militant effort by the public librarian to become an active teaching force. It would be unreasonable to let pupils in the schools select their own textbooks; yet librarians sometimes followed "much of the popular enquiry for books" and thus loaded library shelves with "worthless and pernicious" literature. The class of books in the library called "sociology" had the most need for close management and the greatest possibilities for producing evil or good. False ideas in sociology or those "visionary in theory" should flatly be excluded from the public library, Brett declared.[40]

A corollary of the argument that ignorance and violence went hand in hand was the belief that the library could blunt the impact of the class consciousness which was growing in proportion to the rate of immigration, the number of strikes, and the intensity of economic distress. The recognition that existing institutions of education had not adequately served the needs of industrial workers and uneducated adults of all classes brought the public library into a prominent position in the late Victorian period. Librarians billed their institution as one of the best hopes for improving the knowledge of the restive lower classes and for bringing the community into a higher, better form of life and thought.

Larned had been moved by the tensions of the time to set up a lecture class in 1897 at the Buffalo Public Library on the "labor question."* Talks on unions, socialism, anarchy, and the single tax were presented to the audience of workers, union leaders, businessmen, and curious ladies. Larned did not explain how the heterogeneous crowd was brought into intellectual harmony but he did report that all present gained "some understanding of the economic laws that dominate every possible solution" of social problems.[41] By 1880 the public library had long been touted for its ability to defeat delinquency, crime, poverty, and intemperance. With the increase of economic dislocation and disorderly protest that marked the last two decades of the century, librarians placed a new emphasis upon their mission to do something about "harmonizing opinion" and to bring about a toleration of class differences.[42]

Larned, later librarian of the Buffalo, New York, public library and president of the ALA in 1894, was in 1876 the superintendent of education in Buffalo. In that year he published his book *Talks About Labor,* which combined in fascinating proportions advanced liberal ideas, empathy for the downtrodden, and rock-rib conservatism. The book is an imaginary series of conversations that stretch over five evenings between a comfortable middle-class family and a "judge." The judge makes clear the aim of their talks: an attempt to discover the rules that govern the relations of capital and labor, on the assumption that what is just and what is practicable have a fixed relationship. A distinction between the immutable economic laws and those which are merely customary will enable the discussants to outline a more equitable adjustment of resources than that which presently exists.[43]

The judge immediately states that he favors a more just and secure procedure for dealing with the needs of labor. A young man, the suitor of the daughter of the family, becomes somewhat confused. Is it not the plan of the Creator that the capitalist, whom the Lord has made more capable, deserves more reward than the laborer? he asks. The judge gently leads the young man to an understanding that the harsh tenets of Social Darwinism are a denunciation of Christian principles. This enunciation of what will later be called the Social Gospel excites the interest of the wife, who has heretofore been intent on "some kind of foolish sewing, as women like to be in their leisure time." The wife is now eager to participate in a discussion of this "masculine topic."[44]

As the group ponders the grim state of labor's plight, the conversation lags. But the wise judge has an answer at hand. The co-op system he rules out

---

*Larned and other elite reformers formed at Buffalo, in January 1896, a local branch of the National Educational and Economic League, an organization intended to educate workers about economic "laws" and to prepare them as voters. (Shelton, *Reformers in Search of Yesterday,* 168.)

at once, for he says that workers cannot understand the intricacies of efficient moneymaking. The judge's solution to all of labor's just discontent is simplicity itself — profit-sharing between the capitalist and his workers. The young man present is relieved: "I begin to see, sir, that your views are not so radical as they seemed to be at first."[45]

More confident now, perhaps, of the judge's basic stability, the young man asks his opinion of labor unions. The judge replies that though he is sympathetic to the discontent which causes workers to organize, unions limit the worker's individual freedom and lower working standards. The judge has frequently emphasized the basic goodness of human nature that prevents the capitalist from using his full power against the worker, but curiously, he does not apply this same reasoning to the power of labor. He seems to believe that the laborer is more vindictive in the use of his strike power than is the capitalist in the exercise of his control over wages and production.[46]

Larned, like Thorstein Veblen later, was aware of the connection between wasteful use of profits and the barbaric past. Less philosophically detached than Veblen, he wished profligacy could be controlled by strict laws. Waste, he said, is the consumption of wealth which has no object outside of itself, "which is for the sake, in other words, of displaying the ability to consume and which consumes objectlessly for that purpose."[47] Wasteful consumption appears in ladies' fashions and in the housing of the rich, whose only purpose is to measure against one another the spending power they possess. The mansion of the rich is the "monument of a barbarian who has survived beyond his age."[48]

In *Talks About Labor* the judge concludes that the only realistic way to persuade the rich to part with their excessive profits is to ask them, not to give up what they already have, but to divide their *future* gain with the workers. Unfortunately, the judge admits, such an adjustment between capital and labor is at least 100 years away. In 1876, however, Larned had a strong faith in the final evolution of justice among men, "before human history ends."[49]

Like many gentlemen reformers, Larned detested the "irresponsible" party politics of post–Civil War America. Party machinery, he said, had created "a state of rottenness in American politics which has become a stench in the nostrils of the world."[50] He suggested that proportional representation instead of territorial representation might serve to break up the current political parties, which corrupted individual judgment.[51] Real political independence, he believed, would result in parties of the left, center, and right and would give the principled vote greater power. By 1911 Larned came to fear that socialism had gained a momentum which would carry it to ultimate victory. But if America was pushed into government ownership and management of productive industries "without a previous reformation of our political system," the country would "inevitably be carried to a disaster so great that imagination can hardly picture it."[52] He believed that the party system, with its partisan spoils and graft, would be even more destructive within a socialist government.

As politics and business became more openly allied after the Civil War, librarians assured each other that men of the highest capabilities did not go into business. They viewed the real pioneers of human progress as men who invariably rejected the moneymaking qualities as essentially ignoble. A contempt for practical profit-seeking was a frequent theme among librarians of this period, who reminded prospective candidates that the rewards of library work were not monetary but spiritual. Like pastors they should be content with limited incomes, taking an elitist pride in monastic-like allegiance to charity and poverty.

Concurrent with their disdain for practical men of business was the librarians' support of the idealists' panacea for the ills of the nation—civil service reform. William Foster was one of the many library leaders active in the numerous reform clubs organized during these years to bring the pressure of stern, simple morality upon government officials. Foster joined the almost-universal educational effort of gentry leaders in the early 1880s to convince the public of the evils of the spoils system. Civil service reform was more than just a moderate, businesslike measure for efficient government. Foster saw the Pendleton Act as basically an attempt to return government to the care of men of high character and repute.[53]

At the base of library-reform thought was a belief that the American masses were being corrupted by the selfish greed of demagogues and miscreants. Early in the 1880s library leaders feared the rapacious, irresponsible men of wealth and the grasping politicians who threatened the moral basis of society. Later, many library chieftains would find a target in the newspapers and mass literature, which were bringing the uneducated into sensuality and moral decay. By the middle of the 1890s the enemy had been expanded to include men and women of anarchistic and communistic inclinations, whose aim was to interfere with The Nature of Things in economic matters. Doubtless it was the acceptance of the absolutes of an archaic economic orthodoxy that chained early librarians most firmly to the recent past. They did not often question the conventional wisdom that out of the free play of individual desires and the profit motive would emerge a just society in harmony with "natural laws."

While actually seeking orderly acquiescence to the established economic order, the public library emphasized its claim of democratic service to the masses. But as the public library system developed to maturity after the Civil War, its narrow social foundations became more apparent. The New England towns in which the earliest libraries had been formed differed from modern urban areas in an important feature: their feeling of homogeneity. This enabled the library to develop as an institution with a feeling of largeness about it when in fact it was frequented by a relatively small portion of the population. This feeling of community participation characterized the evolution of the public library, even though a library system had never been a vital working-class issue.

Although librarians spoke of their institution as if it was as important as schools, hospitals, utilities, or police protection, many American urban workers did not really feel the same way. Most people probably felt that a library was a valuable addition to the community, good to have but not essential to daily life, an educational luxury that was a source of local pride. When public libraries were established, urban workers used them, to be sure, but not in the numbers for which librarians had hoped. Despite the best intentions of librarians, the subtle library paternalism—with its nineteenth-century formula designed to support and stabilize the status quo—tended to repel many working-class readers.[54]

Indeed, labor opposition came early to Andrew Carnegie's gifts of library buildings to various communities. When Carnegie donated one of his first libraries to Pittsburgh in 1892, local labor organizations petitioned the city council to return the money, on the grounds that it was tainted by the way in which it had been earned. Workers often charged that Carnegie wished only to glorify himself by his philanthropy. Especially after the violence of the Homestead strike, organized labor and the left frequently opposed the erection of Carnegie libraries, as in Detroit in 1901 and Indianapolis in 1903. This worker opposition to the wealthy's gift of libraries was not scattered, but was general and consistent. Socialist Eugene Debs promised laborers that they would have public libraries in "glorious abundance when capitalism is abolished and workingmen are no longer robbed by the philanthropic pirates of the Carnegie class."[55]

In 1906, Wisconsin librarians had a rare opportunity to hear directly from laborers themselves why they did not often use the library. In his report to the district library meeting, a local union man scoffed at the library's call for "librarians of a new order or [for] a different class of books to attract the working man." What was needed, he said, was an awakening of public consciousness that would prohibit the exploitation of labor through long workdays. If laborers had more leisure, then they could use the libraries built for them by the privileged class. Another spokesman told the assembled librarians that they must develop a different library atmosphere if they were to attract male readers. The feminized propriety of the public library carried with it a "rigidity of rules and a general air of stiffness and conventionality." The use of the public library actually had been reserved, albeit "unconsciously," for members of the educated middle class—"those who need it least and use it little." When a workingman entered the average public library he was apt to be greeted with concern as to whether or not his umbrella was in the proper receptacle and his rubbers left in the lobby. After an inspection to see whether or not he had "a clean shave, a clean collar and a recent shine," the worker was often steered toward the "better class" of literature, in an attempt to elevate his literary standards.[56] Regardless of the validity of these criticisms, it seems safe to conclude that most laborers experienced the environment of the average public library as alien, if not unwelcoming.

One reason, no doubt, why organized labor did not give more support to public libraries was because the library was governed by a narrow social stratum. Library government was almost universally composed of a board of trustees — generally selected by the mayor or elected by the city council — and this board consisted of the eminent people in the community, members of the middle class and up.* Thus the librarian was practically forced to conform to elite demands rather than the wishes of labor.

As librarians struggled to establish their professional status, they often relied upon the group of sympathetic and like-minded trustees to prevent their positions from becoming purely political appointments within often-corrupted city governments. Many librarians felt, too, that board members, with their greater political skills and higher social standing, could make a plea to city officials for sufficient library income more successfully than they. It is also possible that library leaders, whose professional pretensions were not generally accepted and whose status did not command wide deference, could associate through their boards with the leading powers in their communities. Some librarians may thus have been given easier access to higher social circles than they otherwise would have been allowed.

Furthermore, the feminization of the library profession encouraged the subservience of librarians to their trustees. The woman librarian in particular would have been apt to stand not only in awe but in fear of the board. Her low salary, professional insecurity, and allegiance to "femininity" made it necessary for her to play an especially passive role with her trustees. She might have also felt an acute helplessness in dealing with the wholly male world of politics, thus increasing her reliance upon the board's expertise.

All these factors worked in many cases to create a certain passivity in librarianship and an emotional as well as financial dependence of librarians upon the approval of their governing board. It was only when gentry opinion was firmly behind them, or when library circulation was threatened, that librarians as a group risked bold action in initiation of change. For example, they vigorously fought for innovation in the matters of Sunday openings, open shelves, and the reform of the public school curriculum.[57]

In the period 1879 to 1900 the leaders of the public library movement waged a hard campaign for the introduction of supplementary reading into

---

*The evidence is overwhelming that public library trustees have been almost entirely male, white, well-educated, well-to-do, and usually professionals or businessmen. See Carleton Joeckel, *The Government of the American Public Library* (Chicago: University of Chicago Press, 1939); Oliver Garceau, *The Public Library in the Political Process* (New York: Columbia University Press, 1949); Ann E. Prentice, *The Public Library Trustee* (Metuchen, N.J.: The Scarecrow Press, 1973).

the classroom. They initiated contacts with teachers and school administrators, especially in the large cities, and convinced reluctant or apathetic educators of the value of bringing library books into the school. Criticism from librarians set the educators to considering the content of school readers and encouraged the tendency to use literary works in their entirety, rather than extracts, in reading texts. Librarians compiled graded book lists and made the first systematic studies of the reading preferences of children.

In a period when most schoolchildren received only a rudimentary knowledge of the three Rs, librarians perceived the obvious wisdom of training children to enjoy books and to use the library. Librarians were forced to a consideration of educational conditions and found that the rigid structure of the school provided little encouragement of self-education. The very methodology of rote memorization, they saw, served to disgust pupils with books, reading, and learning. Espousing change, librarians were pushed to ever-sharper criticism of the existing system.

The substantial contribution of public librarians to school reform has gone unrecognized by historians of education. Yet without the librarians' drive, it is possible that the introduction of supplementary reading into the average school curriculum might have been delayed a decade or more. Certainly, the educational reformers of this period freely acknowledged their debt to the pioneering work of public librarians.[58]

The librarians' crusade for the "new education" was allied to wider intellectual movements of the late nineteenth century. Darwinian theory—in both its conservative and reform versions—and the new philosophy of pragmatism challenged the traditional authority of religion, which taught that truth was eternally fixed. Proponents of the "new education" believed that instruction should be reformed to accord with the interests of the pupil and with the real problems encountered in daily living. This emphasis upon interest and meaning in education was in harmony with the individualism of American life, with the ideas of scientific progress, with secular development, with the new interest in childhood, and with all the scientific and philosophical implications of evolution.

Herbert Spencer's influence on American thought has been substantial, and his book on education probably found its widest audience in America. In his persuasive style, Spencer argued that a subject gained in educational value as it increased in practical value. Although he was opposed to the provision of state schooling, Spencer's challenge to traditional education brought attention to the cultural lag between the time-worn curriculum of the school and the industrializing world outside. Spencer was also one of the most outspoken proponents of the value of interest in learning: "Of *all* the changes taking place, the most significant is the growing desire to make the acquirement of knowledge pleasurable rather than painful—a desire based on the more or less distinct perception that at each age the intellectual action which a child likes is a healthful one for it."[59]

Like Spencer, G. Stanley Hall and William James were also potent defenders of educational reform during this period. Both men stressed that practical activity and utilitarian knowledge should form the predominant content of an education. Hall, a messiah of the child-study movement, advanced the idea that the curriculum must proceed from the needs and development of the students, not vice versa. No pedagogical topic received more attention from James than that of interest. The motive power of interest — to him, the very basis of all education — was so indispensable to learning that the teacher's first duty was to bring interest forth where it did not naturally exist. James's writing on pedagogy cast aside the last bits of faculty psychology still flourishing in the 1890s. If learning was distasteful or if the subject of study had no practical value for everyday living, he said, interest would be almost impossible to arouse in the child. Both Hall and James taught that only when subjects were correlated, so as to make cross-references to one another, would effective education begin in American schools.[60]

These new conceptions of the educational nature of human beings possessed two aspects. One aimed at a metaphysical formulation of men and women as environment-shaping creatures. The other, practical and concrete in nature, attempted to work out a specific methodology of teaching. The men representing the practical movement — Johann Heinrich Pestalozzi and Johann Friedrich Herbart — greatly influenced American pedagogy during this period. The Pestalozzian wave of reform, introduced at Oswego, New York, in 1861, was replaced by the Herbartian wave of the 1890s. With Pestalozzi, learning came to mean not the gathering of facts alone but the employment of those facts to solve practical problems.[61] To Pestalozzi's study of the physical world through sense perception, Herbart added the study of the moral aspects of daily life. Because Herbart was chiefly concerned with ethical instruction, he espoused a coordinated unification of all subjects around the central cultural core of history and literature. But Herbartians also stressed the importance of firing the learner's interest. The Five Formal Steps of Herbart's teaching method became high-fashion pedagogy during the last decade of the nineteenth century. Under his influence teachers gave increased attention to a scientifically based educational psychology and to the control of interest.[62]

Firmly supported by the new and soon-to-be victorious ideas, the public librarians of this period found themselves riding the crest of the wave of school reform. The demand for relevance caused a reevaluation and expansion of the curriculum that gave literature a new prominence in the American school. Before 1890 librarians had criticized the rote method because it annihilated interest. They wished to enrich the educational experience of children by exposure to varied materials and methodologies. After 1890 the then-popular Herbartian doctrines were perfectly suited to advance the librarians' educational goals. They began to emphasize the moral lessons to be gained by a reading of literature and history. As custodians of the varied types of printed knowledge, the public librarians stood eager to serve the emerging goals of the American school system.

The library's effort to introduce supplementary reading into the public school curriculum was necessitated by the failure of the states to establish adequate school-district libraries. The pioneer efforts of Horace Mann and Henry Barnard to provide non-textbook materials for use in the schools had brought relatively small results.[63] Between the 1830s and the formation of the ALA in 1876, twenty-one states did pass laws that established a school library system. However, the reports of the state superintendents of education to the Bureau of Education in 1874 were all but unanimous in agreeing that the majority of school library books were stale and little read. Most states permitted the school districts to raise money for libraries without providing for adequate state grants and often set limits on the size and usefulness of the library by diverting its funds to teachers' salaries or to the purchase of school equipment. The library funds were sometimes siphoned off into illegitimate uses. The selection of books was not well supervised, and because there were few salaried librarians at work the collections were seldom catalogued or publicized. This early failure of the states to provide a satisfactory library system for the schools was a result of both defective legislation and inadequate administration, as well as substantial teacher apathy.[64]

For three decades following the Civil War, the paucity of competent teachers, as well as the increase in schoolchildren and the inadequacy of physical facilities, had all served to reduce education in many places to a drill system of rote learning. The business of the pupil was to learn by heart and then to recite the facts to a teacher, who in turn was governed by a rigid course of study and narrowly defined examinations. Discipline was authoritarian and repressive. For the most part any movement or conversation in the schoolroom was considered out of order. The formal character of the school was designed to keep students quiet and busy at assigned tasks, submissive to the rule of the teacher.

Spelling, grammar, and oratory were stressed in the schools to the virtual exclusion of reading for pleasure or meaning. Reading texts were apt to be composed of literary "scraps" — selections from English and American authors concerning morals or conduct — rather than of whole units of imaginative literature. In 1890 Charles Eliot investigated the limited exposure to literature that students received in Massachusetts. He found that although 37 per cent of the school time of six years was allotted to the study of grammar, the "time it would take a graduate of a high school to read aloud consecutively all the books which are read in this school during six years, including the history, the reading lessons in geography, and the book on manners . . . was [only] forty-six hours."[65]

Progressive teaching techniques, after the example of Pestalozzi, were often popularized only after herculean efforts by some capable leader like Edward Sheldon, who established a teacher-training school in Oswego, New

York, in 1861. The Oswego movement was the first publicized and popular revolt against the reliance on rote learning. It espoused a teaching method that attempted to respect individual differences and to adapt the curriculum to the child's stage of knowledge. The Oswego-trained teachers became conscious of a new professionalism and of their ability to direct classroom activity without dependence upon a text. Language usage and vocabulary growth became more important with the use of class discussion.[66]

In 1875, at just about the same time that Oswego had reached the height of its influence, the schools of Quincy, Massachusetts, won national renown for the innovative teaching techniques introduced there by school reformer Francis W. Parker. Library involvement with the public schools began as an offshoot of the "new education" in Quincy, which was widely publicized by Charles Francis Adams, a member of the Quincy school board and also a trustee of the Quincy Public Library. Adams's library work never gained the national attention that his efforts with the schools did, although he was so intent upon improving library service that he personally spent himself in the laborious routine of cataloging volumes. In 1876 Adams addressed the teachers at Quincy and complained that he had given each of the public schools a copy of the public library catalogue only to discover that in most schools it still lay unused in the principal's office. He announced that a new public library rule made it possible for teachers to choose books for their students and to bring these books directly into the classroom.[67]

Charles Adams's appeal to the teachers at Quincy attracted the immediate notice of the *Library Journal*, organ of the fledgling ALA. Charles Cutter, who was then the librarian at the Boston Athenaeum, commented on Adams's speech: The use of library books in the school is "a question . . . only just beginning to attract the attention which it deserves." Cutter was quick to use the occasion as a source of professional aggrandizement, to elevate the librarian's work to a refining function at the apex of the collective educational system.

> The . . . [librarian] must continue what the teacher has begun; he must make a beginning, if he can, where the teacher has failed, and for those with whom the teacher has not come in contact; like the teacher he must add this to duties already engrossing . . . or else his work . . . is only the work of a clerk or of a bookworm.[68]

Cutter's comments foreshadowed the concerns of those librarians who would pioneer the use of library books in the schools. First, there was the barely concealed contempt that the cultured and better-educated librarian felt for the social status and intellectual ability of the average teacher. Secondly, there was the tone of the missionary with work to be done. The librarian would need to impel educators to the use of library books in the classroom. Lastly, Cutter briefly touched on one of the major reasons why teachers were reluctant to encourage outside reading: The teacher of this period was so pressed for time that she had difficulty enough in presenting the prescribed curriculum. The proliferation of new subjects introduced into the schools in the 1870s, usually taught in addition to the traditional Latin and math courses, forced the teacher to cram everything into the six hours originally intended for the three Rs. Examination procedures and college entrance requirements were specific and rigid; the teachers, particularly in the high schools, were hard-pressed to prepare their students for graduation. At a time when most teachers were women under twenty-two years of age, without a college degree and often dependent upon political appointment, many teachers covered their weakness by almost complete reliance on the textbook. It is little wonder that many teachers refused to add library readings to their already crowded schedules.[69]

At the same time that Charles Adams was publicizing educational reform at Quincy, Samuel Green, the public librarian at Worcester, Massachusetts, began his campaign to introduce supplementary reading into the classroom. This kind of initiative and drive seems surprising in light of his previous lack of purpose. Green was thirty-four when he became the librarian at Worcester. Before that time he had spent years of ill health at home, traveled in the Near East, taken his degree from the Harvard Divinity School (preaching one sermon before he gave up the ministry), and done nothing much else of note except to shower a morbid devotion on his mother. Green was of slight build, handsome, with dark feathery lashes. He was rejected for army duty in 1861, for reasons of "ill health and undersize [*sic*]." After he gave up the Unitarian ministry he worked for less than a year as a bank teller, in 1864. In 1871 he was offered a library post, primarily through the influence of his uncle, who had donated the library to the town.[70]

A more unlikely crusader could hardly be imagined, yet Green came alive in his new job and gained a national reputation among librarians for his progressive vitality. Worcester, in 1872, was the first library of any size in New England to open its doors on Sunday, an action that no doubt was a reflection of Green's growing religious doubts. In addition to his work with the schools, Green stirred the library profession by his free mingling with the readers of low social class and his specialized services to workers and employers.

In 1879 Green organized a meeting with the superintendent of schools in Worcester, a member of the school committee who was also a trustee of the library, and the principal of the normal school. These three officials agreed that they would back Green in his efforts to introduce library materials into the classrooms. The details of the plan were left to him to devise. Green began personal visits to the schools of Worcester, carrying with him illustrated travel books that he showed to receptive teachers. The common method of teaching geography at this time required literal memorization of questions and answers in the geography textbooks. Children did little else but recite data about boundaries, capitals, products, exports, and imports. Green pointed out to the teachers the interest that would be aroused by display of books and pictures about the countries being studied.

Green offered two library cards to each teacher. One card was for personal use; the other would entitle the teacher to withdraw six books for the use of the students. In the first year Green convinced 119 of the 200 teachers to take a library card. Of these, 77 teachers accepted both cards.[71] Three years later, 550 books were in use in the school each day. Between February and June of 1881 700 books per day were being read by students.

Within a few years Green's initiative had made the public library an important adjunct to Worcester's educational system. Literature and history had been added to the original fare, and students at the normal school learned how to use library books in teaching. Reading lists on various subjects were distributed to teachers and students, and the list of new library acquisitions was sent promptly to each principal. A well-lighted room, with tables and couches, had been set aside at the library for the sole use of students and teachers. Classes were brought there daily to see exhibits, books, and pictures on special subjects. Whenever a new teacher came to Worcester, Green sought her out to explain how the library could be of service in her teaching. It was his conviction that "the librarian is just as much a teacher as the public school teacher in Worcester, he just works after school hours."[72]

William Eaton Foster, public librarian at Providence, Rhode Island, is the other librarian who must be credited, along with Green, for early involvement in school reform. Foster, unlike most library leaders of this period, had no previous profession from which he came to library work. He became a librarian immediately after graduation from Brown University in 1873 and served at the Providence Public Library for fifty-three years.[73] Like Green, Foster encouraged the transportation of books from library to school, but Foster had a more conservative view of how children's reading should be monitored. Foster, who was shy and self-effacing, limited his personal contacts almost entirely to school administrators.* In Providence, it was the principal of the school, rather than the classroom teacher, who read and selected books. These books, numbering several hundred volumes in 1883, were kept at the school. The students were allowed to keep a book one week and then were required to give a written and oral report to the principal.

This close surveillance of student reading of library books was the method at first adopted by most schools; firm direction made more acceptable the use of non-textbook material. The view of R. C. Metcalf, master of Wells

*Apparently Foster was held in wide esteem by public library chieftains, for he was continually asked to contribute his views to library conventions or periodicals. However, the Dewey correspondence contains extensive evidence of Foster's lack of decisiveness or self-confidence. Foster repeatedly indicates his uncertainty about a project he has taken on or begs in a last-minute request to be released from a previously accepted responsibility or duty. In Foster's last years at Providence, he required his staff to send in an advance request if they wished to talk with him.

School in Boston, illustrated the teacher's early resistance to library books in the schools. In a speech given in 1880 Metcalf noted that

> for a long time the public library has been looked upon by teachers as an enemy of the public schools. We have valiantly fought against the introduction of light literature within the sacred walls of the schoolroom. . . . We have coaxed, we have scolded, we have advised, and yet the library would give us odds and beat us every time.[74]

Metcalf brought library books to his classroom and assigned individual readings to the students. Each child then recited to him in class each day a summary of the story as it had progressed so far. Despite his rigid structuring of reading enjoyment, Metcalf was impressed by the student interest his program excited. This stimulation of student interest by supplementary reading is a revelation common to all early descriptions of cooperation between library and school. The experimental nature of Metcalf's reading program was apparent.

> My experience teaches that there is a greater degree of readiness on the part of librarians to serve the schools than of teachers to accept such service. The latter class are so sure that they already have more to do than can well be accomplished, and that the introduction of extra reading matter is an extra load to carry, rather than a help to bear what is now imposed, that it is well nigh impossible to find a respectable minority to undertake the work.[75]

The impetus given to pedagogical reform by librarians received, in 1890, the benediction of one of the most commanding figures in education during this period, William Torrey Harris. The influence of Harris can hardly be overestimated; his address to the 1890 ALA convention marks a turning point in the librarians' crusade to interest teachers in the use of non-textbook reading. Thereafter, Harris's speech was often cited by librarians as a means of winning the cooperation of teachers.

The period since 1876, Harris reflected, had been an era of unparalleled activity on the part of the librarians of the country. The ALA was the center of this "beneficent movement" to introduce library books into the public school curriculum. Because only one out of four Americans finished high school in 1890, Harris viewed the library as an essential feature of American education. Indeed, the prime mission of the school was to teach the use of the public library—"that . . . is the central object toward which our American school methods have been unconsciously guided."[76] Even with allowance granted for oratorical munificence, this was lavish praise. Harris confirmed the educational significance that librarians had long claimed for themselves.

By 1892, William Brett of the Cleveland Public Library could report that there was hardly a city library in the country that was not making a special effort to introduce books into the schools. Brett made a survey of all public libraries containing over 5,000 volumes, asking them to describe their work with the schools. "Librarians throughout the country" were alive to the importance of the work, he reported, distributing thousands of books to the schools, and providing annotated book lists and special rooms within the library for the use of students. Brett's home library in Cleveland began its school program in 1889. His survey of Cleveland teachers documented the now more or less generally accepted notion that library books not only enrich and enlarge the school course, but also serve the auxiliary purpose of bringing approved reading into the homes of immigrant parents.[77]

A high school teacher speaking to the Library Association of California in the mid-1890s provided a good summation of library-school cooperation. He had a sensitive understanding of the history of public library efforts in the schools. On entering the library, he said, teachers would find

> the most cordially welcoming hand stretched out to greet us. . . . The books are at once at our disposal, privileges of all kinds are granted to us, any amount of labor is most cheerfully entered into for our sakes. . . . Most particular[ly] is the teacher welcomed, for as [the librarians'] records show, he is the very individual on whom for years they have been seeking to lay hold.[78]

In 1896, at the instigation of John Dana, the National Educational Association created a Library Department

> to find out what has been done by teachers toward the direction and study of the reading of children; to find out what librarians had done to encourage and assist teachers in this work; to bring teachers and librarians into more mutually helpful relations; to determine the best books for various purposes and their adaptability to children of different ages.[79]

The Library Department was an active disseminator of reading information from 1897 to 1922, and its eventual demise was chiefly a result of how well the librarians had done their work. The prevalence of school libraries and school librarians had ended the necessity for the public librarian's direction and provision of supplementary reading in the school.

Beginning in the late 1870s and reaching its crest in the 1890s, the librarians' determined effort to introduce supplementary reading as an educational reform had gradually gained the support of the organized teaching profession. By 1900 the change of tone of both librarian and teacher was unmistakable. Library books within the school had become such an accepted part of education that school libraries were by then common in the cities. The support of library reading by school officials had become obvious, unargued. By the end of the century the librarian could praise the teacher as an indispensable ally in the direction of children's reading. Notes of the discussion in an 1899 meeting of the Massachusetts Library Club indicate the profound change that had taken place, for librarians were then petulantly complaining that teachers neglected to tell them of their needs in advance. Suddenly a mass of students would swarm into the public library, all demanding information on the same subject and overtaxing both the librarian and library resources. Progress was uneven, of course, especially in rural areas, but by 1900 the librarians had prevailed.

The librarians had found it necessary to create a mass use of the "popular" institution they headed. To rouse the complacent citizenry and to create a public demand for their services, they used every trick known to the propagandist. What they lacked in numbers, they made up for by the heartfelt intensity of their campaigning. They formed national and state associations, wrote numerous articles, and exhorted each other to greater effort and higher sacrifice. They advertised their wares in newspapers and in business establishments and factories. They devoted much time to devising cataloguing systems that would make the buried knowledge in books accessible to even the most uneducated user. The librarians opened the stacks and welcomed people to the library even on Sunday. To reach the public-spirited, they appealed to democratic ideals; to reach employers, they promised informed and contented workers; to reach the masses, they told of the financial rewards and emotional sustenance to be gained from the reading of library books. Naturally, such propagandists did not neglect the indoctrination of the children in their community.

Still, it is most important to note that the librarians did not attempt a serious analysis of the value of supplementary reading in the schoolroom. In all the hundreds of pages they filled with descriptions of their crusade for educational reform, the emphasis is almost entirely upon the practical tactics to be pursued in the task of pushing books upon teachers and students. Because the new educational concepts so well served the librarians' personal and professional needs, they accepted as evident fact the social desirability of an effort to transform the curriculum. Their only apparent problem was how to convince teachers of that fact.

In the developing body of literature on the process of professionalization, we are often left with a general impression that the early professionals were driven more or less unhesitatingly and directly along a predetermined continuum, by large forces of which they were usually not aware. Robert Wiebe's description of a nation seeking order places professionalization within a broad framework of the middle class acting as agents for irresistible scientific, technological, and bureaucratic forces. However, as historians move to specific studies of the differences both between professions and within professions, we may find that it is very often chance and limited personal and professional interests that most strongly determine the professional's goals at any specific time. If a constant develops, it may well be the professional's frequent resort to a narrowly self-serving mode of behavior. In the librarians' case, at least, their crusade for supplementary reading in the school seems to have effected institutional change, not because they understood the profound implications of the "new education" for a modern world, but chiefly because they were energetic men and women intent upon increasing their market value by advancing the demand for their wares. If the library profession stood slightly in advance of the educational bureaucracy in its support of reform, it was chiefly because the library, unlike the school, was relatively untrammelled by tradition, was peculiarly sensitive to popular opinion, and was freer to evolve as conditions warranted.

In recent years there has been much revising of complacent, congratulatory views of American institutions. Scholars in the history of education and in other areas have emphasized the way in which institutions function to legitimate, reinforce, reflect, and transmit ideology congenial to a capitalist society, so as to socialize the populace to the economic inequality fostered by a capitalist mode of production and instill the beliefs required to support it. Certainly the social ideals held by public library leaders shaped the public library to perpetuate the social relations of production. But it is important to recognize the way in which the complex, conflictual relationship between the American economic structure and the institutions within that social system generates protest and countercurrents to the reigning elite forces. To dwell almost exclusively upon the elite and their intentions would tend to ignore the compromises made by powerful groups — accommodations that are central to the process of American history. A revisionism that does not recognize this abrasive interaction leaves little room for popular victories, multiple outcomes, chance consequences, and the irrationalities of life. We should abandon the terrain wherein sunshine conservatives maintain the meritocratic character of American life and the dissenters show the consistent oppression of the passive or mystified weak by the mighty. Our present social reality is more complicated than this; it is probable that our past was also.

Thus, an understanding of the institutional development of the public library must center upon the interaction of the social ideals held by librarians with the popular taste they hoped to direct. In this encounter between the genteel code and public demands, the library, meeting resistance, was forced to continually modify and redirect its often elitist presumptions. During these significant years of the missionary phase of public library development, a sophisticated sector of the still culturally dominant group was moved to define conventional religious dogma and educational theory as moribund. At the same time, it continued to label mass culture as lowbrow and worker protest as dangerous. Eventually, the new professionals who replaced this group came to articulate a reform ideology within the perspective of a state more oriented to the general welfare. By 1920, progressive reform, as well as government and private repression, had sapped much popular discontent. The American economic system was refurbished as new groups, especially skilled workers and educated women, were granted a larger share of privilege.

Throughout the period of economic strife and sexual conflict in the last decades of the nineteenth century, the genteel struggled in the public library, not for instrumental social control, but for symbolic cultural dominance. There is a distinction here between instrumental acts — legislation, court decisions, and official responses — which are aimed at direct control of the people, and symbolic acts — public affirmations of moral norms — which are forms of moral suasion directed at a deviant group. It is the symbolic designation of norms which confirms the status of that group which formulates proper standards of behavior and which degrades those whose behavior is condemned as deviant.[80]

The battle of opposing groups for social power is sometimes reflected in the struggle over whether or not a moral norm will be maintained or changed. If the ideology of the still-powerful group is under serious attack, there may be an attempt to enforce the threatened norm by instrumental controls. Thus, the Comstock laws were gentry-inspired strictures designed to combat changing sexual mores and the emergence of mass culture. Similarly, Prohibition came as the culmination of an effort by the native, Protestant rural middle class to control the immigrant, Catholic or Lutheran urban working class. Ironically, it is often when value consensus is least attainable that the establishment of instrumental controls seems most appealing to the group maintaining the ideals being displaced from cultural influence. The progression of a deviant act from one defined and chastized through symbolic affirmation to one controlled by instrumental acts is an indication that the legitimacy of the norm is meeting a strong challenge.

The effort to enforce conservative literary standards in the public library, however, was clearly symbolic and ritualistic in nature, rather than instrumentally coercive. Although librarians filled hundreds of pages with their denunciations of "immoral" literature, it is apparent that they often stocked these books in abundance. Their censorship was observed more in the fanfare than in the reality. Like religious oratory, the denunciations were there less for what they accomplished than for the ideals they expressed and promised.*

If we understand the librarian's concern with the "fiction question" as a ritual of faith, a form of political theater, then it makes a certain sense. Like

---

*Despite the large amount of space and energy accorded to the fiction question in the *Library Journal* from 1876 to 1900, no definitive standard of judgment was ever seriously attempted. I conclude that this paradox can be explained if one assumes that most librarians, conscious of their community standing, were giving heavy lip service to the genteel code while in reality providing the books most demanded by their readers. A check of the catalogues of the Worcester, Massachusetts, library in 1884, the Coldwater, Michigan, library in 1896, and the Chicago Public Library in 1898 seems to support this conclusion, for these libraries had large numbers of duplicate copies of most of the questionable authors discussed in Chapter 4. For example, Worcester had 16 copies of Ainsworth, 13 of Hentz, 11 of Marryat. Coldwater held 6 Fothergill and 12 Holmes. Chicago had 4 Broughton, 10 Lawrence, and 21 Stephens. All libraries held at least 2 copies of each suspect author, with the exception of Reynolds and Mathers, who were missing from all three categories.

works of art, rituals of this type can be understood in terms of the expressive values and states of mind they convey to a target audience. What upholds social ritual of this sort is not empirical truth, but a shared sense that the ritual names and celebrates a legitimate underlying order.

Because education is, in many respects, the American faith, it was natural that the public library, like the school, should have become a rich focus for expressive meaning in Victorian America. In the public library important cultural ideas were given form. The belief that America was a radical democratic experiment in government; the sense of urban crisis and chaos; the fear of immigrant intruders; the emphasis upon the family as guarantor of tradition; the discontent of women and labor; the hope that education would right the wrongs of poverty and crime; the hunger for education among the poor; the ambiguous paternalistic and humanitarian motives of reformers — all were as important to the content of library ritual as the need for a contented, disciplined, and busy wage force. Like the school, the library tended to be progressive as society was, in fostering civil liberties and political representation, and to be oppressive as the economic system was, in maintaining inequality of income and opportunity by a division of the citizens along lines of class, race, and sex. Yet the library's rhetorical ritual must be understood as more than just a cultural poem or drama; it was, after all, a tale with a purpose, a story that was being told to some people by other people. The library's rejection of realistic fiction was an encounter between the declining gentry — who sought to shape and articulate cultural meaning — and those who listened and sometimes responded.

Although public librarians professed to be most interested in the provision of education and uplift to the poor and the workingmen, in fact their overpowering concern was with the threat to conventional standards of sexual conduct created by the preference of their feminine clients for new types of best-selling fiction. No other question engaged them more than this one. The library's exceedingly prudish attitude toward light fiction is one of the best examples of the way in which public librarians approached public service. Unlike the school, however, the public library did not have the power to force the people to make use of its offerings. Thus librarians found it necessary to serve the new literary taste in order to attract a clientele. The tension between felt ideals and unpleasant social realities is reflected in the librarians' confused and often contradictory attempts to establish some precise standard by which to judge "immoral" literature. Because of the librarians' concept of reading as moral instruction — strengthened by the conservative attitudes of library trustees — the public library only slowly, halfheartedly, accepted the popular demand for recreational reading which expressed modern concerns.

In this analysis of the library ideology that was devised in response to economic conflict and sexual change, two major approaches to a study of the social determinants of beliefs have been utilized. One is "interest theory." According to this approach, idea systems are determined by the economic motivations of those who adhere to such systems, and these motivations are dependent in turn upon class position and perceived economic advantage. The great value of interest theory is that it roots societal thought-systems in institutional structures and exposes the effect of social class upon individual motivations and actions. The other major approach to the analysis of ideology is "strain theory." Strain theory conceives of ideology as a production of ideas designed to ameliorate the social and psychological stress experienced by those who profess the ideas.[81]

The use of strain theory, in combination with interest theory, allows us to see the role ideology can play in draining off emotional tensions, in sustaining groups, and in bringing social problems to public attention. Library ideology functioned in some sense as a cathartic means to displace sociopsychological tension onto scapegoats — the grasping rich, the corrupt politicians, the ignorant immigrants, the immoral fiction, the dangerous radicals. By naming symbolic enemies, the library could ease somewhat the pain experienced by individuals whose cultural influence was being diminished. Library ideology also served to knit librarians together as a group. To the extent that it existed, professionalization rested to some degree upon a common emotive and expressive orientation. Finally, library thought worked to focus public attention upon the social problems and social stress that impelled the defense of the genteel code in the first place. Without the proponents of a conservative literary ideal, there could have been no debate about all that was implied in the newer forms of fiction.

It was, in fact, when American society began to free itself of received religious tradition, conventional moralism, and laissez-faire philosophy that the genteel ideology was most clearly enunciated. It was the confluence of economic conflict with religious doubt and female rebellion that produced sociopsychological stress, exacerbated by the absence of cultural constructs by which to make sense of that strain. The library's effort to shape public morality was closely related to the larger movements of urban philanthropy and the social purity crusade of the time; both, in turn, were essentially an elite response to deep-seated fears about the drift of city life. But literary censorship in this period was not primarily a matter of suppressive attacks by genteel adherents; "it was simply the sum total of countless small decisions made by editors, publishers, booksellers, librarians. critics and — occasionally — vice-societies, all based on a common conception of literary propriety."[82]

Social movements to redefine morality may lead to what Joseph Gusfield has described as a moral passage: "a transition of the behavior from one moral status to another."[83] Moral crusades of this type, supported by those who are losing control over public statements of morality, will tend to generate a countermovement of unrepentant deviants. In the late nineteenth century, as public librarians valiantly struggled to uphold the genteel tradition in literature, they presided over such a moral passage. In the process, they encountered the strong challenge posed by the defense of pluralistic literary standards in an industrializing, often democratic, secular society.

PART 2

Moral Passage: The Fiction Problem

Then the first thing will be to establish a censorship of the writers of fiction, and let the censors receive any tale of fiction which is good and reject the bad; and we will desire mothers and nurses to tell their children the authorized ones only. . . . But if there is an absolute necessity for. . . mention [of bad tales] a chosen few might hear them in a mystery. . . .

—Plato, *The Republic*

If the school-house and the church made New England, the public library preserves it.

—*Library Journal* (1896)

4

Immoral Fiction in the Late Victorian Library

ONE OF THE MOST IMPORTANT changes in the late Victorian age, perhaps the furthest reaching of all in its revolutionary implications, was the triumph of mass culture. Blithely ignoring the warnings of their betters against the evils of reading "salacious" fiction, the American masses, with unrepenting self-indulgence, consumed the "volumes of trash poured forth daily, weekly and monthly" in the form of imaginative literature.[1] Above all it was the American woman who found in light reading a temporary escape from isolation and discontent. In the last quarter of the nineteenth century, the shelves of the American public library began to reflect the influence of the new mass readership upon library standards. By the turn of the century, the young generation had abandoned many of the fixed values of the past and had begun to experiment with new modes of thought and behavior that embraced change, variety, and experiment. The quest for change and the resistance to modernity created a cultural crisis that in many ways America has yet to overcome.

Codified in fiction-fantasy, the alteration of fundamental values expressed in many best-selling novels aroused the indignation of those Americans who resisted the value change. Significantly, the objection to deviation in literary standards, as revealed by the public librarian's preoccupation with "the fiction question," was made largely on moral grounds. Esthetic complaints were minor matters compared to the moral ire of those who sought to shape popular reading taste. Library censorship of fiction was erected to resist or to channel rapid value change. Perhaps conservatives recognized that deviance in moral theory was a good index of radicalism in general. The person who questioned sexual standards was also likely to entertain heretical views regarding the efficacy of prayer, the concept of private property, and the benevolence of political parties.

Until the end of the nineteenth century the early library chieftains demonstrated a deep concern over the quality and quantity of light reading provided to the public.[2] Upper middle class to the core, by birth, education, or imitation, they feared that their missionary work with the masses would be subverted by the popular passion for suspect fiction. Through the late 1880s many public libraries regularly published and analyzed the figures for the percentage of fiction in the total yearly circulation. An increase in the percentage brought dark self-questioning. A decrease of one-tenth of a point was cause for joy.*

Ever since the invention of the printing press the better educated have feared, despaired over, or clucked over the reading taste of the common folk, but the unprecedented expansion of popular culture in late Victorian America was a new development. The threat posed by the large numbers of readers touched off the production of a great body of articles and books designed to give reading direction to the less educated. These literary guides had titles like *Books, Culture and Character, The Abuse of Reading, Books and Ideals, Good Habits in Reading,* and *The Reading of Books: Its Pleasures, Profits and Perils.* Early library leaders frequently quoted these how-and-what-to-read books and offered these and similar writings to public library patrons. An analysis of the literary guidebooks recommended by leading librarians will reveal the standards by which traditionalists judged good and bad in best-selling fiction and how they presented their guidelines in popularized form to the public they were seeking to control.[3]

There is a striking homogeneity in this group of writings, a similarity of tone and repetitious quoting of the same authorities that exemplifies a common purpose and a clearly stated artistic creed. Confronted by the ever-widening gulf between the earlier idealism and the reality of mass tastes, these traditionalists stationed themselves at a fork where two paths diverged—one, almost deserted, leading toward the esthetics developed through generations of religious and social formalism; the other, toward an acceptance of contemporary actualities. While the mass movement streamed by them, they pulled fretfully at the public's coat-sleeves, disheartened and

---

*In 1878 the Mercantile Public Library in San Francisco reported 71.4 per cent of its circulation was fiction, while .6 per cent was religious works. In the same year the Indianapolis library crowed that its fiction circulation had dropped from 80 to 72 per cent, after heroic efforts had been made by the librarian to reduce fiction reading. The St. Louis library reported a "remarkably" small circulation of fiction—53.9 per cent. In 1887 a speaker to the New York Library Club declared that "the great mass of reading done by the people is devoted to novels and romances," ranging from 60 to 87 per cent. Three prominent California libraries in 1895 had collections that were 11 to 13 per cent fiction, yet recorded the percentage of fiction in circulation as from 53 to 79 per cent. The percentage of fiction circulated had varied little from 1876 to the present, usually between 65 to 85 per cent of all books loaned during the year in an average public library.

vexed because their warnings had no appreciable effect on the direction taken by the moving hordes. Their moral certitude gave their writing strength, but there was also in their pages a note of resigned bafflement, for they realized that fewer and fewer people shared their fears.

A predominant theme in this commentary was the knowledge that the mass production of printed material had ushered in an entirely new conception of the educated class in society. These defenders of traditional esthetics clearly remembered the educated generation who were familiar with relatively few books, who "were well-acquainted with the greater Greek and Roman classics . . . , who had read and reread Locke, Bacon, Milton in prose," and were not "tempted to hurry through a book because there was a public library across the way offering a thousand others equally worthy of their attention."[4] That golden time, when measured reading developed the intellect and trained men to "habits of accuracy and perseverance," was recognized as irretrievable, however, even by the most conservative spokesmen. In general, these writers defended the public passion for certain types of light reading. Because they were addressing the masses—those "earnest readers to whom books and reading are . . . amusement . . . inspiration and relaxation"[5]—the literary traditionalists stifled their lament for the time when classical learning marked them apart as the educated class. They sensed that a generation which would read Zola would no more read Homer than it would attempt a cuneiform inscription.

Even as they accepted some of the revolutionary change brought about by mass publication, their shock at the multiplication of books was so great as to seem humorous to the modern reader, who has long been reconciled to the impossibility of reading all that is worth reading. Again and again these literary conservatives emphasized that the average reader should not be ashamed to admit that he or she was wholly ignorant of a great many books. Arithmetical discussions were often offered as proof of the point.

> One can read only a small proportion of the twenty-five thousand volumes now published every year. . . . An English critic has estimated that more than three thousand years will be needed for the merely mechanical process of reading the books which either are or have been standard works of literature. A book read each week in a lifetime would aggregate only twenty-six hundred volumes.[6]

"IT IS OUT OF THE QUESTION TO READ EVERYTHING," librarian Frederick Perkins assured his readers in bold print.[7]

The literary traditionalists were aware that one effect of the growth of mass literacy and popular culture would be to decentralize the influence once held by a small group over American letters. They hoped to retain a measure of control over popular taste by convincing the public that only clear principles of guidance would suffice "to keep the head cool in the torrent and din of works . . ., the storm of literature around us."[8] The masses, in moral peril, were much in need of the "influence of trained thinkers and students in directing the choice and valuation of books, and times and modes of reading."[9] Only professional guidance and clearly defined standards would establish order in the anarchical provinces of popular taste.

It should be understood that when literary conservatives spoke in general terms of the power for evil exerted by morally doubtful books, they were usually thinking of the terrifying effects of domestic and sensational fiction upon the "gentle sex." By the 1870s American fiction had fallen almost entirely into the hands of women. Not only were the great majority of novel readers women, but feminine standards shaped the form of fiction in many magazines. This feminine reading class had been growing and gathering momentum since the 1830s. Women readers had been, at first, even until the middle of the century, generally content with tales of heavy sentiment and syrupy heroines.[10] After the Civil War, however, Americans felt the sand shifting under old totems as the general process of social evolution brought change in women's economic and legal status, on a scale that seemed irreversible. With this social change, a fictional literature that embodied female discontent was also born.

Only against the background of our contemporary understanding of the long-term feminist revolution just beginning to be articulated in the last half of the nineteenth century can we place in proper perspective the menace to tradition presented by many books of popular fiction.[11] It was preeminently the woman reader who was supposed to be protected against the inflammatory literature that unsettled morals, "not only because her delicate, impressionable nature may be more easily injured by worthless or harmful literature than man's, but because to her it is given to shape the destiny of man and of nations through the *Home*, which is the great center and strength of both individual and national life."[12] With so much resting upon feminine acceptance of woman's customary role, those books that stimulated her rebellion against the nature of things were a threat to the entire social structure. Modern fiction, the traditionalists knew, had a tendency to agitate rather than confirm.

New types of fiction encouraged female readers to desire wider experiences than could be found within the limits of their normal routine. Their virtuous, uneventful days were set against "dashing deeds and passionate joys . . . and appear all the more dull and profitless by the comparison." Even the mild works of Mrs. E. D. E. N. Southworth depicted imaginary conditions and possibilities that stimulated thoughts which resulted "in terrible revolt against the laws of social safety."[13] The tranquil and industrious home life was held up to scorn in pernicious fiction. A dangerous new type of heroine emerged: "the silly and the weak-minded woman, the fast and slangy girl, the intrigante and the 'shady' . . . to drag us forever along the dizzy, half-fractured precipice of the seventh commandment . . . to force us to sup . . . on misery and sensuousness."[14] By genteel standards, the

American woman's duty was to teach self-denial to man and to thus refine and spiritualize civilization. Deprived of body and mind, women were chiefly composed of soul. New forms of fiction threatened traditionalists on two counts. It featured vivid, sprightly heroines, who not only chafed under domestic isolation but also had an excess of sexual energy that denied the basic degradation of sensual delights.[15]

Many of the new "immoral" books of fiction constructed a theoretical model of female oppression and dramatized wronged womanhood. Designed to appeal to middle-class women, some novels sketched an all-out war between the sexes. Much of the best-selling suspect fiction, while couching antimasculinity in a conventional framework, yet expressed female anger and frustration through a criticism of the marriage market and monogamy. Late Victorian feminism was full of contradictions; some of the new fiction called for more self-control for men rather than new license for women. The new ideas were disseminated through novels to thousands of potential converts and encouraged a kind of covert solidarity among women readers.

The reading of salacious books not only prompted a general female rebellion; it also threatened to unleash the emotional, unreasoning element in human nature. To the Victorian-shaped traditionalist, it was important to retain emotional control — to practice self-discipline, self-denial, and rationality. The fusion of ascetic Protestantism and democratic capitalism had internalized a set of cultural values that insisted upon control of sexual expression, spontaneity, and emotion.[16] This value system persisted far into the post-Civil War era even though its religious justification was fast losing credibility. Newer notions of morality, which sanctioned sensual indulgence, were in the late nineteenth century drawing strength from the relativism engendered by new research in the biological and sociological sciences. Meanwhile the older, collapsing morality held tenaciously to the concept that the deliberate excitation of feeling and frivolity should be deplored.

One of the most detailed examples of the way Christian and utilitarian tenets worked together to support older literary standards was Noah Porter's *Books and Reading*, first published in 1870. It carefully defined the special dangers and temptations which awaited the unwary reader. A certain class of romantic novels was said to excite "mischievous expectations of extraordinary turns of fortune, and beget, even in sober and sensible people, a romantic and dreamy habit of mind in respect to the chances of success in life, and the conditions by which it is to be achieved."[17] Besides this yearning for status beyond reality, the inveterate novel reader often acquired a craving for constant excitement. So stimulated, a reader lost his sober judgment and his resignation to life's afflictions. Fictional characters and scenes that gave false conceptions of duty, honor, and life would unsettle the morals of even the most virtuous reader. Porter obviously sensed that faith in the beneficent order of the universe, with its emphasis upon self-denial and acceptance of patriarchal authority, was a shaky tenet in the 1870s.[18] Since only a slight jolt might topple it, it was better to avoid entirely any literature that increased doubt.

Porter also warned that reading was serious business and ought never to be aimless or free from the restraints of conscience. One should have a fixed aim in mind, even if the aim was only to while away an hour. Indiscriminate reading excited the sensibilities and relaxed the power of attention. One method of controlling attention to reading that Porter recommended was to hold one's breath through each sentence, the breath being released as the sentence was finished.[19]

But the literary conservative's wistfulness for vanished days was expressed most subtly in his defense of the "ideal" in literary treatment. The genteel tradition in literature held to a concept of beauty that rested on the belief in a universal, divinely appointed, beneficent order. Yet, to present life as it was in reality was to touch upon the absurdities, the commonplaces, and all the disagreeable aspects of human experience. The danger of realism, however, lay not in the portrayal of human doubt and ugliness but in the conclusions pointed out to the reader by that portrayal. Evil, if discussed at all, was supposed to reflect the shame and the remorse of sin as well as its glory and short-lived triumph. If fiction mirrored social disorder and meaningless existence or effaced the lines between virtue and vice, then the reader, especially the feminine one, might be led to question the fundamental truths of a benevolently ordered world.

This staunch defense of things as they were was the most prevalent theme in the how-and-what-to-read books that librarians recommended to their patrons. Rarely does one of this group of authors miss a chance to quote the following statement by Robert Southey in its entirety:

> Would you know whether the tendency of a book is good or evil, examine in what state of mind you lay it down. Has it induced you to suspect that that which you have been accustomed to think unlawful may, after all be innocent, and that that may be harmless, which you hitherto had been taught to think dangerous? Has it tended to make you dissatisfied and impatient under the control of others? and disposed you to relax in that self-government without which both the laws of God and man tell us there can be no virtue, and consequently no happiness? Has it attempted to abate your admiration and reverence for what is great and good, and to diminish in you the love of your country and your fellow-creatures? Has it addressed itself to your pride, your vanity, your selfishness, or any of your evil propensities? Has it defiled the imagination with what is loathsome and shocked the heart with what is monstrous? Has it disturbed the sense of right and wrong which the Creator has implanted? . . . If so . . . throw the book into the fire![20]

The traditionalist also feared the influence of imaginative literature because a clever author could arouse sympathy for sinners. The reader who felt compassion or understanding for the fictional character who did not follow traditional patterns in behavior and thought might extend that sympathy into dangerous fantasizing about the possibility of challenging the accepted value system. If in a book evil triumphed just as much as good, or if life were given no God-sanctioned meaning, then the reader might internalize "a fevered and fantastic vision of utter unreality."[21] In 1883 Charles Dudley Warner's widely read attack on modern fiction declared that in immoral books "life, we are told, is full of incompletion, of broken destinies, of failures, of romances that begin but do not end, of ambitions and purposes frustrated, of love crossed." Warner longed to see again the "lovely heroine, the sweet woman, capable of a great passion and a great sacrifice . . . at the end in a blissful contemplation of her troubles, and embued with a new and sweeter charm." Instead he found in modern literature an obsession with the tempter and the temptress, with unhappy marriages and with a frivolous view of life that widened discontent with domestic and social order and lessened sensual constraints.[22] Since fiction's effect on moral principles was so powerful, it was essential that literature describe an idealized world, where examples of thought and actions were more noble than actual contact with life could possibly furnish.

The genteel defense of the ideal in literature was also an attempt to dignify the standing of the cultural elite. By defining art as the perception of an ideal world transcending the normal, the genteel could inflate the image of the artist, with whom they identified, and could make the writer into a genius with an elevated, almost mystical, insight into Beauty and Truth. The implication of this doctrine of poetic genius was that the artist was an agent of general perfection, revealing to corrupt or less perceptive persons the grand design of life.[23]

A corollary to this idea of the writer as prophet was the genteel conception of literature as primarily educational and disciplinary in function. The didactic purpose given to reading was of old standing, having evolved partly as a result of the reverence once paid to a literate minority and to the Bible. The traditionalist, as revealed by the tone of the how-and-what-to-read homilies, had an overriding desire to instruct and elevate the public. By emphasizing a noble and idealized world, genteel culture above all sought to teach people how to behave.

The aspect of literary idealism which has been most remembered is the excessive prudery regarding any discussion of sexual love. The censorship of literature in matters of the flesh reached remarkable proportions in the late nineteenth century. Such a basic change as the New Woman represented would probably not have activated such intense apprehension if it had not been aggravated by the other painful concerns felt by the genteel mind — fears of the effect of declining religious faith, of economic strife, of the conservative's slippery control of culture, of dissolving standards and clashing creeds. The appearance of the New Woman, bent on shattering the unconscious dual imagery of Goddess of Life and Vagina with Teeth, was a culminating blow. One way in which the champions of conservatism fought back was to purge women of the promptings of the senses and to separate Art from erotic desire.

Guilded as they were by the standards of literary conservatism, public librarians made a bold attempt in 1881 to define the best-selling fiction that offended genteel sensibilities. In that year the American Library Association Cooperation Committee sent a questionnaire to 70 major public libraries to determine if they had ever held, or had later withdrawn, the works of certain authors. The list was limited to those "whose works are sometimes excluded from public libraries by reason of sensational or immoral qualities."[24] As might have been expected, the librarians did not entirely agree on the objectionable authors, but the list does give a good indication of the suspect fiction which, because of its popular appeal, was most troublesome to them.

An analysis of the major themes in these widely read but "injurious" books provides clues not only to the genteel conscience but to mass thought. It is in popular fiction, Arthur Lovejoy has argued, that the tendencies of an age may appear most directly. Writers of genius "are for all time. . . . But in the sensitive, responsible souls of less creative power, current ideals record themselves with clearness."[25] Yet there is serious disagreement among scholars as to how accurately popular fiction reflects the reader's curiosities, values, and views in the context of the characters to which he responds. Is mass culture the "number two brain in the withering tail of the dinosaur? Or the antennae of the race?"[26] Does widespread fantasy that violates established standards precede value change, or does such fantasy-making more often tend to be antirevolutionary because it permits vicarious discharge of conflict?

These are extraordinarily complex questions, and historians who puzzle over popular culture must be exceedingly cautious in their imputations of collective behavior. Certainly any analysis of popular fiction that does not mesh with extensive outside historical evidence of a more traditional nature can be justly criticized as "presentism" or as a fallacious jump from information about the limited book-reading public to inferences about the "collective mind" or the "average American." However, when fiction is both "immoral" and immensely popular we can be certain that it does catch cultural reverberations which are disturbing to the group that designates it as deviant. Because there is abundant outside evidence of a questioning of the traditional role of women during this time, we can safely assume that many readers of the period's fiction were responding to its themes not with confusion and anger, but with excitement and interest. Above all, an understanding of the themes of immoral fiction gives insight into the troubled concern of the time with intellectual and ethical problems. Amid the whirl of social change in the late nineteenth century, the small literary flurry over book selection in the public library serves to dramatize not only esthetic concerns but important questions of morality and religion that perplexed the age.

The librarians' committee listed sixteen questionable authors.[27] Ten of these can be generally classified as domestic novelists, writing chiefly for women and about feminine experience: Ann Sophia Stephens (1813-1886), Mrs. E. D. E. N. Southworth (1819-1899), Mary Jane Holmes (1828-1907), Caroline Lee Hentz (1800-1856), Augusta Jane Evans Wilson (1835-1909), Jessie Fothergill (1851-1891), Rhoda Broughton (1840-1920), Florence Marryat (1837-1899), Helen Mathers (1853-1920), and Mrs. Forrester (1850-1896?). Mary Elizabeth Braddon (1837-1915) and Ellen Price (Mrs. Henry) Wood (1814-1887) represent the school of domestic criminals in their tales of outwardly ordinary women who commit adultery, bigamy, and murder. A little less oriented toward feminine readers are George Alfred Lawrence (1827-1876) and Ouida (1840-1908), with their muscular heroes and wild, sensuous women. William Harrison Ainsworth (1805-1882) and G. W. M. Reynolds (1814-1879) wrote the "Newgate Novel" of complicated action, violence, and unabashed emphasis on sex.

Common to all these best sellers is a rejection of traditional authority, particularly in domestic life, in religious faith, and in matters concerning class distinction. The rebellion is sometimes blatant and crude, more often subtle and half-hidden by platitudes. Indeed, it is the embedding of covert antimasculinity within a strongly conventional framework that may be the crucial factor in the popularity of these works with women readers. Feminine protest is made more acceptable when served in a traditional setting. These authors strike out at the clergy, the pompous rich, the penal system. Receiving the most vigorous blows is the marriage system itself, as its faults are perceived through the eyes of women. And throughout most of these books is one dominating theme—how strong woman decisively conquers and slyly manipulates weak man.[28]

"Women must marry—it is their vocation!" exclaims the simpering Miss Alton as she plots an alliance with the repugnant but wealthy Lord Clayton.[29] Even so self-sufficient and lively a young woman as Nell Adair has to agree that a spinster is a poor and powerless creature. "No wonder men call themselves lords of creation!" Nell muses. "It is not for what they are, but for what they give, that they are of so much importance; all good things come to a woman through a plain gold circlet, apparently!"[30] Most of the heroines of this fiction acknowledge that even an unloved husband, assuming that he is at least not cruel, is preferable to none at all. The overriding interest of the unmarried girl is to trap a husband, and the main concern of the married woman is to be content with the man she has—or failing that, to escape into fictional dreams of domestic bliss or wild abandonment.

The domestic novelists of immoral fiction met their woman reader's needs; their work was a kind of strategy manual for prospective brides and unhappy wives. In their novels the male figure is frequently stupid, wholly submissive to feminine whims, or in some way an emotional cripple. Those male figures who show spunk and strength are finally brought to heel by the more dominant female. Nor do women fail to recognize the true meaning of their performance. It may be a man's world, but the fictional heroine in these novels knows she is the real ruler on the throne, her realm gained and held by the tender mechanisms of "weakness" or "love." So far there is nothing really new in these depictions of woman reacting to her ancient state of "powerlessness"; manipulation of the male toward female-selected goals is an old and honored preoccupation.[31] What *is* new about the morally objectionable popular authors of this period is their much more open discussion of the female's plight: the necessity of selling one's life to the best bidder in exchange for security, the indignity and injustice of such a system, and the wearisome isolation of the woman within her home. New, too, is the bold heroine, with more energy than virtue, who scoffs at convention and wins a worthy husband despite her uncommon approach.

Rhoda Broughton's outspoken Belinda is such a heroine—full-bodied, intelligent, and caustic. Belinda and her sister Sarah cavort through Europe "chaperoned" by a bright-eyed grandmother who harbors memories of an exciting past beneath her ruffled cap. Granny always lets the girls go where they want, so long as they do not ask her to accompany them. Frivolous Sarah takes full advantage of the situation, but Belinda is too proud to copy her sister's light coquetries and masks her tumultuous inner passion with a "cold hard voice and chill set face." Yet young David Rivers finally succumbs to her will and proposes to her, after Belinda has lured him into going alone with her into a romantic spot in the forest. Rivers is aware that Belinda's outward conformity to Victorian propriety is merely a cover for her eager sexuality. He would not mind if a woman treated him like a dog in public, he tells her, "if she were—if she were—as I would have her when we were alone." But Rivers forsakes Belinda because he feels he is too poor to support a wife.[32]

Our heroine finally enters a loveless marriage with a flat-footed, aged pedant from Oxford. "It is a mere matter of business," she explains to her husband. "You want a secretary, housekeeper, nurse for your mother; I want a home of my own, and a guide, philosopher and friend." In less than a week her marriage goes sour.

> Belinda had been married three days . . . recollecting how many lumps of sugar he likes, as she has already discovered that he has no objection to repeating. . . . Nor is it less monstrous to be warming his overcoat, and cutting his newspapers, and ordering his dinner with that nice attention to digestibility and economy which she finds to be expected of her. They have been enormously long, these three days.[33]

Her life becomes that of a sullen coolie in harness as she responds to her hated husband's calls—to the "voice she had given the right to command Belinda; to chide Belinda; immeasurably worst of all, to caress Belinda."[34]

When Rivers reappears upon the scene, now a rich man, Belinda responds to his longing for her with only the barest twinge of conscience. She feels more anger than shame. What, indeed, is sin? she rebelliously questions. "Is it to fulfill with nice scrupulosity every tasteless or even nauseous duty of a most dreary life? To sing as she walks her treadmill? To forego her own hot bright youth? . . . To be secretary without pay, a drudge without wage?" After pages more of maneuver, yearning, and husband's cruelty, Belinda and Rivers, in one "drunk, oblivious moment," embrace with "loud blood dinning in their ears and hammering their temples."[35] Belinda decides to risk ultimate disgrace and run away with Rivers. Happily this is unnecessary, since her husband falls dead on the last page of the book. When she finds his body, Belinda is apparently overcome by sheer delight and falls in a faint—thus succumbing to a feminine stratagem that she has heretofore scorned in women. The book ends on a note of high glee, with illegal love triumphant.

More respectable than Belinda, but just as unconventional in thought, is Jessie Fothergill's heroine May Wedderburn, who at age seventeen manages to escape her dull existence as the daughter of an English clergyman. Living alone in Germany while she studies for a singing career, she falls in love with a mysterious gentleman named Eugene whose eyes shock "with a kind of tameless freedom in their glance."[36] May moves into Eugene's hotel, where she has a room so conveniently situated that she can spy on him through his window. Obviously sensual and competent in love, May is continually washed with "wave after wave of wild emotion," especially when brushing against Eugene as they pass each other on the stairs. The author often emphasizes May's passionate nature: "Sometimes a subdued fire glowed in her eyes and compressed her lips, which removed her altogether from the category of spiritless beauties."[37]

Eugene is finally won over by his apparent weakness for the female form draped in clinging wet clothes. After some maneuvering on her part, he rescues her from drowning and carries her home in his arms. Trembling in his embrace, May thinks, "In the midst of the torpor that was stealing over me there shot every now and then a shiver of ecstasy so keen as to almost terrify me."[38] May—bohemian, talented, irreligious, and "that most dreadful of all abnormal growths, a woman with a will of her own"—does have some qualms about her adjustment to married life: "Should I not be shocking him by coarse, gross notions as to the needlessness of this or that fine point of conduct? by my ill defined ideas as to a code of honor—my slovenly ways of looking at questions?"[39] The reader, though, feels little doubt that May's steel center will ever collapse or that she will allow herself to remain in any situation that she does not control. Eugene, of thin ankles and worshipping heart, is no match for dauntless May.

Whereas Belinda and May verily throb with sexual energy, the incredibly popular heroine of *St. Elmo*, Edna Earl, seems to be free of all drives except the urge to dominate her world. In St. Elmo Murray she finds a worthy opponent in the battle of the sexes. Edna, an orphan, has been taken into St. Elmo's home by his wealthy mother. With unremitting application, Edna tackles the whole of knowledge, learning along the way Sanskrit, Chaldean, Arabic, Cufic, Greek, and Latin. Edna does not approve of bluestockings or of pushy women who want the vote. Nonetheless, she remains "obstinately wedded to the unpardonable heresy, that, in the nineteenth century, it was a woman's privilege to be as learned as Cuvier, or Sir William Hamilton, or Humboldt."[40]

Edna and her learning provided wits with numerous opportunities for ridicule; as one commented, she cannot bring home a cow from the pasture without a dozen classical allusions to fit the occasion. Words like epoptae, chrysolegent, and lotophagi; places like Alfrasib and Demophaon; and references to "meleschott's dictum" and the "incipient Isotta Negarole" abound in her communication with others. Even when crying into her pillow she speaks in grandly structured sentences: "Commit me rather to the horny but outstretched hands, the brawny arms, the untutored minds, the simple but kindly-throbbing hearts of the proletaire!"[41] It is easy to laugh at Edna's high-flown language, less easy to be amused at the woman reader's pathetic hunger for status through knowledge reflected in the popularity of *St. Elmo.*[42] Edna, who eventually becomes a famous author, understands her public's longing for education.

The major theme of *St. Elmo*, however, is the reduction of the strong and sinful hero to a blob of jelly by the indomitable Edna. St. Elmo Murray admits to having killed his best friend in a duel and to having jilted his fiancé at the altar. The shock caused that unfortunate bride-to-be to have a hemorrhage of the lungs on the church steps, and she died two months later; thus St. Elmo is responsible for two deaths. The effects of these happenings, he says, warped his nature and deformed his soul. He entered a life of wandering and hatred: "I drank, gambled, and my midnight carousels would sicken your soul, were I to paint all their hideousness."[43] Edna is unbending; St. Elmo must become purified if he is ever to be worthy of her love. She defers marriage to him until she has won fame and fortune on her own and he has become a spineless ghost of himself — a mild-mannered minister, inferior to her even in his religious potency. Thus do Edna, and her readers, realize their dream: a marriage in which the real psychological and intellectual power is firmly held by the wife.

Sometimes the hero of domestic fiction is not merely subjected to female domination but is literally destroyed by his love for the heroine. This fate awaits Paul Vasher in the very popular *Coming Thro' the Rye*, perhaps because the heroine, Nell Adair, has very early in her childhood rejected male supremacy.[44] Nell decisively repudiates a decorative femininity and glories in her delight at feeling "more than half a boy." She even resents her restrictive clothing.

> How cumbrous, and useless, and ridiculous they are; how my gowns, petticoats, crinolines, ribbons, ties, cloaks, hats, bonnets, gloves, tapes, hooks, eyes, buttons, and the hundred and one et ceteras that make up a girl's costume, chafe and irritate me! What would I not give to be able to leave them all in a heap and steal . . . Jack's cool, comfortable, easy grey garments?[45]

Her heart abounds in joy when she dons knickerbockers for the first time to play a game of cricket. Nell is as emotionally rugged as any man. Tears are to her a cowardly refuge for suffering women. She would "far rather storm" through a crisis than simply weep and bear the pain.

Unable to locate a man who shares her advanced views, Nell drifts into a betrothal with Paul, who is heavily traditional in his ideas about female passivity: "Paul Vasher is like the rest of his sex, who value their privileges too highly to permit women to encroach the merest jot upon them, and would build so prickly a wall of propriety around us, that we shall not be able to climb up and see what is going on on the other side."[46] The conflicting views of Nell and Paul provide the author with numerous opportunities to discuss the relation of the sexes. Invariably Nell enters a debate:

> "The Man should always rule," says Paul, in his masterful way; "and you may say what you like, Nell, but you would love to be ruled, you would like to be kept in order."
>
> "No, no," I say gravely . . . "a man grows tired of treating his mistress or wife like a goddess or baby; he wants more solid stuff to live on, and the one everlasting dish palls him. If she will look the knowledge in the face that such is the case, and putting sentiment on one side enter heartily into his ambitions and aims, and hopes, and amusements, she becomes not only the beloved woman, but the bright, pleasant comrade, who is bound to him by fifty ties of mutual interest and support; they are equals, and he considers her as capable of giving advice as taking it."[47]

Despite the running battle he fights with Nell, it is clear that even strait-laced Paul prefers a girl with spunk. But Paul, who mistakenly believes that Nell has wed another man, is tricked into marriage to a stock villainess. Realizing his error, Paul offers to leave his wife and run away with Nell, but Nell refuses to endure such disgrace. Broken and tortured, Paul ages thirty years in two years' time and finally escapes to a merciful death on the Sudan battlefield. Nell elects to remain a spinster, supremely confident of her ability to function independently of men.

Unlike the heroines above, who are not physical beauties, Rachael Norreys combines all the characteristics of beauty, will, intelligence, and passion. Rachael eloped when she was sixteen but her father found the errant couple before the marriage was consummated. When her husband, Raymond, returns after an absence of five years to claim his bride, Rachael finds that she is not ready to settle down to domestic life. But the celibacy that she imposes on herself and her husband is not easy for either of them to endure. Her sensuality is the one force that

> could subdue her pride. . . . No one could help seeing it who saw anything. It flashed out of her liquid eyes; it hung upon her ripe, tremulous mouth; it made itself known in the sensitiveness of her nervous little hand; in the sudden flushing of her cheek—the low, impassioned accents of her voice. Yes, she could love, and she should love![48]

When Raymond unjustly accuses her of having a man in her bedroom she is too proud even to explain the truth to him. She moves out of their home in a rage. "With fire flashing from her irradiated eyes, with her delicate nostrils distended,"[49] she determines never to return. Even when Raymond begs her forgiveness, she refuses to submit or to allow him to "lay his feet upon her neck." Only many months later, when he is near death (and has also, incidentally, inherited a baronetcy and rich estates), does Rachael accept his apology and return as his wife. Raymond has presumedly learned a lifelong lesson: "However unpleasant they may be at times, it is your stormy women, after all, that can love the best, although they may be the most dangerous when crossed."[50]

The preoccupation with manipulating and trapping men characteristic of domestic fiction is particularly blatant in *Fair Women*, a tale of matchmaking in high society. Rich Lord Clayton makes the point clear in his assessment of marriage: "Why the devil should I bind myself to one woman, of whom I should get heartily sick in a month, when I can indulge myself with all the pleasing varieties of the sex at half the cost? . . . Of course you can buy them—it only depends on whether you're willing or able to pay the price."[51] Miss Alton, who is plotting to marry Clayton, realizes that he is malicious and cruel, and yet she imagines that she can use his money to escape him: "If you lived in the country and were to be bored with him all day long, it would be the most awful thing conceivable; but you know that fashionable wives are not much troubled with their husband's company, and can always get away from it." The less fortunate middle-class woman reader who was also caught in an unhappy marriage must have been glad to see that Miss Alton's freedom, once she became Mrs. Clayton, was as severely limited as her own. However, bold Mrs. Clayton's married life is enriched by a love affair with a handsome colonel who begs her to run away with him. Lord Clayton's behavior drives her to heretical thoughts: "We hear sometimes of women leaving their husbands, and then the world cries them down, and they never dare show their faces in society again. If people could know [half] of what a wife may suffer, I wonder if they would be so harsh?"[52]

It is what an unhappy wife suffers that these novels present in rich detail. The morally suspect authors could not always defy convention and allow a runaway wife to live in full contentment forever. Therefore they often killed off the husband in one way or another—in Lord Clayton's case, with cholera—before they could assure lasting joy to the rebellious heroine. But even the unhappy runaway is given more than enough reason to escape the repression and isolation of a loveless marriage.[53] The reader is strongly encouraged to sympathize with the wife rather than with the betrayed husband. Interestingly, too, the husband's sins are not the obviously distressing ones of adultery, desertion, drunkenness, or physical cruelty, from which most states provided legal escape via divorce, but are instead the core traits of his tyrant personality: intolerance, stupidity, and insensitivity. In essence the morally questionable authors effectively argued that the difficulty of divorce and society's intolerance of the divorced woman kept many wives in painful, lifelong servitude. And in these books the innate strength of the heroine is constantly stressed. Either she escapes from the chains placed on her by an unhappy marriage or she successfully enslaves her compliant husband.

The six domestic novelists discussed above make their women daring and unconventional; in other equally popular forms of domestic fiction the heroine's steel fist is concealed in a prim silken glove. The writing of Mrs. E. D. E. N. Southworth, Mary Jane Holmes, Ann Sophia Stephens, and Caroline Lee Hentz is of low quality; the characters are often wooden and the involved plots move along only by ridiculous coincidence and unbelievable incidents. Each novelist, however, has an easy flowing style, and all but Mrs. Southworth display a real talent for writing fast-moving dialogue. But if their faults of expression are many, their forte is the intuitive understanding with which they catch and communicate the rebellious feelings of their feminine characters. In 1872 the Boston Public Library reported that the books of Southworth, Hentz, and Holmes were called for more than any other volumes held. Holmes sold a total of 2 million books, and Hentz more than 93,000, in one three-year period. Southworth sold more books than any female author in American history. Even in 1936, eighty-four years after her first bestseller, one publisher still printed 27 Southworth novels. Only in the 1940s did her work generally drop out of print. Stephens is best known for *Maleska*, a dime-novel which probably sold over 300,000 copies. The remarkable similarity of the lives of these four best-selling authors can be used to question the charges so often brought against them by later critics that they were sympathetic supporters of the traditional concept of woman's place and nature. Southworth and Hentz suffered gravely in deeply unsatisfying marriages, and each of the four women very early surpassed her husband in energy, intellect, and achievement. They all struggled desperately to succeed in the male world of action and were all personally incensed by the restrictions imposed on them by the operating assumption of male supremacy.[54]

Linda Walton, the most popular creation of Caroline Hentz, exemplifies the heroine of mighty, though hidden, strength. In the ultimate rebellion, Linda refuses to marry Roger, the husband selected for her by her father.

She runs away with Mr. McLeod, a local schoolteacher who has offered to help her escape. When McLeod begins to hint at their destination as "a secluded place," Linda realizes she has misplaced her confidence. To escape his embrace she dives from the boat in which they are making their getaway and is picked up on shore by Tuscarora, a noble savage. It is her amazing good luck that he speaks perfect English. For several adventurous years Linda prowls the wilderness, with her brave (and apparently celibate) Indian protector at her side. By remarkable coincidence she meets Roger, who by now has forsaken earthly love and has dedicated his life to missionary work among the heathen Indians. Now free to leave her exciting exile, Linda returns to her first love, a young steamboat pilot. Amid sunlight and music, we leave her supremely happy.[55]

To understand the deeper implications of Linda's popularity with female readers, it is useful to compare her with Edith Lyle, Mary Jane Holmes's well-known heroine. Fifteen-year-old Edith has been brought to the United States from England by her mother, who hopes to make a brilliant match for her with a wealthy man. Edith upsets her mother's plans by a secret marriage to a poor carpenter, who is almost immediately killed in an accident. Disgraced and pregnant, Edith is returned to England by her disappointed and domineering mother. After the loss of her child, Edith enters into a long state of depression and illness. Eventually finding a job as companion to a spinster, Edith meets a wealthy American widower who proposes marriage. Her suitor feels "a thrill of exultant pride as he [sees] her in his fancy at the head of his table and moving through his handsome rooms, herself the handsomest appendage there."[56] Edith, however, refuses to "sell herself for a name and a home," for she believes: "He does not love me, but he admires my face and form, and would no doubt be very kind and careful of me, just as he would be kind and careful of a favorite horse . . . he would hang on me jewels rare, and silks and laces and satins."[57] Only after he has convinced her of his appreciation of her individuality will she marry him and return to his wealthy estates in America. A major crisis occurs when her aristocratic-minded husband discovers that she has been the wife of a lowly carpenter. His devastation is greeted by her magnificent disdain. Chastened by the withdrawal of her approval, he eventually adjusts to the knowledge that he must accept her as used merchandise, and he becomes more devoted to her than ever.

In both style and plot these two novels are literary rubbish. Of course, it was not any artistic merit that gave them their wide popularity, but the forces of psychological attraction. Both Linda and Edith are placed in sharp conflict with the authority that attempts to force them into traditional feminine passivity. Each girl escapes successfully from psychic oppression and feels the confidence proceeding from proven self-sufficiency. In contrast to the strong heroines, their male lovers are pitifully ineffectual and compliant. In a society that bolstered the social and legal authority of the male, some women readers could find confirmation of their own value in the pages of popular domestic novels like these. The long-lashed heroines, despite their glossy curls and physical fragility, were clearly women in revolt—feeling, establishing, and maintaining a strident female protest in the fantasized world of "immoral" fiction.

Mrs. Southworth's extremely popular creations, Capitola and Ishmael, also illustrate the feminist message. Capitola, a foretaste of the New Woman, is vigorous, daring, and radiant. This adventuress, sometimes disguised as a boy, fights duels, outwits villains, scoffs at ministerial sanctimony, and once even "put[s] her thumb to the side of her nose, and whirl[s] her fingers into a semi-circle, in a gesture more expressive than elegant."[58] Ishmael is, on the other hand, so saintly and subservient to woman's will that Mrs. Southworth felt compelled to assure her public that his exalted character was real: "Reader! I am not fooling you with a fictitious character here."[59] In his first law case he defends the rights of a deserted wife, and he works his whole life "to modify those cruel laws which . . . [make] woman, despite her understanding intellect, an idiot, and despite her loving nature a chattel—in the law."[60] Ishmael finds his place with the feminine gender, at their feet.

Ann Sophia Stephens, the last of the morally suspect writers of domestic fiction, does not so often portray the subtly rebellious heroines found in the books of Southworth, Hentz, and Holmes. Perhaps her greatest appeal lay in the sheer excitement of her feminine characters' lives—set in rapidly growing cities, with thrilling glimpses of poverty, crime, luxury, and sin.[61] But Stephens made Maleska, her famous Indian heroine, with whom Beadle began his dime-novel series, into a woman whose heart beat at one with her lighter-hued sisters. Although Maleska's "sentiments were correct in principle and full of simplicity," she, too, toiled all her life, "in piling up soft couches for those she loved, and taking the cold stones for herself. It was her woman's destiny, not the more certain because of her savage origin. Civilization does not always reverse this mournful picture of womanly self-abnegation."[62]

Mrs. Stephens, the other domestic novelists, and their millions of women readers had each in her own way learned to resent the "mournful" feminine passivity induced by cultural pressure. To their tremendous audience these ten novelists spoke of the pressing concerns of a woman's daily life, of how to assert individuality, of how to win a man as a trophy and then cut him down to manageable size. Feminine discontent, vaguely defined but deeply felt, permeates the domestic fiction judged "immoral" by leading librarians and literary conservatives. Indeed, the Victorian librarians judged it rightly, for it does reflect the unsettling cultural shift in the nineteenth century from an idolatry of women to a more realistic consideration of feminine needs and abilities.

Startling as it was, the work of these ten novelists was not considered so shocking as was the writing of the six remaining authors judged questionable by the American Library Association in 1881. Whereas the writing of the popular domestic novelists was apt to be sneered at as the "pablum" of the uncultivated masses, the work of the "sensational school" was condemned with real horror by persons of genteel literary taste.[63] The single common element in the works of Ainsworth, Reynolds, Braddon, and Wood—the use of the criminal as an important character—does not preclude a wide variation in their treatment of the fallen man or woman. Ainsworth and Reynolds tended to use low-life settings; Braddon and Wood used a middle-class or upper-class background. The genteel objection to these books was that they brought to their readers a dangerous familiarity with vice. The extraordinary popularity of the humanized criminal made the "Newgate Novels" of Ainsworth and Reynolds the most fearful.[64]

The strain of the sensuous in *Jack Sheppard* and *Robert McNaire* is undeniably startling. Physical pain and sexual passion are fully experienced and described with gusto.[65] Feminine beauty is portrayed with considerable physical detail. McNaire's paramour, Maria, wore "a morning wrapper, which was as yet open at the breast; and her young and beautiful bosom, which the garment only half-concealed, heaved with frequent sighs."[66] "Voluptuous" is one of Reynolds's favorite words. The criminal heroes are made to seem dashing, acceptable, and even admirable. Daring deeds of murder, robbery, and extortion are described with a lighthearted suspension of moral judgment, and in fact the reader is often impressed with the criminal's virtuous traits.

Ainsworth and Reynolds turned genteel ethics upside-down. In their books women are loose *and* lovely, and while the hero and heroine do not always escape punishment they have a wonderful run for their money first and really enjoy themselves, free of the reproaches of tortured conscience. The aristocracy and clergy are repeatedly lashed; the vices of the wealthy are contrasted with the restricted lives of the poor, who cannot afford sensual indulgence.[67] Despite incredible coincidence, involved action, and flighty dialogue, the story moves along in pizzicato style and the criminal characters are usually convincing persons, with real human mixtures of virtue and vice. Beginning in the 1830s in England, Ainsworth and Reynolds drew heavy ire from those of discriminating literary taste, but their books continued to have great appeal in the United States until the end of the century.[68]

Following the example set by Ainsworth and Reynolds, Mary Braddon and Ellen Price (Mrs. Henry) Wood had a large public following in the United States. Their immensely successful books, *Lady Audley's Secret* and *East Lynne,* were sprinkled with murders (real and attempted), bigamy, adultery, insanity, endless complications, and painful predicaments.[69] In their books the rigid conduct expected of proper Victorian heroes and heroines decidedly gives way to a wider freedom. Young maidens cavort with married men and wives solemnly plot their husbands' betrayal, or sometimes death. It is all great fun for everyone involved, and when retribution comes it is given brief treatment by the authors. Often insanity is offered as explanation for the heroine's general infamy. Underlying these action-packed tales one finds a most tolerant attitude toward human frailty, an engaging portrayal of feminine character against the background of a world that is generally indifferent to justice.

Similarly, the novels of G. A. Lawrence and those of Ouida—who is the best of a large group of inferior imitators of Lawrence—displayed a strong sympathy for actions that greatly violated the prim moral codes of the Victorian world. The principal source of Lawrence's popularity was his portrayal of the superhuman hero. Guy Livingstone, his best-known creation, is a gigantic patrician of unparalleled strength, passion, and lust for general risk-taking. This superb male animal is also cynical (especially about the purity of women) and strictly amoral. Unhampered by any religious injunctions, contemptuous of parental and societal controls, Guy forces his will upon the world and upon the women who love him—amidst a constant round of hunting, warring, and revelry. Guy attracts and enjoys women with all the "confidence of one who knew his subject well."[70]

Guy's female counterpart is Flora Dorillon, the quintessential femme fatale. Needless to say, Flora is beautiful. But what attracts Guy to her is her "daring disregard of opinions, conventionalities, and more sacred things yet, which carried him on straight to the accomplishment of his thought and purpose."[71] In a scene highly unusual by Victorian standards for its suggestive eroticism free of moral judgment, the reader sees the unmarried couple off to bed, and the narrator, watching them go, comments: "I know men who would have given five years of life for the whisper that glided into his ear . . . ten for the Parthian glance that shot its arrow home."[72]

Ten years after the publication of *Guy Livingstone,* Ouida began to write her florid novels. In her heyday "she was considered an apostle of insidious immorality. . . . She was smutty and 'not nice'; therefore everybody read her."[73] Bertie Cecil, the Life Guardsman in *Under Two Flags,* is a hard, masculine, unintellectual Lawrentian superman, adored by women. Although aristocratic Bertie's goings-on and the incidents that lead him to a long exile in Africa, all told in purple prose, appear truly absurd to the modern reader, it is in her depiction of the gamine, Cigarette, that Ouida exceeds her natural literary limitations and creates an original and enchanting heroine. This little creature is a camp follower and mascot of the Foreign Legion. Reared in a barracks-room, Cigarette can toss off brandies and shoot from a gallop as well as the toughest Legionnaire. In admiration, Ouida pauses to ponder Cigarette's future death:

> Well, she will die, I dare say, some bright day or another, at the head of a regiment, with some desperate battle turned by the valour of her charge. . . . That is what Cigarette hoped for—why not? There will always be a million of commonplace women ready to keep up the decorous traditions of their sex, and sit in safety over their needles by the sides of their hearths. One little lioness here and there in a generation cannot do overmuch harm.[74]

But this sun-browned girl is not entirely unsexed. She has had

> a thousand lovers, from handsome marquesses of the Guides to tawny black-brown scoundrels in the Zouaves, and she had never loved anything, except the roll of pas

de change, and the sight of her own arch, defiant face, with its scarlet lips and its short, jetty hair, when she saw it by chance in some burnished cuirass, that served her for a mirror.[75]

Long accustomed to demure and spotless damsels for the most part, the reading public of the late nineteenth century must have found Cigarette and Lawrentian heroines like Flora extraordinary beings, deliciously designed to shock the stolid bourgeoisie.

Clearly, the major themes of these "immoral" bestsellers were in opposition to convention. Most prevalent was the depiction of a new heroine—sensual, active, defiant. Parental authority was repeatedly denied and was openly resented. The major characters, if they were not overtly antireligious, were at least rebelliously critical of clerical pomposity. There was also a sympathetic presentation of the inner conflicts of the sinners, whether their sins were actual crimes or simply revolts against sexual and religious mores. Emphasis was placed upon the responsibility of the social structure itself for the miseries of the world, rather than upon the individual's deliberate and willful choice. In short, the traditional procedures and idolatries of society were unquestionably under pressure. The lines of battle were drawn in the pages of these subtly revolutionary, sensibility-jolting, extremely popular novels.

The great majority of readers of these novels were women. Here, in the domestic and sensational novels which they consumed by the tens of millions, they could read of the wildly independent heroine putting the lie to the premise of masculine superiority and gaily negating societal controls. In these pages emancipated women ruled over slavish men, and new answers to the question of the place and meaning of sex were devised. A new consciousness of thwarted sensuality emerged. Desire became alluring and women not so pure, sex not so degrading, as literary idealists would have had them believe. And all about them, toward the end of the century, women readers could find abundant signs that men, too, were impatient with the narrowness of life and wished for new ideas and modes of behavior.

In effect, a demand for greater individual autonomy, triggered by previous changes in relationships to religious and political authority, was being expanded in the late nineteenth century to include a liberalization of controls over sexual and familial norms. Specifically, as women's older role-performance became increasingly archaic under changing historical circumstances, a disturbing demand for change surfaced in many forms—one of which was "immoral" fiction-fantasy. The longer-term process of structural and cultural change was related to the shorter-term process of the library's institutional effort to channel and slow the suspect novel's desacralization of the status quo. The new moral order that gradually emerged was more differentiated than the old. As a sociologist could remark by 1908, "Virtue no longer consists of literal obedience to arbitrary standards set by community or church but rather in conduct consistent with a growing personality."[76] Today the trend toward personal standards of morality is so well established that it would be difficult for most present-day readers to understand what the late-nineteenth-century librarian's fuss was all about. The difference lies in the high degree of Victorian opposition to sensual stimulation and challenge to patriarchal authority.

The advent of mass culture worked to negate the ancient presumptions that enclosed the individual in community structures and standards maintained, at least in principle, from the top. No matter how well stocked its rooms, the public library could not attract the public without providing the reading that reflected mass concerns. By 1900 public library leaders had all but given up an attempt to discredit best-selling fiction. Because the mass literary movement supported by women novel-readers aided the general nineteenth-century trend toward individualized morality, the decline of library paternalism was a sign of the times.

5

The Shift in Attitudes
Toward Popular Fiction

As THE NEW CENTURY BEGAN, a generation of librarians who felt less concern with moral direction of their patrons assumed control of the ALA. Twenty-four of the thirty-six librarians upon whom this study centers were either dead or retired by 1910. The contribution of these men and women to library development was very considerably lessened after about 1900. The prominent librarians who had created and shaped a profession and a philosophy became library legends of the past as a whole new crop of names began to spread through the pages of the professional literature. As the generations transferred control, the trend toward an acceptance of mass taste became more pronounced.

Increasingly, any distrust of mass preferences was ridiculed by younger librarians. By 1902 a woman librarian could comment that the truth was that the people did *not* thirst for elevating reading. "What an amount of misconception it would save if we would all admit that the order of things is pretty fairly established, and a part of it seems to be that people with tastes for the highest literature are few and far between." It was time for librarians to go "out of the miracle business."

> Timid librarians who a few years ago were trying to prevent us from circulating many pleasant harmless books are now by a natural reaction throwing wide their doors and admitting almost everything. It takes some degree of personal courage to urge the exclusion of a book when you know that the library ten miles away has just put in twenty or thirty copies.[1]

Miss Emma Adams timidly agreed: "I want to enter my feeble protest against our rather pharisaical attitude about fiction. . . . I mean that the error seems to lie in the narrow conception which leads us to try to get people to read non-fiction."[2] Edwin Gaillard added, "Let librarians avoid cant. . . . The real truth . . . is that librarians have assumed a pose . . . they meet together, quote self-satisfying statistics and tell each other of the noble work that the new profession is doing. They seek ways of disguising the fiction percentage."[3] Charles Bolton pointed out that the libraries which did not buy a novel until it was one year old were driving off influential and educated patrons. Bolton, librarian at the Boston Athenaeum, had a college-professor friend who told him that his family was "tired of being 'educated' by a librarian with whose standards of culture we are not in sympathy." Bolton wondered "if, after all, we do not need in our public libraries men and women with an outlook on the world . . . quite as much as we need Minerva with her aegis forever shielding her temptation-loving and tax-paying children."[4]

Such a marked change from the library rhetoric of the past was not simply the result of a shift in generational control. From the beginning of the formation of the library profession there had been some opposition to those leaders who advocated paternalism. The shift in librarians' attitudes toward the public's right to read was chiefly indicative of the changing perception of the institution's social purpose.

It is evident that there are four main trends in the development of the objectives of the public library movement, although the question of priority among the four cannot be categorically stated at any one time. In general, however, the first objective of the public library had been reformative, an effort by the "better people" to uplift and control the thinking of the masses. By the 1890s librarians had recognized their need for mass support, and library leaders began to emphasize the objective of education as well as reform. The library as a chiefly educational institution, however, did not attract a sufficient number of patrons. It became evident to librarians that further wooing of the public was necessary. Next followed a period when the recreational function of the public library began to vie with the educational objective as a primary goal. This theory in turn was gradually supplanted by a shift to a more democratic position: The people themselves were given authority over what they ought to read. This last opinion was more or less current among librarians by 1920.

Inasmuch as these four objectives were not independent of each other but interacted together, there was much confusion over the criteria of book selection. This confusion is particularly evident in the many anguished library discussions of what constituted questionable or approved novels. As the emphasis shifted from an educational to a recreational objective, the library as an institution lost much of its former pretension to intellectual authority. Moreover, within the library profession the increasing predominance of women had the effect of causing the library to become more and more demand-oriented, since most librarians did not feel strong enough either as individuals or as professionals to assert themselves in the face of public demands. Thus, after considerable controversy, especially over "immoral" fiction, the course of the American public library was set.

The reformative objective was prime in the formation of the first true public library, as we know it, in Boston in 1852. A committee, consisting in part of Edward Everett and George Ticknor,[5] was requested to prepare a statement of the "objects to be attained by the establishment of a public library, and the best mode of effecting them." This report emphasized that the Boston Public Library would have the special purpose of serving the class who could not afford books of their own. To attract this sector of the populace, the library would provide in ample numbers the "living, fresh and new" popular books of the time. The committee, nevertheless, was careful to defend the necessity for proper control of the people's reading. Popular taste would be followed — "unless it should ask for something unhealthy."[6] In this phrase is capsuled the conflict between public library objectives in the period under study. Clearly the public library was designed to serve mass taste. Just as clear was the determination to uplift mass taste through exclusion of undesirable books. Catering to the popular passion for suspect fiction was originally justified only as a means of creating a love for reading that would eventually lead the public to higher literary levels.

> When such a taste for books has once been formed by these lighter publications, then the older and more settled works in Biography, in History, and in the graver departments of knowledge will be demanded. . . . This taste, therefore, once excited, will, we are persuaded, go on of itself from year to year, demanding better and better books, and, can as we believe, by a little judicious help in the selections for a Free City Library, rather than by any direct control, restraint, or solicitation, be carried much higher than has been commonly deemed possible; preventing at the same time, a great deal of the mischievous, poor reading now indulged in.[7]

By the late 1890s, librarians had made a strong case for using tax funds by stressing the library's function as an educational organization. The library profession preferred to describe their institution as an agency coordinate with the public school, serving teachers and students, and as a people's university, serving the unskilled and the artisan throughout life. This latter concept of the library as a lifelong educator caught the imagination of many human-itarians and made them allies of the library profession.

In the 1876 government report librarians had sanctioned the existence of large fiction collections, but only because it was believed that readers could "be made to glide into what is commonly called instructive reading"[8] by a conscientious librarian-guide.

> The old recipe for cooking hare, which begins with "first catch your hare" may well be applied to the process of elevating the tastes of the uncultivated masses. Let the library, then, contain just enough of the mere confectionary of literature to secure the interest in it of readers of the lowest — not depraved — tastes; but let

this be so dealt out as may best make it serve its main purpose of a stepping stone to something better. . . . Then by care in the matter of advising readers whose most desired books are "all out" very much may be done to give them an introduction to these writers, who will, in many cases, win them to a higher level of reading.[9]

This recipe for cooking hare—in various guises—was repeated by library leadership for the remainder of the century.[10] Although a few librarians did not agree that "bad" reading could be justified,[11] the majority of the library profession accorded a large place to fiction on their shelves, while continuing to argue, in extremely vague terms, about where the line of exclusion of really dangerous literature should be drawn.

Still, with the hare caught, there remained the problem of how to cook it. The question of how to bring about reading improvement was a basic element in all the discussions of the fiction problem. It was first argued that the librarian's personal influence was the most important factor. But guidance had to be diplomatically extended; American readers were unusually resentful of overbearing interference in their reading choices. A frequently mentioned method for raising reading levels was to prepare special lists and bibliographical aids that would cite approved fiction of a high level, along with references to related historical and biographical works.[12] Another method considered even more effective was to permit readers to browse through the shelves themselves. For this reason open shelves were common by 1900 in most major public libraries.[13] While reading lists, displays, and open shelves became permanent features of the public library service, another system for raising reading taste, called the "two-book system," did not survive to modern times.

This interesting innovation, it must be remembered, came about at a time when it was common to have a great many regulations governing the use of library books.* It seemed natural, then, to formulate precise rules to control the amount of fiction reading. The two-book system became a popular device in the 1890s. This system permitted a reader to take out two books at a time if one was not a novel.† It was believed that the inveterate novel reader would thus be led to books of solid nonfiction. Proponents of the system believed that it would enable the sly librarian "to educate without trying to

---

*Most libraries in the 1870s had stringent regulations concerning the age of borrowers, the number of books issued, and the types of books allowed to different classes of readers. The older concept of the librarian as warden was slow-dying and is reflected in the many discussions in the *Library Journal* about how to apprehend and punish book thieves. A minor received a four-year sentence in reform school for stealing two reference books from the Providence library in 1879. As late as 1892 a young man was given an eight-year suspended sentence in Pennsylvania for stealing twelve books from the Pratt Institute Free Library. The librarian there remarked that the thief "has been confined to his bed since the trial, and it is hoped that the shock may have been a salutary lesson."

†As late as 1912, when the New York Public Library allowed patrons to check out four books at once, it was stipulated that only one could be fiction. When the Pratt Institute Free Library in 1916 allowed patrons to check out two novels at a time, there was no reported increase in fiction circulation.

reform his patrons, to teach without compelling them to learn; . . . in a word, it enables him to aid their mental growth, without . . . making his patrons feel they are the objects of a reform."[14]

But once the emphasis was shifted from an educational to a recreational objective, the librarian was free to justify the choice of books by reliance upon majority approval. Throughout this process of institutional change, it is apparent that the librarians were pushed along by the demands of mass readership.[15] They very quickly learned that any drop in the purchase of new fiction invariably led to an alarming decrease in the total circulation. Although their subservience to their clientele's wishes was strengthened by the feminization of librarianship, their passivity was also a result of the library's peculiar position as a tax-supported institution. The public library, unlike the public school, had no means of coercing the people to make use of its service.

Along with all the magnificent music made by librarians in praise of their altruistic, patient, sacred service in the elevation of their communities' reading habits, it is possible to pick out another tune in the background. It is a light, unsophisticated little ditty, heard only faintly at first but gathering in force by the 1890s as librarians began to accept the fact that American patrons could not be driven in their reading. In 1890 Frank Hill asked the pertinent question that had been all but ignored at the ALA conferences: "It is all very well to speak of educating the people, but if they refuse to be educated, what is to be done about it?"[16] In 1894 a hesitant "yes" was given by the respondents in a series of papers presented to the ALA on the question "Is a free public library justified in supplying to its readers books which are neither for instruction nor for the cultivation of taste; which are not . . . good literature; which are books for entertainment only—such, for example, as the ruck of common novels?"[17] George Cole warned that "the librarian should not carry his head so high in the clouds as to forget that the vast majority of people are bowed down by their cares and burdens, and care more for mental relaxation than instruction."[18] Thus, by the last decade of the century, the library, now firmly established as a worthy recipient of tax dollars, moved into an open defense of the supply of reading for recreation only.

A new tolerace of mass taste had first been formally enunciated, at the ALA convention in 1883, by the man who replaced Winsor as chief of the Boston Public Library, Mellen Chamberlain. At age sixty-two, Chamberlain had a long career of lawmaking and teaching behind him before he entered library work. Perhaps his less intense professional identification enabled him to view the library's function more objectively. He gently chided the holier-than-thou spirit of his colleagues: "Neither libraries nor librarians will altogether enlighten the world. Least of all will they succeed when they undertake to set themselves about it."[19] Public taste could not be forced. The editorial clout of the *Library Journal* was applied in support of Chamberlain:

> Hitherto the complaint of the tax payer has always been that so much rubbish, meaning fiction, was bought. . . . Eulogium of a city library has always made great use of the phrases, "judicious selection," "standard books," "works of permanent value." Is it possible that all this is to be changed? Are we approaching a new era. . . . Has the reaction against . . . puritanism already set in?[20]

In 1884 J. N. Larned's complaining tone revealed that he was finding it more difficult to maintain older literary standards. "I do not know that . . . the library's right to exercise upon literature the criticism which discriminates art from rubbish is formally disclaimed or formally denied; but it seems to stand in doubt and to be exercised with hesitation, if at all," Larned told the American Social Science Association. "There seems to be much hesitancy in the movement [to set library standards] and a want of positive principles to govern it."[21]

The peak of conflict in the ALA between the old paternalism and the new liberalism was reached in 1895-1896, when the old guard of the East made a kind of final stand for pure fiction against the less moralistic representatives of the West and Midwest. In 1893 Tessa Kelso, librarian at Los Angeles—an outspoken dissident and one of three women who headed sizable collections—had thrown down the gauntlet in the pages of *Arena* with an attack on those public librarians who deprecated the reading of light fiction.[22] In 1896 the ALA held its first open discussion on immoral fiction that mentioned precise titles and authors.[23] But perhaps more than any other factor, it was the presence of John Cotton Dana and his supporters that fomented hot dissension between old and new.

The early library had its mavericks, of course, and chief among them was Dana. Descended from a prominent New England family, Dana graduated from Dartmouth in 1878. He next spent two years as a surveyor in Colorado. After an unsatisfying attempt to practice law in New York City, he returned to frontier life in Colorado as a railroad engineer and rancher from 1883 until 1889. During these years Dana suffered a "mild attack of socialism," cast off religious dogma, and supported the single-tax system of Henry George.[24]

When Dana took charge of the Denver library in 1889, he immediately removed the rails that had fenced off the delivery area and the alcoves. He also established there, in 1894, one of the first children's libraries.[25] Dana introduced open stacks and a business and medical collection into the Denver library. The library was opened seven days a week, twelve hours a day—a radical innovation at the time. When Dana took over at Denver the library held 2,000 books. Five years later, in 1894, the library loaned 7,967 books during the year. As Dana left Denver to go east for his first American Library Association meeting, his last words to his assistants were, "Remember that rules were made to be broken."[26]

The inveterate rebelliousness of Dana won the support of many younger questioners of the status quo. Arthur Vanderbilt, chief justice of the New Jersey Supreme Court, recalled how he and his high school friends had been influenced by Dana: "There was not one of Mr. Dana's scrapes that I failed to remember, since we had been on his side in every one of them—was he not against old-style fogyism and tradition and for all that was right and sensible?"[27] Dana's impatience with old dogmas also shaped his outspoken religious heresy. When in 1905 the New York Public Library excluded some of George Bernard Shaw's books on the grounds of immorality, Dana took a public stand against the "whole Sweet Branch of Very Pure Librarians" and suggested that librarians pay close heed to Shaw's point that morality should be shaken before it could be redefined.[28] Dana was one of the few prominent public librarians who did not succumb to the anti-German censorship hysteria during World War I. Because Dana kept German books on the shelves of the Newark, New Jersey, public library during the war years, the *New York Journal* suggested that he deserved an Iron Cross.[29] Dana politely refused to accept the decoration. Arthur Bostwick believed that Dana loved controversy and would automatically take the unpopular side on many questions simply for the sake of argument.[30] Perhaps this is true, for in his last years Dana shifted from his earlier support of novel reading to a frequent denunciation of worthless fiction. Throughout his life Dana taught the "danger of submitting too much to authority."[31]

John Dana was a catalyst for new ideas in the library world, but he was too cynical and alienated from others to draw to him a core of followers in the way that Melvil Dewey did. He functioned as a gadfly to the library profession, discounting library missionary work and opposing the staid propriety of the library world. Although Dana was a religious and sexual radical, he admired the practical world of business. As librarian at Newark, from 1902 to 1929, he created the first business library in the country. By the turn of the century Dana had effectively challenged library conservatism and won the respect of less liberal librarians than himself.

Dana's first appearance at the American Library Association conference of 1891 caused unrest. He was markedly opposed to the genteel spirit of the bookish "best men" in the library. He charged that many members of the ALA were

> sometimes dying and quite unmindful of the fact, and never as effective as opportunity permits. They are often too conservative. They think it is their wisdom which restrains them, when in fact it is simply their mediocrity. . . . They repress the aggressive and the original. They fear they may do something improper and, clothed in perfect propriety, before they are aware of it they reach a Nirvana of futility.[32]

Too often, Dana noted, the members gathered "solemnly . . . [to] glare at one another across a crowded room," parading their well-worn speakers "until their meeting [became] little more than one voice crying in a wilderness of inattentive ears."[33] Dana confessed that he stayed away from the first session of the ALA meeting where novels were discussed because he "knew what would be said about certain virile authors" and knew that he would react with a "fit of wrath of no use to others" and hurtful to himself.[34] Dana found most librarians to be inflexible, timid before change, and "diseased with 'satisfacto-conformitum' — because they are bookish and not open to competition with others."[35]

Dana had a less elevated conception of the people's desire to absorb "culture" than did many library leaders. He spoke up instead for the pure recreational function of the public library.[36] Throughout his career Dana chided librarians who appointed themselves missionaries to their communities while, in fact, they kept out fiction not agreeable to them personally.[37] He believed that the library should present the whole range of human thought, "should bar out nothing because it is strange, no doctrines because they are heresies."[38] Many librarians, Dana knew, were rigid conservatives. Unfortunately, "the type of mind that is attracted to libraryism is usually conventional. To it the new is painful and therefore evil."[39] Dana claimed to "get his recreation mainly by startling the soberminded . . . or baiting them with radical paradoxes."[40]

It was Dana who replied to Larned's and Brett's conservative defense at the conference of 1894. The "fact that the people are in a state of unrest" made those librarians fearful, Dana said, but made him proud. "Well nigh every step in advance in the past has been taken in the face of opposition, often the opposition of sheer stupidity, and still more often the opposition of direct protest against change."[41] Public libraries, Dana hoped, could add to the social disquiet, if they would extend to the people the opportunity to judge for themselves.[42]

Dana led several revolts against voting procedures in an attempt to further democratize the electoral machinery of the ALA. He was much in evidence at the 1894 convention, especially active among the lesser lights — the members who were librarians or assistants at small libraries. His strong liberal stand against Larned and Brett won him the support of those association members who felt unsympathetic to the philosophy of the leading chieftains. Dana was elected president in the next year after a change in voting procedure had been adopted by the membership. Previously the elected executive board had chosen the officers of the ALA. In 1895 Dana and the other officers were elected by a democratic vote of the entire membership. The shift in emphasis from the genteel East to a more democratic West was symbolized in another way in 1895, for the annual conference was held in Dana's home city of Denver. This location was farther west than any ALA meeting held since 1876, with the exception of the small gathering at San Francisco in 1891. The membership who elected Dana was small in number, only 147 (87 women and 60 men); 52 chief librarians and 39 assistants were present.

In 1907 Dana led another attack against established ALA procedures. In the election of that year the council's nominations for officers were opposed for the first time by independent nominations. The polls became a "center for electioneering hitherto unprecedented in the annals of the Association. . . . There were strong cross currents of agreement and disagreement . . . and a regrettable amount of 'coralling' of uninformed delegates," the *Library Journal* reproved editorially.[43]

Dana found sympathetic listeners among those librarians who were farthest west from Boston. In 1889 Frederick Crunden commented from the St. Louis Public Library that only well-to-do people were apt to be "satisfied with the status quo and to enter upon no troublesome investigations, but those who, in their own discomforts and privations, see the time reflected out of joint, are more inclined to inquire the why and wherefore."[44] Crunden had also given liberal support in 1894 when Dana replied to J. N. Larned's and William Brett's conservative addresses.

In 1896 Crunden delivered the most radical speech ever presented to the members of the ALA. The progress of man was very great in the area of scientific thought, Crunden told his startled colleagues, but in economic or sociological questions the advocate of new ideas was still repressed and feared. Reformers were invariably labeled as socialists, Communists, or anarchists. "From the beginning of time every social advance and until recently, every forward step in science or religion, has been regarded as menacing the very foundations of society."[45] In an obvious stab at the old guard, Crunden called them the "real revolutionaries," for it was they who blocked the onward flow of the stream and thus caused the eddies and whirlpools that created change. Crunden believed that the strongest conservatives of 1950 would find it "almost inconceivable that rational beings could ever have defended the system which prevails in America today." The unrest of labor was justified, and the worker's demand for relief had to be answered by something more than the old saws. Amidst

> millions of workers in enforced idleness, and its attendant want and destitution, we are offered the absurdity of "overproduction" of the very things for which millions are suffering; when we see men and women who toil not reveling in luxury, while others who labor sixteen hours a day are barely able to keep body and soul together, we may know absolutely, without further investigation, that there is something fundamentally wrong in our social organization.[46]

Perhaps no other example so dramatically illustrates the alteration of the librarian's attitude toward mass reading rights as does the comment of Melvil Dewey in 1897. A proponent of the educational mission of the library at one time, Dewey was, as always, pragmatic. He had been in library work for twenty-three years when he delivered his somewhat disillusioned and tired "Advice to a Librarian": "Look at your position as a high-grade business one, look after the working details, have things go smoothly, know the whereabouts and classification of books, and let people get their own meat or poison."[47]

In 1899 a dirge was sung for the missionary direction of reading in Lindsay Swift's much-quoted "Paternalism in Public Libraries." Swift castigated the scheme that had "unquestionably been grafted" upon the library system—the "tendency to regulate and decide for others, which is antipathetic to the democratic principle of least possible government." In the selection of books the paternal spirit "will most show itself toward the classes of supposedly objectionable literature, vulgar books, books dealing with the problem of sex in all its phases, and books thought to be generally menacing to the social structure." Only those persons whose respectability rests on pretense oppose realism in literature, while "robust men and women with steady nerves and wholesome natures . . . recognize in others what they know to be true of themselves, that the sex problem in all its complications is of absorbing and continuous interest to mankind."[48] Harmless books are mediocre books, Swift said. If a new idea in morals or in society is sounded, "the suggestion of a possible injuriousness at once arises." Discontent among the masses sometimes causes the throwing of bombs and the guillotining of fine ladies and gentlemen, but "it is simply and absolutely none of the librarian's business what the mental and moral processes may chance to be in the public which pays us to run its literary shop."[49] Swift urged librarians to drop "patronizing and depressing" methods and to stop "being so confoundedly serious" about their sacred pretension to responsibility for culture. It is the opinion of some . . . minds among us that . . . we have a certain charge laid upon us to treat the bulk of mankind as if it really were incapable of self-guidance. . . . This theory in regard to the helplessness of mankind in vicious."[50]

Of course there were still librarians who could not shed the pastoral concern implanted in them by their training. John Ashurst, a Philadelphia librarian, told of meeting a noted Greek scholar and philologist coming out of the library, in the summer of 1899, with ten or twelve novels under his arm. "He greeted me with a sickly smile," recalled Ashurst. " 'One of those young women in there,' he said, 'stopped me as I was going out with my novels and told me that if I would come back she would be very glad to pick out some good "class" books for me.' This sort of thing would be funny if it were not sad," Ashurst said.[51] The manner in which this incident was reported indicates the movement of the public librarian from a conviction that the library was a medium for social improvement and education, through the recognition that people must first be given access to the books they manifestly liked, to a final belief that people were entitled to read whatever they wished, instead of what any authority asserted they ought to read.

By 1900 many librarians could agree with this female poet who had given up library maternalism:

> Should we rare ones who inhabit the superior realms of thought
> Dictate to the Unenlightened what they oughtn't or they ought?

. . . .

Or shall we abandon flatly this whole altruistic fight
With the philosophic dictum that "Whatever is, is right?"
. . . .
Let us stop our futile task of pointing to the open door,
Let the Enlightened cease enlightening and the Cultured cult
     no more.[52]

Despite the influence of liberals like Dana and Crunden, however, many library leaders maintained a conservative stance in economic and political matters throughout the 1890s.

In 1901 Richard T. Ely, who had helped to make the University of Wisconsin into a center for dissidence in economic thought, requested twenty minutes' time on the American Library Association's conference program to respond to a recent article by George Iles in *World's Work*. Ely had been "especially stirred up" by Mr. Iles's "vicious" attempt, in his view, to introduce the "system of papacy into literature."[53] Iles had suggested that a Central Bureau be established to judge and appraise the mass of literature so as to sort out the enduring and worthwhile from the vapid and ephemeral. This body of experts, Iles believed, would be able to guide the uninformed reader by a system of annotations and remarks that could be printed on the library's catalogue cards.[54]

Ely, in answer to this proposal, was determined to "speak plainly" against what was to him a "grave menace to the progress of science." Ely insisted that there was no possibility of assembling a group of judges who would be all-wise enough to perform such a task without an "assault on liberty." Book reviewers were notoriously wrong or small-minded, Ely reminded the librarians. Most literary reviews, he felt, were simply examples of "an inferior passing judgment on a superior." Librarians must guard free thought, Ely said, "must watch with impartiality the struggles among tendencies and schools of thoughts, and above all things, endeavor to keep open a free way for new truth."[55]

In the discussion following Ely's paper, many librarians seemed mildly offended at his lecture to them on their responsibilities. Their creed had long included a denunciation of censorship in economic, scientific, and political matters. Iles had not been defending censorship, the librarians agreed, but had merely been attempting to deal with the serious question of how best to discover the useless and immoral in the deluge of printed material.

Ely misunderstood the deepest concerns of the library professionals. It was not the reading of new theories in science or economics that they opposed. It was the interest of the public in new trends in fiction that most perplexed them. Here they had defended a form of censorship from many angles for many years. The librarians who discussed Ely's speech did not consider the larger implication of his words—that "objectivity" is generally either noncontroversial or harmonious with established ways of thinking. The somewhat miffed reaction of librarians to Ely's horror at the establishment of a literary judiciary reflected not only their earlier identification of themselves as literary experts but the early strength of their missionary attitude toward the public.

After 1900 references in library literature to the "fiction problem" became increasingly scarce, although interest in the subject peaked again in 1903 and 1908. Here and there, the older library fears reappear—in the instruction of library school students how to build ladder systems designed to lift the reader step by step from Rhoda Broughton to George Eliot, or from Mary Jane Holmes to Walter Scott;[56] and in the brief revival of interest in Emerson's idea that no work of fiction should be purchased until it had stood the test of popular demand through one year's time since publication.[57] Andrew Carnegie, it was reported, believed the testing period could be safely extended to three years.[58]

Indicative of the librarian's new attitude toward popular reading was the reaction to an attempt in 1903 to classify fiction in a subject index with categories like philosophy, ethics, and sociology. The purpose of this classification was to better estimate the quality of reading done by the public. The *Library Journal* responded with scorn to the proposed index: "Why not accept the fact that the novel is today the dominant form of literary expression, and not seek to label it as something that it is not?"[59] In 1906 the idea of the subject index was still alive. In that year the ALA's Committee on Prose Fiction received only ten replies from its national canvass of prospective compilers. One of these replies flatly advised the committee "to stop this nonsense." The committee promptly dissolved itself because of the profession's lack of interest in the further classification of fiction.[60]

The group of library leaders who had maintained their duty to discourage reading of the modern fiction so popular with the public had few defenders left. In 1903 James Hosmer, the newly elected president of the ALA, presented his indictment of the "over-officious" librarian and defended the public's right to have whatever books they chose, in whatever quantity.[61] In what was to be a last restatement of the older paternalism by one of the earlier set of library chieftains, William Foster answered Hosmer with an appeal to those librarians who did not wish to give up their position as moral guards of their community. Foster, who was fifty-three years old, had been a librarian since 1873. If the ideas motivating librarianship should change, Foster knew, then shortly afterward would come the change in practice.

> It is at present only the first stage that we have to deal with, the change of ideals, but here the change is sufficiently marked, if we make comparison with ten years ago. Already it is proposed . . . [that] the librarian should become a mechanical medium for the transferring of books to readers. . . . If the modern library no longer represents a need for a man who shall develop in readers the conscious selection of the best (an anti-Philistine doctrine which seems to be frowned upon), or who shall help the reader to advance from one stage of literature to another,

then the race of librarians of which Dr. Winsor, Mr. Cutter, Dr. Poole and Dr. Hosmer himself were typical representatives . . . will gradually die out.[62]

Foster's vision was not to be realized; Hosmer's advice was to prevail. The race of librarians who had dominated professional thought in the 1880s was literally dying, and with them went not only their often-arrogant presumptions but also their dream of the public library as a center of cultural life and of the librarian as a leading moral force in the community.

In 1908 a new consensus on the question of suspect fiction was reached among librarians at the national convention. Their decision was to succumb to the public's desire for novels that discussed "undesirable moral teachings" but to either refuse to purchase or to lock away those bestsellers that did not provide an appropriate punishment for their sinning characters.[63] This curious transitional view, which retained only a portion of the genteel code, was enunciated by Arthur Bostwick in his 1908 presidential address. Only prissy lady librarians were still apt to hold the belief that *all* "ugliness is sin," he said, whereas a book was really only bad if it taught "that evil is good or that it makes no difference." Bostwick urged the guardian at the library door to stand firm before the menacing tide of popular fiction, to say, "Thus far shalt thou go and no farther."[64]

In the years just prior to World War I, however, as the genteel tradition collapsed, public librarians found it less necessary to justify their existence through reference to their position as self-appointed censors of public morals. In 1911 J. I. Wyer, director of the New York State Library in Albany, noted the "unfortunate twist" and "unhappy stigma" given to library work by the early belief that librarians were "peculiar people to whom has been given the final revelation," and Mary Plummer, in her 1916 presidential message, made a strong attack upon the almost-discarded genteel code.[65] By 1920 the painful analysis of the library's moral duty to its patrons had all but ended. Although a survey of thirty-three public libraries and state commissions in 1922 revealed that there were still locked-away collections, it also found a widespread acceptance of mass reading demands.[66] Gradually overt paternalism was discarded and the public library became a provider of best-selling fiction to Ms. and sometimes Mr. Mid-Cult. However, the seclusion of the most "immoral" books behind glass doors or in uncatalogued collections assured that only the most brazen adults would dare sample the library's forbidden fruit.

This solution to the library's "fiction problem" has persisted, in some places, into our own time. Outside the limits of this study is the detailed history of how the immoral books, almost always a euphemism for discussion of sexual topics, came to be hidden away on locked shelves and in back rooms, ostensibly for the protection of the young, in reality to reflect the fastidiousness of individual librarians or the limited tolerance level of the community. Beginning in the 1890s, the influence of the "new professionals," led by Melvil Dewey and his supporters, increasingly deemphasized the earlier mission of moral instruction assumed by the public library, replacing it with a commitment to efficient "library science." Thus did paternalism, professionalization, and solid middle-class pretensions blend with the really radical idea of free thought through free books to produce that unique institution—the American public library.

PART 3

Melvil Dewey: Mission and Mechanics

Successful public men are not merely themselves. They are records and gauges of the activities and aspirations of their own day. It is futile to praise them or blame them except as we remember that in so doing we are appraising the time and the people that produced them.

—John Dewey

6

Formation of a Savior

MELVIL DEWEY WAS A DRIVEN MAN, tense, complicated, concentrated, hounded by a fear of death and decay. He was a man for whom nothing was ever completed; each achievement was only a challenge to accomplish more. His dreams and projects were superhuman. To fulfill any one of them would have required the span of ten lifetimes. Dewey was a librarian the like of which the country had never seen — a one-man profession. He was a man who bridged two Americas, his early years formed by the hard Victorian demand of duty to God and work, his final years devoted to the rationalization of a technocratic culture. From frontier farming America of the 1850s to the Depression of the 1930s, he spanned his time in a remarkable way, rashly moving from missionary of culture to prophet of business. He was a man of massive influence, force, and enthusiasm, and of equally massive insecurity. The volume of his achievements never lessened the inner fears that impelled him to incessant activity.

He was a complex of incongruities. He achieved fame through the Decimal System that bears his name, yet others did most of the work for him. He was highly intelligent and consecrated his life to education but he lacked the flexibility of a first-rate mind and could not feel any real affinity to intellect. Although he was literally obsessed with the saving of time, his most striking characteristic was the manner in which he wasted it, in inordinate amounts, in his effort to save it. A lifelong apostle of thrift, once holding on to a postcard for twenty-one years before using it, he was incredibly reckless with his personal finances. While earning great wealth, he remained perpetually balanced on the very edge of financial ruin. Tall, powerfully built, handsome, personally magnetic, he was beloved by many and drew to him a group of unusually talented and otherwise self-sufficient women whose loyalty to him was supreme and who followed him, harem-like, for decades, from one of his homes to another. Yet he was fiercely hated by many others, to whom he had been cold, tactless, and cruel. No one who met him found it possible to hold a neutral opinion of Melvil Dewey, for he had "an indisputable . . . inner power—chemical or/and electrical—that was evidenced in a few seconds when in his presence."[1] A schoolgirl who saw him briefly in 1892 never forgot her impression.

> I was ushered into an office where a black-haired, black-bearded, black-eyed gentleman in a pepper-and-salt suit was working away with a kind of furious quiet at a big desk. I was struck by the speed and accuracy of his movements. It was like watching a fine machine, an electric machine—the air about him was vibrant with energy. . . . His decisiveness, the sparkling darkness of his face (dominated by his vivid eyes), his intense energy impressed me deeply. Indeed, I was a little awed . . . I had come into contact with an immense force.[2]

More than any other single person Dewey shaped the development of the public library in the United States, forcing it forward into the path he believed it should take. Almost alone he set the pattern for library education. His paeans to professionalization not only affected the growth of librarianship but also influenced educational standardization in all the professions, especially in New York State. But we must remember that to Dewey the library was only one area of operation for his educational work. He decided when still a boy that he would be above all else a "seed-sower"—a man who expanded his own life many times by inspiring others to work toward new and great ends. Despite the grandiose nature of his goal, it is startling to discover how often he reached it. Wholly outside the library profession and entirely aside from the crusades he directly initiated, his influence propelled others to organizational activity in forms as varied as the establishment of Barnard College, the founding of the American Home Economics Association, and the bringing of the Winter Olympics to the United States in 1932—to mention only a very few of his sown seeds.

Dewey was intensely aware of his place in history and preserved the documentary vestiges of his life from the time he was fifteen years old until his death sixty-five years later. Despite his belief that he would be remembered as a foremost educator, however, Dewey's name has survived almost entirely because of his identification with the decimal system of classification. He formulated this when he was twenty-two years old and an assistant at the Amherst College Library. Within the library profession, his reputation was permanently affected by the sexual scandal of 1905, which helped to force him out of active library work.

To some modern feminist librarians he has become almost an object of ridicule, remembered for his simplistic preaching of the library mission and his rakish reputation. ("Like what did you *really* have in mind, Mel baby, when you hotly defended the right of women to library education and then made the attracted young ladies put their bosom measurements on their application? . . . Your brother librarians have kept your more goatish gambols out of your authorized biography."* ³) His two biographers have indeed suppressed the remarkable Melvil Dewey. The official biography by Grosvenor Dawe, published the year after Dewey's death, is an unashamed romanticization of his life that was written under the general supervision of his second wife; the book's subtitle gives away its purpose. The small book written by Fremont Rider in 1944⁴ is more valuable because Rider, who married Dewey's niece, knew Dewey intimately, both personally and professionally. Rider's study is a sensitive and detached interpretation, but when he sent his manuscript to readers he was congratulated by them for his deliberate decision to delete any reference to Dewey's less glorious moments or to his "darker side."⁵

Yet Melvil Dewey remains a figure of considerable historical interest despite the lack of attention paid to him by posterity. Aside from his effect upon the American library and his influence upon the larger professionalization movement that took place in the United States during his lifetime, his life can be studied for the insight it provides into at least one type of reforming "savior" mentality. Because he left such a wealth of evidential material and was a man of such unusual inner force, it is impossible to ignore Dewey's personal disorder and its connection to his social impact.

It is apparent that Dewey manifested in his personality a particular complex of thoughts, feelings, ideas, and behavior characteristic of a general mode of functioning that is most often dubbed "obsessive-compulsive." This personality structure is marked by a tendency toward order, perfectionism, and concentration on detail; an emphasis upon intellectualization; an overcompliance with and hyperconcern for rules; a reliance on verbal fluency; and an overriding commitment to work. The central idea is control—governance over oneself and over the forces outside oneself. The ordering of self and others is achieved in most instances through the assumption of grandiosity. This posture allays anxieties about being in danger either because one cannot meet the requirements of others or cannot be sure of their acceptance.⁶

But how to tease from the biographical record these matters of compulsion? When evidence allows, the historian can trace the interaction and interdependence of three themes—the historical impact of the innovative "great man," the personality constants that reappear throughout his life, and the needs and characteristics of a particular period in history. In our post-Freudian age, it seems self-evident that the contribution of theory in any area of thought is inevitably stamped with the subjective concerns of the theorist.

---

*Apparently this *Library Journal* editorial refers to the application form at Dewey's library school at Columbia University. However, while the form asked for data on height and weight, it did not request bust measurements.

As the following pages will attempt to show, Melvil Dewey's contribution to library development was related to his personal conflicts. But it will not do to merely dismiss him as a neurotic personality. Dewey was a prophet of the new professionalism, an evangel of efficiency and standardized methods, and a decisive contributor to the social upheaval that made mass culture a way of life. Let us simply recognize that here was an uncommon man whose attempts at resolving inner conflict stamped our library system, and hence our lives.

Dewey's mother had been married nineteen years and borne three children when Melvil was born a few weeks after her forty-third birthday, on December 10, 1851. The Dewey family was solidly middle-class and Protestant. Melvil's father, whose Welsh ancestors had migrated to Massachusetts in 1630, owned a few acres and operated a general store in Adams Center, New York, a village of a little over three hundred people. The family practiced constant industry and scrimping in order to maintain their sober existence. Dewey received a rude education at the local schools and worked at the family store, learning from his father something of the craft of bootmaking. After his graduation from Adams Center High School, he held his first job at the age of sixteen when he taught a twelve-week school term at nearby Toad Hollow. At his urging, his family moved to Oneida, where he attended Oneida Seminary and Alfred University in preparation for his entrance into Amherst College in 1870.

Dewey's mother was an austere and undemonstrative woman whose life centered around thrift, work, and the Baptist Church. To judge from her letters, she was poorly educated and of only moderate intelligence, a woman not given either to sensitive contemplation or to the enjoyment of life's small frivolities. In her mundane letters to her son she constantly directed him toward saving and hard work, with the ultimate goal of a cash return. But she set him a nearly impossible task—to be both altruistic and rich: "I want you always to try to benefit the world but you cannot afford to do it without being well-paid. You are working hard enough to command big wages."[7] Perhaps it was this double-bind message that helped to set up a painful conflict within him, which, as we shall see, he resolved only by a habit of self-deceit that was evident to almost everyone except himself.

Dewey never spoke of his childhood environment in any but solemn or resentful tones. His mother, he recalled, was "so over-worked . . . she had no time to fuss with babies, so my older sister had practically the entire care of me from infancy." His relationship with his sister "Mate" remained warm and close throughout her life. After her marriage he spent long periods of time with her on her husband's farm until he reached his teens. Away from Mate, living again at home with his parents, he felt sadly alone and brooded about the future: "I was so unhappy over many things that seemed wrong, wasteful and foolish."[8]

Dewey's hunger for parental empathy and affection sometimes grew very strong. Home for spring vacation from Amherst, the twenty-year-old Dewey basked in the admiration of one of his former students, a small girl of twelve. He wrote in his diary:

> The look of affection and trust she gives me so bashfully is very precious and touches me deeply. . . . I am so jealous in my nature that it requires an effort to trust and believe in older people . . . I know my own unworthiness so well I guess that I can hardly believe anyone does care particularly for me.[9]

A few months later, during his summer at home, and in a romantic mood, he strolled around his birthplace hoping to experience a "delightful" or "sad" nostalgia for his childhood days. Sadly he recorded:

> My home was not very calculated to inspire such sentiments. . . . There was not that home influence and intimacy that are necessary to the ideal home and which makes all memories and thoughts so pleasant. It was hurly-burly, scolding, etc. too much, and neither of my parents ever practiced any confidences with me. I of course regret very much this fact but it cannot be altered and I must make the best of it.[10]

Although he felt his parents had worked hard to provide for his "education and character," he had missed as a child their genuine concern and sympathy.

> I often think how precious a place home would be should all one's early life be passed pleasantly with no jangles and quarrels to mar the memory. If life is spared I'll try and profit by my lesson and make a home that my children will look back to with pleasure.[11]

"I often regret exceedingly," Dewey wrote to his brother, "that there was never much affection manifested in our immediate family. However much there may have been it was somehow smothered, so much. I suppose mother's natural disposition made a great difference, for she don't like much demonstration and you and I certainly do."[12] After Dewey graduated from college he rarely returned home to visit, despite the accusing self-pity of his mother, who repeatedly begged him in her letters to come and see her "at least once a year."

Dewey never mentioned the effect of his father upon his life, and one may conclude, from the absence of such a statement and from the tone of the family correspondence, that Joel Dewey was overshadowed by the more decisive personality of his wife. When Dewey did refer to his father it was generally in a belittling or contemptuous manner. The general store was described by Dewey as a "God-send to the ne'er-do-wells for ten miles around."

> He [father] did plenty of business to have been a rich man . . . but he never could refuse credit. The result was that poorly paid people whom nobody else would trust would come to our store for groceries, food, supplies, shoes, etc., and never paid cash and seldom paid anything on account.[13]

When he was seventeen Dewey waited on customers and "tried to improve store methods."

> I finally made a complete inventory, to get rid of the guess work, and my figures were convincing that the store was a loss rather than a gain, so I devoted my energy for months to persuading father that it ought to be sold . . . it was very hard for him to give it up.[14]

Perhaps some of the quarrelling that Dewey reported in his home centered upon his father's inability to provide more for his penurious wife.

Shortly before his sixteenth birthday Dewey began a diary in which he wrote sporadically until he was twenty-five years old. This, along with his speeches and literary efforts, is a revealing record of his struggle to define his goals and diminish his anxiety about himself. His diary was not a recital of boyish enthusiasms or a youthful effort to conceptualize the mysteries of existence. Rather, it began with a careful description of his weight, height, and "stock of worldly goods" and continued as a detailed account of a dull round of school and work. Life, to the young Dewey, was shorn of spontaneity and perceived as wholly serious and purposeful. "If God sees fit to grant me life and health there shall be at least one man who will not fear to . . . cast his whole influence on the side of right in every crisis,"[15] he wrote with characteristic humorlessness on his eighteenth birthday. At about the same time he purchased a pair of bone cuff buttons and surreptitiously marked each with the initial "R"; only he knew that this stood for "Reformer."

When he was fifteen Dewey began his lifelong crusade to eradicate the evils of drink and tobacco. Predictably, his strongest objection to the use of tobacco was the amount of money "blown away in smoke" each year.[16] Asa O. Gallup remarked years later to Dewey: "It is not enough for you to do your duty, but you must make others, as far as possible, see your duty in the same light."[17] As a young man Dewey always felt it necessary to police the morals of those around him; he reported one of his friends for violation of the temperance pledge and talked his fellow students at Amherst into abstinence from tobacco. "Got Parker and Fisk to swear off from smoking for a week and got Parker's last cigar," he reported to his diary with self-satisfaction.*

As a boy Dewey was riveted to the internal life: "thinking" as opposed to action, solitude rather than gregarious activity. He spent his leisure hours studying Latin, math, or shorthand, reading philosophy or history. The visit of a circus to his small town held no attraction for him.[18] Nor did he interest himself in the wider events of the world. Not once in his boyhood writings does he refer to public affairs except to comment: "Town meeting today; did not attend; have no time for such things."[19] At Amherst a game of billiards he had come to enjoy was given up because it offended his hypercorrect sense of propriety: "It's a fine game but I can't stand the loafers that put their

---

*Diary, January 9, 1875, MDP. Dewey set himself a difficult chore. In the Amherst yearbook of 1874 it is recorded that 74 per cent of the students played cards, 46 per cent danced, 30 per cent smoked, 67 per cent drank ale and cider, and 25 per cent drank stronger beverages.

heads into the door, and all those things. It makes me feel too much as if I were one of their class."[20] Dewey sensed the lack of naturalness in his deliberate existence. His diary often records the felt oppression of his effort to conform to the moral directives he imposed upon himself.

> My poor mind has been sadly racked for two or three days and I have wished so many times that I might fly away from my thoughts and rest.[21]

> I feel very peculiar. . . . Oh, how the thoughts crowd on my weary brain. A great dreamy, dizzy future looms up before me, so strange and sad . . . Wearily, drearily, swaying from world to world, I feel so strange.[22]

It is not surprising the Dewey suffered all his life from headaches, nervous indigestion, difficulty in breathing, and a myriad of minor complaints.

Dewey was too upright to have been popular or to have made many friends. Entering Amherst he made good his pledge to "mingle in society very little during the next four years; in term time almost none."[23] He collected programs of many college events, but his name does not appear on any of them. Later he took a deep pride in his alma mater, attended reunions, and donated money for a scholarship fund. But Dewey never quite fitted in at Amherst gatherings, not even at reunions, for he was apt to be too rigid and stuffy to meld easily into the rites of male conviviality.[24] Dewey was remembered at Amherst as a tall, gangling, active man of highly nervous temperament, one "full of enthusiasm for a number of good causes; and he was fluent and convincing in advocating them."[25] Behind his nervous energy and incessant talk was an aching loneliness, which appears in the uneasy bravado of statements such as "My social expenses are less than other boys because I keep clear of nearly all of them and am satisfied."[26] This serious do-gooder was once lampooned by his classmates in a manner that caught perfectly the essence of his protective armor, the guard of quick repartee and assumed gaiety that was his habit, and a sense of their bemused boredom with him: "Dewey will remain after the division has departed to attempt an oration on 'Practical Jokes on Serious Subjects or How I Didn't Get Married.' "[27]

Dewey was typically and intensely involved all his life in serious work.[28] In any endeavor he functioned as his own supervisor, issuing himself directives as to how he should act and even how he should feel. It is important to understand this feature in Dewey's cognitive process. Although he was fully aware that he was his own overseer and that the commands came from within, still he functioned in the curious capacity of an agent or representative *to* himself, in the service of some quasi-external necessity or imperative. It is as though he were always reminding himself of some compelling directive, coming from within himself, but with a higher authority than his personal will or choice, which he was obliged to obey. Thus he stood ready to *try* to conform to the commands he transmitted to himself. This is in sharp contrast to the more ordinary intrinsic experience of a sense of self-direction, autonomy, and choice that we usually describe as a sense of "will."

Nothing so well illustrates the rigid directiveness of Dewey's emotional life as in the way in which he made even the writing of his diary into a demanding chore—one he could not enjoy, could not perform to his own satisfaction, yet could not give up. Within a few months after beginning the diary he was already chiding himself because his words did not seem significant enough to him: "I have made up my mind it is all foolishness writing a journal every day unless there is something unusual going on." He berated himself for lack of inconsistency and wrote only from "fear I shall get in the habit of neglecting my journal," or wondered if "the biggest half of what I have written isn't about worthless to me or to anyone else." He lamented his failure to live up to inner commands: "I am sitting in my room . . . wondering whether I had best write in my journal or not. I have commenced to do so in a mechanical way and so will finish." A few weeks later he worried because he was "writing in this poor book when I had quite resolved to give it a little rest." And finally, in frustration, he admitted: "I never seat myself with this book without having the question, 'Does it pay?' come up in my mind. I do so wish some competent person would tell me these things."[29]

But the central key to an understanding of Dewey's personality is his overriding preoccupation with death and the passage of time. Although the fear of death is not always so predominant an obsessive trait as is true in Dewey's case, a preoccupation with death fears and a distorted concept of time is commonly noted to be present to some degree in every obsessive personality. The obsessive feels besieged, at every moment. The *forced* drivenness of his existence is to him a real life-and-death matter and if he does not do as he is driven to do, he is filled with panic. Dewey behaved as if his existence were continually threatened; he seemed to live in an imaginary jungle where the threat of death necessitated a constant guard. Hence his obsessional defenses: grandiose thinking to assure omnipotence; intellectualization to ensure certainty; indecision to avoid mistakes; verbal juggling and ritualistic interests to maintain control.

The attempt to control all eventualities presented time as a special problem to Dewey. Time, an enemy to be overcome, was a threat to all his plans and projects. Since a guarantee of the future was his prime concern, he experienced time in the present as being wasted unless it were filled to the brim.* The present did not have significance in itself because his interest was solely in the future; it was relevant only insofar as it could be used to enhance that future. Day after day was consumed in a futile and desperate struggle to control the passage of time itself. Unable to tolerate ambiguities and unpredictabilities, Dewey sought to dismiss time as a realistic limitation on his life. He craved certitude—desired to foretell, foresee, and exert control

---

*In an interview with an old employee at the Lake Placid Club, Lake Placid, New York, in October 1976, I was told that in the 1920s Dewey once fiercely scolded a new reception clerk because the clerk consumed valuable time by saying "Good morning, Mr. Dewey."

before the fact. Thus Dewey's lifelong concentration on detail is best understood as a measure of self-protection.

Before he was eighteen Dewey was preaching the value of the four great timesaving crusades of his life—the adoption of simplified spelling, the metric system, shorthand, and abbreviations in writing. He believed that the time spent by children in learning standard spelling and compound numbers were the "two chief reasons why it takes America so much longer than Germany or Italy to teach efficient reading."[30] The scores of abbreviations, or "breves," that he worked out and spread through any organization he controlled were devised for the purpose of saving the seconds that made up the minutes and hours of life. Dewey insisted that his family, friends, and business associates correspond with him in Lindsley's Takigraphy, a phonetic shorthand, which he learned in 1867. Because "truly in the midst of life we are in death," every wasted letter, number, or motion became a crime against life itself. His constant resolve was to be more zealous "of my God-given time which I fear is short."[31] Dewey feared that every day might be his last. His consolation was that we "live in deeds, not years, in thoughts not breaths, and the man who thinks and does twice as much in reality lives twice as long, in the same time."[32] When he was seventeen Dewey made a decision to advance the human condition through education. His major contribution, of course, would be the saving of time.

> I wish to inaugurate a higher education for the masses. .. . . If my life is spared . . . I believe it to be a great sin for those who have controll [*sic*] of youth to allow or rather indirectly compell [*sic*] them to waste so much time in acquiring so little knowledge. . . . When one looks back and finds that he has spent ten years in what might be more easily and much better learned in five he sees and laments the error. . . . I believe the masses should be fully educated . . . They should spend much less time but by more perfect allotment and application of that time they should acquire more and better knowledge.[33]

Birthdays, recording the passage of time, were naturally of great significance to Dewey. On these days he was in the habit of totaling up the year's wasted moments and outlining his hopes for the future. "Little by little time creeps on and life grows shorter and more earnest. . . . It is a terrible sight to see so many precious years going to waste. . . . The measured tick of the clock warns me that unyielding time is steadily and surely marching on."[34] His composition "Life" again stressed his attention to death.

> As we pass through this part called life, we feel deeply that life is very short, eternity very long. We see the sands of life flowing surely and with almost fatal rapidity from a fountain which to us is hidden. We cannot look within. We . . . know that it might contain enough of the golden sand to supply the waste of a hundred [grains]. It is possible but not probable. . . . How much it *may* contain, how long the rapid wasting *may* continue, is a secret known to God alone. . . . If life is *so short* and eternity so long, nothing but earnest, persistent endeavors will enable us to look back on a finished work.[35]

To accomplish good, to control others, to save time, to preserve and extend his life—how to combine all of these driving forces within one career? Dewey puzzled over the question and found an ingenious answer when he was twenty-two years old. Once he formulated his solution, the rigidity of his personality never allowed him to stray from it for the next fifty-seven years of his life, although he was sometimes required to perform considerable mental gymnastics in order to rationalize his every interest and action to fit it. His graduation from Amherst was near when he finally hit upon the answer.

> I thought I would like to teach mathematics, [or] study, practice and teach architecture where one could build his ideas into *permanent* form; but I always realized that out of a score of things that had greatly attracted me, I could do only one with one life and so I determined that my higher usefulness would be not to do any one of these things, but to stimulate others to take up the work. I thought I might on the average each year induce one person to do some important work that he would not have done except for my influence. Thus in fifty years I would really have accomplished fifty things instead of one by raising myself to the second power, seeking out and inspiring and guiding others to do the work for which my *one life did not give time*. So, instead of "teaching," I always use the word "education" in naming my chosen profession. [Italics mine.][36]

Such extraordinary vigor and purpose made Melvil Dewey a unique teacher, a teacher who did not seek to impart knowledge so much as to fire enthusiasms in others that would remain long after he had gone. Home education, not the classroom, was his ground, and the library, not Turkey or China, was his mission field. Each book, carefully chosen and well placed, was *his* influence living on in others, *his* life lengthened and protected from decay. It was Dewey's inner imperatives that determined the formal motto of the ALA: "The best reading for the greatest number at the least cost." The least cost could only mean the least time. The library had to be standardized and mechanized. Life was a dangerous power-struggle to Dewey, and his compulsive timesaving was in the service of his own deep alienation from a loved and secure self.

In 1872, during Dewey's junior year at Amherst, he began work in the college library as an assistant. Dewey began to read about library work and to visit other libraries in New York and New England, in an effort to solve what was for him the central problem: "the waste of time and money in the constant recataloging and reclassifying made necessary by the almost universally used system where a book was numbered according to the particular room, tier and shelf where it chanced to stand on that day, instead of by the class, to which it belonged."[37] After "months of study," Dewey claimed to have received his inspiration while in chapel.

> The solution flashed over me so that I jumped in my seat and came very near shouting "Eureka!" It was to . . . [use] the simplest known symbols, the arabic numbers as decimals with the ordinary significance of nought, to number a classification of all human knowledge in print.[38]

Dewey had realized the obsessive's dream—to place all of human knowledge into *ten* tight holes.

The decimal classification plan was presented to the Amherst faculty in May 1873, and Dewey was quickly given permission to apply the plan to the reclassification of books in the college library. After his graduation the young library assistant was made the assistant librarian, and he stayed on at Amherst for two more years before his move to Boston in 1876. On his twenty-first birthday he wrote that he had found "my World Work—Free Schools and Free Libraries for *every soul.*"[39]

Fortuitously, Dewey found a mother substitute during his last years at Amherst and, more important, discovered that she was willing to lend him a large sum of money that would enable him to establish himself in business. He began to board with his new friend, Mrs. S. F. Pratt, the moderately well off widow of a missionary, in early 1875. "Mrs. Pratt is now 'my folks,' " he wrote in March.[40] Dewey took charge of the investment of her money and in the summer began to lecture her on budgeting. In December 1875 he made a decision to move to Boston. His last day in Amherst was strangely depressing to him.[41] He had several "big cries," as did "Mother" Pratt. His diary for that day ends in a curious manner.

> It was to me a sad day for I feared it might be really my last. So with an earnest prayer that God will do with me what seems to Him best I closed the book, for it is written and no entry can be altered.[42]

Dewey set out for Boston on April 10, 1876, dramatically aware that he was leaving his school boy environment to meet the tests of manhood. For the next eight months he managed to increase the relentless pressure he created to drive himself toward the realization of his goals. By the end of the year, however, even he seemed to sense the limits of his endurance, bitterly complaining in his business letters of physical fatigue, insomnia, indigestion, and emotional exhaustion, repeatedly forecasting to his correspondents the possibility of his impending breakdown. Yet the commands from within dominated his actions—the next generation must be saved from the loss of time in the gaining of education, the literary laborers of the nation must be taught to work efficiently, the masses must be weaned from false ideals and given the tools of self-education. And, incompatible with his other goals as it might seem to anyone else but Dewey, he must somehow win a fortune with his unselfish labor.

Compartmentalization is the essence of Dewey's cognitive processes, and nowhere is it better illustrated than in his lifelong attempt to balance his equally strong needs to be both altruistic and mercenary. Juggling these disparate elements in his personality forced him into strange contortions of reason. It was his ability to work mightily for his own advancement while genuinely believing that he cared only for the good of others that so in-furiated his many enemies and frustrated his friends.

Thus in 1879, after he had established his three great organizations to reform spelling, metrics, and the library and had incorporated his first business, he could publicly describe his Readers and Writers Economy Company as a cooperative endeavor solely designed to provide a forum in which literary workers could share labor-saving ideas, while arguing privately that he was "convinced that a fortune was before me and that all my society work . . . was . . . to become of great commercial value in making a constituency for the new company."[43] His interest in the adoption of the metric system, a reform into which he put much militant effort in the 1870s, was touted by him as an altruistic effort to free the child from the time wasted in learning compound numbers. Less publicized was the American Metric Bureau's interest in copyrights and supplies of certain metric apparatus, the sale of which "would amount to a practical monopoly of the business when the missionary work of the metric is given up."[44] Later Dewey could believe that the Lake Placid Club, his phenomenal multimillion-dollar development in the Adirondacks, was not simply a successful vacation resort but a humanitarian venture devoted to the interests of educational workers.

He was often a slippery businessman, especially during those periods when his debts far exceeded his income. In the 1890s he several times ordered supplies for the Lake Placid Club and then returned the unsold merchandise to the manufacturers with the "reminder" that he had only accepted the goods on consignment. When the manufacturers responded that they had no memory of such a prior understanding, Dewey would react with the hurt innocence of a wronged philanthropist. In 1897 the Eastman Kodak Company stuck to its guns and insisted that Dewey pay for the materials he had ordered. How could they treat him so dishonorably, Dewey wrote, when he had sold their cameras and even built a darkroom for the use of their customers, all because he fervently wished their success? It would be a mistake to assume that Dewey was feigning idealism. He was perfectly sincere, certain of his own noble motivations. R. R. Bowker, a prudent man, had once been burned by Dewey's unique business methods during their association with the *Library Journal* and had no illusions regarding Dewey's peculiar concept of truth. In answer to Dewey's request for advice regarding a job offer at the University of Chicago in 1892, Bowker wryly commented:

> Your assertion of purely philanthropic motives, coupled with the demand for more salary on the ground that you have debt on your shoulders, must make an exceedingly unfortunate impression on businessmen. That is the plain English of your letter, as I think it will strike almost any outsider trained in business habits of thought. I have come to learn that your mind acts curiously in these matters and that the letter really represents a feeling of altruism coupled with peculiar pecuniary relations, about as the two exist in your own mind. But you would be a great deal easier person to get along with if your mind could be trained to treat these two relations somewhat as other minds are accustomed to treat them.[45]

Still, one can only marvel at the determined energy and spirit of the young Dewey. If many thought him a fanatic, put off by his high-pitched voice and nervous intensity, it is, after all, the committed zealots of the world who move and shift it a little now and then. His powers of persuasion were formidable. Within the first year in Boston he had negotiated large loans, been the major organizing force in the ALA, taken over as managing editor of a new magazine for librarians, established the headquarters of the Spelling Reform Association and the American Metric Bureau, and planned the publication of two bulletins to advance the cause of spelling and metric reform. From his office on Hawley Street, the correspondence came pouring out in impressive volume: letters exhorting others to join one of his crusades, requesting information on metric items, arranging innumerable meetings, praising the reform activities of another educational worker—inquiring, instigating, encouraging, arguing, scolding, exalting the virtues and practicality of better and more efficient methods in the educational "suburbs of the holy field." With every tick of the clock life grew shorter, and more earnest.

Less than two weeks after arriving in Boston Dewey received a business offer from Edwin and Fred B. Ginn. Ginn and Company agreed to finance the establishment of a library journal and a bureau to sell items pertaining to Dewey's interest in takigraphy, metrics, and the library. The brothers were to receive three-fourths interest, Dewey to have one-fourth interest and to draw an annual salary of $2,000.[46] Although he had a business card printed showing himself as their agent, Dewey was apparently not satisfied with the share they offered him.[47] On May 13 he used Mrs. Pratt's bonds as collateral to borrow $12,000 from Edwin Ginn. Four days later he was in New York City, planning with Frederick Leypoldt the establishment of a library journal.

Leypoldt, an immigrant from Germany, was already well known in the book trade. He was a romantic idealist and a bibliographical scholar, with an enormous capacity for work and an almost total lack of business sense. Due chiefly to the shrewd help of his associate, R. R. Bowker, his *Publishers Weekly* became by 1876 the principal organ of the book trade in the United States. Like Dewey, Leypoldt longed for the time when all agents of book dissemination should be recognized as members of a learned profession. As early as 1874 Leypoldt had published a "Library Corner" in the *Weekly* at the suggestion of Dewey, then a librarian at Amherst, and discussed with Bowker the desirability of printing a separate library journal to encourage the use of better library methods and to provide librarians with an organ of communication. In May 1876, Bowker, Leypoldt, and Dewey began the organization of a national association of librarians, which would meet at the Centennial in Philadelphia, and planned the publication of the *American Library Journal*, which would appear for the first time in October.[48]

Dewey was able to drive a hard bargain. Leypoldt would assume all financial risk. Dewey was to carry on the work of the new magazine, providing material and soliciting advertisers and subscribers. Bowker's only job was to edit the copy that Dewey was to send. For this Dewey would receive 20

per cent of the gross, not the net, receipts; an annual salary of $500; and of
fice expenses for the year, promising that he would devote at least half o
each day to work on the *Journal.*[49] Mrs. Leypoldt, already driven to despair
by her impractical husband's denial of financial realities, was certain the
venture would end in disaster. She judged Dewey to be "as miserable a
specimen of a gabbling idiot as I ever beheld."[50] Her insight was prophetic
Although the *Library Journal* survived and eventually became self-
supporting, it steadily lost money for many years, while the wrangling between Dewey and Leypoldt grew to such proportions that Leypoldt came to
believe himself "persecuted,"—hounded, literally, to death.

As Leypoldt and Bowker soon discovered, Dewey, the missionary of efficiency, was one of the most disorganized of businessmen. Perhaps he simply
attempted too much in his first years at Boston. He had not yet assembled the
loyal coterie of women who in later years would provide the organization
necessary to the realization of his grand conceptions. Dewey was an inspirer,
an enthusiast, a dreamer of great dreams; he was not a responsible or dependable worker. His verbosity was legendary. Once he began to create his
visions aloud, time was forgotten, although not always by his dazed listeners.
He used words as a magical tool to control his immediate environment. Yet
time moved relentlessly on, despite all his efforts to control it. He was so intent upon the perfect use of every moment, trying to accomplish too much
too well, that he became sidetracked and lost in the pursuit of endless
minutiae.

Dewey would not get his copy in to Bowker on time. His letters were, he
admitted, "wholly without organization." He could not keep an accurate account of his monthly expenses and would not send in to Leypoldt even the
chaotic account he kept. In January 1877 Bowker insisted on a new contract
that raised Dewey's salary to $750 but put a firm limit of $450 on his expense
account.[51] By April, when subscriptions totaled only 300 and losses were
nearing $1,800, Bowker decided to take charge of the management of the
Journal. Through the remainder of 1877 relations between the New York
and Boston offices continued to sour.

Dewey felt little remorse. He excused his inefficiency by reminding
Bowker of the overriding importance of his reform activities in spelling,
metrics, and the library. All his life, Dewey was always in the right; it seemed
obvious to him that a man with his high ideals and standards deserved more
than ordinary consideration. He should be free from criticism because he
tried so hard to achieve more than other men—and he should not be criticized if he sometimes failed to reach perfection.

Along with his frenetic work activity, Dewey was falling in love. He had
met his future wife, Annie Godfrey, in the Harvard Library, only a few days
after his move to Boston. She was the daughter of a deeply religious shoe
manufacturer whose wealth had allowed her to mix socially with cultural

figures like Longfellow, Lowell, and members of the Beecher family. Annie seemed a perfect match for Melvil—intelligent, well educated, earnest, and ambitious. One of that pioneer group who attended the new elite colleges for women, Annie entered Vassar in 1872 and left there in her junior year to assist, as librarian, in the opening of Wellesley. Like so many of her sister reformers—women like Jane Addams, Lillian Wald, Ida Cannon, and Ellen Richards—Annie was too well educated to be content simply with conventional domesticity. Yet, in common with the other founders of service professions for women, she did not question "biologically ordained" sex-typed work for women. Her later activity in establishing professional careers for women in librarianship and home economics was chiefly a glorification of women's service role in society.[52] In 1876 she was twenty-five, a slightly plump, eminently serious and hard-working young woman, happy to be ballast for Melvil's high-flying spirit.

Annie and Melvil exchanged warm letters in 1877 and 1878, their courtship marred only by the necessity for Annie to choose between Melvil and an ardent steamboat captain who was pushing his suit with great skill.[53] In August they traveled together to Paris, to attend the international conference of librarians, where she was impressed with Dewey's devotion to duty and unfailing energy. On October 8, 1878, her other suitor conceded defeat and on October 19 she married Dewey. Predictably, Dewey almost missed the train on the way to his wedding ceremony because he was involved in talk with a bookdealer.

Annie brought order and continuity to his life, supplementing their income during the lean years at Boston by her work at indexing in various libraries, straightening out his chaotic bookkeeping, tempering his enthusiasms, smoothing his stormy relations with others. Depending on one's point of view, her household record books are either awesome in their completeness or humorous in their detail. She counted and recorded every penny and every item that went in or out of her home, from jars of fruit canned to buttons purchased. She could have given the exact number of guests in her home for the past few years, including the number of meals they had consumed.

For at least the first ten years of their marriage, she and Dewey compiled weekly "time budgets," even to the point of blocking out hours for "vacation." Annie allowed herself one half-day a week for such frivolity, on "Wednesday, if pleasant, or first pleasant day thereafter." They also devised a tortuous regime of self-discipline, complete with a self-rating and a fine system. Dewey had over forty resolutions—among them, to be "punctual," not to "talk loud or in [a] high voice," to "eat slowly," to "sing daily," to use "no slang," to "breathe deeply," to get to "meals on time," and to "behave with dignity." He rarely rewarded himself with over 70 per cent achievement for the week, sliding once on "accuracy in print" to 48 per cent. On Annie's side, she cautioned herself, "On Sundays don't scold," and summed it all up in one grand entry, "Don't waste a minute."[54]

During the Albany years, from 1899 to 1906, Annie spent more and more time away from home, perhaps because of ill health, possibly because of marital strain. During those years she was the real organizing force at Lake Placid, drawing to exact scale the building plans and supervising the overall operation. At Placid she was known as the lady invariably dressed in starched white, with especially made colored pockets to fit the matching colored notebook and pencil she carried.

The new responsibility of a wife made it necessary for Dewey to rethink his business investments. By 1878 he had given up the idea of making money from the sale of metric goods[55] and the Library Journal was clearly not earning enough to successfully cover his expenses. Actually Dewey was the only person profiting from the Journal, having received almost $3,900 in cash, goods, and advertising space by the end of 1878, while Bowker and Leypoldt were almost $1,600 in debt.[56] Considering the erratic and undependable nature of Dewey's work for the magazine, Bowker felt his compensation was exorbitant, and Leypoldt was for canceling the association with Dewey altogether. Bowker soothed his two excitable associates. Under the final contract of January 24, 1878, Dewey was given 150 pages of advertising space and his annual salary was lowered to $600. Leypoldt agreed to pay Dewey one-fourth of the gross receipts but with the understanding that Dewey's total payment would not exceed $1,200 for the year.[57] Dewey, of course, felt he deserved much more.

In early 1879 relations among the three men exploded when Dewey threatened to withhold copy and to open his own periodical in Boston. Bowker felt betrayed; he offered to turn the entire matter over to the ALA executive board for arbitration. This was never done, probably because of Winsor's disdain for messy feuds over money, and the Journal managed to survive through more issues until the suspension of publication was announced in June 1880.[58] Meanwhile Dewey extracted another $485.69 and Bowker's debt increased to nearly $2,400.

Dewey had probably already lost much of his previous interest in the Journal, for he had a grand new moneymaking scheme which he felt was so original in its conception and would appeal to such a large untouched market that he was sure to gain all the riches he had failed to accumulate after three years in Boston. The fact that he was heavily in debt and had no capital was but a temporary barrier. He had all the bluster and optimism that mark the successful entrepreneur. Yet Dewey was psychologically incapable of recognizing within himself such a low motivation as a desire for wealth. Like all his business endeavors, this one was to be an unselfish act of labor on his part, directed, at great personal cost, toward a high purpose. The Readers and Writers Economy Company, organized in March 1879, was actually a business house that supplied library and office equipment to its customers, chiefly through catalogue orders. As Dewey described it, however, it was a cooperative union of literary laborers throughout the nation to increase the personal efficiency of each—"the great commercial tree, sprung wholly from a literary root." Its "members," mostly "college-bred men," were urged to send in their suggestions to save time, money, and labor. The company would test all such ideas and appliances and manufacture or provide whatever apparatus passed trial, at 5 per cent "discount," to advance the great cause.[59]

The capital for Dewey's new venture was provided by Frederick Jackson, the superintendent of the Newton, Massachusetts, free library. Dewey had negotiated the purchase of a tract of land near Boston for one of Annie's relatives,[60] and then, no doubt making use of his remarkable powers of persuasion, had used the land as collateral for a loan of over $4,000 from Jackson. Jackson soon became seriously ill and Dewey claimed to have bought out his interest in the business in late 1879. The details of this business deal are exceedingly murky,* but apparently it was in December 1879 that the Economy Company was incorporated as a joint stock company capitalized at a heavily watered $100,000.

The first meeting of the stockholders was held in late 1879. The board of directors consisted of Dewey, Frederick Perkins, and H. E. Davidson. Dewey was elected president and treasurer. In January 1880 Charles Cutter, who eventually was to contribute $1,150 to the enterprise, became one of the vice-presidents. Initially business was good, and plans were made to open branches in New York and Chicago. By May Dewey was pressuring the stockholders to determine the amount of credit he was to receive for goodwill. He pushed them, especially, to set the amount of his salary and to make a decision about how much stock he should be given for origination of the company.[61]

At this point dissatisfaction among the largest stockholders was very high, for they had become aware of the confused system of bookkeeping that Dewey maintained. A special committee to go over the books and to report on the question of the president's salary was appointed on May 12, 1880. In June the committee recommended that "a set of books be opened to be kept in the manner usual among merchants and corporations."[62] Dewey continued to press for a decision about his salary. His demands were naturally not modest—$5,000 a year and $14,000 in stock to be held as security and purchased by him as he could afford it.

Beginning in July serious conflict developed. A series of resignations occurred during the summer. The notable Brahmin Edward Wigglesworth, the largest investor, who had previously worked with Dewey on metric reform, forced Dewey's resignation as president on October 11.[63] The same day Wig-

*I have found three contradictory versions told by Dewey of the arrangements with Jackson. Certain, however, is that in the summer of 1883 Dewey paid back to Jackson all but the interest, $1974.71, on a $4,000 loan made on October 31, 1879. (Frederick Jackson to Dewey, June 23, July 13, and August 24, 1883, MDP.)

glesworth, Cutter,* and Herbert Coolidge filed an injunction against Dewey that made it impossible for him to manage any part of the business or to have access to any of the goods or papers in his office.

The bill of injunction listed many grave charges. Dewey was accused, among other things, of holding 1,084 shares that he had not paid for; of crediting himself on the books with cash for assets that were not worth what he claimed or were totally worthless; of granting himself an unapproved $3,000 salary; of using the company money to pay his private debts, including interest on those debts; of withdrawing for his private use at least $3,800, perhaps as much as $5,800, in cash; and of extracting over $1,500 from the company on a Metric Bureau note. In summation the bill charged that the books were so "artfully" done that no one could understand them. It was clear that Dewey's credit side of the ledger continued to swell in volume and that "if the said Dewey is allowed to continue in his past course the company will soon be ruined and the greater parts of the assets appropriated by the president himself."[64]

Perhaps it is true, as Dewey claimed, that he was not guilty of fraud, only of inattention to detail and careless supervision of the books. Still, the scope of his naivete is notable, especially in a man of twenty-nine who had been entrusted with large sums of money and who even as a child had been noted for his facility with numbers — a man, moreover, who was an apostle of efficiency. For example, the investigation revealed that he kept only one set of books, in which he recorded — all as part of one balance — the funds from his personal account, including some of the money from the *Library Journal* and his many personal loans, as well as the treasury of the ALA and the money of the Metric Bureau *and* the Economy Company. Therefore, it was literally true, as the bill charged, that he paid private debts with company money, for the monies were mixed indiscriminately. At those times when his funds were temporarily low or when an expansion of liabilities seemed wise, he habitually advanced money from the total to his credit.

In fact Dewey's bookkeeping was such an intricate jumble that even he admitted confusion. When the final adjustments were made he "discovered," among other errors, that he had been credited twice in one month for his monthly *Journal* salary, had incorrectly given himself another salary advancement for $291.67, and had wrongly charged the Economy Company for a $200 personal note. It is also apparently true that he had issued himself large amounts of stock along with a high salary. This action seems justifiable, for the company was after all his own creation, although it was chiefly financed by others. Dewey admitted that he had sold some of his stock to his secretary, financing this by a raise in the employee's salary. Thus, while nominally raising her salary, he in fact credited the $150 premium to

---

*Cutter resigned as an officer of the company on October 12, 1880. He later invested more money, losing $2,500 in all.

himself. The metric note transaction was equally complicated. Dewey had held an old note from the Metric Bureau that represented money he had borrowed and loaned to the Bureau. Using this note as collateral, he had borrowed an additional $1,543.17 for the Economy Company, thus in effect passing liability to the Economy Company for the money he had originally borrowed and then had loaned himself! With his remarkable talent for self-justification, Dewey argued that he had merely offered credit to the Economy Company on his account. One must sympathize with the plaintiffs here. At best, the procedure could only be described as highly irregular.

Yet Dewey, when faced with the shambles of his bookkeeping, sincerely contended that his books were no different from anyone else's, "except that they had greater clearness and greater clarification of accounts."[65] It is likely that because he saw himself as morally superior to other persons, since he was striving toward such high goals, he was offended and surprised when he met with criticism or dissatisfaction. Grandiosity is maintained by an assumption of a privileged status and by the denial of realistic limitations upon oneself, in order to overcome all doubt. Feelings of omnipotence are a defense mechanism to counteract the constant state of jeopardy experienced by deeply insecure personalities.

While the obsessional system is intact, the illusion of perfection can remain. However, in the event of a major crisis, when the obsessive is forced to acknowledge a loss of status or an inability to control every aspect of his life, he will commonly take one of two routes — toward paranoia or depression. The first response represents an extension and expansion of his defenses, the latter a total breakdown of his integrative capacities. Dewey, throughout his life, most often relied on paranoid delusions to control any threat to his self-esteem, but in the 1880 fiasco he apparently fell briefly into depression. His letters reveal wild swings from supreme confidence to the most un-Dewey-like self-pity, fear, and self-derogation. The physician Wigglesworth, his major "enemy" in the conflict, reportedly feared that Dewey might be suicidal during this period.[66]

A week after the injunction was filed, Dewey was writing frantic letters to his friends and opponents. Dewey feared the loss of his metric interests as well. To F. A. P. Barnard, the president of Columbia University, Dewey wrote that overwork "has nearly cost me my life. I've learned a severe lesson." He vowed to "redeem" himself metrically.[67] On October 21, Dewey wrote a long and plaintive letter to Wigglesworth:

> I can't stand this. I shall be sick abed. . . . If we both live I will prove my worthiness and be called your friend. . . . My wife joins me in throwing ourselves entirely in your hands. . . . Everything we have is yours if you say it is. . . . We would rather live on a crust of bread and wear rags than have one who has been my warm friend and trusted me as you [have doubt me]. . . . I cannot live and feel that you think I have wronged you. . . . We are in your hands.[68]

In early November, because his assets had been commandeered, Dewey wa
forced to beg the Economy Company for money to pay his bills.[69] During thi
time he kept up a stream of entreaties to Wigglesworth.[70]

Perhaps the gravest wound to his ego came from his loss of face before the
patrician Winsor. In December, Winsor, in order to "observe appearances,"
sent J. L. Whitney to collect the ALA papers from Dewey and to hold them
during Dewey's "interim of uncertainty," as Winsor so delicately phrased it.
(Gentle Samuel Green had already infuriated Dewey by a patronizing letter
in which he said that because Dewey had done so much for the library world,
he, for one, would "show him mercy.") Dewey was mortified. He wrote Winsor in December 1880:

> I am much surprised by your letter. . . . it seems as if my most trusted friends
> were glad of a chance to hear something to my discredit, to believe it themselves,
> and take such action as to confirm it in the eyes of others. I am hurt very deeply by
> this feeling supposing that my associates of the ALA knew too well the sacrifices I
> had made for that work, to be ready to do me injury and injustice at the shadow
> of an opportunity. . . . I must protest against the rank injustice of the
> Board. . . . it is to my mind contemptible to take a course that . . . means
> judgement against me . . . I feel more hurt than words can express . . . and if
> I say more shall use very strong language.[71]

The Brahmin leaders were unquestionably shocked by this unseemly scandal.
Poole's reservations regarding Dewey seemed to have been verified. Dewey's
friendship with Winsor and Cutter decidedly cooled from this point on,
although their relationship was not ended.*

The case was decided out of court in January 1881. The ALA was returned the full amount of its treasury, $400.14, and Annie was paid about
$130 for some secretarial work. Dewey gave up all his stock in the Economy
Company and all right to future gain but retained the right to the metric
records and to perhaps some of the metric goods.†

The decision was a resounding defeat for Dewey.[72] He was considerably
chastened by the experience. In the little over three years since he had been
in Boston he had tried to establish three reform organizations and to make
his fortune as well. Now he was without profitable work, was thousands of
dollars in debt, and had alienated the library leaders in Boston, as well as
Leypoldt and Bowker. His small kingdom had fallen about his ears.

The years of 1881 and 1882 were emotionally wearing and financially
uncertain. Annie's indexing work brought in a small income and Dewey

---

*An additional difficulty for Winsor was the temporary confiscation of the ALA mail in Dewey's
possession. This was because Dewey had only one post office box at which he received correspondence for all his business interests as well as his personal mail. (William Nichols to Winsor, December 27, 1880, MDP.) Dewey told Cutter "you will be ashamed" of your small part in
this matter, for you did it "all on hearsay." (Dewey to Cutter, n.d., MDP.)

†Dewey told Bowker in 1891 that the Economy Company settlement had netted him $19,000 in
stock, supplies, notes, and securities, but that most of this had gone to pay off his debts. (Dewey
to Bowker, June 6, 1891, R. R. Bowker Papers, New York Public Library, New York City.)

probably earned some money from consultant fees at small libraries in the area. With little else left, Dewey returned to the metric reform that he had all but given up some months before. At first he seemed interested only in the Metric Bureau's educational efforts, but as the reorganized Economy Company began to flounder, Dewey gradually separated the business side from the reform work of the Metric Bureau. In January 1882 he bought the Economy Company's stock and revived his old "co-operative club." Three months later he reopened in triumph, as the Library Bureau.

In the first year business was reasonably good. With the aid of H. E. Davidson, Dewey helped to lay the foundations of what later would become, under the management of Davidson and W. E. Parker, an immensely profitable concern. The Library Bureau was a pioneer in the revolutionizing of business equipment and methods that took place in the United States around the turn of the century, developing such items as the vertical file system and the two-color typewriter ribbon.* Dewey gained substantial dividends from his investment, but in the 1890s he gradually began to sell all his Library Bureau stock in order to finance the Lake Placid Club. Ironically, Dewey chose to give up his share of what proved to be his most successful business endeavor begun at Boston.

In the early days of the Library Bureau, Dewey's influence was not always favorable. Davidson was in constant battle with Dewey until the Library Bureau's failure and reorganization in 1888 — alternately protesting, threatening, and pleading in an unsuccessful attempt to force Dewey into a more conservative management position. Dewey was restless in business life, never content with slow and steady growth, always pushing outward in new and different directions, rarely considering and often suffering the consequences of risk. When an unexpected opportunity came to him in early 1883 to return to library work, Dewey eagerly accepted the offer.

---

*In 1926 the Library Bureau became a subdivision of the Rand Kardex Bureau, Inc. It is now a full-fledged division in the Remington-Rand Division of the Sperry-Rand Corporation. A 1976 publication of the Library Bureau headlines Dewey's founding of the company and states, "Oh, if Melvil Dewey could only see us now."

7

Columbia College, 1883–1888

IN 1876, THE SAME YEAR that Dewey left Amherst, his popular professor, John Burgess, also moved to a new post as professor of political science, history, and international law at Columbia College. Burgess was committed to the German-style university system with its emphasis upon research and seminar teaching. He was appalled by the lethargic nature of the faculty at Columbia and began a determined effort to institute a modern university there. Burgess, to whom the library was the central tool of scholarship, was most of all aghast at the Columbia book collection, run by a Reverend Beverly R. Betts, of whom it was said that "were . . . a jellyfish endowed with the faculty of speech, it would talk as he does." The library held a little over 31,000 volumes, "few of which were rare and none of which were modern,"[1] and was open for one and a half hours on some weekdays. Betts developed an immediate hatred for Burgess, a feeling that was shared by the other members of the faculty who had also been exposed to Burgess's criticism of their educational practices.

Burgess found an unlikely-looking ally in the sixty-seven-year-old president of Columbia, F. A. P. Barnard. Already infirm in 1876, Barnard was invariably dressed in black frock coat and trousers. With his exceedingly long white beard and hair he seemed a man of the past, yet young and radical ideas danced in his head. Burgess described his first faculty meeting, where he encountered Barnard presiding at the head of the table. The president, who was deaf, carried an enormous ear trumpet, which he directed toward the person with whom he spoke. For faculty meetings, Barnard had installed speaking tubes that ran to each seat. Because the board of trustees at Colum-

126

bia retained almost total control of the operation of the college, approving even the most minor details, Barnard had little real power, and the faculty habitually did not use the tubes but conversed among themselves, while Barnard sat with a dazed, confused expression, sometimes banging on the table for order. Burgess endeared himself forever to Barnard by speaking directly into the tube at his seat.

Working closely with Barnard, Burgess pressed the trustees to provide more money and a modern librarian for the new library building that was nearing completion. In early January 1883, Barnard, as chairman of the Library Committee, was charged with the responsibility of recommending changes in the library staff and in the arrangement and selection of books. Both Barnard and Burgess thought first of the young librarian at Amherst who had devised the Decimal System there. They invited Dewey to meet with the committee several times, and he "proposed so many and so novel views in regard to library management, that he greatly impressed the minds of the members."[2]

Dewey, although feigning reluctance to leave Boston, in fact sent urgent letters in April to leading librarians requesting them to communicate with the Columbia trustees regarding his qualifications for the job.[3] Significantly, Winsor, the foremost librarian of the period, did not send a letter, causing Barnard to comment on its absence.[4] Poole, irritated by Dewey's mechanical mode of thought and by his sophomoric enthusiasm, was properly supercilious.

> I am very glad to hear that you will write your name *Dewey*. Now pray lay aside some, at least, of your orthographical peculiarities, and spell like common folk. It will help you very much in your new position. Let the world reform itself as best it may; but do you attend strictly to business, and not antagonize conservative people by sharp-pointed, bristling peculiarities in spelling.*

As for Dewey's plans for a library school, Poole asked tiredly, Why not establish it first and get it into operation before asking for the profession's approval? "I shall be glad when your plans are matured to learn about them," he added.[5]

Dewey, perhaps uncomfortable with the chiefly commercial nature of his Boston endeavors, was eager to resume the missionary work of the library. The prospects were grand—a new building, adequate finances, a steady salary, and a friendly president. Most giddy of all was the opportunity to establish a library school, a plan Dewey had been polishing for at least ten years. Barnard more than supported the idea; he was enthusiastic about it, perhaps having already recognized it as a means of bringing coeducation to Columbia. Dewey, effervescent with new plans, his confidence restored by

*Frederick Poole to Dewey, April 23, 1883, MDP. A little over a year previously, Poole, in a letter to Winsor, had snidely remarked that he really thought "Dewy" was a more appropriate spelling—in celebration of naiveté. (Cited in William Landram Williamson, *William Frederick Poole and the Modern Library Movement* (New York: Columbia University Press, 1963), 102.

this unexpected and complimentary job offer, would certainly not follow Poole's advice to trust the world to reform itself without assistance. Nor was Dewey psychologically suited to let stand, unchallenged, the attitudes of those who did not share his certainties of right and wrong. Ready for combat against all the forces of darkness, Dewey accepted the position of librarian-in-chief at Columbia College on May 7, 1883, at $3,500 a year. The opening guns of the "Barnard-Burgess-Dewey revolution"[6] were fired.

Dewey immediately began to select his staff, some of whom were to double as faculty for his library school. With the help of Annie and of Alice Freeman, the president of Wellesley College, he chose the famous "Wellesley Half-Dozen" from the June graduates of 1883, each at an annual salary of $500. From the beginning Dewey openly recruited cultured and educated women to library service, appealing to their unsatisfied need for useful work and paid employment. Spinsters were welcomed, for he stressed that only those who desired permanent, lifelong work need apply. (He warned the applicants not to lie about their age in an attempt to appear younger.) Above all Dewey played upon women's proclivity to fulfill the traditional feminine role — as sacrificial servants, as ministers of morality, as cultural guides.

The collection of letters from hopeful applicants that poured into his office offers a fascinating sample of the tentative, yearning mood of many middle-class American women in the 1880s, as they timidly began to test the boundaries of Victorian womanhood and to seek for themselves a wider and more interesting share of the world. The letters are articulate, intelligent, often desperate and pitifully eager. Many came from women who were past the promise of girlhood, already "old maids" in their society. Some who wrote were poor. Some wrote only after receiving papa's permission and on fine stationery. Some were forceful and self-assured. But all were aliens within their society — for they were educated, ambitious, and restless women, either denied marriage against their will or refusing it for reasons of their own.[7] Among them were Florence Woodworth and May Seymour, Dewey's most intimate friends and most devoted lieutenants. Woodworth stayed with him for eighteen years. Seymour followed him until her death thirty-four years later.

Dewey took thirty pages of fine print in the president's report of 1884 to describe the transformation of the Columbia Library. The six old libraries had been combined into one and placed in a new building; 10,000 volumes had been added, and books had been classified, catalogued, dusted, and repaired. Twenty-five thousand volumes were now on open shelves in a reference room. The library had been open 4,382 hours during the year, in contrast to the old yearly average of 438. The staff had worked at great speed, each allotted a specific task in assembly-line fashion. A total of 10,780 catalogue cards had been prepared, and Dewey expected to complete the reorganization in two more years. The library was filled with students; sixty reading tables had been placed for 200 visitors at a time. The library pro-

vided ice water, mail service, reference advice, and speedy book delivery to
its amazed patrons. Dewey labelled, classified, designated, sorted, and
organized every hallway, room, and niche to his heart's delight. Even the pictures of the former presidents and professors of the college were cleaned,
framed, and arranged around the rooms in — naturally — chronological
order.[8] By the end of the year he and his crew had created one of the first
modern college library services in the United States. Barnard, the young-
hearted old rebel, was ecstatic:

> The principal service which Mr. Dewey has rendered has been the inspiration
> which his fervent zeal and enthusiasm has infused into the whole body of students
> which are taught in the classes, and stimulated to endeavor to produce something
> original of their own. In this respect his influence has been invaluable and has
> been of more important service to the college than that of any other officer.[9]

Unknown to all but a few, the Library Bureau, with Davidson protesting
bitterly all along the way, had made a prominent contribution to the library
at Columbia College. Indeed, so heavily did Dewey bleed the Bureau, in
order to sustain the library, that this, probably more than any other factor,
led to the Bureau's collapse in 1888.[10] When Dewey left for Columbia he had
"loaned" Davidson the money to buy an interest in the Bureau, secured by a
mortgage on the goods. Davidson agreed to manage the Bureau and to
assume all liability for its debts. Dewey, as chief creditor, had a controlling
interest in the stock and also retained the right to write checks, order supplies, and borrow money on the Bureau's behalf.

From the summer of 1883 through the spring of 1884 Davidson's letters to
Dewey became progressively more frantic as Dewey proceeded to strip the
Bureau of funds. Dewey took half the working capital in the summer of 1883
alone.[11] He used the money to pay off his old debt to Jackson, purchased
hundreds of dollars of supplies and furniture for the library without paying
for them, and even met part of the payroll at Columbia with Bureau money.
By August 1883 Davidson wrote that the Bureau was nothing "but a shell"
and that a business without goods or capital had "but one ending" in sight. A
fire in 1883 and Davidson's illness in 1884 added to the Bureau's difficulties.
Amazingly Davidson held on, perhaps because he sensed that with proper
management the Bureau had a good future. And then, of course, he had little alternative except personal bankruptcy, for he had agreed to be liable for
all the Bureau debts.

From 1885 to 1887 Dewey attempted from afar to revive the failing
business. W. E. Parker, his former assistant at Columbia, was sent to Boston
to help with the management. Davidson's letters grew colder and more
hopeless, while Dewey judged Davidson to be "incompetent" and "reckless."[12]
By March 1888 Dewey had negotiated further loans to save the Bureau, but
the company could not recover from the 1883–1884 depletion of its capital,
partly because Dewey insisted on such a low margin of profit from its sales. In
mid-April the Bureau was bankrupt. To those who remembered Dewey's

peculiar business methods it was no surprise to discover that the mortgage Dewey claimed to have given Davidson in 1883 had somehow never been recorded.[13] Bowker wrote to Dewey that neither he nor Cutter would print in the *Library Journal* Dewey's claim that the Library Bureau had been prosperous under his management and gone bad only because he left for Columbia. Such a statement, Bowker said, "would be seriously publicly controverted."[14]

Dewey, with the help of a loan from his brother,[15] bought out the seventy-six creditors of the Library Bureau for forty cents on the dollar in 1888 and reorganized the Bureau, but this time on very different terms. Davidson and Parker insisted that they be given complete responsibility for the day-to-day operation of the business and retain most of the profits. The business prospered steadily from that time on, growing in the early twentieth century to a multimillion-dollar concern. Before Dewey eventually sold all his Bureau stock to finance his investment at Lake Placid, he drew a sizable income from the Bureau as the dividends and stock increased in value. And of course he continued to quarrel with Davidson and Parker. In 1899 they finally convinced him that they had gained majority control of the business. Dewey claimed an undue share of the profits because he had established the business, but, as Parker reminded him, "You know that doesn't count much in this country."[16]

By September 1886 Dewey was engrossed in planning the first professional training school in librarianship. Several of the elder statesmen of the ALA were less than enthusiastic about the school, probably suspicious not so much of the idea itself as they were cautious about making too close a commitment to the as-yet-unspecified details of an operation directed by Dewey. After ten years of association with him, they had learned to approach him with some reserve, to anticipate the presence of hidden truths behind the face value of his words and behavior.

The story of the opening of the first library school at Columbia is now a cherished part of the librarian's heritage. It has been told and retold, and the farther we progress from 1887, the more wondrous grows the opposition of the Columbia trustees to women on campus. Twenty-four hours before his school was to open Dewey was informed that he was not to be given a room on campus because the first class of twenty had seventeen women in it. Since the school had already been denied funds, faculty, and equipment, a less committed man than Dewey would have been stopped cold long ago. President Barnard retreated home, made ill with nervous exhaustion. But Dewey rounded up some janitors, cleaned out an unused storeroom above the chapel, nailed legs on broken-down tables, "picked up odd chairs where we could get them without encountering the police, sent a truck for some more to my house in New York, and with smiling face, without giving a hint of the volcano on which we all stood, I welcomed the first class and launched the first library school."[17]

It was perhaps his finest moment, or so it always seemed to him to be. Years later he thanked the Lord who "let me be the particular Moses to lead those particular children of Israel into the promised land." For Dewey, library work was not a job, but a sacred mission. "Dewey wasn't directing a school," said Fremont Rider, who knew him well; "he was preaching a crusade. . . . He invited you to enlist under a marching banner. AND YOU DID!" "Whatever else it may accomplish or fail in, this School will not send out a race of dawdlers," Dewey promised.[18] And so, for three remarkable years, Dewey and his students kept the faith high at Columbia, so much so that an ALA committee reported concern about the frenzied school pace. Dewey promised to guard the health of his pupils so that they might go out with the spirit of "a great awakening." And "when our every pupil is, each in his own sphere, doing his all and his best . . . then we shall feel that our first skirmish line has begun the march. . . . At this particular time in library history . . . the fields are white already to the harvest, and the air is full of hope."[19] The results of this type of training *were* inspiring. Librarian William Foster, a man not given to superlatives, told Dewey that speaking with one of Dewey's pupil assistants was the "most interesting experience I have had for a long time. Such enthusiasm, such determination and complete absorption in one's life-work are not often found except in the Jesuit missionaries."[20]

In 1886, despite the injured protest of Bowker, Dewey began to publish *Library Notes,* a quarterly magazine that publicized his school and his reform ideas. Its pages are an entrancing blend of mission and mechanics. Platitudes lie next to inspiring passages, which rest alongside statements of highly original ideas and devotion to long-lost causes like spelling reform. Interspersed among all this are sections discussing the most minute details of library mechanics. "Literary Labor Savers" and "Library Economy," Dewey entitled these sections. Here he wrote countless abbreviations, computed the best width for columns of pamphlets (6 cm.), described how to store paste, wrote four pages on the standard size of library cards, and showed how to cut paper without waste, complete with diagrams. Here is a representative sample of a nine-page discussion of library handwriting (during which he pauses at one point to chide those who are bored with so much "fussy detail"):

> The standard card has lines 6 mm. apart, or four spaces to the inch. Of these the small letters should be 2½ mm. high; and b,f,h,k, and l, 5 mm. high, thus leaving 1 mm. margin below the top of the tallest letter and the line above.[21]

The length of 1 mm., in case anyone wanted to compute it, was about the width of six hairs. Perhaps it really is not possible to truly comprehend the intricacies of Melvil Dewey's mind.

The appearance of women as members of the library staff and as students at a library school was a matter of great import to Barnard, Burgess, and the trustees. Dewey's later exit from Columbia often has been attributed to other factors such as his lack of tact and discretion; an application form for the library school that requested personal data on height, weight, and color of hair and eyes; insubordination; overly boastful library reports; and wasteful use of funds. All these factors were certainly irritating to Columbia officialdom, but the hottest conflict centered around his unauthorized establishment of coeducation at Columbia. On this question he and Barnard stood almost alone against most of the trustees and faculty, including Burgess. When Dewey arrived at Columbia in 1883 the trustees had already been beleaguered for several years by Barnard and others who demanded that women be admitted to the college. Dewey jumped wholeheartedly into the fray. Perhaps Barnard had even selected Dewey partly because he hoped that Dewey's library school would serve as a wedge to open Columbia's doors to women.

New York had fallen behind other cities in the provision of a degree-granting institution for women, for only the normal school admitted women in 1883. Since 1873 a few women had been allowed to sit in on some classes at Columbia, but when one of the trustees found that his own daughter was among the brazen ones the practice was immediately stopped. Petitions from groups of women to enter the medical school had also been denied, a decision that created much protest against the trustees in the press.

In 1879 Barnard threw a panic into the board of trustees by a long argument in his annual report in favor of coeducation. He spoke out again in 1880. In thirteen closely reasoned pages in 1881 he continued to insist that Columbia be opened to women. His words were wholly modern in tone. With no trace of doubt Barnard asserted that women were both intellectually and physically equal to men. This was certainly a more radical view than Dewey held, for Dewey, more in line with the liberal thought of his time, was more apt to speak of women's disabilities—their physical weaknesses and overly emotional nature.[22] Not so Barnard. He pointed out that experiments at other educational institutions had already proved that women could perform college work with distinction. Barnard insisted that coeducation, not separate schools, was the only rational solution, that two plants were a waste of resources, that the best professors were in established schools, and that separate education was illogical in conception because it rested on the invalid assumption that men and women required different modes of instruction. He concluded that "whatever may happen this year or the next, Columbia College will open her doors widely enough to receive all earnest and honest seekers after knowledge, without any distinction of class or sex."[23] By 1882 the trustees had had enough. They referred his annual report to a committee for revision, and his support of women's education was reduced to a brief statement of his views. But Barnard had the last words; he added that Columbia "may not in our own day be opened to women: but that it will be so in that better coming time which awaits . . . appears . . . to be as certain as anything yet beneath the veil of the future can be."[24]

In 1883 the controversy received national attention. A public meeting, held at the Union League Club in New York and presided over by the editor of the *New York Evening Post,* led to the presentation of another petition to the trustees to allow women into Columbia. It was signed by over one thousand persons, many of them too influential to be ignored. Trustee Morgan Dix, the pastor at famed old Trinity Church, was so aghast at the agitation that he preached a sermon the following Sunday foretelling the destruction of womanhood portended by the demand for coeducation and the "fantastic proceedings of female suffrage."[25]

Barnard and Burgess, battling together in the attempt to modernize Columbia's curriculum, were bitterly split over the woman question. Burgess opposed mixing the sexes in the classroom because women would distract males from study and because women, "on account of physical infirmities," could not be expected to demonstrate even scholarshop and faithful attendance in class. But the clincher to this argument, one that "took like wildfire" with students and alumni, was that if Columbia opened its classes to women the well-off Jews of New York would send their daughters there, creating a "female academy and a Hebrew female academy" at that.[26]

The trustees, at the very same meeting in which Dewey was hired, were forced to a sort of modus vivendi in answer to the latest petition. They agreed to open Columbia College to women, but by use of a remarkable stratagem, they forbade them to attend classes! The Collegiate Course for Women gave women the right to receive credit for those courses in which they could pass the final exams, but they were to have no access to lectures or classrooms. From 1883 to 1888, the period of Dewey's stay, fifty women attempted the course. The first woman graduated with a B.A. in 1887. Winifred Edgerton, a close friend of Dewey's and the Wellesley six, and probably employed for a time in the library, was the first woman to receive a Ph.D., in 1886.

Among the women students was the intrepid Annie Nathan, who "at the age of eighteen . . . had with pathetic eagerness accepted from the authorities of Columbia College the stony substitute for knowledge known as the Collegiate Course for Women." Daughter of a prominent Jewish family, Annie Nathan studied secretly. When she finally told her father about her work he drew her to him and said sadly, "You will never be married."[27] Given the circumstances under which she and the other women students labored, the library became all-important—their classroom, professor, and school. Fortunately, the Columbia library was almost unique in the United States at the time, devoted to progress and filled with eager assistants. What a haven it must have seemed to the small band of women, a place where they were greeted warmly by the librarian himself and where they could receive friendly support and service. Annie Nathan and the other women students agonized over decisions regarding the proper decorum. The heavy doors of the library required some force to open. Should they exert their strength and go through unassisted? Some women felt that such behavior was clearly unseemly. On the other hand, if male students held the doors for them, it was unladylike either to say "Thank you" to a stranger or to accept help without acknowledgment. Such lascivious mixing at the library doors was precisely the sort of letting down of bars that conservatives had warned would lead to unimaginable consequences once women were allowed on campus.

Against heavy odds, Annie Nathan Meyer, now married, continued to struggle with her studies, and she was befriended by the enthusiastic librarian, whom she came to idolize. Once, momentarily discouraged, she expressed her frustration at the educational barriers she was encountering in an angry outburst to Dewey. He reacted with all the overbearing positivism with which he was endowed.

> It was as if a lighted match had been thrown upon a ready-built bonfire. His enthusiasm was contagious. Of course there must be a college for women in New York; there must be! We must obtain one! He agreed with me that the present scheme was utterly absurd. Obviously, if women could get for a few examinations all that men get for daily intercourse with Faculty and with students, and from hundreds of lectures and work in the laboratories, then either women were miraculously gifted or else — and this was an alternative pretty serious to contemplate — all the millions and millions at the moment locked up in college endowments, in laboratories and lecture halls, were just so much sheer waste!
>
> To all of this I wholeheartedly agreed. But what was to be done about it? What could *I* do about it?
>
> Why, start a college for women myself. That was all![28]

Annie Nathan Meyer always spoke of that moment as the beginning of Barnard College and of Dewey as the real initiator of the idea.

The "joint efforts of Melvil Dewey, Mary Mapes Dodge and Annie Nathan Meyer"[29] produced the petition to the Columbia trustees that was signed by fifty-two notable citizens of New York and that led to the approval on May 7, 1888, of the Barnard College annex for women. Barnard College, "in its prenatal days," Dewey later said, "was probably discussed more in my private office in the Columbia library than anywhere else."[30] By June 1889 Dewey had moved to Albany as secretary to the New York regents. It was his fortuitous presence there that allowed Barnard College to open in October, despite the lethargy of the trustees, because Dewey issued the college a provisional charter, even though it had, as yet, no property and no money.

Actually, the establishment of a separate annex was a defeat of President Barnard's plan for coeducation. But the constant agitation of the woman question, creating such unpleasant pressures upon the board of trustees, made Dewey's unauthorized coeducational experiment at the library school and his vocal support of women's rights the chief irritants among the other provocations that eventually led to his expulsion. "My whole five years at Columbia was a constant struggle against the Anti-woman element," Dewey later wrote to one of the trustees, Silas B. Brownell.[31]

From the time when Dewey first opened his school in January 1887 until the time of his resignation in December 1888, he was in more or less constant conflict with one or another of the factions among the trustees and the faculty. In May 1887 the trustees' exasperation with Dewey led them to reject Barnard's request for money to provide more floor space in the library and to obtain furniture for the library school. They also ruled that after July 1887 no women would be admitted into the college without the special order of the trustees; this action gave the trustees the power to overrule Barnard's decision to admit women to the library school. By October, Barnard was thrown on the defensive by an article in the *New York Tribune* which stated that there was strong dissatisfaction with Dewey among the faculty at Columbia. Barnard sent a circular letter to the faculty, asking them to name their complaints, if any. Although most of the replies praised the remarkable transformation of the library wrought by Dewey, several faculty members commented upon his abrasive personality and questioned whether the large amount of money allotted to the library had been spent in the most efficient manner.[32]

When Barnard, due to ill health, submitted his resignation as president on May 7, 1888, Dewey lost his strongest defender. Moreover, the man appointed acting president, Professor Henry Drisler, had long been the strongest opponent of the Barnard-Burgess effort to modernize the curriculum. Those who were hostile to Dewey moved quickly after Barnard's retirement. On November 5 a resolution to dismiss Dewey was referred to a special committee of the trustees, and Dewey was suspended as librarian until such time as the committee reported its findings. Dewey was charged, among other things, with general insubordination, with making boastful statements "not in accordance with academic propriety and the dignity of the College," with dispersing unauthorized printed material, and with being "impatient, and unwilling to follow accepted precedents."[33] Although the committee's report on December 3 did not recommend his dismissal, it was evident that his library school would not be allowed to reopen in 1889.[34] As W. T. Peoples remarked from a distance, Dewey, by his resignation on December 20, 1888, took "time by the forelock" and accepted the inevitable.[35] But Dewey was as pleased to leave Columbia as the trustees were eager to have him go, for on December 12 he had been offered a new job — one in which he could continue his treasured library school.

8

Albany, 1888–1905

In mid-1888 the purposeful librarian of Columbia College was invited by Whitelaw Reid, editor of the *New York Tribune* and a member of the New York State Board of Regents, to visit Albany and to recommend to the regents a plan for the reorganization of the New York State Library. Reid, chairman of the regents' Library Committee, introduced Dewey to some of the other board members at a meeting in January 1888, where Dewey impressed them by his vision of how state library service could be enriched. That summer Dewey outlined his ideas in an impassioned speech in the Senate chamber to the annual convocation of New York educators.

It was perhaps the best speech of his career, important for its vision and for its effect upon his listeners. In 1888 the modern library service that he described was a new idea to most of his audience. He placed the library in an educational trinity, alongside the church and the school, and played upon the educator's fear of the restless uneducated masses, who without the library were "left without guidance, supervision, stimulus or support." Dewey intended his audience to notice that he was the man responsible for the library milestones he stressed—*Library Notes*, "especially devoted to the modern methods and spirit," and the library school, begun by "the same influence which had before started the association, *Journal*, Bureau and *Notes*." He ended with an outline of how New York State, and especially the regents, could take the national lead in educational reform.[1]

This was exactly what the regents most wanted to hear, for the governor had been calling for their extinction as a body since 1886.[2] The regents, chosen by the legislature and retaining office for life, had originally been given supervisory power over all the public schools in the state. In 1854, with the appointment of a superintendent of public instruction, a rival department of education was established to oversee public schools. Over the years the line of function between regents and superintendent had become blurred. By the mid-1880s the regents controlled the curriculums of the schools in the state through the examination system that they supervised. They had also established a tenuous authority over entry into the medical and legal professions. Still, chiefly because of their historical lack of sympathy to the needs of the public secondary schools, they were quite generally ridiculed as well-meaning ancients whose presence retarded educational progress in New York State.[3]

On November 24, 1888, just two and a half weeks after his suspension at Columbia, Dewey addressed a circular letter to the leading librarians and educators of the country, asking whether they thought him qualified for the new job of secretary to the regents and state librarian of New York.[4] He also wrote an ingratiating letter to Regent Reid in which he laid out an ambitious educational program that he recommended the regents adopt. His letter was a transparent bid on his own behalf for the job at hand. In his letter to Reid, Dewey stated what the "experienced, skillful man" who undertook the great work should *not* do. The list of prohibitions sounded like a guilty recital of all the mistakes Dewey had made at Columbia: One must not exceed proper authority, entangle oneself in partisan alliances, or push forward with progressive policies faster than the authorities "could digest the new ideas."[5]

The board of regents—unorganized, threatened with extinction, manned by persons of diverse interests who met irregularly—was attracted to the idea of a strong executive at their helm. Dewey's proposals offered change, direction, and a major role for the board in the educational system of the state. He was elected secretary of the University of the State of New York and director of the New York State Library on December 12, 1888, at an annual salary of $5,000.[6]

In January 1889 the board of regents resolved to accept "the proposition submitted by the Trustees of Columbia College . . . to transfer to the State Library . . . the Columbia College School of Library Economy." The Columbia trustees replied somewhat testily in February:

> It is obvious that this resolution must have been adopted by the Regents of the University under an erroneous impression of the facts . . . as the proposal to transfer the school to Albany did not come from us . . . but from the late librarian of the College, and the part of the Trustees . . . consisted simply in consenting to Mr. Dewey's suggestion. So great, however, was the anxiety . . . to have this matter ended and to close the School of Library Economy with the least possible delay, that [we consider] it best to overlook the error of the Regents . . . and to facilitate the plan submitted to them and substantiallly approved by the Regents.[7]

Thus did the Columbia trustees rid themselves of their unwanted child, the

School of Library Economy—so named, Dewey quipped later, because he thought "of getting the most possible out of the appropriations not available."[8]

By 1889 Dewey was thirty-eight years old and had won a reputation as one of the foremost librarians in the nation. Hundreds of letters asking for advice came to him each year from librarians all over the world. The volume of his letters, articles, and speeches; the single-minded, often simplistic and ingenuous nature of his proselytizing; and the force of his energy and enthusiasm had brought librarianship a sense of pride and profession for scores of persons he had never met. The influence of the Albany graduates upon librarianship was so powerful that before long a jealous fear developed on the part of some that the whole field of library work was being shaped by one man.

Yet from the time he left Columbia, Dewey moved progressively farther from the center of the library profession. His school at Albany was turned over almost entirely to the direction of his staff and the revision and improvement of the now-famous Decimal System was carried on by others. Although he continued to speak and write about the library, he fashioned no significant new ideas but merely repeated the old ones, delivering them over and over to his audience with never-ending zeal, predictably repetitious to some listeners, invariably inspiring to others. In his seventeen years at Albany he turned to other interests—adult education, the advancement of professionalization in general in New York State, and most of all, the development of his resort at Lake Placid.

Dewey's personality noticeably hardened in these years. His enemies increased in direct proportion to the growth of his arrogance and pile-driving force. One senses, beneath the surface of his recorded activity, a kind of building frenzy, in his life and in his relationships with others. Perhaps he attempted too much in those years. Undoubtedly his nervous intensity worsened and affected his physical health. Despite his intent to profit from his experience at Columbia, Dewey continued to create at Albany some sort of minor or major conflict to fill almost every moment of every day. He was always set for attack and always able to find it, distorting his experiences so that he invariably emerged a victim. At the time of his expulsion from Albany, the rising crescendo of his emotional life can only be described as having ended in paranoid delusions about his moral superiority and the malevolent many who envied and sought to humiliate him.[9] During his stint at Albany, the alliance of anti-Deweyites became stronger within the library profession. Even today, it is accurate to say that the old antagonisms of so many years ago have permanently affected Dewey's professional reputation, just as his personal abrasiveness has tended to obscure the real value and constructive work of his Albany years.

During Dewey's eleven years as secretary he transformed the public image and the educational importance of the Board of Regents of New York State.

Under his direction the regents moved into a position of commitment to public high schools. By 1894 he had raised the standards of secondary schools across the state by upgrading the requirements of the regents' examinations. Dewey wrote almost single-handedly the University Law of 1892, a revision and reorganization of school law. By 1897 Dewey had also laid the foundations that enabled New York, through the Regents' Office, to become the first and for a long time the only state with an effective agency to supervise and regulate the standards of the professional schools. Dewey accomplished all this while being assailed, for purely political reasons, by a variety of persons whose attention was centered upon graft, office-seeking, or office-holding rather than upon the educational needs of the state.

Yet Dewey's supreme executive defect was a compulsion to concentrate on detail. For example, year after year, rather than use a rubber stamp, he signed by hand each regents' certificate issued to the children of the state — over 279,000 in ten years. Dewey was a master of persuasion, not an executive. Regent St. Clair McKelway, a political enemy of Dewey's, said that he had seen Dewey talk the regents into a unanimous vote to approve some plan of action and then, six months later, give the opposing arguments with such force that they would unanimously negate their earlier decision.[10] Dewey inspired; others executed.

There was one far-reaching reform idea that Dewey could not persuade others to accept. He hoped to make the library into a true people's university by the creation of a system whereby any citizen could earn any degree, from an elementary school certificate through the doctorate, by studying at home and passing a regents' exam. Dewey first formally presented his plan to the Convocation of 1890. He convinced the legislature to grant him an unprecedented $10,000 to establish an Extension Department in 1891. Opposition began to build at once among the educators of the state. In vain Dewey assured them that the college professors of the state would prepare the examinations, which could be made so strenuous that only qualified persons would pass them.[11] In 1892 the Convocation resolved it "inexpedient and unwise" for the regents to give degrees "on examination, however strict."[12] In 1893 Dewey pressed the idea of "credentials" rather than degrees, but he was discouraged by the reception given to his plan.[13] The Extension Department eventually became a sponsor of lectures, study clubs, correspondence courses, and summer schools, and the 1891 appropriation was never repeated.

Under Dewey's direction the state library underwent the same dramatic change in operation and organization that had occurred at Columbia. When he arrived the library was in such a condition of neglect that he found a priceless collection of colonial papers being used as kindling for the fireplace. By 1891 Dewey had almost tripled the number of volumes, increased the staff from 15 to 103, and developed a legislative reference service, a medical library, and mail service for the blind, as well as instituting a system of traveling libraries. By 1903 the New York State Library had grown to the fourth largest library in the nation, ranking below the Library of Congress, Harvard, and the New York Public Library.

As at Columbia the students in the library school served as glorified apprentices and a cheap source of labor. After paying their fee to the state for admission and buying their own books and supplies, they were expected to give a liberal amount of their time each week to work in the library. In 1902 Albany became the first library school to require a college degree prior to entry. By 1926 thirty-two of seventy-eight American cities with libraries of over 100,000 volumes had Albany graduates at their head, and thirteen state university libraries and six of the fourteen library schools were directed by Albany graduates.[14]

Dewey reigned over his admiring staff and students like a benevolent but imperious lord. He received them at his home several times a week, regaled them with entertainment, enthralled them with his visions, and took a close interest in their professional and personal lives. The loyal spinsters Florence Woodworth, May Seymour, and Mary Salome Cutler had followed him from Columbia to Albany. Florence Woodworth, vivacious and barely five feet tall, shared his home for seventeen years and acted as mother to his son Godfrey, born in 1887, on the many occasions when Dewey's wife was away. May Seymour — unmarried, brilliant, and comely — was his closest confidante. She served for thirty-four years as his private secretary and retired with him to Lake Placid. Cutler, much nearer Dewey's own age, was the real director of the library school. Even after her marriage to the Reverend E. M. Fairchild in 1897, she continued to work at the library until her relationship with Dewey ended in the disastrous schism of 1905.

The explosive growth of the departments of the Regents' Office caused an increase in expenditures of 78 per cent within three years after Dewey's arrival. In 1890 Dewey reduced the already meager clerical salaries by 25 per cent and hired more employees with the savings. He installed in that year a system of tubes, electric bells, "pigeon-holes and files" and reported that "our office is known to take greater pains than any other to increase in this way its working efficiency."[15]

During the same period of time when he boasted that he had cut salaries by 30 per cent, Woodworth and Seymour were given constant salary increases. Both were hired at $800 in 1889; Woodworth had advanced to $1,800 by 1899, and Seymour to $2,100. In 1896 both Woodworth and Seymour passed Cutler in salary range. It may have been actions like this that led to the charges against Dewey of favoritism in hiring and promotion. In 1897 Dewey found it necessary to defend the efficiency of the departments under his charge, perhaps partly because postage costs alone had grown from $32,000 in 1893 to $66,000 in 1897, increasing $10,000 between 1896 and 1897.[16]

Dewey was in a constant stage of siege at Albany. In 1893 he was accused in the press of running a boardinghouse and making his employees live there, of profiteering from Library Bureau sales to the state library, and of being a tyrannical employer. Political infighting grew so fierce by 1895 that Dewey demanded an investigation of the charges made against him by an Albany paper. *The State* accused him of storing books in the corridors of the state chamber in such numbers that the legislators were barred from their washroom, of paying factory wages to women with college degrees, of forcing employees to buy bicycles, of attempting to gain control of the state museum, and of generally seeking to magnify his position.

The investigation conducted by a legislative committee in 1895 completely cleared him of wrongdoing, finding "that a man endowed with the progressive spirit, energy and will displayed by Professor Dewey might be expected to incur opposition, if not hostility to his conception of duty and responsibility of office."[17] Dewey acknowledged that he paid very low salaries. He had installed time clocks to ensure that an employee would lose half a day's pay if she were even five minutes late, he boasted. His description of the wage scale led one member of the investigative committee to protest that Dewey might be a little more liberal in wages without doing injustice to the taxpayers.* During the course of the investigation Dewey could not resist getting in a few licks of his own at his ever-present "enemies." He dramatically announced to the committee that the aged and venerable state geologist, James Hall, had sold a state-owned collection of fossils for $75,000 and pocketed the money. Investigation revealed, however, that the fossil collection had been Dr. Hall's private property. The committee's final report reprimanded Dewey for making unsubstantiated public charges against Hall. In *his* report to the regents, Dewey remarked upon the committee's shameful effort to "shield" Hall and magnanimously concluded that he did not intend to make a further fuss about the matter.[18]

While he was in Albany, Dewey's attention to state affairs or to library interests was overshadowed by the amount of time he gave to his investment in the Lake Placid area of the Adirondack Mountains. Dewey and his wife believed that this region of the state offered them the best relief from their chronic allergies. Dewey began to buy land there as early as 1891. Although others had built hotels at Lake Placid before the 1890s, it was Dewey's development at the Lake Placid Club which brought the region its reputation as *the* fashionable watering place in the early twentieth century. Working closely with Jeremiah W. Jenks, professor of political science at Cornell University, Dewey urged some of his friends to form a cooperative club in

*In 1894 Cutler complained to Dewey that the senior class of the school was working 800 hours overtime without pay; she was annoyed when Dewey responded by cutting the overtime hours to only 690. Joseph Gavitt recalled that the library staff were "wrapped up in library work to the detriment of their physical and social health." (Joseph Gavitt to Grosvenor Dawe, July, 22 1932, MDP.)

1895 for vacation purposes. Of course Dewey began to quarrel with Jenks at once—over the details of the agreement, over what Jenks felt was too rapid an expansion, over debts, over an unprofitable boat business. In 1897, using some of Annie's money and borrowing the rest, the Deweys bought out their first investors and assumed all the risk and profit for themselves.*

Dewey's plunge into debt was truly breathtaking. His vision seemed to have no bounds. His technique was to buy land for a bargain, up its value to a potential creditor, borrow on the inflated value, and use the loan to buy more land and repeat the process. In 1895 he had title to 513 acres; within three years he had accumulated 1,671 acres and forty-five buildings, and still he continued to buy. His estate in 1919 encompassed over 7,800 acres of forest land and farmland, 118 buildings, a large general store, a golf course, and fifty miles of maintained trails. The Club's most prosperous days came in the early 1920s. In 1922 retail sales alone grossed $758,000, and the Lake Placid Company had expanded to include forty farms, a dairy, three modern commercial kitchens, a theater under construction with a floor that could be made flat to serve as a gymnasium, and a library with over 6,000 volumes.[19]

During the time he was in Albany, Dewey frequently could not meet the payments on his huge debt. Only a man with his mathematical talents could have developed to such a high degree the art of juggling figures. When cajoling creditors and postponing due dates did not suffice, he always managed to take out another loan just in time to stave off disaster. Frank K. Walter recalled to Fremont Rider his memory of Dewey's financial adroitness.

> I remember that many years ago . . . [I] happened to meet Ledyard Cosswell. Possibly you remember him from Lake Placid days as one of Mr. Dewey's financial reserves in the Albany banks. He had come across from Lake Placid. He told us that he had been [at Lake Placid] at Dewey's request to check on the club's finances as a disinterested party. He spoke of Dewey's skill in drawing up reports. He stated that he had no doubt that all the items were true; but, he said, he did not know whether the Club was in debt or worth a million dollars![20]

Of course Dewey was not content to merely develop a successful mountain resort. He thought of Lake Placid as a "university in the woods," a great philanthropic institution devoted to simplified spelling, the home economics movement, eugenics and birth control, the thirteen-month calendar, the metric system, billboard control, conservation, business efficiency, and international fellowship. The Lake Placid Club was also a place where "teachers,

---

*See Lake Placid Folders and Letterbooks, Box 91, MDP, for insight into Dewey's unorthodox business methods in regard to the boat company. The 1897 reorganization was accomplished only at the price of much hostility between Dewey and the other investors. Lucy Salmon, one of the investors, believed, as did Jenks, that Dewey had cheated them out of a fair compensation. (See Lucy Salmon to Dewey, April 8, 1903, MDP.) Jenks, who chaired the American Social Science Association's Department of Finance in the late 1890s, was also heavily involved in professional organization, being the prime mover in the formation of the American Political Science Association in 1903.

librarians and other educators of moderate means who have become incapacitated by overwork" could be restored to health. In fact the Club was so successful because it was an unusually comfortable and pleasant vacation spot for those persons who could meet the financial and social requirements for membership. Dewey made lavish provisions to ensure safety, nutritious meals, sports, amusements, fine music, and expert personal service and childcare for his guests.

The uniqueness of the servant class at Lake Placid was legendary. The employees, usually young college students, were selected for character and conformity. They were required to sign a pledge to do one good deed a day and to refuse any tips, and they had to produce three letters which testified that they never smoked, drank, or used profanity. Any backsliding in behavior, the employees agreed, was to be promptly punished by the loss of two weeks' pay.

But it was the rarefied social atmosphere of the Club that made it most attractive to its exclusive guests. To the very end Dewey prohibited the entry of Jews, blacks, Cubans, or any newly rich person who was "lacking in essential social standards."[21] Morris Longstreth, who once lived at the Lake Placid Club, revealed the existence of a continually revised catalogue that graded the guests. "A" was for those who were to be given every inducement to join; "B" designated desirable members of "distinguishing traits"; "C" was applied to common clients; while "D" meant deficient and "E" defined those who should be eliminated from the list, if already members, or excluded if they were not.[22] Club "customs" (Dewey disliked the dictatorial sound of the word "rules") were strictly enforced. He forbade women to smoke, either sex to drink, and gambling or noisy activity after the ten o'clock curfew. Nor could one flaunt these rules in the privacy of one's room; club "customs" were expected to be observed behind bedroom doors too. The Lake Placid Club stood as proof "against all inroads of mere fashion or display."[23] Until the late 1920s, Dewey had no trouble finding members congenial to its purpose.

Within the library profession Dewey's single-minded drive toward the mechanization of library work was meeting stiff resistance by the mid-1880s. Poole, Winsor, Cutter, and William Fletcher provided the leadership for the anti-Dewey forces. These men felt that they knew Dewey from the Economy Company fiasco of 1880 and they did not entirely trust his motivations or judgment. They found his conception of efficiency to be an assault on the scholarly image of librarianship. Moreover, they were simply of another generation; they could not feel comfortable either with his personal style or with his attempt to dominate library development. As the elders, they resented his egotism, tactlessness, and brash exuberance. Neither could they believe that the formation of library schools was the panacea that Dewey thought it to be. They questioned his notion of curriculum and worried at the bustling simplicty of his technical approach to training.

In his presidential address to the ALA in 1886 Poole was obviously thinking of Dewey when he derided "librarians who surround themselves with short-hand writers and much routine. Every emergency is provided for by a rule or contrivance, and every sort of business transaction, by an armory of handstamps." Only the librarians who were "not swamped in an ocean of detail" would have time to "attend to the higher and bibliographical wants of their library."[24] At the same conference, Fletcher, joining with Poole in the attack on Dewey's leadership, argued that bibliographical scholarship, not mere technical competence, must be the "watchword of the future for us." Dewey's emphasis upon library procedures substituted "machinery for brains" and filled what should be a place of culture with a "set of cog-wheels."

> If the library system of our day has one mission more strongly set before it than another it is that of furnishing the means of *culture* to a people the whole current of whose life is in danger of being drawn out into the straight canal of a fatal specialization. May God forbid—I say it with reverence—that the library system itself should add another to the narrowing and specializing tendencies of these times; that it should encourage the disposition to save time at the expense of culture, by being itself an embodiment of the labor-saving, time-saving and superficial spirit of the age.[25]

Fletcher's criticism of Dewey was not persuasive because he chose to ridicule Dewey's effort to produce more efficient service rather than to speak plainly against the spirit of anti-intellectualism implicit in Dewey's emphasis upon standardization. Furthermore, Fletcher's belief that the library should furnish "culture" to the masses was not convincing to those librarians who already suspected that the "masses" were disinterested in the "higher" forms of reading. To many, Fletcher sounded only nostalgic and negativistic.

Dewey confidently dismissed Fletcher's critique. "There are two schools . . . one for progress, one for stagnation," Dewey said. Young librarians would have to choose "time-saving, labor-saving methods or stick to the . . . ways in which our grandparents made their reputations." Undaunted, in the following year Dewey even attempted to impose efficiency upon the ALA's discussion period itself. "Time is precious," he reminded them. "Give us the points in five minutes if there is not the half-hour you would like. . . . The ALA has won [the] reputation of doing its business with an unusually small amount of talking against time."[26]

In 1889 Dewey was defeated by the combined power of Cutter, Fletcher, Winsor, and Poole in a final showdown on the question of whether or not the ALA should officially endorse specific systems, procedures, and rules. Dewey was intent upon forcing recognition of "the one best way" (his way) of performing any library job. The ALA constitution specifically stated, he

ALA Presidents 1876-1903. Left to right, top to bottom: *Justin Winsor, William Poole, Charles Cutter, Frederick M. Crunden, Samuel Green, William Fletcher, Melvil Dewey, J. N. Larned, H. M. Utley, John C. Dana, William Brett, George Putnam, W. C. Lane, R. G. Thwaites, Henry J. Carr, J. S. Billings, and James Hosmer. (Courtesy University of Illinois Library.)*

Melvil Dewey, Amherst College, 1874. (Courtesy Columbia University Library.)

Melvil Dewey, Columbia University, 1885. (Courtesy Columbia University Library.)

Left to right: *Frederick M. Crunden and John C. Dana, 1900. (Courtesy of University of Illinois Library.)*

Berkshire Athenaeum, Pittsfield, Mass., ca. 1910. (Courtesy University of Illinois Library.)

Left to right: *Frederick M. Crunaen, Mary Ahern, Melvil Dewey, Katherine Sharp, and M. McIlvaine at the St. Louis Fair, 1904. (Courtesy University of Illinois Library.)*

Ex-Presidents of the ALA on the Alaskan Cruise of 1905. Left to right: (standing) *John C. Dana, Ernest C. Richardson, Frank P. Hill, Henry J. Carr, H. M. Utley, and C. W. Andrews;* (seated) *Melvil Dewey, Frederick M. Crunden, and Samuel Green. (Courtesy Columbia University Library.)*

Class of 1895, Armour Institute Library School. (Courtesy University of Illinois Library.)

Philadelphia Public Library Reading Room, ca. 1905. (Courtesy University of Illinois Library.)

Atlanta Public Library Children's Room, ca. 1910. (Courtesy University of Illinois Library.)

ALA Group at Nantucket, Mass. Public Library, 1906. (Courtesy University of Illinois Library.)

Dayton, Ohio, National Cash Register Travelling Library, ca. 1910. (Courtesy University of Illinois Library.)

Scene from a Typical Camp Library, World War I. (Courtesy University of Illinois Library.)

Chicago Public Library Circulation Desk, ca. 1920. (Courtesy University of Illinois Library.)

argued, that "we are . . . organized, not alone to exchange views but to *reach conclusions.*" The older leaders countered by suggesting that the *Library Journal* should make a practice of printing both sides of any arguments about methodology. People reading two views, Dewey said hotly, would not be able to make up their minds: "You all change like shuttlecocks."[27] The next day Dewey's opponents brought in their heaviest guns, Winsor and Poole, who expressed their annoyance at Dewey's practice of using simplified spelling and abbreviations in ALA printed matter. Poole protested the printing of his name as "W: F:" by asserting stormily, "My name is William, not a W and a colon. My name is Frederick, not an F and a colon."[28] Winsor offered a resolution that the words in the ALA constitution "to reach conclusions" were not to be understood to mean the adoption or endorsement by the association of "any principles of action or usage."[29] But Dewey was able to close off the discussion, and Winsor's resolution was referred to a committee (of which Dewey was a member), where it eventually died through inaction.

Dewey fought the coalition of older leaders by leading a successful attempt to democratize the structure of the ALA. In 1887 the membership for the first time voted by informal ballot for president. This was not an election, Dewey assured the conservatives, but simply the quickest way of asking members who they would like for president next year. In the same year the nominating committee was thereafter forbidden to choose the same person for president two years in a row. Until 1889 only Winsor, Poole, and Cutter had held the top position. In that year Dewey suggested that the informal ballot be followed by a formal one, rather than having the executive board appoint a nominating committee as before. The ALA must be careful, he said, not to give the impression that the executive board was controlled by "leading spirits." The new system would give each member a "chance to express his preference . . . and is all there is left to us of democracy in an election."

Dewey's election as president in 1890 was a triumph for standardization in library work. His influence prevailed partly because he was so wholeheartedly involved in the quest for dominance, whereas Winsor, Poole, and Cutter were primarily interested in other matters and could not think of the conflict with Dewey as a personal challenge. In a gesture of conciliation Dewey declined the presidential office in 1890. Fletcher rose to say that he believed that Dewey disclaimed the right to office because of the antagonism displayed toward him "by a class in this body, of which I am representative, and which is known as belonging to the other school from that represented by Mr. Dewey." At the membership's urging Dewey did accept office, but he was unable to attend the conference in his presidential year because of ill health.

In 1892 Dewey's national reputation brought him a flattering job offer from William Harper, president of the University of Chicago. Dewey at first seemed eager to accept the dual position of head of the university extension program and dean of the library school. He wrote a letter to Harper in which he outlined his plans for development of the school, much as he had done before in his letter to Whitelaw Reid before his hiring as secretary to the regents.[30] Dewey also wrote to the chancellor of the board of regents that his personal debt of $22,000 was so overwhelming that he could not continue as secretary without a larger salary. To Harper, Dewey stated that he could not come unless he were made a full professor at Chicago. But Dewey was unable to wring a salary of $8,000 or $9,000 from Harper. Harper was "considerably disturbed" that Dewey now demanded more than the $7,000 they had originally agreed upon and urged Dewey to reconsider. Although Dewey denied it, it is clear that the major reason he did not move to Chicago was because of this disagreement over salary.

After Poole's death, Dewey, who had led the attempt since 1885 to weaken the power of the conservative coalition, felt secure in his position of leadership. Accordingly, Dewey opposed any further democratization of the ALA election machinery. He spoke against the direct election of officers by the membership and wished to return to the method whereby the executive board chose the next year's officers. Apparently he feared that the growth of the association and the wide dispersal of its membership would prevent him from maintaining close control of its affairs. He opposed the popular selection of officers because there was "great danger of electing now and then the wrong men and the Association will suffer very severely for a matter of mere sentiment."[31] The membership decided against his arguments, and in 1893 the first president was elected by popular ballot.

Through the 1890s Dewey continued to be prominent at the ALA annual meetings, but the work of the association was more and more turned over to others with whom he had only infrequent contact. In the mid-1890s a new "western influence" became a factor in ALA affairs, marked by the election of John Cotton Dana as president in 1895.* Dewey professed to welcome the change: "We want to make the ALA national and not let the idea get abroad that it is a New England affair. I wrote Dana . . . to call upon me . . . I do not care for any official position or prominence. After twenty years my place is on the back seat."[32] As his investment at Lake Placid grew, Dewey became less involved in association infighting. But he continued to quarrel, as always, with the ALA leadership.

Dewey called his arrogant and abrupt treatment of others "frankness" and prided himself on his no-nonsense openness. Even his devoted employee

*The question of sectionalism was still an issue in 1900. Elizabeth Browning, a proud westerner, tendered her resignation from the Library School Committee in 1900 because she felt there were too many people from the West on the committee. She said, "I am aware of the fact that there are a great many members of the ALA who are positive that there is a geographical limitation to the culture of the ALA. This is no time to do missionary work with them, to teach them better. . . . Something must be conceded to prejudices that are rooted in Plymouth Rock." (Browning to Carr, November 14, 1900, Henry Carr Correspondence, 1900-01, Folder B, ALA/Archives, University of Illinois, Urbana.)

and friend Florence Woodworth was aware of how his egotistical forth-rightness could become boorishness or outright brutality.

> I want to ask you to *please* be careful what you say about MSC [Mary Salome Cutler]. She has served you long and faithfully and has done more than anyone else to help you make your cherished plan at the library school a successful reality. . . . You have high ideals for those who work with you, and you see their faults on that account. . . . You are quite inclined to enlarge on those faults to people whom it is unnecessary to take into confidence. You say little unkind things . . . things which stick long in the memory and make you appear unap-preciative. I have noted this tendency in a marked degree . . . this past year. . . . When I hear you say these little slighting things it always gives me a shock. Somehow it seems as if your regard for your friends ended when they ceased to be especially useful.*

Dewey's temperament did not improve with time. The librarians whom he had alienated steadily grew in number. In 1899 many ALA members were annoyed by the amount of time the association gave to Dewey's library school interests, and they complained that the ALA had been "worked more for this purpose than anything else."[33] By 1900 Dewey seemed more a revered relic than a forceful chief to many younger members. As W. E. Parker remarked to Dewey in 1898, Dewey had little influence over Library Bureau operations because he "was no longer involved personally" with librarians as before and did not bring in the business as he once did.[34]

Throughout Dewey's tenure at Albany the Department of Public Instruc-tion, which had authority over the public schools of the state, had gradually enlarged and centralized its educational activity. Andrew Sloan Draper, superintendent from 1886 to 1892, had invigorated the role of the depart-ment just as Dewey had done in the Regents' Office. Draper was forced out of office in 1892 when party control of the legislature changed.[35] After his exit conflict increased between the two departments, chiefly because both agen-cies had been assigned duplicate functions under the law. In 1899 Superintendent Charles R. Skinner demanded that his department be given control of all the public schools. The regents resisted this attempt to take the public high schools from under their jurisdiction. Finally Governor Theodore Roosevelt named a commission representative of the warring interests to form a plan for the unification of the educational administration of the state.

The commission, of which Dewey was a member, brought in a divided report in 1900. Dewey headed the minority who were opposed to the reconstitution of the Regents' Office and the diminution of their authority.[36]

---

*Woodworth to Dewey, August 4, 1895. Even so close a friend as Woodworth could not escape his temper. In 1898 he fined her one month's salary because of what he felt to be her insubor-dination to him. (Woodworth to Dewey, July 8, 1898.)

Although Roosevelt heartily endorsed the majority proposal of the commission, political warfare stalled any attempt at legislative action at that time.

As a result of the unification fight, Dewey resigned as secretary to the regents. Actually, Dewey may have been ill and overworked as he claimed, or he may have hoped that his resignation as secretary would clear the way for his own eventual appointment as the new executive head when unification came about.* Meanwhile, Dewey continued as state librarian and as director of the Library School and the Home Education Department.

In 1904 Governor Benjamin B. Odell, disgusted with the years of political bickering, pushed through the Unification Act of that year. The new law created a commissioner of education who was to assume executive power over all the educational interests in the state. Andrew Draper, president of the University of Illinois since 1894, was chosen as the first commissioner. The offices of secretary to the regents and superintendent of public instruction were abolished by the act.[37] For the first time since he had come to Albany, Dewey found himself serving under a superior executive, a situation made all the more difficult because he and Draper had once shared equal powers before Draper's political defeat in 1892.

Draper moved quickly to consolidate the departments under his charge. In the summer of 1904 he surged into Dewey's bailiwick to reorganize the Library School and the Home Education Department. Draper was opposed to "many of the projects which commend themselves to the intellectually prolific and widely experienced Director Dewey," with whom he had "worked long and differed much in years gone by." Dewey argued for the necessity of more employees and for the expansion of his responsibilities. Draper felt that the New York State Library should strive to be "great, rather than merely big, enduring rather than popular" and that Dewey tended to "start something new because it is new, or set up something different because it is different." The commissioner found a "lack of systematic and regular procedure" in Dewey's administrative practices. Above all Draper was annoyed by the disorderly system of procedure in the appointment and work distribution of employees. Dewey's staff members complained to Draper about their work load. "The course of a public office is not to be shaped by personal sympathies or passing impulses," Draper warned. Draper announced that appointments and promotions were henceforth to be made exclusively upon considerations of merit and that the time clocks Dewey had installed would be removed in order to institute a more professional office atmosphere.[38] Dewey was unable to knuckle under to the direction of a man whose personality was as strong and uncompromising as his own. Within a few months their relationship had hardened into one of mutual distaste.

*See *Report of the Regents* (1900), R78–R84, for details of the resignation. Dewey claimed to be "under daily medical treatment" and said that "the nervous strain of these unfortunate discussions is more than I have physical strength to endure." In 1902 Dewey felt real concern for his health. He complained of dyspepsia, rheumatic fingers, and a wandering pain. He was especially troubled by the fast beat of his heart, which woke him just as he was falling asleep—a common symptom of chronic anxiety. (Dewey to Dr. Alder, n.d., 1902.)

Dewey's final fall from favor came in the years of 1905 and 1906. His troubles began with a petition to the regents in January 1905 that requestted his removal from state office and were compounded by the events of the ALA convention's excursion to Alaska in July. The dual conflict of Dewey versus the regents and Dewey versus segments of the library world culminated in June 1906, in forced resignation from his job and expulsion from active leadership in the library profession.

The conflict with the regents centered upon Dewey's long-standing prejudice against Jews.* From the beginning the endeavor at Lake Placid had included an effort to prevent Jewish property-owners from buying in the vicinity. In one of his many letters intended to drum up visitors to the Club, Dewey had written in 1896 to a prospective client that a look at Lake Placid's handbook would assure that "no Jews or strangers or consumptives or other guests who can fairly be annoying to cultivated people are received under any circumstances."[39]

In early 1905 a petition was presented to the regents calling for Dewey's removal from state office. Enclosed was a circular from the Lake Placid Club that stated:

> No one will be received as member or guest against whom there is physical, moral, social or race objection or who will be unwelcome to even a small minority. . . . It is found impracticable to make exceptions to Jews or others excluded, even when of unusual qualifications.[40]

The petition against Dewey was signed by the prominent attorney Louis Marshall; by Adolph Lewisohn, donor of a $200,000 building to Columbia University; by Daniel Guggenheim, who had given Columbia $500,000; and by eight other Jewish philanthropists.

The protestors did not question Dewey's legal right, as president and stockholder of a private club, to exclude Jews, even though this action pandered "to the lowest prejudices of which man is capable." They demanded, however, that Dewey not remain as a state official

> who can so far forget himself and the duties which he owes to the entire public as to spread broadcast through the land a publication which tends to make of the Jew an outcast and a pariah. . . . There is but one course to pursue and that is to remove from the service of the State the official whose act undermines the very foundations of our governmental system.[41]

In a public reply printed six days later Dewey claimed to have no personal prejudice, citing Jewish members on his staff and Jewish visitors to his home. He defended the right of a "social club" to restrict membership and denied that he had ever used his position as state librarian to enhance his investment

---

*Lesser charges were that he neglected state work during his long stays at Lake Placid, which averaged about two months of every year. There was also a complaint that the state library's connection with the Library Bureau was suspect. On February 9, 1905, a newspaper clipping reported that the attorney general of New York had ruled that all connections between the Library Bureau and the state library must be broken so long as members of the library staff had an interest in the Bureau.

at Lake Placid. Of course neither of these charges had, in fact, been made. Moreover, the latter statement was not literally true, and Dewey was certainly twisting the truth when he went on to claim that he allowed no club business by mail with his office in Albany.[42]

Actually, Dewey had been taken in by a successful ploy of the petitioners to prove his use of his official position to encourage the sale of club memberships. A decoy letter from a William Taylor, addressed to A. O. Gallup, his manager at Lake Placid, had asked for more information about the Club and its president. Gallup forwarded the letter to Dewey at Albany. Dewey wrote a reply to Taylor on stationery that listed him as state librarian, answered Taylor's inquiries, and enclosed in his letter to Taylor the circular that the petitioners cited.[43] Dewey later claimed that only the Lake Placid circular printed in 1901 had specifically mentioned Jews. The 1904 circular had simply noted that exclusion was applied to those "against whom there is any reasonable physical, mental, racial or social objection," Dewey said. The old 1901 circular had inadvertently been mailed to Taylor, Dewey explained.[44] Dewey's self-righteous denials were unconvincing to others besides Commissioner Draper. Cyrus Sulzberger wrote a sarcastic letter to Dewey on February 13, 1905.

> You answered Mr. Taylor's letter yourself. . . . Your name appeared on a single printing of the business letterhead. . . .Wonderfully enough, that printing was used in replying to Mr. Taylor. The offensive rule has not been printed since 1901 and these words were omitted in the later printings, yet the only copies that happened to fall into my hands were issued in 1904 and contained these words. Fate has certainly been unkind to you.[45]

On February 2, 1905, Dewey was called to face his accusers at a hearing before Draper and the Library Committee of the regents. Attorney Louis Marshall led the questioning. Marshall first established Dewey's controlling ownership of the Lake Placid stock. Dewey argued that because he was not a member of the council of the Lake Placid Club he had no influence upon the exclusion rules. Marshall expressed unbelieving wonder at such reasoning from the man who had founded the Club, still owned it, and drew the largest profit from its operation. In a stirring summation of the petitioners' case, Marshall pointed to John Singer Sargent's picture of the prophets of Israel which hung above their heads in the meeting room, reminding them that everyone portrayed there would be banned from Mr. Dewey's club. He accused Dewey of "hiding behind his wife's petticoats" with the claim that he could not control her share of the voting stock. "I never knew an anti-Semite yet who did not claim his heart was full of love for the Jews. They claim not to like the ignorant or immigrant Jew, but in fact they ban all Jews. Patronizing good fellowship is worse than original insult," Marshall charged.[46]

Dewey was obviously shaken by Marshall's argument. His reply was almost incoherent at points. Lake Placid had saved his life and the life of his puny baby boy, Dewey whimpered, referring to their "frail" health. His self-sacrificing wife had made up the Placid deficit each year from her own small savings. His family, barely surviving from the sale of land, was in Lake Placid almost six months of the year. Yet in spite of the fact that hay-fever attacks would surely kill him and that he would have to give up even Sundays with his family, still he would do whatever the regents wished of him. He offered to resign as director of the Lake Placid Company and to expunge all offensive language from the Club literature if the complaint against him were withdrawn. Draper abruptly ended the meeting with a promise of a Committee recommendation by April 1.[47]

Considering Dewey's position as a relatively minor state official, there was enormous coverage of the conflict in the New York press.[48] Obviously the controversy had sparked the prevailing anti-Semitism of the time. Much attention was given to a defense of Dewey by a Jew, I. F. Funk, of Funk & Wagnalls fame, who argued that the petition had only served to *create* race problems and should be withdrawn. Marshall reminded Funk that Dewey had issued "no word of regret for the wrong that has been done — no apology, no recantation, nothing but patronizing and nauseating slobber . . . while your clerical friends stand by and raise not one word of protest . . . but, on the contrary, voice the gospel of hate, of intolerance and of bigotry."[49] And a *Harper's Weekly* editorial patiently explained to its readers the reasons why Jews, even educated ones, were not fit for polite circles.[50]

Perhaps the fury of the debate forced the regents to an early decision, for on February 15, nearly a month and a half ahead of schedule, the Library Committee issued its report. Dewey was unanimously censured by the regents for his "circulars containing matters considered to be a reflection upon Jewish citizens," and was warned that "formal control of a private business which continues to be conducted on such lines is incompatible with the legitimate requirements of your position."[51] The regents effectively forced him to make a choice between his job as state librarian and his involvement at Lake Placid.

Dewey probably could have survived the censure. Because anti-Semitism was so widespread, he found many supporters who saw him as a martyr.* There seemed to have been no immediate plan to force Dewey to a decision about Lake Placid. But Dewey was too pugnacious to simply let the question rest. Sometime in February he and his manager, Gallup, mailed a pamphlet to interested persons, among them the Club members and the regents. It concluded smugly: "The Jews are too important an element nowadays to be discriminated against by anybody who holds a public position. Jews may be despised, but their vote is respected."[52] In defiance of good sense, the pamphlet was sent out in a New York State Library wrapper. The pamphlet may not have been mailed until late spring because the petitioners' furious response did not peak until the summer of 1905. Dewey, typically, was now

---

*Dewey received many letters of support, many of them from librarians. Some were openly racist in tone; others indicated that this was just another attack by political partisans.

ready for conciliation; he insisted that the pamphlet was not his but Gallup's doing.

By the summer of 1905 criticism of Dewey grew to crisis proportions among his staff. No doubt one major problem was Dewey's tendency toward pompous megalomania, a trait that was most prominent at those times when his sense of self-esteem was threatened. Some staff members probably rallied to Draper, drawn to the countervailing presence of a strong executive force, agreeing with Draper that the atmosphere of library and school was more chaotic than inspiring, "more disturbing than logical, and more confounding than progressive."[53] Perhaps another factor in the breakdown of staff morale was the coincidental emotional collapse of Mary Salome Cutler Fairchild, the real leader of the school.* In June 1905 the advisory committee of the New York State Library School Association reported the students' complaint that the general curriculum was too enmeshed in "minute details" of library work, especially in the first year, when the students' labor in the library was most heavily exploited.[54] Florence Woodworth wrote to Annie Dewey about the Albany situation in September. She had been approached by Mr. Fairchild, then on the Moral Education Board, who implied that she should tell Dewey that his staff "would like to give you a model and a monument and let you go in peace," but might be forced to "disagreeable" revelations if Dewey did not go quietly.[55]

Dewey's and Gallup's pamphlet had caused a revival of tension. As the pressure to remove him increased, Dewey found it necessary to invent malicious enemies in order to explain his dilemma. In two wildly paranoid letters to his old friend Regent Pliny Sexton, Dewey accused Draper of alliance "with the Jews for my overthrow." Draper was "hopelessly broken in health" and emotionally unstable, Dewey said.

Dewey told Sexton that he would resign as state librarian in October, but would remain as director of the library school until January, although he hinted that he was thinking of taking the school with him when he left.[56]

Only a few days later, at a hastily arranged regents' meeting, Dewey's resignation as state librarian was accepted under conditions which indicate that his exit from office was not completely voluntary.[57] In October he wrote to Chancellor James Day at Syracuse University, an anti-Semite who had offered him a job as librarian, that Draper was "pitiable for New York education" and that if Dewey left it would mean disaster for the Albany library school.[58] By November, Dewey had unearthed a new villain. It was Mr. Fairchild who had driven his wife "out of her mind and sent her to the asylum as a result of his persistent efforts to make her a tool for undermining our work

---

*Salome Cutler married, at age forty-two in 1897, a Congregational minister, the Reverend Edwin Milton Fairchild. In May and June 1904, she almost had an emotional breakdown when her husband became seriously ill. (Woodworth to Annie Dewey, May 31, 1904, and June 5, 1904, M) Mrs. Fairchild retired from active library work on the same day that Dewey resigned as state librarian.

here."* Thus did Melvil Dewey leave library work—ingloriously and with a whimper.

From January to May Dewey worked sporadically at the library, supposedly on the preparation of a library school manual. Early in February he asked permission from Edwin H. Anderson, the new state librarian, to remain at the library indefinitely to work with May Seymour on the revision of the Decimal System.[59] Perhaps unknown to Dewey, Anderson had the day before given one month's notice to Seymour, who had held her job for seventeen years. Her work on the Decimal System was not essential to the work of the library, Anderson told her, but was for Dewey's personal advantage.[60] In light of their long association, it seems unlikely that Dewey and Seymour would have agreed to work apart from each other. In late February Anderson curtly denied Dewey's request that Seymour continue her work and told him that the many complaints to the commissioner that the Decimal System was being revised with state funds forced him to require Dewey to move the revision work elsewhere.[61] When Dewey left Albany, having drawn no salary since January 1, he claimed he had to borrow money to finance his trip home to Lake Placid.[62] Later, when he tried to collect six months' back salary, his old technique of claiming "misunderstanding" about oral contracts no longer worked to his advantage. Draper informed Dewey through a clerk that his salary had ended on January 1 and that if he had performed any lecture work at the school he should submit the bill to the state.[63]

In the late spring of 1906 Dewey was settling into the secure surroundings of Lake Placid. But another storm cloud was building, and its effects were to prove the most devastating of all. From within the library profession itself came a new shower of innuendos and personal attacks. He was accused of sexual misconduct on the ALA Alaska excursion of 1905, and the dispute over his guilt or innocence nearly ripped apart the ALA convention held at Narragansett Pier, Rhode Island, in June 1906.

There could hardly be more conflicting tales of what actually happened. There were "four prominent women in the ALA, ready to testify to improprieties and two who would resign" if Dewey would not.[64] They charged Dewey with forcing unwelcome attention upon some unidentified woman during the Alaska trip. Mary Ahern, one of Dewey's most loyal defenders, told Seymour that she "was made the recipient of several tearful confidings from girls that [Dewey] had disturbed." Ahern "understood the situation and quieted their fears" but "disapproved" of Dewey's inappropriate behavior.[65]

---

*Dewey to F. B. Hill, November 11, 1905, MDP. Dewey marked this letter as "not sent" to Hill. Dewey remained at the library even though the Home Education Department and the business affairs of the library were taken from his control. On December 14, 1905, he was removed from his position as director of the library school. The next day, Edwin H. Anderson, librarian at the Carnegie Institute and a graduate of the Albany school, was appointed as State Librarian of New York. Dewey's relationship with Anderson, at first relatively cordial, quickly deteriorated.

An anonymous letter, probably addressed to Lake Placid, threatened to expose Dewey and to force his expulsion from the ALA.

The first warning of slanderous rumor came from Woodworth and Seymour. Woodworth wrote Dewey a letter that she cautioned him three times to burn.

> My advice is to keep perfectly quiet. It is thought you will be "cowardly" and force the woman to give their names which they say they are perfectly willing to do. . . . Mrs. Dewey is thought a noble woman and a martyr. The whole matter is terribly grave. Everyone in the library will soon know. . . . Shall I resign here or would it be better to go on as if nothing had happened?[66]

In mid-June Annie Dewey wrote scorching letters to the two persons whom she believed were responsible for the "plot" against her husband.

> I learned that my long absence from home in the past few winters, together with some criticisms of Mr. Dewey's unconventional ways has been so misunderstood as to occasion gossip. . . . Mr. Dewey was free to entertain the library school as usual and to invite guests to 315 [Madison] and so feel my absence as little as possible. Women who have keen intuition know by instinct they can trust Mr. Dewey.[67]

> There is a point at which righteous indignation must find expression. . . . Since the day your name was bulletined for a course of lectures before the library school, without Mr. Dewey's knowledge, and it was necessary for him to withdraw them at once, you have plotted and schemed in underhand ways to injure him. You have poisoned your wife's mind and made her disloyal to her executive head. In your intense egotism and conceit you fancied you could secure Mr. Dewey's position. . . . You pose as a minister of the gospel . . . yet your own words betray your real character. Your mysterious anonymous letters are transparent and despicable . . . . However careless and unconventional his manner, [Dewey] is free from any impure motives or actions.[68]

Edwin Fairchild denied Annie's accusations and assured her that he had done all he could to "crush these attacks." He offered to confirm in writing his faith in Dewey's integrity.[69] To Woodworth, Fairchild wrote:

> Both Mrs. Fairchild and myself think that it would be very wise for you to avoid reference to members of the Dewey family for the present. . . . We quite understand that you instinctively seek to have it known that Mrs. Dewey has no unfriendly feeling against you. . . . Neither of us think it possible that any serious immoralities can have been practiced by Mr. Dewey during his Albany career and we hope you will not feel under suspicion at all.[70]

James Canfield, librarian at Columbia University, served as arbiter and consultant to the Deweys in this matter. He told Annie that Dewey's speech and actions had seriously alarmed at least three women, two of whom were of the highest character and had not been hostile to Dewey before this time. Canfield urged the Deweys to stay away from the 1906 ALA conference, lest they "precipitate a crisis which none of us could control."[71] Annie agreed that Dewey "had been most unwise in his unconventional manner with women" in a way she did not "in the least excuse, but this is not the way a man with evil intentions goes about it."[72] Dewey, after almost two months at Lake Placid, seemed to have regained much of his emotional equilibrium. He wrote Canfield a thoughtful letter in late June.

> I always thank God for a pain. It tells me that I have been doing something I ought not to do. . . . I am sorry I did as much as I did over the Jew business. If it were repeated today I would cooly ignore the whole thing. Certain people have evidently taken a vow to ruin me, if possible. I think this must mean I have needlessly offended, have been too outspoken in my criticisms and in my zeal and independence have failed to consider weaknesses and vanity and other personal qualities. I do not doubt that considerable fault is mine. . . . The grafters and politicians of both parties have hated me supremely for years but this last attack is from a smaller more contemptible source. . . . I have discussed this fully with Mrs. Dewey and the ladies of my family. . . . The many women in the ALA who have known me long and well will be the best witnesses to the deep respect and confidence I feel for women. . . . I was so different from other men and had so much more trust in women. Pure women will understand my ways.[73]

The Narragansett Pier conference of 1906 was abuzz with stories. Frank K. Walter remembered over thirty-five years later "the sharp divisions between Dewey friend and foe" that split the gathering.[74] Katherine Sharp reported that "the enemy is *very* busy. Mr. Hill is furious that people are trying to spoil his meeting. Some say they will go home if annoyance does not stop. They are being warned and forced to listen. . . . We think you will walk into a trap if you came. . . . May [Seymour] says that if she wears nothing else she will wear 'an inconsequent air.' "[75]

The scandal of 1906 helped to push Dewey out of active library work and left bitter and long-lasting grudges.* Even today the vestiges of that long-ago quarrel survive in wry jokes and knowledgeable smiles within the library profession. It may be that modern librarians, saddled with a professional image of uncommon dullness, indeed deserve and certainly relish the memory of at least one rogue among their pioneer heroes. That Dewey was guilty of indis-

---

*Edwin Anderson complained to Bowker in the summer of 1907 that J. N. Larned, who had suggested that the library profession erect a statue of Dewey, obviously did not understand the situation. "It would be a serious blow to decency if . . . Larned should rise and champion Mr. Dewey," Anderson said. "I am deeply concerned for the reputation of American librarianship." (Anderson to Bowker, May 15, 1907, R. R. Bowker Papers, New York Public Library.) Mary Plummer, reported to be one of the offended principals in the 1905 scandal, wrote to James I. Wyer in 1915, in regard to Dewey's expected presence at a library meeting, "If Mr. D. is to be asked, I shall want to know at once. . . . I should not come. . . . There is no demand on the part of librarians for Mr. D's presence. . . . Quite aside from the scandal of some years ago, it seems strange to me that those who know the man's character as well as we do can wish him to figure again as a representative of the profession and exercise an influence over the younger . . . members that in the long run would be unfortunate, since they too would finally come to know his essential falsity. I shall never, as long as I am a member of the profession, consent to meet him." (Plummer to Wyer, August 3, 1915, James I. Wyer Autograph Collection, ALA Archives.)

cretion and familiarities that were susceptible to decidedly harmful misconstruction is undeniable. Yet there is little real evidence to indicate exactly how Dewey offended the moral conventions of his time.

From his earliest manhood Dewey had shown an unusually strong desire for feminine company and an equally strong indifference to the presence of men. He preferred women as colleagues and friends, especially women who were young, intelligent, and attractive. His defense of women's talents drew to him a devoted group of spinsters who served his interests for many years of their lives—in return for his recognition and appreciation of their work. He habitually spent his leisure hours with women, on carriage or bike rides, on vacations, in his home. And from the time of his move to Albany, and later at Lake Placid, he shared his home with one or more warmly intimate female friends. Add to this Dewey's vital, unstable, and inconsistent emotional makeup and it becomes easier to understand why he continually shocked those who were cramped into a more cautious life-style. Indeed, the 1906 scandal was not to be the last of its kind that he would face.[76]

An interesting footnote to Dewey's exit from library work is the story of his organization of the American Library Institute, an ill-fated attempt to form a group of "leading spirits" who in their wisdom and detachment could guide the future growth of the library profession. The idea came to Dewey in 1904 when he decided that the ALA meetings had grown so large that he and his disciples could no longer be certain of control over decision making. "The best men in ALA" were forced to sit outside, Dewey wrote to Bowker, unable even to get into the crowded ALA meetings when important questions were being discussed. He proposed an elite organization of leading librarians, akin to the American Academy of Letters, that would debate important issues and serve as a forum for the exchange of ideas. He intended that election to this group would be considered the highest honor the profession could bestow on its leaders. Bowker was not enthusiastic; he warned Dewey that his passion for organizational activity "is so overflowing that it is sometimes in danger of bursting the dam."[77]

Dewey pushed ahead with his idea and in 1905 won the approval of the ALA for the fifteen ex-presidents to organize an elite group. The Institute was to have a membership of one hundred, with the first members selecting the others and with a three-fourths majority vote necessary for election. There was much opposition to the idea from the beginning. Many were contemptuous of the idea of a self-chosen elect, especially one sponsored by Dewey. The first board of the ALI chose Dewey as president and was composed of John Dana, Frederick Crunden, James Canfield, Henry Carr, and Frank Hill—all loyal Deweyites. The first members were elected by correspondence. Dewey husbanded his votes and cautioned some of his friends to do the same, so that when all the ballots were in they could be sure to throw their votes to the "most valuable" persons.[78] By 1908 fifty fellows had been selected.

Because of the lack of enthusiam for the new ALI, Dewey sent out a circular letter to the elected fellows in late 1907 and asked them to choose one of three options: to find a vigorous new president, to let the ALI "continue in quiet slumber until the right man rises up to wake it," or to abandon it altogether. Only thirty-three members bothered to reply, and of these only fourteen voted to press forward with the original plan.[79] Despite this lack of interest the ALI held its first meeting in 1908, with only seventeen members attending. Dewey, the first president, was absent. He suggested that the ALI might be revived if the dues could be raised as a means of forcing out the uncommitted fellows. He wanted to "steer it so a lot of people will resign" and then to hone the membership down to twenty "of the wisest," who would consult by correspondence.[80]

The membership of the ALI in 1911 was chiefly an honor roll of the old guard. In that year only twenty-two of the ALI "best men and women" attended the ALA convention, and only fourteen of these saw fit to attend the ALI meeting held in conjunction with the convention.* An amused ALI member wrote an ode to the self-selected elite in 1912:

> Men and women, high in station —
> Cease thy mutual admiration,
> Lend thy fellows some assistance,
> Justify thy own existence.
> . . . .
> All these years you've been a-brewing
> What on earth have you been doing?
> . . . .
> And you met and yawned and fiddled,
> And your thumbs you duly twiddled,
> Till your moribund condition
> Has become a fixed tradition
> And your guns are spiked and dusty
> And your armor very rusty.[81]

The ALI, created by Dewey at just the time when his library career was ending, never won the support of the new leadership of the ALA. "Born under the auspices of a semi-antagonistic spirit,"[82] the Institute seemed to many to have neither a goal nor a representative composition. In 1916 the new president, E. C. Richardson, outlined a new purpose for the ALI of per-

---

*"American Library Institute," *LJ* 33 (1908), 147; "Editorial," *Ibid.*, 483. John Dana led the opposition to the ALI in 1909. In a letter to Mary Ahern on December 18, 1912 (ALA Archives), he said, "It [the ALI] is a joke. It is worse. It makes our calling ridiculous. Let it do or die."

forming research in library science. For a brief time the group seemed rejuvenated. In the mid-twenties it met several times at Lake Placid, but attendance was always poor. After the last meeting held in 1941, Dewey's academy of elite spirits disappeared without a trace, its passing not even graced with a proper funeral.*

*George B. Utley, "The American Library Institute: A Historical Sketch," *Library Quarterly* 16 (April 1946), 152-59. In 1932 the Carnegie Corporation gave $5,000 to the ALI for the "study of professional library problems." A letter to the fellows in 1950 brought sixty-nine replies in favor of dissolution of the ALI. The ALI treasury of $1,706.85 was turned over to the ALA. (Paul Rice to Fellows, July 3, 1950, ALA Archives.)

9

Final Diversions, 1906–1931

ALTHOUGH DEWEY SPOKE A few times to librarians' gatherings and wrote occasional articles that were printed in the library literature, he effectively dropped out of active participation in library affairs after 1906. When a new building was dedicated in 1912 to replace the New York State Library, which had burned down, Dewey did not attend the ceremonies. The *Library Journal* commented that "it would be unfortunate to allow any questions of personality to obscure at such a time an acknowledgement of the great and very real debt that the state of New York, as well as the whole library profession, owes to [Dewey's] . . . initiative."[1] Dewey did not return to an ALA convention until 1918; the audience at the ALA session of the League of Library Commissions gave him a standing ovation when he spoke to them about the librarian's obligation to advance the cause of simplified spelling. He attended his next convention in 1921, maintaining a low profile, and again spoke to the ALA in 1926, on the anniversary celebration of its fiftieth year. Dewey continued to welcome librarians to Lake Placid for "library week," a period of time each year when the Club encouraged them to visit.[2]

During these years Dewey's library interests turned almost exclusively to the improvement of technique and methodology. But his rhetoric toward that end was exceedingly hazy. Rather than contribute new ideas himself, he urged other librarians "with a gift for that kind of work" to study "their last detail as the experts now study a great factory," to eliminate "every useless motion . . . organize into a recognized system a mass of petty economies that many a librarian would feel 'beneath his dignity.' " The modern librarian must be more than a missionary of the book; men were needed whose altruism "was sanctified by hard business sense as its balance wheel."[3] As Dewey grew older his description of his own influence upon library development became more complimentary. Indeed, "as I look back over my fifty years' work for education, the man of sixty-five finds that the boy of fifteen had seen clearly the problems and their solution."[4]

Thrust out of the library world, Dewey in his later years channelled his still-considerable energies into reform interests of a more diverse and general nature. Until 1912 Dewey had remained essentially apolitical, although in good Mugwump style he had supported free trade, civil service reform, and reformist city governments.* Not until "the greatest moral issue since 1860" brought him out to campaign for Theodore Roosevelt and the Progressive party in 1912 did he "face the fact" of the Republican party's "degeneracy." Dewey's admiration for Roosevelt, whom he had idolized at Albany as the first governor to attend the regents' meetings in seventeen years, knew no bounds.[5] To doubt the success of the Progressive crusade was to doubt "that God is in his heaven and that right . . . will prevail." The Revolution is coming "but with votes, not swords," Dewey said at a political rally. Electoral victory in 1912 was not so important as the certainty that by 1916 Progressive ideals would triumph as surely "as the sun is to rise."[6]

The revolution that Dewey foresaw was not the triumph of the poor over an economic system run for the benefit of the privileged few. Rather, he saw a Progressive party victory as the realization of his long-time hope that the "great army recruited from the best elements in American life" would wrest control from "grafters" who represented the "most dangerous elements in American life." This Progressive army would "break away from party principles" and destroy the "professional politician . . . [who] is the greatest menace to the public good."[7] As Dewey saw it, Roosevelt's victory would mean the command of the country's life by the right-thinking, educated, new professionals who would elevate the lower classes to settled principles of conduct and impose restraints upon the predatory "money power." All his life Dewey maintained a naive faith in the ability of persons of social and cultural refinement—with their supposed inbred sense of honor and decency—to solve the serious problems created by the Industrial Revolution. His ideal was a social system that rewarded "exceptional men" rather than "the people," that emphasized distinction rather than equality.

Despite his pronouncement in 1912 of sympathy for the poor who were "enslaved" by "politicians" and "millionaires," Dewey was convinced that trade union members were natural malingerers who were misled by their leaders into striking for higher wages than they deserved or the natural operation of the economy would allow. Dewey believed that the average businessman paid the best wages he could afford and that proper considera-

---

*Dewey was a member of the Boston Free Trade Club in 1877 and supported municipal reform as a member of the Civic League of Albany. Annie was district head in New York City of the women's suffrage party organized by Carrie Chapman Catt.

tion and kindness to employees made union organization unnecessary. He felt that much of the opposition to him at Albany had come from labor leaders who hated him because he had accused the construction workers at the library of low productivity. When the local carpenters' union at Lake Placid struck for higher wages and delayed the erection of Club buildings, Dewey blamed worker discontent on the local labor leader — a "reputed jailbird and bad lot." Dewey directed his management to hire only nonunion labor who would work for eighty cents a day and who were not subject to the orders of a "disreputable chief."[8] Because he provided his workers with a steady all-year job and had their best interests at heart, Dewey insisted he must have "loyal, family-type" employees who understood that their interests and his own were precisely the same.

Basic to Dewey's labor view was his belief that laborers did not work hard enough, partly due to sloth but mostly due to their ignorance of the economic "laws" or their reaction to archaic management systems and wage policies. Under his efficient scientific management, he believed, wages, hours, and working conditions became subjects for scientific determination rather than bargaining. The laws of efficient management, like the older concept of the natural laws of God, were above class prejudice. Enlightened management meant social harmony, the leadership of the competent, and the greatest welfare for the many.[9]

Dewey's economic ideals were marked by the same ambivalence and confusion that beset so many "best men" of his generation. He detested the dominance of the capitalists, who he thought lacked both morality and culture, yet he revered "progress" and admired the man of property. He was convinced that many businessmen made immorality part of their daily routine with their buying of legislators and government officials and their flaunting of greed and luxurious possessions. In reaction he saw himself — as did many economic conservatives of the period — as a self-appointed guardian of virtue, the defender of the sterner, simpler value of work and duty. He knew that businessmen represented property and property represented order and stability. He realized that undermining mass confidence in the business community might lead to an attack on the economic system as a whole. Dewey placed his faith in efficiency and professionalization. He would work to elevate the "college-bred" into a key position of influence, all in the interests of social harmony.

Thus the efficiency movement that swept America from about 1910 to 1917 was greeted with enthusiasm by many members of the educated new middle-class. Scientific management promised something to everyone — higher wages, higher profits, social peace, control by the educated few, and a refurbishment of the Christian work-ethic. Dewey moved quite naturally into a position of leadership in the efficiency craze that hit the United States "like a flash flood, at first covering almost the entire landscape."[10]

Dewey's field of expertise within the efficiency movement was to be in the saving of "time, money or labor in office, library or study." Just as the "services of high salaried men who work at desks are more valuable than those of mechanics, so . . . are literary labor savers worth more to the world than the highly prized machines of manufacture and commerce." His aim was to accomplish more intellectual labor with less expenditure of time and strength. "If the principle is admitted that time and labor should be saved for brain work as for hand work, it follows that the minutest saving is worth attention." Thus Dewey could recommend that since color coding saved time it was wise to sit at one's desk with four pens or pencils carried between the fingers "so that a check mark may be made instantly in either of four colors." Paper clips were important in his system, for "the few seconds spent in unfurling or uncreasing a paper so [that] it can be read aggregate in a year an extravagant waste."[11]

Dewey urged the use of typewriter, duplicator, and dictaphone and laid much emphasis upon a properly fitted desk and a careful selection of cards, files, boxes, bells, rulers, stationery, shelves, and fountain pens. Brevity was the goal; abbreviations, shorthand, simplified spelling, and shortened forms of expression were the means to that end. Mastery of his system would enable one to write:

> w advis, howev, i circumstanes whr a certain variation fr majority practis, tho clearly a improvemnt, wd be offensiv t mo readers, to er o e cservative side & follow e older r mo comm usage, introducing desirabl changes gradually along e line v least resistance i sted v rousing hostility twd all by refusing to postpoe r sacrifice a fu.*

Seated at his carefully designed desk (78 cm. high, middle opening 60 cm. wide, 120 pigeonholes in 6 labelled tiers of 20 boxes each), the brainworker could "acquire the easy habit of resting by change of work instead of idleness." And directly in front of his eyes, if industry flagged, was the reminder of fleeting wasted moments: "Keep a watch or clock hanging before you. An accurate alarm clock if set closely enough calls attention to the next engagement, train time, etc."[12]

In 1915 Dewey became president of one of the three centers of the efficiency movement in New York. The Efficiency Society of New York was organized in 1911 by a group of businessmen, educators, and engineers. The group met in convention for several years at the Lake Placid Club, where they heard speeches by politicians, ministers, professors, and the warden of Sing Sing on how to apply the principles of scientific management to their diverse areas of work. In 1914 Dewey was chairman of the society's Language Committee, which sought to increase efficiency in written expression. Dewey

---

*"We advise, however, in circumstances where a certain variation from majority practice, though clearly an improvement, would be offensive to most readers, to err on the conservative side and follow the older or more common usage, introducing desirable changes gradually along the line of least resistance instead of arousing hostility toward all by refusing to postpone or sacrifice a few." Melvil Dewey, "Office Efficiency," reprint from *The Business of Insurance* (New York: The Ronald Press Company, 1912), p. 45; MDP.

urged the brainworker to omit *the*'s and other articles and to use the shortest form of expression—for example, replacing "due to the fact that" with "because." He reminded those who scoffed at minute saving that the Philadelphia telephone exchange had saved the equivalent of fifteen operators working eight hours a day just by asking all operators and patrons to drop the word "please."[13] Dewey taught the omission of initial and final curves when writing letters like *f, j,* and *g,* and the dropping of periods in punctuation except at the end of sentences. For Dewey, efficiency equalled morality.

Yet as Dewey aged he became more and more disturbed at the state of modern morality. The young Dewey had delighted in shaking old traditions; the aged Dewey was a querulous man who shuddered to see his value system rejected by the younger generations. Dewey especially disliked women smoking. In an exchange of letters with *Outlook,* Dewey defended the Club policy of profiting from the sale of tobacco to men while refusing it to women guests: "Women are more highly organized and more susceptible to the poison." The editor replied that "if such a position is logical, then we live in a topsy-turvy world." In 1928 Dewey gave up entirely on restoring the magazine to a sane editorial policy:

> You had a great constituency of America's best families . . . reaching . . . higher class people. [The new editor] . . . doesn't speak our language and doesn't understand or appreciate our family standards and ideals. . . . Your effort to revive the discussion of which the public was so thoroughly sick, of the Sacco-Vanzetti case, was badly mistaken . . . the best of the public was nauseated by the years of delay over technicalities.[14]

After Annie's death in 1922 Dewey married again, less than two years later, when he was seventy-three.[15] His second wife, Emily McKay Beal, was a widow who had worked at Lake Placid for some years as an administrative aide. For years Dewey had maintained a kind of communal household. Living with Dewey and his wife in two large houses at Lake Placid had been for a time their son and his family, Margaret Miller, Katherine Sharp, May Seymour, Emily Beal, and others.

Dewey and his second wife began to look for a spot in Florida on which to build a new resort. In 1927 they established the Lake Placid Land Company in central Florida, near Lake Stearns, and secured title to 3,000 acres. In December 1929 clearing of the land began and the first group of buildings were erected. Even Melvil Dewey did not have the financial genius to weather 1929. In June 1931 he reported that he and Emily had $300 in the bank and owed $10,000 in bills.*

The Lake Placid Club in New York was also caught in an overextended

---

*Dewey to "MJ," June 9, 1931, MDP. Having provided for a life income for their only son, the Deweys established in 1922 the Lake Placid Club Education Foundation and turned over to it their common stock in the Lake Placid Company. Dewey retained for himself a life income of $18,000 a year. The Foundation was to aid educational institutions or workers and to foster "other movements to advance public welfare through education."

position. By 1931 Club "customs" no longer appealed to those who could afford its pleasures. Dewey discovered that even the children of the best families could not be trusted to stay away from speakeasies, dance-halls, and cigarettes. Guest business went down in 1931 by 15 per cent, chiefly because of the depressed economy and more directly because of the rigid ban on smoking women. Despite the plea of his financial advisors, Dewey refused to change his rule, for "this one item of women smoking in public [is] merely the gateway through which the other more important standards [will] disappear and . . . in three or four years this little militant group [will] abolish all restrictions and . . . have exactly the same freedom as [in] a public hotel."[16]

Dewey had maintained an iron-code dictatorship over his estate for twenty-six years and he would not consider abdication.

> The Lake Placid Club is not a democracy where a majority . . . is stampeded . . . into overturning something better that most of them after second thought, would greatly prefer . . . The popular currents are always drifting downward. . . . The world is afloat and drifting rapidly from its old moorings and drifting is always downward.[17]

Dewey was deposed in 1931 by a revolt of twenty-five women Club members who threatened to station themselves in prominent spots around the Club and all light up at once. His perilous financial position and the pressure of his managers forced him to give in. He installed "temporary" smoking rooms for women in his main clubhouse. The Club did not survive the Depression. It passed into a friendly receivership and was eventually reorganized, although for the most part it remained physically intact. Dewey's dream for a center of enlightenment in the Adirondacks died with him.

Dewey had been seriously ill only twice, with typhoid at Amherst and with pneumonia in 1914, but he continually suffered from minor ailments — hay fever, nervous indigestion, fatigue, headaches, colds. At age seventy-six he had a small stroke, and when first stricken, he dictated what he thought would be his last words. His self-identification as savior and guide is prominent in his final words to "my Associates in many good causes":

> If I must finish my life-work now, I am very sorry because for my fourth quarter-century, I had planned so many splendid things which I know would be of great service. But I am profoundly grateful that I have had seventy-five years with so much of the supreme joy of hard work; so little pain and so many opportunities to help make a better world. . . . I leave no definite instructions because I believe supremely that you will be guided to the wisest solution of your many problems. I hope on the other side I may know how loyally you carry on.[18]

And who else but Dewey could say so confidently, in the same simplistic vein:

> As I look back over the long years, I can recall no one whom I ever intentionally wronged or of whom, I should, now, ask forgiveness. Doubtless, I have made many

mistakes but according to my light, I have tried to do right and so if my race is run, I can go down into the last river serene, clear-eyed and unafraid.[19]

But Dewey recovered, and realized he had some life left, and four years later he wrote one last defiant challenge to his old enemy, time.

Melvil Dewey is not a watch that wears out to be discarded, but like a sun dial where no wheels get rusty or slip a cog or get tired and long for rest.[20]

Dewey spent the Christmas day after his eightieth birthday at the Lake Placid Club in Florida. The next morning he arose very early and went into his wife's room to discuss their problems with the faltering Club. Suddenly his speech thickened and he became unconscious. Melvil Dewey died a few hours later of a cerebral hemorrhage. His ashes were deposited in the Lake Placid Chapel in New York next to those of his first wife, Annie, and his two grand-sons.

10

From Missionary
to Professional

IT IS DIFFICULT TO RECAPTURE the intensity of Melvil Dewey's relationships with his contemporaries. He was loved and hated with equal passion. Most reacted to him, sooner or later, with varying amounts of dislike, but all expressed his impact upon them in terms of energy. William Warner Bishop met him first in 1897 when Dewey was at the peak of his Albany career. Bishop's first response was aversion. But Bishop, too, experienced the surging force radiating outward from the man and even considered a theory that Dewey's bloodshot eyes were red as a result of "too great mental activity."[1]

Dewey's steamroller qualities allowed him to almost single-handedly organize and nurse into survival a new profession. After the initial meeting of the ALA in 1876, as the busy men and women dispersed and returned their attention to everyday problems, it was Dewey, especially through 1883, who continued to prod and push them together and forward, chiefly by his insistence that they actually were an important, influential, and organized unity. There is little doubt that without Dewey's attention to mundane organizational activity the ALA would not have so quickly prospered and grown into self-consciousness.

To a great extent Dewey worked within a vacuum. He did not meet very powerful opposition even from those who strongly disagreed with his purpose and method. Dewey was so devoted to his blend of mission and mechanics that he was able, within a relatively short time, to build a professional structure, to create an identity and spirit, and to set a pattern for library development. One senses that those who found his person or his ideas alienating were grateful, at the same time, that someone else, even Dewey, was willing to

166

assume the heavy and dull burden of organizational activity. And then, when convention time rolled around, it was so pleasant to travel to a distant place, meet with like-minded others, exchange mutual assurances, and hear inspirational sermons which proved that one's daily work was part of a great national movement.

There is an element of breathless ambition and moral overstrain in Deweyian rhetoric that impressed itself upon the still-warm wax of the ALA. To be sure, the "professionalization" of librarianship required the solemn treatment of commonplace problems, but the way in which librarians decked out library events in the sumptuous dress of noble objective is indelibly stamped with Dewey's mark. If a collection of accurate catalogue cards seemed a sound idea, for example, a paper would appear on the elevated theme of "The Social Responsibility of the Library to the Uninformed Reader." When librarians decided that adults would read selected books that were attractively displayed near the checkout counter, they praised the vastly improved reading tastes of the community engendered by the library's unremitting dedication to evangelism. Was it necessary to control the behavior of a disorderly youngster in the children's room? If so, a librarian was apt to launch into descriptions of how the library's expulsion of a wayward child had aided the development of national honor and democratic principles. It is true that Dewey, a past master of this art of exaggerated moralism, led the way, but it is important to remember the impetus given to library rhetoric by romantic ideals of femininity and by the moral atmosphere of progressivism.

Dewey's crusade for the standardization and mechanization of library science was achieved at the expense of genteel cultural ideals and an intellectual stance for the public librarian. Elite determination of what was and was not proper reading for the public could not have survived at any rate. Literary idealism was moribund already under the onslaught of the economic and social changes that were producing a pluralized culture. The genteel notion of the function of culture was altogether too conservative to endure. The public library, dependent upon public monies and use to survive, had of necessity to popularize its collection in order to serve a majority of its patrons.

The possibility of an intellectual role for the public librarian poses different questions. There is no intrinsic reason why the public library, following Fletcher's prescription, could not have evolved with an educated scholar-librarian in charge of distribution of books to the public. Although Dewey's influence made this outcome less likely, the foremost barrier to the realization of Fletcher's hope was the overwhelming presence of women in librarianship. Women librarians could not be accorded intellectual leadership, because they were women, and the standards of "femininity" prevented them from seeking such a role for themselves. The presence of women also helped to lessen the attraction of educated men to the profession and to keep wages low, thus ensuring continued feminization.

Nevertheless, Dewey's emphasis upon mastery of technical detail as the mark of a librarian, while strengthened by cultural imperatives and by the national movement toward rationalization and specialization, also had a significant impact upon library development. Dewey was intent upon providing rapid, efficient distribution of printed material to as large a number of people as possible. In no sense can he be understood as an intellectual; he scorned the consideration of theory and concentrated his energies upon administration and organization. Like most educational reformers in this period, Dewey did not stress a commitment to intellectual values of free speculation, social criticism, and disinterested intelligence as a goal of mass education. Rather, like many of his contemporaries in the schools, he exalted numbers over quality and emphasized the utilitarian economic benefits and political stability to be gained through universal education. The thoroughly technocratic mind does not necessarily display the ideal assumptions of anti-intellectualism; it is simply nonintellectual in structure.

But perhaps Dewey's chief effect upon the development of the library profession was through his shaping of library education. The curriculum for library education that he devised at Columbia College in 1887 and later amplified at the New York State Library School — attention to mechanics and apprenticeship within the training school, to the neglect of theory or general learning — went almost unchallenged for three decades. His students, like Katherine Sharp at the University of Illinois, dominated library education for many years after Dewey's exit from active library work. Not until 1921, at the time of the publication of the Williamson report, did librarians begin to seriously reconsider the Dewey model.

Dewey designed library education so as to tap the considerable unused energies of educated women who in the late nineteenth century had little source of economic opportunity outside teaching. The role he offered women in the library gave them a new power but did not challenge the traditional boundaries placed on their activities. The belief of the tender technicians in the library that they, as women, had special qualities which fitted them for moral reform work and sacrificial service was embellished by the touching and persistent American faith in the efficacy of education itself.

The career of Melvil Dewey supports historian Robert Wiebe's hypothesis of the growth of a "new middle class" at the turn of the century. Wiebe describes this new group of professionals and specialists in business, labor, and agriculture as intent upon imposing order on urban-industrial development through organizational activity that brought them a new identification by way of their skills, rather than their class or community. Dewey, unlike the older library leaders, felt little need to assert cultural dominance over the library patron. Rather, he was bent upon the formation of a new profession that would bring librarians a self-conscious pride in their position as skilled technicians serving a literate nation. His stress on technique and entry requirements implied that librarians shared the mysteries of a specialized knowledge. This gave them identity and purpose and opened an avenue from their fragmented communities into a national whole. Their organizational activity, although it served narrow goals, was national in scope. Like other professionalizing groups, they made a practical accommodation to the business leadership of the nation. The early group of gentry professionals had been isolated from the mainstream of urban-industrial development by their allegiance to a genteel New England–based concept of culture and by their felt alienation from the unruly urban masses. Dewey and his followers bypassed the older definitions of class and community by a Progressive commitment to bureaucratic order, functional specialization, national cohesion, optimistic idealism, and a touching faith in something called "science" that was best ensured by the allotment of power to disinterested experts.

The concept of scientific management that Dewey preached all his life became a national craze during the Progressive period, when the ideal of social control was developed into a scientific program directed by the efficiency expert. Support of efficiency served an important purpose for those of the educated middle-class who resented their loss of dominance in business and politics and who feared the leveling tendency of mass culture. The objective approach of the expert was theoretically motivated only by a desire to increase productivity, unlike the selfish motivations of the financier and the union leader, who both supposedly obstructed productivity. The guiding expert would attack materialism and greed and restore societal harmony in the best interests of all, while gaining a crucial position of control over the whole.

In a society that had slipped its religious moorings, the efficiency gospel strengthened the traditional call to virtue and duty. Without any reference to God's law, Dewey's efficiency sermons conserved the Christian moral code and projected it into every secular area of life. Scientific management represented a restatement of old religious instructions—control of sensuality, self-denial in hope of future gain, hard work, and passive submission to knowledgeable leadership. The new professionals drew from gentry professionalism many of the latter's qualities and incorporated them into a higher synthesis. Dewey's followers in the library promoted a Progressive, pluralistic belief-system, albeit an antiradical one, which was more in keeping with the needs of an urban-industrial state.

Melvil Dewey harnessed the historical forces of his time and rode them to fame, with the instinctive understanding of the "great man" whose influence essentially rests upon his intuitive understanding of the direction in which his followers are already moving. Dewey's particular plan for the professionalization of librarianship was triumphant because it promised to provide, in the proper proportions, a new power base and entry route for the new middle class, romantic reform in the service of national rationalization and bureaucratization, an amelioration of class conflict, moral values for a disordered society, an outlet for the changing needs of women, and an acceptance of the force of mass culture in an urbanized nation. As Dewey struggled to satisfy his personal needs, he helped to make a workable revolution for his society. His incessant energy and obsessive need for control fed a grandiose belief in his savior-like qualities. Melvil Dewey's mission was shaped by a reforming mentality well suited to his day—devotion to technocracy in combination with zealous moral purpose.

PART 4

The Tender Technicians

The *A-L-Adies sailed one day,*
To voyage up the Saguenay,
Gay and grim, stout and slim,
Twenty-five hers to every him.

— *Library Journal* (1912)

11

Feminization:
Symbol and Reality

"THE LAW OF NATURE DESTINES and qualifies the female sex for the bearing and nurture of the children of our race and for the custody of the homes of the world," stated the Wisconsin Supreme Court in 1875 when ruling that women could not be admitted to their bar. The judges conceded that the "cruel chances of life" might leave some women free of the sacred female duties. "These may need employment, and should be welcome to any not derogatory to their sex and its proprieties."[1] Most Americans of the time would have agreed with the court that only financial need justified a woman's going to work and that only limited jobs should be opened to her. But in the decades before and after 1900 Americans became unobservant participants in a social revolution, as the changes that took place in the attitudes toward women and their work influenced the development of the feminized service professions—nursing, social work, teaching, and librarianship.

The American public library played an important role in the revolution, for the feminization of librarianship proceeded rapidly. In 1852 the first woman clerk was hired at the Boston Public Library;* by 1878 fully two-thirds of the library workers there were female.[2] In 1910, 78.5 per cent of library workers in the United States were feminine. In that year only teaching and nursing surpassed librarianship as the most feminized "professions."[3] By 1920 librarianship, composed of almost 90 per cent females, employed a larger percentage of women than either social work or teaching.[4]

*The Athenaeum Centenary (Boston: The Boston Athenaeum, 1907), 42. William Poole is generally credited with the hiring of the first woman librarian at the Boston Athenaeum in 1857. Poole's predecessor had barred women from the staff on the grounds that parts of the library should be closed to impressionable female minds.

Educated women, while meeting resistance in the more established male professions, flooded into library work during the last quarter of the nineteenth century for a variety of reasons. Librarianship was a new and fast-growing field in need of low-paid but educated recruits. With a plentiful number of library jobs available, male librarians offered no opposition to the proliferation of women library workers, partly because women agreed that library work matched presumed feminine limitations. Librarianship was quickly adjusted to fit the narrowly circumscribed sphere of women's activities, for it appeared similar to the work of the home, functioned as cultural activity, required no great skill or physical strength, and brought little contact with the rougher portions of society. For all these reasons, Melvil Dewey could predict, when writing at the turn of the century of the ideal librarian, that "most of the men who will achieve this greatness will be women."[5]

The feminization of librarianship, however, had unexpected long-range results. The prevalence of women would profoundly affect the process of professionalization and the type of service the library would provide. The nature of library work itself, one of the few sources of economic opportunity open to educated women in the late nineteenth century, would serve to perpetuate the low status of women in American society. Above all, female dominance of librarianship did much to shape the inferior and precarious status of the public library as a cultural resource; it evolved into a marginal kind of public amusement service.

The rapid growth of libraries in size and number was an important cause of the feminization of librarianship. The monumental government report on public libraries in 1876 listed 3,682 libraries containing a little over 12 million volumes.[6] Total yearly additions of library books in the nation passed the one-million mark in 1876.[7] A conservative estimate raised the total to 40 million volumes held in 8,000 libraries in 1900.[8] Because a heavy demand for trained librarians corresponded with other national developments, particularly the advance of women's education and the increase of middle-class workers, many women found employment in library service. Very probably, women would have flocked into any new field into which their entry was not opposed. Because male librarians heartily welcomed women into library service, the eventual feminization of the library staff was assured.

The low cost of hiring women, who were notoriously low-paid, was perhaps the most important reason that male library leaders welcomed women assistants. The public library, supported by taxes and voluntary donations, was by necessity obliged to practice thrifty housekeeping. Trustees and taxpayers expected that the major portion of the yearly income would be invested in books, not administration. In about 1860, the male librarian told an inquirer about opportunities for women at the Boston Public Library that

> much of the labor performed by males is the same as that performed by females; but in every instance, save one, paid for at higher rates. . . . Ladies are employed in preference to men because they are competent, because it is a good field for female labor, because they have a good influence on those who transact business with the library, and I doubt not, because their work can be had at less rates than men's.[9]

Frederick Perkins, in an 1876 article entitled "How to Make Town Libraries Successful," recommended that "women should be employed as librarians and assistants as far as possible." Perkins was no crusader for women's equality; he only pointed out that the hiring of women, along with the use of "mechanical appliances . . . better arrangements of book rooms and . . . other sufficient contrivances of that American ingenuity," would lessen the excessive cost of library administration.* Justin Winsor, speaking at the 1877 conference of British and American librarians in London, again emphasized the importance of women workers in American libraries.

> In American Libraries we set a high value on women's work. They soften our atmosphere, they lighten our labour, they are equal to our work, and for the money they cost—if we must gauge such labour by such rules—they are infinitely better than equivalent salaries will produce of the other sex. . . . We can command our pick of the educated young women whom our Colleges for Women are launching forth upon our country—women with a fair knowledge of Latin and Greek, a good knowledge of French and German, a deducible knowledge of Spanish and Italian, and who do not stagger at the acquisition of even Russian, if the requirements of the catalogue service make that demand. It is to these Colleges for Women, like Vassar and Wellesley, that the American library-system looks confidently for the future.[10]

Thus the feminization of the library staff neatly coincided with the arrival of college-educated women on the American scene, as a new female generation came of age among middle-class women who rejected their mothers' role of piety and passivity played out in the isolation of the home.[11] These educated women, although few in relative numbers, excited much comment from social critics of the time. They were to be found in college classrooms, in professional life, and in women's clubs, drawn there by increased leisure and boredom, the wane of religious authority, and the preachings of suffragists and more radical feminists. In 1890 almost one out of every fifty women broke the bonds of conventional femininity and attended college. By 1900 almost 40 per cent of all undergraduates were women. Female college enrollment tripled between 1890 and 1910.[12]

---

*U.S. Bureau of Education, *Public Libraries in the United States of America: Their History, Condition and Management,* Special Report, pt. 1 (Washington, D.C.: U.S. Government Printing Office, 1876), 430. Perkins, who deserted his family to go West and to become the surly librarian at the San Francisco Public Library, left behind his young daughter, Charlotte Perkins Gilman, who later became a noted spokeswoman for women's rights.

College attendance violated the feminine role and rendered these advanced women "unsexed." The majority of the first groups of educated women remained spinsters—partly because there was a surplus female population in New England and in the cities between 1890 and 1910, and partly because society forbade them the male option of combining a family with a career. Of women college graduates from Vassar, Smith, and Wellesley who were between twenty-six and thirty-seven years old in 1903, 75 per cent were unmarried. As late as 1915, only 39 per cent of all living women graduates from eight major women's colleges and Cornell had taken husbands.[13]

In common with most educated women of their time, library school graduates at the Armour Institute of Technology and the University of Illinois in the 1890s were forced to choose either career or marriage. As William Poole noted, "When an unmarried lady goes into library work as a profession, the chances are that she leaves behind her matrimonial expectations and probabilities."[14] The alumni files at the University of Illinois contain the records of fifty-seven students who attended the library school before 1900. Of these, only 18 per cent married.[15] Many of those graduates who did marry expressed guilt over what they felt to be their betrayal of a sacred trust. "I fear you will call me a deserter," one woman wrote to Katherine Sharp, the director of the library school, "but truly I had not thought of this [marriage] when I entered . . . school." The ex-student vowed to keep alive the "best ideals and deeper motives" of library work as a citizen in her community. Another married graduate wrote plaintively that she still remembered a library school class about "married women and mental stagnation." She promised Sharp that despite her motherhood she would do her best to remain mentally active.[16] Even as late as 1920, only 7.4 per cent of women librarians were married; among all gainfully employed women in 1920, only stenographers and typists had a lower marriage rate.[17] Many spinster librarians felt compelled to find a high social purpose in their work, partly as a means of defining and justifying their own lives as deviant career women. As pioneer women professionals, they believed they were charged with a strong social and moral responsibility to make use of their training.

The limited opportunities open to educated women for paid employment served to bring larger numbers of competent women than competent men into low-paid library jobs during this period. In view of the constant references made in library literature to the necessity of finding educated workers with a knowledge of books, a high intelligence, and preferably a familiarity with a few langauages, it is safe to assume that most women entering library service at this time were either self-educated or formally educated to at least the extent expected of an urban schoolteacher. The same economic factors were at work in librarianship and teaching, for educated women, with few other job opportunities, flooded into both fields, with a depressing effect on wages. Library work required similar qualifications to teaching and was little worse in pay. In librarianship women could exercise their presumed special feminine talents and could also remain isolated, in a way teachers could not, from the rough workaday world.[18]

The feminine movement into occupations like nursing, social work, and teaching or into clerical and industrial employment soared in the last decades of the nineteenth century when both the right to individuality and the myth of women's "sphere" held extremely important places in American popular thought. Two such conflicting ideas could not exist together unless individualism was reserved for men alone. Thus men took the world and all its activities as their sphere, while confining women to domesticated work roles and the guardianship of culture. Women, too, were guilty of inconsistency. The gradual expansion of women's claim to the right of individual choice was on the whole unaccompanied by any feminine calls for radical social change. Instead, as each new job became filled by women, charming theories were developed by both sexes to explain why the feminine mind and nature were innately suited to the new occupation. Thus it was decided that teaching was much like mothering; women, it was said, were uniquely able to guide children into piety, purity, and knowledge. Women were cleared to work as writers, musicians, and artists because of their inherent sensitivity, elevated moralism, and love of beauty. Women doctors and nurses were intuitively kind, sympathetic, and delicate of touch. Women social workers expressed inborn feminine qualities of love, charity, and idealism. Factory, business, and clerical work fit the feminine nature, for women were naturally industrious, sober, and nimble-fingered, as well as better able than men to endure the boredom of detailed or repetitive tasks. These various expansions of the work of women served to modify the concept of their proper sphere, but the process was gradual and involved little threat to traditional social ideals.[19] Yet each expansion led to others, with a snowballing effect, so that within a hundred years the limits of women's claim to individuality had undergone drastic change.

This redefinition of women's sphere, always in accord with the characteristics presumed to be innately feminine, also came to encompass librarianship as one of the proper fields open to women. The course to library work had already been cleared for women because libraries held books and books denoted Culture with a capital *C*. By the late nineteenth century, women's sphere decidedly included the maintenance and enjoyment of culture. It was believed that through their refining and spiritualizing influence women could exalt all human society. It would be almost impossible to overemphasize the Victorian conviction that men were physically tamed and morally elevated by the sway of the gentle female. Therefore the advent of women to library work required little stretching of the popular ideal regarding the female, for "books . . . should be tended by reverent hands . . . should be given out as a priest dispenses the sacrament, and the next step to this ideal ministry is to have them issued by women."[20]

> The librarian . . . is becoming . . . the guardian of the thought-life of the people. . . . The library, in its influence, is whatever the librarian makes it; it seems destined to become an all-pervading force . . . moulding public opinion, educating to all of the higher possibilities of human thought and action; to become a means for enriching, beautifying, and making fruitful the barren places in human life. . . . Librarians have an important part to play in the history of civilization and in the conservation of the race.[21]

Women in librarianship were merely making more visible the female position as the custodian of cultural ideals.

Just as the concept of culture had been gradually accorded to the care of women, so the functions of providing education and of overseeing charity to the poor had been deemed suitable fields for female concern. The provision of education and moral uplift to the masses was a prominent mission of the early library; thus, women library workers, with their supposed inborn talents and temperaments, seemed uniquely suited to the new field. The popular library brought the librarian "in hourly contact with her constituency of readers, advising, helping and elevating their lives and exerting a far-reaching influence for good not to be exceeded in any profession open to women. . . ."[22]

The great mass of men in all fields worked to secure prestige or a higher income, but the librarian worked "with as distinct a consecration as a minister or missionary. . . . The selfish considerations of reputation, or personal comfort, or emolument are all secondary."[23] For Melvil Dewey, library work offered more opportunity to the altruistic than did the work of the clergyman or teacher. The woman librarian could reach those who never entered a church or who did not go to school.

> Is it not true that the ideal librarian fills a pulpit where there is service every day during all the waking hours, with a large proportion of the community frequently in the congregation? . . . [Is not the library] a school in which the classes graduate only at death?[24]

Dewey encouraged educated women who might ordinarily have become teachers to consider a library career. Physically the library was less exacting than the school. The librarian avoided the "nervous strain and the wear and tear of the classroom" and escaped the bad air of crowded rooms. Dewey could think of no other profession "that is so free from annoying surroundings or that has so much in the character of the work and of the people which is grateful to a refined and educated woman."[25] The genteel nature of library work would compensate, he believed, for the regrettable fact that women librarians normally received half the pay of male librarians and often received even less than urban teachers did.

As women became dominant in library work, the professional literature began to reflect the concept that the ideal library would offer the warmth and hospitality of the home to its patrons. To nineteenth-century man, of course, woman's sphere was above all the home, for which she was originally intended and which she was so exactly fitted to adorn and bless. Not surprisingly, it was anticipated that the feminine influence of the librarian would soften the library atmosphere. The librarian stood "always ready to serve," to anticipate wants, to do "the honors of a library as a hostess."[26] Like a visitor to a home, the reader was to be welcomed, to be given kind and individual attention, to be treated with tact and gentle manners. Not the cold impersonality of the business world should pervade, but rather the warmth of the well-ordered home, presided over by a gracious and helpful librarian. The reading room could be made inviting by "a bright carpet on the floor, low tables, and a few rocking-chairs scattered about; a cheerful, open fire on dull days, attractive pictures on the walls, and one can imagine a lady librarian filling the windows with plants."[27]

It was this ideal of the genteel library hostess that Theresa West had in mind when she said that "the personal equation of the librarian may easily become the exponent of the power of the library."[28] On the surface the comparison of the library to the home was but one of several devices that library leaders used to entice the reluctant patron and to make the library into a more "popular" institution. Operating more subtly, underground, were the effects of the prevalence of women in library work. So, too, had the schoolroom been redesigned and identified with the home, in order to make more acceptable the dominance of women teachers. And as women entered the new profession of social work, the same impulse drove them to center their work in the settlement-house domicile—a homey haven of beauty and order amidst the slums. The lady librarians in America were praised for their ability "to make the library a bright and beautiful home." The position of librarian required a certain "gracious hospitality" in which "women as a class far surpass men." Women would not feel humiliated by serving, by playing in the library the part they played in the home: "Here it is said her 'broad sympathies, her quick wits, her intuitions and her delight in self-sacrifice' give her an undoubted advantage."[29]

Women library workers were also preferred, it was generally conceded, for the tedious job of cataloguing. Again, it was the unique nature of woman that qualified her for this work because of her "greater conscientiousness, patience and accuracy in details."[30] Because women had greater ability than men to bear pain with fortitude, women had stored great reserves of patience and thus could perform the most monotonous tasks without boredom. All the routine, repetitive work of the library was quite generally agreed to fall within the scope of women's special talents, "especially those of patience, of enthusiasm and of loyalty—which have served to confine chiefly to women that vast mass of detail incidental to the organization of rapidly growing collections."[31]

It is evident that the role of domesticity imposed upon women also worked to create the emphasis which was early given to library service for children.[32] By 1900 the children's library had "passed its first stage—all enthusiasm and effervescence";[33] it had moved into its current position as a major department of the public library. From the beginning, the supervision of children's reading was given over to the woman librarian.

> The work for children in our libraries, like many other of our best things, is woman's work. To them it owes its inception, its progress and present measure of success, and its future is in their hands.[34]

Here in the children's section was woman's undisputed domain. And here the librarians waxed eloquent over the attributes and accomplishments of the reigning queen. Work with children is "the most important, and in its results, the most satisfactory of all library work," reported Minerva Sanders. "As our personal influence is exerted, in just such a proportion will our communities be uplifted."[35] Another librarian commented that woman, alone, has "that kind of sympathetic second-sight that shall enable her to read what is often obscure in the mind of the child."[36] Edwin M. Fairchild summed up the prevailing attitude toward woman's natural role in library work — not as a bluestocking, but as a traditionally defined female with intrinsic traits. The children's librarian "needs to be . . . a woman grown, herself the realization of the educational ideal, which by the way is not the smart, but the intelligent, great-souled woman."[37]

Originally conceived and theoretically maintained as an educational institution, the children's department was, in fact, even by the turn of the century mainly a provider of recreational reading for preadolescents.[38] Misgivings over the nature of library service to children were rarely expressed, however. Most often, sentimentality overruled any attempt at a realistic assessment of the work being accomplished in the children's department. The romantic air of enthusiastic tenderness so prominent even today in any discussion of children in the library is in sharp contrast to the more normal tendency of librarians to indulge in searching self-criticism in every other phase of library work. This incongruity becomes more understandable when it is remembered that the children's section of the library was created and shaped by women librarians. Here, as in no other area, library women were free to express, unchallenged, their self-image. Because their activities did not exceed the Victorian stereotype of the female, their endeavors remained substantially unquestioned and unexamined by male library leaders.

Despite the respect paid them, however, women soon learned that they were seldom paid the same as men who were doing the same work; and that even though women easily dominated the library field in numbers, male librarians headed the largest and most prestigious libraries. Yet in the library literature before 1900 there is hardly a hint that the hundreds of women librarians across the country were seriously disturbed at the inequality that was freely admitted to be their lot.[39] Rather, one finds feminine pride repeatedly expressed at the prevalence of women in the library; at the increased participation of women in the national association; and at America's flattering contrast with England, where women were meeting resistance in library work. A situation that really amounted to the exploitation of women in the American library was publicly touted as a liberal concession to women in America and was contrasted with women's less favorable position in the Old World to indicate the superiority of American freedoms and the liberal attitudes of the male leaders of the American library movement.[40]

While recognition of women librarians in the national professional association is historically high in comparison with other professions, here, too, women have been underrepresented in official positions. Although since 1879, when three women presented papers, women have continued as an important percentage of participants at the annual ALA conventions, this has not been in relation to their numerical attendance or their overall strength in the profession. Significantly, women were early handed major responsibility for the topics that pertained to reading for children or standards for judging immoral literature. But while women since 1880 have been regularly elected to the ALA Council, through the 1890s they tended to compose only about one-fifth of the Council members.* Feminine representation on the Council rose to about 30 per cent by 1920 and remained there until World War II, when the percentage rose dramatically. In 1945 women held about 70 per cent of the Council positions. After a decrease in the late 1950s, the percentage of women Council members has hovered around 60 per cent. As far as the higher positions were concerned: In 1893 Caroline Hewins, the first woman to have spoken publicly at an ALA convention (in 1877), was elected as the first woman vice-president. In 1911 Theresa West Elmendorf became the first woman president, following a precedent already established by the National Education Association† and the National Conference of Charities and Corrections. Women have held the presidential power in the ALA two times per decade between 1911 and 1939 and three times per decade since 1940. Because, as Melvil Dewey pointed out, the secretary, as "the mate of all work"[41] was the prime executive officer, no woman has yet served as executive secretary, except for one joint appointment in 1890–1891.[42]

The twelve women present at the first meeting of the American Library Association in 1876 set the submissive tone that few women librarians were to challenge. They were "the best of listeners, and occasionally, would modestly take advantage of gallant voices, like Mr. Smith's, to ask a question or offer a

---

*It is important to note that in the nineteenth century it was a few favored women who were repeatedly elected to official posts. For example, between 1880 and 1900, although fifty-four council seats were given to women, only thirteen different women served in them.

†David Tyack, in *The One Best System: A History of American Urban Education* (Cambridge: Harvard University Press, 1974, pp. 265–66), tells the story of the fierce women's rights struggle to win power in the NEA, led by reformer Margaret Haley against the old-guard male leadership. Ella Flagg Young became the first woman president of the NEA in 1911. The NEA battle was self-consciously feminist in tone; the ALA election was not.

suggestion."[43] The next year Caroline Hewins had the distinction of being the first woman to speak up at the national convention; she asked if the dog tax was used to support a library outside Massachusetts. Perhaps this small temerity earned her the reputation of fearless spokeswoman, for it was Hewins who presented in 1891 the first general discussion of the "woman question" in the *Library Journal.*

Library work was difficult for women, Hewins said. For a salary varying from $300 to $900 annually, a library assistant had to write steadily six or seven hours a day, know half a dozen languages, be absolutely accurate in copying, "understand the relation of all arts and sciences to each other and . . . have . . . a minute acquaintance with geography, history, art and literature." A successful woman librarian would work eight to ten hours a day, and "those who are paid the highest salaries give up all their evenings." Hewins added that "librarians and library attendants sometimes break down from overwork." With unconscious humor, the intrepid Miss Hewins had a remedy for impending exhaustion: "plenty of sleep and nourishing food, with a walk of two or three miles per day."[44] Presumably this stroll was to be taken in the hours of early dawn or late evening.

The year after Hewins's article appeared there was an abortive attempt to establish a Woman's Section in the national organization. The sole meeting of women in 1892 was a tame affair, with only the barest expression of distress over women's low wages and subordinate position. An official statement secured from twenty-five of the nation's most prominent libraries revealed that "women rarely received the same pay for the same work as men."[45] But no matter. "The palm of honor and of opportunity waits for her who shall join a genius for organization . . . to the power of a broad, rich, catholic and sympathetic womanhood." In "the long run" the woman librarian "will win appreciation."[46]

The Woman's Section of the American Library Association did not meet again, although the 1892 session appointed a committee to report at the next conference in Chicago. There was no formal explanation of the failure of this committee to report, but it may be that a protest movement, sparked by Tessa Kelso of the Los Angeles Public Library, would explain the demise of the Woman's Section. Kelso stoutly disapproved of any deference paid to women as a group.*

> In the . . . 14th American Library Association Conference I note that there is a movement toward establishing a woman's section. . . . For years woman has worked, talked, and accepted all sorts of compromises to prove her fitness to hold the position of librarian, and to demonstrate that sex should have no weight where ability is equal. In all these years the accomplishment is seen in the table of wages

---

*"Library Association of Central California," *LJ* 22 (1897), 308. Kelso later became a successful businesswoman in the field of publishing and remained an outspoken feminist. In 1894 she sued a minister in Los Angeles because he prayed for her publicly after she placed a French novel in the library.

paid women librarians in comparison with those paid men. . . . For women to now come forward with the argument that a woman librarian has a point of view and such limitation that they must be discussed apart from the open court of library affairs is a serious mistake. . . . The use of the name of the association should not be permitted in such a direction.[47]

Such a truculent defense of women's equality, however, was not in accord with the expressed attitude of most women librarians. They accepted with little protest the traditional view of women as inherently limited in the working world. Of course they wanted to do things not customary for women in the past, such as managing a library with pay equal to men's, but this they considered as no more than a slight modification of tradition, and certainly not as a basic change in the male-structured view of women. As late as 1896 the influential Mary Ahern, editor of *Public Libraries,* warbled that "no woman can hope to reach any standing . . . in the library profession . . . who does not bring to it that love which suffereth long and is kind, is not puffed up, does not behave itself unseemly, vaunteth not itself, thinketh no evil." Every woman owed it to herself to live up to the ideals expected of womanhood; "no woman striving ever so hard to play the part of a man has ever succeeded in doing more than to give just cause for a blush to the rest of her kind." Every woman in library work should seek not "to detract from the reputation so hardly earned of being faithful conscientious workers." Eight years later librarian Frances Hawley firmly held to the inheritance of female self-abnegation:

> At the very top there is no room for us. . . . Ambition must mean more to us than a desire for good pay and perhaps a little honor and authority. . . . It must mean there will not be a single working day in all our lives when we will not see or hear or think something that will make for the betterment of our library.[48]

In 1904 one hundred representative librarians were asked by the ALA to comment on the limitations of women library workers.[49] Economic reasons were most often cited to explain women's low pay scale; women who did not demand as much salary as men were in abundant supply. Women were generally acknowledged to be hampered by their "delicate physique" and "inability to endure continued mental strain." Mary Cutler (now Mrs. Fairchild), an important woman library leader, commented that she could not see how women's physical disability could ever be eliminated. Whether women would ever hold high positions in the library "may remain perhaps an open question." While having decided advantage wherever "the human element predominates," Fairchild went on, women too frequently lacked the will to discharge executive power, and most trustees "assume that a woman would not have business capacity." Reviewing all the facts, she concluded that "on account of natural sex limitations, and also actual weakness in the work of many women as well as because of conservatism and prejudice, many gates are at present closed to women."[50]

Recognition of women's limited potential was probably justified when applied to women library workers in general. The average woman accepted the doctrine which taught that her success in life would be judged by her marriage and not by her work. With this concept central in her mind, she was being wholly practical if she spent much of her time conforming to the popular ideal of "femininity" rather than thinking about professional achievement. Women librarians who had given up hope of marriage were also less apt to strain for advancement, since they realized that society would further censure them for a display of "male" aggressiveness. Of course, some talented and energetic women librarians did realize their ambitions to a considerable degree, primarily because these ambitions were exceedingly modest and did not threaten the prevailing notion of woman's place.

Although the number of professional women increased 236 per cent between 1890 and 1920, most of these women merely left the home, not woman's sphere. They became segregated in the woman-dominated service professions, where femininity was newly defined on a vocational basis. Even if women of higher education and social class were drawn into professional life, they settled "like sediment in a wine bottle"[51] — along with their unskilled, uneducated, and poor counterparts — to the bottom of the American working world. The library hostess was as much victimized by the national movement toward professionalization as she was aided by it, for the process worked to drive women from some occupations and to isolate them in the low-paid, feminized areas of work. It is absurd to think that a society which invariably barred women from equality in law, religion, politics, or the economic structure, which denied them even the right to vote, would accord power or prestige to women's work or to women's vocational spheres in the community.*

One major function of a sexually segregated work force is the maintenance of sexual controls and of a socially homogeneous marriage system.[52] Whenever men and women are mixed indiscriminately, without supervision, the potential for socially unacceptable sexual relationships is present. The sex-typing of occupations is thus closely related to the fact that vocational segregation of men and women ensures less contact between the sexes. Wives fear career women as competitors for their husbands, while husbands face competition for their wives if their wives share tasks with men of their own class. It should not be surprising, then, especially in Victorian America, that as middle-class women entered professional life the professions became so strongly sex-typed. The feminized professions developed as the preserve of the unsexed spinster.

*The jobs for which there was an increase of 100,000 or more women between 1950 and 1970 numbered eight: babysitter, charwoman, fountain worker, file clerk, domestic servant, stewardess, musician, music teacher, and receptionist. (Marijean Suelzle, "Woman in Labor," *Trans-action* 8 [November–December 1970], 50–58.) In 1970, 80 per cent of female professionals and technical workers were concentrated in teaching, librarianship, social work, nursing and other types of health work, and dietician's work. (Shirley S. Angrest and Elizabeth M. Almquist, eds., *Careers and Contingencies* [New York: Dunellen, 1975, p. 13].)

Because the first generations of professional women did not openly question sex-roles, there was no possibility that this group of educated women could conceive of themselves as disciplined intellects operating freely in all areas of human competence. In library work, as in the other feminized professions, the only legitimate area for the operation of female intellect, which in some obscure way was believed to be complementary to that of the male, seemed to be through an extension of women's domestic service. Professional women stressed the social value of their work. They rarely described their right to work as an individual need for human expression and happiness. For library women, the expanded maternal role was to result in their early definition as the mechanic in the library—thrice blessed as moral guardian, cultural guide, gracious hostess.

Even if some women librarians did not subscribe to the concept of woman's sphere, with all its connotations, they had to appear to do so in order not to offend the many who did. Not to surrender to the Victorian mystique was to run the terrible risk of being judged deviants in their society, or being judged abnormal because of a challenge to well-established values. Even today the instrumentally active and intellectually aggressive woman is popularly suspected as showing signs of neurotic disturbance. Critical commentators who have studied the dominance of women in the conservative "moral uplift" efforts of the late nineteenth century have generally failed to acknowledge the supreme courage that would have been required of any deviant group of women who sought emancipation from sexual role-playing and thereby suffered the loss of economic security and social isolation and ridicule.[53]

Instead the great majority of newly restless, educated women spent their energies and talents in extending their role as housekeepers into the society at large. Their activity had the added value of not being seen as competition for jobs that men had the right to perform. Altruistic work for middle-class women filled the void in their lives created by increased leisure and rising expectations. It is not surprising that they, like males, defended their class interests. They upheld the sanctity of the family, of the capitalist economy with its formula of hard work and delayed sensual gratification, of Protestant nativism, of parental discipline, and of their nurturing, expressive functions—for these were the ideals that had traditionally given meaning to their lives.

Perhaps, too, both male and female librarians wished to avoid any real discussion of the injustice that library women suffered because of the eagerness of all library leaders to establish their profession. To publicize the prevalence of women in the library or to increase their influence could only harm the drive toward professionalization. A woman-dominated profession was obviously a contradiction in terms.

12

The Effect on Professionalization

LIBRARIANS HAVE BEEN ABSORBED to a marked degree, from 1876 to the present, with the question of professionalization. The 1923 Williamson report on library education forced librarians to recognize that significant elements common to professional schooling were lacking in librarianship.[1] In the effort to gain more professional standing, librarians have concentrated upon improvements in their system of library schools. The education of librarians, it has been commonly lamented, includes too much detail and attention to method, whereas true professional education should present as a foundation a systematic body of theory and scientifically based abstract knowledge.

Throughout the debate among librarians as to how best receive recognition as professionals, the dominant influence of women on librarianship has been strangely shunted aside, buried under a multitude of words concerning recruitment, accreditation, library school curriculums, and other factors thought to be inhibiting professionalization. There has been no systematic consideration given to the way in which feminization has shaped, most significantly, the development of library education and the entire range of activities associated with the field of library work. Carl White, who has written one of the best studies of library education as it developed before 1923, gave thoughtful attention to the social and educational setting in which library education began and related it brilliantly to the traditions which remain today from that early inheritance.[2] Yet White curiously refrained from considering the effect of the prevalence of women workers upon the shaping of those traditions. Sociologist Peter Rossi, in a symposium of 1961, was one of the first scholars to tackle the existence of feminization head-on and to apply it to library development. Rossi commented upon the puzzling absence of any real consideration being given to the influence of women upon library history.

> I kept expecting . . . some comment on the *major reason* [italics mine] why librarians find it difficult to achieve a substantial spot in the array of professions. Any occupation in which there is a high proportion of women suffers a special disability. . . . Women depress the status of an occupation because theirs is a depressed status in the society as a whole, and those occupations in which women are found in large numbers are not seen as seriously competing with other professions for personnel and resources. It is for this reason that professions such as education, social work, and librarianship develop with themselves a division of labor and accompanying status along sex lines.[3]

Rossi added that the status of librarianship could be raised by a radical division of labor such as that accomplished in medicine, where nursing was done by females and doctoring by males. A sharp differentiation between male and female librarians, however, runs counter to the central development of library history. Once formed, the solutions—both planned and accidental—found workable by nineteenth-century librarians closed the possibility of starting over with a clean slate. For this reason, it is important that librarians assess the basic meaning of feminization and give precise attention to their early history, for the dominance of women is surely the prevailing factor in library education, the image of librarianship, and the professionalization of the field. Women's role in the library was established in the last twenty-five years of the nineteenth century. An examination of this period of library history should include an emphasis upon the underrated effect of women students in library schools and its relationship to the librarian's search for professional status.

Although sociologists and historians are generally agreed that professions have certain characteristics differentiating them from other occupations,[4] there is no agreement on the precise nature of those characteristics. The conceptual model for this study will be devised so as to examine the professionalization of librarianship under three headings: service orientation, knowledge base, and degree of autonomy. These components will be examined first as they apply to nineteenth-century librarianship in general and then as they relate to the feminization of the field.

The service orientation of librarianship exhibits most of the elements expected in the lip service given to the ethical code of a profession. Professionals, in contrast to nonprofessionals, are theoretically more concerned with their clients' needs or with the needs of society than with their own material interests. A profession also has direct relevance to basic social values on which there is widespread consensus. In law and medicine, for example, the services provided by the professional are presumed to further justice and

health. In librarianship, the basic social value served is supposedly education. Early librarians were firm in their commitment of the library to educational purposes; they definitely relegated its recreational function to a secondary place. William Poole's comment typifies this view:

> Our public libraries and our public schools are supported by the same constituen-
> cies . . . and for the same purpose. . . . If public libraries shall in my day
> cease to be educational institutions and serve only to amuse the people and help
> them to while away an idle hour, I shall favor their abolition.[5]

The librarian thus showed a professional type of allegiance to the ideal of
community service. Additionally, librarians, like the ministers and educators
with whom they frequently compared themselves, sensed a professional identity as a group, sharing a common destiny, values, and norms.

The service and collectivity orientation of librarianship, then, conforms
to certain important characteristics of a profession. (The characteristics used
in the definition of the term "profession" are variables, forming a continuum
along which an occupation's rise to professionalism can presumably be
measured.) But although librarianship certainly has shown a number of professional traits, significant elements of a truly professional code of service still
are missing. Specifically lacking are a professional sense of commitment to
work, a drive to lead rather than to serve, and a clear-cut conception of professional rights and responsibilities. The feminization of library work is a major cause of these deficiencies.

The concentration of women certainly served to lower a professional
work-commitment within librarianship. The culture defined woman's
responsibility to the home as her primary one, and this definition was all-
pervasive before 1900. It was perfectly understandable, for example, that
Theresa West would leave her job as the leading woman librarian heading an
important library when she married Henry Elmendorf in 1896. Indeed, it
would have been shocking if she had chosen otherwise. Nineteenth-century
complaints of high turnover and low commitment to excellence among
library workers are directly related to the place that women accepted in
society. For the library assistant of the nineteenth century to become highly
work-committed required from her an atypical value orientation.[6] The majority of librarians were no doubt eager to marry and to leave library work.
Of the eight women among the early group of library leaders selected for this
study, five were unmarried and one was a widow. Of the two who married
while they were librarians, late in life, both continued to work in the field,
although not as head librarians. All eight of these women were highly
educated by the standards of their time. In each case professional success, extensive training, and spinsterhood served to increase their vocational commitment. Nevertheless, it remains generally true that within the field of
librarianship, from 1876 to the present, the dominance of women significantly lessened a trend toward professional, lifelong commitment to the field
of library service.[7]

In established professions, the practitioner supposedly assumes the responsibility for deciding what is best for the client. Whether or not the client agrees is theoretically not a factor in the professional's decision. Thus a doctor does not generally give whatever treatment the patient requests, but prescribes what he or she thinks is correct. In contrast, librarians tend to "serve" the reader.[8] This is partly a result of the tax-supported nature of the library and of its early efforts to attract a large public following. But the passive, inoffensive "service" provided by the librarian is also a natural acting-out of the docile behaviorial role that females have traditionally assumed in the culture.[9]

The assumption of a definitive intellectual leadership did not come to characterize the public librarian. Modern librarians have laid the blame for their general passivity and inferior status upon various factors: the lack of a scientifically based abstract body of knowledge, the public's lack of differentiation between the "professional" librarian and the library clerk, and the inherently weak position of the librarian as implementor rather than creator of intellectual and cultural advance. Rarely given its due as a determinant is the overwhelming presence of women in librarianship. The negative traits for which librarians indict themselves — excessive cautiousness, avoidance of controversy, timidity, a weak orientation toward autonomy, poor business sense, tractability, overcompliance, service to the point of self-sacrifice, and willingness to submit to subordination by trustees and public — are predominantly "feminine" traits.* The conventional ideals of feminine behavior held by women librarians and the reading public had a significant impact upon the development of the public librarian's nonassertive, "nonprofessional" code of service.

The second component of library professionalization — the body of knowledge — does not contain as many attributes as does the service ideal of librarians. Professional knowledge is generally defined as that knowledge which (1) is organized in abstract principles, (2) is continually revised or created by the professionals, (3) places strong emphasis upon the ability to manipulate ideas and symbols rather than physical objects, and (4) requires a sufficiently long term of specialized training for society to consider the resulting skills beyond the reach of the untrained person. William Goode has commented:

> Librarians themselves have found it extremely difficult to define their professional role and the knowledge on which it rests. To use a phrase like "specialization in

*My interviews with a leading university librarian and with several public librarians indicate a recent twentieth-century trend toward male homosexuals in library work. Their presence may be connected to the role playing assumed by librarians in general. That is, to the extent that the homosexual male takes on the characteristics of femininity, he proves quite adaptable to playing a female service role. It may be, too, that male homosexuals, having been driven from most of the high-status professions by prejudice, find women less hostile to their presence and thus feel more comfortable in a feminized working environment. On this point, note the formation of the Task Force on Gay Liberation during the 1970 American Library Association's annual meeting.

generalism" is insufficient. . . . The repeated calls which librarians have made for a "philosophy of librarianship" essentially expresses the need to define what *is* the intellectual problem of the occupation.[10]

In short, librarians do not know who they are. Are they library mechanics, having to do with such clerical, technical work as cataloguing, shelf arrangement, and signing-in-and-out management? Or are they expert guides, with considerable training in knowledge retrieval and organization?

One point, at least, seems clear. Despite the expressed desire of librarians to become admired professionals whose expertise would make available the world of knowledge, the system of library education that developed in the nineteenth century trained women to perform jobs that were chiefly mechanical in nature. This relatively low level of training, which made a small intellectual demand on the student, did not evolve entirely because of the feminine majority in library schools. The rate of expansion in both size and numbers of libraries was the first influence. The demand for a rapid production of library workers encouraged library schools to grind out graduates after only a brief course of instruction in the fundamental skills of "library economy." The older system of in-service training could not produce enough self-made librarians to satisfy the needs of the country. Carl White has outlined the second great influence on library education—the nineteenth-century development of technical education to fill the vacuum created by the breakdown of the classical curriculum and the medieval system of apprenticeship.[11] Library leaders were aware that a concentrated practical training had been demonstrated in other fields to produce the same results as learning by doing, but in less time and more systematically. Moreover, library education originated at a time when the methodology of record keeping and organizing collections was being developed and emphasized in order to provide more efficient service to larger numbers of people. The first schools designed their curriculum to meet the need for librarians who were skilled in the installation of the new systems and who understood the importance of technical accuracy. Thus, detailed instruction in mechanical routines became the solid core of library training. Library education was in no sense designed to cultivate intellectual leadership, to produce trained high-level administrators, or to develop an abstract-knowledge base for library science.

From the beginnings of library education in the late 1880s to the Williamson report of 1923, many librarians (outside the library schools) recognized that one major barrier to professionalization was the lack of distinction drawn between professional education and clerical instruction. The first report ever given to the ALA on library education criticized the "exaggeration of the importance of instrumentalities" by the pupils at Dewey's new school at Columbia. In 1890 a report on Dewey's school at Albany noted that the curriculum was "too practical" and that less time should be given to instruction in the use of the fountain pen and the "library hand." An ALA study of the library schools in 1900 again expressed the common concern that only "scholastic training" would raise librarianship to the ranks of an established profession. In 1912 Chalmers Hadley's accusation that library schools "appeal largely to the housewifely instincts" went unchallenged in the discussion of his paper at the annual ALA convention. In her report, "Women in Libraries," to the Association of Collegiate Alumnae in 1917 Adelaide Hasse flatly stated that library education presented a "dead level of mediocrity" that did not appeal to educated minds, chiefly because the training was too technical. The occupational crisis created by the exit of educated women workers from the library during World War I brought dissatisfaction with the quality of library school graduates into even more prominence in the library literature. Thus when Charles C. Williamson presented his withering criticism of library education in 1923 his ideas were by no means new to librarians at large.[12]

Yet even Williamson did not openly state the direct connection between the mechanical nature of library education and the predominance of women in library schools as students and instructors. Like many others before him, he approached the problem indirectly by bemoaning the lack of males in librarianship. That raising the level of library instruction would attract more men to library work was recognized as early as 1903, when the New York Library Association recommended short training courses for men who "were not willing to undergo two years instruction in library methods which after all were neither particularly abstruse or difficult" to learn.[13] Most librarians believed that the entry of more men into librarianship would raise the level of salaries and increase the librarian's prestige.[14] Thus Williamson took it for granted that the library schools had failed because men avoided library work as a career, since library work was "generally looked upon as clerical" in nature. Although only 5 to 6 per cent of library school graduates had been men, he said, it was significant that over 60 per cent of these men had attended the Albany school, which required a college degree for admittance. "If we are to judge by the statistics, college men prefer a school of the highest standards which comes most nearly to meeting the requirements of a professional school organized on a graduate basis." Williamson argued that few college men, or women, would be attracted to library work as a professional career when so many of the library school catalogues assured them that " 'a ready ability to use the typewriter is an important part of a modern librarian's equipment' [and is] 'necessary for almost any library position.' "[15]

Williamson also criticized the peculiar emphasis placed upon "personality" as a criterion for admittance to professional library schooling. It is indeed difficult to imagine a comparable emphasis in any male-dominated profession. This elusive quality of personality was variously described as "the missionary spirit," "cultural strength," "breeding and background," "gentleness," "sense of literary values," or, as summed up in 1905 by George Putnam, "all the amiable qualities which go to make a hostess."[16] The personality test was commonly applied through a mandatory interview of each prospective student by the head of each library school. As Williamson wryly commented, this test did not inspire much confidence, for "in the first place, no attempt has been made to determine scientifically what qualities are essential." No doubt the selected personalities meshed closely with that of the library school director and this inbreeding in turn contributed to the "excessive conservatism and conformity" that Williamson found in the library schools' faculties and programs.[17] The first and second generation of library school directors in the United States were almost all graduates of the pioneer school at Albany, thus fulfilling Mary Plummer's hope of "carrying on the traditions . . . by a kind of apostolic succession."[18] This form of confinement no doubt contributed to the sameness of women librarians; the emphasis upon "personality" as a test for library fitness, not only in the library schools but in the profession at large, is reflected in the fact that by 1900 librarians ranked second only to government clerks as the occupation in which native white women of native parentage had attained the greatest prominence.[19]

The predominance of women in library schools, on library school faculties, and in library work functioned as an unmentioned but inflexible framework into which "professional" education would have to be fitted. An emphasis upon the influence of women is not meant to downgrade the other elements that shaped library education or to deemphasize the other inherent weaknesses in the librarian's claim to professional status, nor is it meant to impose chauvinistic attitudes upon male library leaders. Nineteenth-century librarians, however, were men and women of their time, governed by conventional views of woman's role in society. They were faced with an unorthodox problem—how to devise "professional" training for young women. Their answer was caught between the upper and the nether millstones. The upper millstone was their hope that librarians would become indispensable educational leaders, with professional scope and value. The nether millstone was the reality of the library school student—a woman who most likely lacked scholarly ambitions or preparation; who had no lifelong vocational commitment; and whose attitudes toward feminine sex roles led her to accept, and expect, administrative controls, low autonomy, and subordination to clerical, routine tasks.[20]

No study of why library training developed as it did would be complete without an emphasis upon how it was influenced by the thought of Melvil Dewey. Dewey so molded library education that the whole period before 1923 is called the "Dewey period." He was, above all, pragmatic and technically minded. Dewey has been called a "man-child," for his idealism, enthusiasm, and impatience with any obstacle. There is indeed something childish and maddeningly pretentious about his simplistic assessment of the world and his mission in it. Yet burning zeal can carry one very far. Dewey's contributions to library development are unequalled by any one man, and his personal drive and unflinching faith in his mission will long be admired. It was Dewey who initiated library school education and aggressively promoted his standards of technical training in library mechanics.

Dewey's compatibility with women gave him insight that was unusual among men of his time. This remarkable statement was delivered before the Association of Collegiate Alumnae in 1886:

> Would a father say to his son, "My boy, your mother and I are lonely without you; you must stay at home, go out to afternoon teas with us, and keep us company in the big, empty house. I have enough for us all, so there is no need of your bothering your head about supporting yourself." Would he expect his son to be happy under such circumstances? Why, then, his daughter?[21]

Dewey had sincere respect for the intellect of women. He has often been praised because his defense of women's capabilities led him at times to suffer real personal sacrifice, as at Columbia. His role as champion of women is a complex and intriguing one, for beneath it lies a grating note of paternalism. He did not call on women to assert themselves but instead set himself up as their valiant spokesman.

The library school curriculum that Dewey devised at Columbia and later continued at the New York State Library School ruled out any "attempt to give general culture or to make up deficiencies of earlier education." Dewey, in a characteristically pragmatic decision, would reconcile the library needs of the country with the status of women in society by concentrating upon schooling that taught the technical skills necessary to perform work on the lower rungs of the library ladder. The American Library Association's committee on the proposed library school at Columbia remarked that those who came to the school would probably wish to become administrators. Dewey quickly corrected it; the committee was told that "the plans all contemplate special facilities and inducements for cataloguers and assistants who do not expect or desire the first place."[22]

By 1905 library education had crystallized around Dewey's core of practical instruction in routine detail to a predominantly female force. Yet even though librarians had established library education as a system of nonprofessional training for library mechanics, they continued to wonder at the "appalling misconception" in the public mind of their qualifications and to bemoan the fact that the public had made them "the poorest paid professionals in the world."[23] In that year the American Library Association convention found an answer of sorts to the dilemma: The great librarians, it was agreed, were born, not made.

> Pooles and Winsors are not and never will be wholly produced by library schools. . . . Such eminent examples are born librarians. The born librarian will not need a school to teach him principles of classification . . . he will evolve systems of classification and cataloguing, and methods of administration without ever going near a school. . . . But there will never be many of him, and there will be thousands of library employees.[24]

It was for the low-level employee "that our schools are at present intended."[25] In the discussion that followed a consensus was reached by important library spokesmen like E. C. Richardson, Frederick Crunden, Samuel Green, Melvil Dewey, and Herbert Putnam.[26] It was agreed that librarians of genius had no need of formal training. Unconsciously the national association had focused upon a central truth. While females from the library schools became clerks and assistants and heads of small libraries, the most honored and best-paid librarians were men. The "best" librarians of the time were indeed not made but born—born male.

The prevalence of women in library work also served to strengthen a non-professional bureaucratic system of control that gave the worker little autonomy. In librarianship, as in teaching and social work, the presence of women made more likely the development of an authoritative administrative structure with a stress on rules and generally established principles to control the activities of employees. In these feminized fields the highest success was secured through promotion to the administrative levels of the organization. This is in contrast to the pattern within established male-dominated professions. In university teaching, for example, the productive practitioner is usually more honored within his profession than is the high-level administrator of the university. Within librarianship and other feminized occupations, compliance with sex roles prevented women from assuming much autonomy. Because sexist attitudes still prevail in the society, this basic situation has undergone little change since the nineteenth century.[27]

The popular image of librarianship graphically illustrates the many alterations feminization brought to library work in the late nineteenth century. To call the public image of librarianship a stereotype does not make it an entirely erroneous concept, for the popular vision of librarians is a byproduct of deeper social realities. In the 1860s the popular concept of the librarian was that of a preoccupied man in black—a collector and preserver who was never so happy as when all the volumes were safely on the shelf. He was thought to be ineffectual, grim, and "bookish."[28]

The public's image had shifted by 1900 to portray the librarian as a woman, and it was consistently deprecatory. "Meek," "mousy," and "colorless" had been added to the description of the original "old" male librarian as eccentric, frustrated, grouchy, and introverted. The public librarian came to be stereotyped as an inhibited, single, middle-aged woman.[29] Librarian Harold Lancour quipped that he had heard so much about this lady, he was "growing rather fond of the old girl."[30]

Howard Mumford Jones, musing in 1960 on the caricature of the librarian, demonstrated a sophisticated understanding of the chief reason why professionalization continued to elude library workers: The training of librarians should include more about the insides of books and "less technical lore about what to do with the book as an object in space." Jones suggested that the stereotype of the woman librarian was "partly the product of limited budgets and in part the product of genteel tradition." Lumping together social workers and librarians, Jones said not all of them were maiden ladies, but enough of them were to rank them as "persons less likely to go to night clubs" than women secretaries or department store clerks.[31]

Jones's analogy was an apt one, for social work and librarianship shared many developmental characteristics. A comparison of the origin and evolution of these two feminized professions is helpful for an understanding of the general movement of professionalization that took shape in the United States, of the process of professionalization itself, and of the changing status of working women within the social order.

13

Librarianship, Charity Work, and the Settlement Movement

DURING THE LAST TWO DECADES of the nineteenth century, when women's suffrage became a symbol for much more than just electoral equality, the "woman question" became as central and intriguing an item for discussion as the class and national conflicts of the time. The attention given to the "new woman"—the pros, the cons, the endless fascination with the subject—were evident in one form or another in almost any popular novel, magazine, or newspaper. It would also be difficult to find major thinkers, writers, or scholars who did not seriously and often passionately address themselves to the implications of the shift in sex relations that followed in the wake of Western industrialization.

In Victorian America the "masculine" virtues were balanced by the "feminine" virtues and the two were deemed complementary, but this artificial parcelling out of human traits to the separate sexes was precisely what the woman question threw open to discussion and doubt. If women were successful in their move to share public power with males, no one could foresee the possible effects upon Western culture. What seemed certain, only, was that a change in women's status would effect society in ways that were difficult to predict.

Yet the first timid ventures of middle-class women into the public arena were not accompanied by any feminine demands for radical social change. Rather, quite the opposite was true. Women did not view themselves as competitors or meddlers in the areas that men had historically dominated. The first groups of women to leave their homes in the 1870s formed an army directed toward the realization of temperance, "social purity," and "child-saving."[1] They assumed special roles as conservators within public life, roles that made use of their uniquely "feminine" qualities and publicly affirmed the moral values of their white, Protestant, and native-born middle class. Even the suffrage movement, the most overt threat to the patriarchal structure, was couched in terms that supported social attitudes prevalent among the dominant class of white males.[2] Other groups of organized women became champions of social outsiders such as the poor and the immigrants and were active in municipal reform. Always, however, the rhetoric that legitimated women's movement into positions of public influence pictured the community as a larger home—a home in which women could play their roles of housecleaner, sacrificial servant, bearer of culture, and teacher of morality. The areas of feminine responsibility were defined as those in which males had traditionally shown less interest than women—work with children, for example, or charitable endeavors, or matters concerning moral purity.

Thus, although women's assumption of public activity was potentially radical in its long-term effects, the first mission of organized women in America was heavily traditional in nature: refurbishing the cherished values of the agricultural past, cleaning up the consequences of political corruption and business greed, ameliorating the brutality of life for the poor in the cities. A typical magazine article of the period enunciating the elements of women's "grand awakening" lauded woman, "inventor of all the peaceable arts of life," as the "vital force which is to make society morally pure," shedding her light "to illumine a new day when righteousness shall reign."[3] Convinced of their spiritual superiority, middle-class women embraced their new public duties with enthusiasm. Very few of them went so far as to deny the value of a social and racial hierarchy maintained by force.

Nevertheless, one cannot overlook the greater emphasis upon social welfare that women brought into public life. The social feminist movement was vigorous and vocal between 1890 and 1920; never before or since have so many women's groups been so active. Organized women played an important role in the Progressive movement. Commentators of that time were certainly aware of the relationship between the woman question and a general climate of social reform. Since women were *supposed* to be more peaceful and compassionate than men, many of them acted that way.

Within this great army of reform-minded, leisured women who were entering public life in the late nineteenth century was that group of educated middle-class women who, in contrast to the majority of female activists, moved into *paid* positions outside the home, within the occupations where the linking of professional roles and sex roles resulted in the creation of the "feminized professions"—notably public school teaching, nursing, social work, and librarianship. In contrast to the other three fields, the professionalization of teaching began long before the Civil War and was thus shaped by considerably different historical forces. Teaching was feminized before librarianship and social work and is the only one of the four fields in which males have continued as a significant percentage of the total. Moreover, in teaching, the highest levels of the bureaucratic administration common to all the feminized professions have been almost entirely reserved for males. Nursing began professionalization at about the same time as librarianship and social work but is different from the other three fields chiefly because it has been all-female. Perhaps this is why the history of nursing contains a colorful strain of militant feminism in sharp contrast to the predominant attitudes of women teachers, social workers, and librarians. Or perhaps the bitter feminist consciousness so apparent in early nursing history is partly a result of the defeat of women herb-healers and midwives by the male medical profession, which had all but excluded women from their time-honored role as healers by the late nineteenth century. The nurse is also unique because of her peculiar position as a professional who is directly subordinate to another professional, the physician.

There is, however, a striking similarity between the development of social work and librarianship. The early librarians and charity workers were at first as supportive of conventional social attitudes as the stuffiest temperance worker or social-purity reformer might have wished. And both occupations were profoundly affected by the emergence of a more questing and less conservative group of feminine activists, the settlement-house workers.

The beginnings of social work as a profession in the United States are to be found in the Charity Organization movement, which began in Buffalo in 1877 and spread quickly to twenty-four other cities by 1883. By 1900 there were 138 Charity Organization societies in existence, functioning as administrative clearinghouses to organize private sources of philanthropy. These private funds had been considerably strained by the growth of the poor and the effects of industrialization. The 1873 depression and the presence of large numbers of urban immigrants had also operated to bring the cost of welfare to an unprecedented and alarming level. The expense of private benevolence was often inflated by the corruption of city officials who administered public welfare funds.

The Charity Organization movement gained its strength from the alarm of the well-favored over the soaring cost of public and private relief. Charity agents sought to better organize private resources, through the creation of a central coordinating agency staffed with persons who would keep accurate records, discover frauds and cheats, weed out undeserving recipients, and distribute aid more honestly and efficiently. The governor of Michigan put the matter bluntly to the National Conference of Charities and Corrections in 1875: "If we can *cure* crime, we make money. . . . If we can *cure* pauperism we make money. . . . This . . . is the legitimate field of social science, to prove, so that people may see, that what you claim to be the correct theory will save them money."[4]

Most early charity agents and librarians placed their faith in self-help as one of the best ways to lessen poverty in a political democracy. Unless destitute individuals made the struggle toward self-dependence, many believed, charity would only further demoralize the poor and destroy their chance for a better future. Thus all available means of pressure needed to be brought upon the poverty-stricken to force them into self-sufficient positions. Some charity agents believed that indiscriminate, "unscientific" alms-giving was itself a cause of pauperism. In the library, regeneration of the poor was to be accomplished by exposure to the proper books and by individual contact with the informative and encouraging librarian. Charity workers had a tougher job before them, the material as well as moral regeneration of the poor, but their motives and their methods were much the same as those of librarians. The miracle wrought by contact with a refined, concerned middle-class friend would help to raise the deficient members of society to economic independence and right thinking.

Charity Organization societies often relied upon upper- and middle-class women volunteers, called Friendly Visitors, to aid in moral uplift of paupers. The personal contact between Friendly Visitors and the poor was seen as beneficial to both groups. Friendly Visitors fulfilled the duties of good citizens; the poor benefited through association with "a patient, persevering, faithful friend, who, by the power of that strongest thing on earth, personal influence, will gradually teach [them] habits of industry and self-control."[5]

In contrast to the pre–Civil War years, the majority of charity workers by the 1870s were women. Who was better equipped, by way of natural talents, to give moral direction than the well-bred American woman? More important, what other group could be found that was able and willing, even eager, to work without pay? Charity literature did not often stress that volunteers were valued for the sake of economy. Rather, an elaborate rationalization of the benefits to be drawn from unpaid labor was devised to encourage the Friendly Visitor. A willingness to work for nothing was described as the real hallmark of a sincere charity worker. As late as 1898 the announcement of the first training course in social work warned prospective students to enter the field for the sake of knowledge to be gained of social conditions in New York rather than from the hope of securing paid employment in the philanthropic field.[6] Fortunately, women were so naturally designed as agents of charity that no special training was really required to prepare them for the work. Warm hearts, cheery spirits, and wise thoughts were qualification enough, and this, the ladies knew, was "a work for which our daily lives fit us."[7] Charity reform, before the participation of women, had been "a man's attempt at woman's work, and of course a failure."[8]

The Friendly Visitor was urged to share her knowledge about the preparation of food and the mending of clothes, but it was her mere presence in the home of the poor which seemed to be the critical factor in their education. By some vaguely understood osmosis, her sympathetic understanding and robust optimism would raise their spirits and would rouse them to make their rooms pretty and bright. So inspired, the poor would learn to seek "little details of comfort and decency," like pleasant games, library books, and clean clothes, "the total disregard of which is at the bottom of much misery and vice." The gracious lady's coming brought in its wake a new "hope and happiness and a new desire to live rightly." "Imagine the result," a charity worker asked, "if every man, woman and child from the laboring classes who needs it in any way had the sympathy and aid of a friend who never lost sight of them, and who was able, by means of a larger cultivation and happier life, to bring comfort and brightness to their weary lives of unceasing toil."[9]

Despite the Friendly Visitors' good intentions, however, it was difficult to be accepted as a friend by those whom they considered to be their social inferiors.[10] The early charity reformers seldom acknowledged that the poor might have special insight into the cause of their poverty. Just as the librarians slowly learned, by experience, that condescension and assumption of superior wisdom did not make their charges grateful and malleable, so did the Friendly Visitors learn that approaching the poor in a spirit of uplift did not often elicit their friendship.

In fact, the use of Friendly Visitors by the charity societies was decreasing steadily from the 1880s on.[11] There were simply not enough leisured and educated ladies who were willing to be dependable and long-term visitors. As the urban population shifted in the last decades of the century, the geographical distance between rich and poor increased. Transportation problems and the development of slum districts inside the great cities became a further barrier to "neighborliness" between the lady visitors and their prospective charges. By the 1880s differences in ethnic background, religion, and language further separated the rich and poor. The trend toward paid workers was greatly accelerated during the depression of 1893, and by 1900 a reversal of roles had occurred. Whereas earlier the routine office labor had been done by paid staff members, by the turn of the century volunteers mostly served as board members or office workers, and the paid agents performed the work in the field. Many upper- and middle-class women moved on to other reform work, in settlements or within suffrage or women's clubs, or to paid employment. The paid charity agent moved in by default to assume much of the work of the Friendly Visitor.

By 1890 the budding profession of social work was predominantly female in numbers, though not in leadership positions. As in librarianship, women became the instructors and administrators within the training schools of the new profession. In the national association of charity workers organized in 1874, the National Conference of Charities and Corrections, women were given recognition as chairpersons of committees. Like women librarians in the ALA, the charity workers were first assigned to committees that concerned the care of children. The first woman president of the national association of social workers was Jane Addams, elected in 1910. Other women presidents followed Addams at intervals of about five years through the 1920s.

In 1891 the first of two session meetings of the Committee on Women in Charity and Corrections was held. These sessions in 1891 and 1892 mark the only time when the work of women in social welfare was formally singled out for attention at the national conference, perhaps because, as one speaker, Anne B. Richardson, commented, "the co-operation of women in charitable work seems in itself so natural an arrangement that at first blush one hardly admits the necessity of its discussion." The committee reported in 1891 that a survey showed that women were serving on state boards of charities in most of the northeast and mid-Atlantic states. The 1891 speaker assured the conference members that women were grateful for the opportunities given to them in social work and had no sympathy for the radical idea of women's equality. The next year, this theme was stressed even more strongly by the main speaker at the women's session. Richardson repeated no less than three times her reassurance that the committee had no intention of advocating the "dreadful doctrines" of women's rights. Women felt qualified for administrative positions and were even better qualified than most men for work with children or female clients, she said, but did not see these positions "as the means to the end of their advancement as women and with a view to final assertions of rights." Rather, the committee sought the advancement of women only because of "their fitness . . . for the duties" of charity work.[12] Thus, as in librarianship, the stage was early set for women to emerge into the public arena without threatening the conservative notion of their proper concerns.

There are other important similarities in the development of the new professions of social work and librarianship. Each group was controlled to a large extent by a governing board composed of educated and affluent members. But the leaders of the new professions were not aliens who held a different ideology from their overseers. Librarians and charity agents were generally men and women who were sympathetic and sensitive to the attitudes and wants of their board members. In social beliefs and in socioeconomic origins, they differed little from the class that they practically represented in their areas of work.

Both librarian and charity agent shared a genuine humanitarian desire to improve the living conditions of the poor and uneducated. Sometimes this desire was founded in religious beliefs but more often it was the expression of a new spirit that represented the secularization of religion, the transfer of the ideal of self-sacrificing service from God to man.[13] Service to the less fortunate was also one means of easing the sense of personal guilt that often underlay the humanitarianism of many women reformers. Beatrice Webb called this uneasy sense of guilt a "class consciousness of sin,"[14] experienced by those who realized how blessed they were by the existent social order in comparison to others. How to close the widening gap between classes of rich and poor, educated and uneducated, native and immigrant, was a problem very much in the minds of both librarians and charity workers in the early days of both reform movements.

The desire to mitigate class conflict was clearly tempered by fear. Without relief or direction the ignorant poor might band together in despair and upset the social system itself; at best the lower orders threatened the virtues held dear by the middle class. Just as library literature was saturated with the promise that libraries would offer protection against social revolution, so too did charity workers vow to restore class harmony.[15] Charity leader Mary Richmond typically promised to lessen poverty and crime among the lower class: "Only let us give . . . [the charitable impulse] organization and direction, and we'll *put out* your bonfire."[16] The possibility that poverty or ignorance among the masses might be caused wholly, or in part, by the political and economic organization of society was not a major consideration of the new professionals in the early stages of the library and Charity Organization movements. Where social evils existed, they were believed to be due chiefly to human weakness and thus to be solvable by reconstitution of individuals.

Both of the newly formed feminized professions sought to use their organizations to mend the moral and cultural fabric of a society that was unravelling into mass diversity. Thorstein Veblen, who so often saw clearly the reality of his time, noted this connection between cultural reformer and charity reformer and questioned the supposedly disinterested motives of both.

> Many of the efforts now in reputable vogue for the amelioration of the indigent population of large cities are of the nature, in great part, of a mission of culture. It is by this means sought to accelerate the rate of speed at which given elements of the upper-class culture find acceptance in the everyday scheme of life of the lower classes . . . [Charity] is in part . . . consistently directed to the inculcation, by precept and example, of certain punctilios of upper-class propriety in manners and customs. . . . The propaganda of culture is [also] in great part an inculcation of new tastes, or rather of a new schedule of proprieties, which have been adapted to the upper-class scheme of life under the guidance of the leisure-class formulation of the principles of status and pecuniary decency. This new schedule of proprieties is intruded into the lower-class scheme of life.[17]

The "principles of status and pecuniary decency" defended by librarians and charity workers can be traced in the professional literature, which, especially before the 1890s, reflected the reformers' nostalgic longing for the idealized American small town or village where the native Protestant had exercised powerful social influence. The swelling social problems in urban and industrial America were still so new they could not be clearly understood. It was the older American community that seemed in jeopardy and that these reformers sought to save. Whatever the reality had been, the older community was remembered as a harmonious, homogenous whole where rich and poor had mixed in mutual respect and understanding. The stress placed by reformers on personal influence and neighborly intercourse with the poor was partly for the purpose of recreating the fancied social peace of the small community so cherished in American memory and folklore.

Librarianship and social work also flourished upon the discontent and boredom of many hundreds of middle-class women who were ambitious and nonconformist enough to desire meaningful activity outside the home. Both library and charity agency made a consistent and determined pitch to attract the labor of the new breed of college women, and this effort was generally successful. In both library and charity work, educated women were welcomed primarily, although not entirely, because their labor was so cheap, or in the case of the volunteer charity worker, actually free. At a time when the number of libraries and charity agencies were rapidly expanding, the economic value of hiring educated and devoted workers at such low cost should not be underestimated as a major reason for the rapid feminization of both professions. As we have seen, a facilitating ideology that emphasized the inherent fitness of women for the new work was very quickly developed to legitimize the extension of women's sphere. Both the charity worker and the librarian stressed the nonrevolutionary nature of their emergence into public life, reassuring their male leadership that feminization posed no real threat to male prerogatives or traditional sex-roles. And in both professions there was an immediate and intense involvement of the women workers in one or another variety of child-related work. The early librarian and charity organizer in New England, at least, were almost identical women, conservative in social philosophy, drawn from the same general socioeconomic group. They were content to join with the male leadership of their profession in defense of the social ideals of a group that was losing cultural and economic dominance at the same time as it was seeking to exert its influence over the new mass society that would reject the genteel code as irrelevant and obsolete.

By the early 1890s, it was becoming apparent to many librarians and charity organizers that the older social philosophy of their organizations was inadequate and unrealistic. This was a period of ideological confusion and turbulence in both occupations, shown in the doubt, debates, and conflicting theories expressed in the professional literature.[18] Experience had taught both groups of workers that the old presumptions about mass needs were simply not true. Librarians had learned that the public would not read the "higher" literature, no matter how cleverly it was presented. Charity agencies could not avoid the knowledge that poverty was often caused by external factors rather than by the moral frailty of individuals. These agencies had insisted upon careful and extensive record-keeping, and it was not long before the accumulation of data made it clear that unemployment, low wages, sickness, accidents, and periodic depressions were major causes of poverty. The suffering of only a small percentage of the poor could be explained by laziness or intemperance alone. Older charity leaders like Josephine Lowell and Mary Richmond began to recognize the necessity of an attack upon the social origins of poverty.

By 1900 the terminology of "deserving" and "undeserving" poor had been all but abandoned by the Charity Organization movement. In 1895 Robert Paine's election as president of the national association of welfare workers marked the general acceptance of the new strain of realism in charity work. He placed responsibility for poverty upon the social system itself in his presidential address and located the problem in unrestrained pursuit of the profit motive.[19] In 1899 the classification of items to be discussed at the national charity conference was revised so as to include two main headings—causes of poverty "within the family" and "causes outside the family." By 1903 the general secretary of the New York Charity Organization Society could declare: "We may quite safely throw overboard, once and for all, the idea that the dependent poor are our moral inferiors, that there is any necessary connection, between wealth and virtue, or between poverty and guilt."[20]

Perhaps the library and the Charity Organization movement would have progressed to this new realism without outside pressure, merely influenced by internal experience and the general awakening of social consciousness in the nation in the 1890s. But this possibility is doubtful; institutions, once formed, move ponderously toward new concepts and new actions. It was the challenge of the settlement movement, born in the late 1880s, partly as a reaction against organized charity, that bankrupted the older ideology and jostled both charity worker and librarian into a different stance. The settlement movement, generally staffed by women, was a significant influence upon both occupations, causing a rethinking and restating of goals, as well as a whole new mode of behavior. As Jane Addams, that endlessly intriguing symbol of the age, put it so succinctly, "the Charitable and the Radical" had at last united together,[21] to produce, for a brief period of American history, a romantic, energetic, optimistic demand for social justice, tempered and channelled by bland conservatism.

The settlement workers spoke of themselves as social reformers and made clear their distaste for the methodology of the charity organizers. Jane Addams thought of many charity agents as stingy religious hypocrites who offered the poor only moralistic advice.* For a few years there was a great deal of antagonism between the two movements, for many charity agents were repelled by the sentimental "would-be saviours of mankind" in the settlement houses. The two movements had similar elements—the use of women

---

*Apparently Addams had little respect for any educated women who did not give some time to social service. Margaret Bingham Stillwell, trained under William Foster and an eminent librarian specialist on rare books, showed Addams through the John Carter Brown Library in 1908. Addams looked politely at the books, then sadly chided Stillwell when leaving, "A young woman like you, so competent and well and strong, when there are so many people in the world who need you." The encounter so shook Stillwell that she immediately began volunteer civic work (Margaret B. Stillwell, *Librarians Are Human: Memories in and out of the Rare-Book World, 1907–1970* [Boston: The Colonial Society of Massachusetts, 1973]). See also Allen Davis, *The American Heroine: The Life and Legend of Jane Addams* (New York: Oxford University Press, 1973).

volunteers from the privileged classes, an emphasis upon collection of facts, the idea of the individual's duty to restore class harmony, the religious tone of humanitarian concern—but in significant ways the social settlements and charity agencies were the antithesis of each other.

Settlement house workers were more inclined to base their work upon the needs and desires of the poor, rather than to ask the poor to conform to a predetermined pattern of behavior. They even encouraged the immigrants to retain and strengthen their cultural differences from WASP America. The settlement workers were interested in the problems of the impoverished community, not merely in individual paupers, and directed their efforts to meet the problems of the poor as a class. Inevitably, their philosophical assumptions led them to broaden charitable activity so as to include provision of clubs, employment bureaus, nurseries, parks, playgrounds, and other services to the neighborhood. Intent upon action based on research, they served as the national conscience and gathered the data that prompted many reforms in the political and legal arena.

From the 1890s until the war years the settlement worker served as an idealized popular figure for the American public. The well-off, native-born American who felt concern for the living conditions of the poor or who feared the threat posed by the immigrant masses to social stability wanted to believe that the settlement resident could ease class conflict and alleviate poverty in the cities. Settlement work was especially attractive to the growing numbers of young college-educated women who felt a social obligation to make use of their training or who did not have an immediate prospect for marriage. Settlement work became a glamorous goal for many young women. Whereas the bright and ambitious college woman of today might choose to enter graduate school, in 1900 she might have been drawn to live and work in a settlement house.

Settlement workers saw that shortcomings in the social and economic order impoverished a large number of Americans. To discover the evils, educate the public, and bring about legal change was their basic task. As "spearheads for reform" they were highly visible.[22] Nearly all their proposals involved in one way or another the elevation of human rights over property rights and the extension of public authority into the sacred precinct of the individual's right to profit. Eventually some of the settlement workers went too far in their challenge to the ordered society. Opposition to war and its foundation of nationalism, a tentative thrust toward racial equality, a too-fervent support of labor rights, and an expressed affinity for the creation of a welfare state were too radical for postwar America to absorb. But before the decline of settlement popularity, the activity of settlement workers had changed the face of the social-work profession and had influenced the activity of the public librarian to a marked degree.

14

Maid Militant:
The Progressive Years
and World War I

FROM THE EARLY 1890s TO World War I, the larger American public libraries, inspired by the popular success of settlement activity, expanded their mission to concentrate upon social work with children and the urban poor. Public libraries opened their doors as never before and sought to function as social centers, with clubs, assembly rooms, lectures, and outreach programs. Librarians joined the army of concerned citizens, chiefly female, who worked to enrich the life of the child, to Americanize the foreigner, and to deal with the urban problems the settlement houses sought to remedy. In the largest cities, the distinction between librarianship and social work became blurred, especially for the branch librarians, who were encouraged to give as much attention to people in the neighborhood as to books inside the library. Arthur Bostwick, elected president of the ALA in 1907 and again in 1918, announced that the library of the future would treat "classes of people" as direct objects of attention, "instead of dealing primarily with books, as formerly."

> It may all be summed up by saying that we are coming to consider the library somewhat in the light of a community club, of which all well-behaved citizens are members. Our buildings are clubrooms with books and magazines, meeting rooms, toilet facilities, kitchens—almost everything, in fact, that a good, small club would contain. If you say "then they have ceased to be libraries" . . . that does not affect me any more than that you show that we are no longer speaking Chaucer's language or wearing the clothes of Alfred the Great.[1]

This new endeavor of the public library in the Progressive period was manifested in three ways. First, the library building was put to use as a community center—a place open to local groups for business, educational, and recreational meetings.[2] By 1912, the year that marked a peak of professional interest in the "social center movement," the St. Louis Public Library reported that in one week it had opened its facilities to fifty-five different community organizations.[3] The St. Louis experience was a typical one in urban libraries, particularly in the branch libraries, where direct community involvement was generally greater than in the main library building. Secondly, public libraries began to sponsor myriad activities not directly related to books, which they described as "library extension" work. The range of such activities was very wide, apparently limited only by the imagination and energy of individual librarians. In both rural and urban settings, public librarians organized clubs, sponsored lecture series, set up contests—from "fly-swatting" to flower shows—devised classes in subjects as varied as crocheting and socialism, installed game corners, held exhibits and festivals, and taught handicrafts, gave cadet drills, and ran correspondence courses.[4] By 1915 the president of the ALA warned that extension activities might be in danger of overpowering the library's more traditional function of providing books to the citizenry.[5] But the development of library service to children was the most important new form of public library activity in the Progressive period. Work with children developed earliest, received the most interest, and was the activity most directly influenced by the example of settlement work, as well as by the library's feminized setting. As women, librarians turned naturally to the nurture of the child.

It was also natural that the first effort of women settlement workers "should be in the medium with which they were most familiar—books."[6] Two years before the first library room for children was opened in the country, settlement workers and librarians in Boston were allied in the joint operation of a children's library at the settlement house. One of the first activities undertaken by settlement houses in other cities was also the installation of a library for children. The books were sometimes donated to the settlement by citizens, but were often provided by the local public library. As women librarians began to specialize in work with children, most settlement houses eventually turned over their book collections to newly opened branch libraries.[7]

As we have seen, the interest of public librarians in children's reading, already evident in the 1870s, was first directed toward cooperation with the public schools. As late as 1893 children under the age of twelve were barred from almost half the large public libraries in the nation. This early reluctance to admit children into the library stemmed from the widespread concern that the use of library books, particularly fiction, would distract the child from school study.

Mary Bean, who in 1890 was the first public librarian in the nation to open a children's room within the library, at Brookline, Massachusetts, had once feared the effect of too much reading on children's minds. In 1879 Bean had protested

> against the freedom which most of our public libraries afford for the daily supply and exchange of . . . books among school children. . . . One teacher said to me . . . that her greatest bane in school was library books, she having to maintain constant warfare against them . . . she had frequently wished that there was not a public library within fifty miles! . . . [T]his craze for books . . . leads to utter neglect of home as well as school duties.[8]

In this first spirited discussion of juvenile reading, at the ALA convention in 1879, librarians agreed that the library should issue young people no more than one work of fiction per week and that the popular "sensational" fiction for children should be eliminated entirely from the juvenile collection.[9]

Public librarians quickly discovered, however, that children, like adults, would not use the library unless it fed their appetite for exciting literature. The children's librarian was thus moved to provide ample amounts of "approved" fiction so as to counteract the effect of the "pernicious trash" that was readily available to youngsters outside the library walls at ten to twenty cents a novel. Minerva Sanders at Pawtucket, Rhode Island, who in 1877 was probably the first public librarian to allow children under twelve to use the books, had displayed in the 1870s a scrapbook filled with clippings that described how boys had been led to lives of crime by reading sensational fiction. She claimed that twenty minutes' perusal of the scrapbook was in most cases enough to cause her young patrons to give up entirely the reading of suspect novels.[10] But by the mid-1880s library leaders had decided that fiction was not really harmful to children and that the library should undertake an aggressive campaign only against certain "corruptive" juvenile books.

Throughout the 1890s women slowly evolved the essentials of library work with children — careful censorship, approved reading lists, separate rooms with small-scale tables and chairs, and a kindly maternal guidance designed to lead the child, unsuspecting, to a higher standard of reading. So important did children's work become in the feminized world of the public library that the first publication of the ALA Publishing Section was Caroline Hewins's *Books for the Young* in 1882; the first separate session established by the ALA was that of children's librarians, organized in 1900; and the first specialized training in librarianship was for children's librarians, begun in Pittsburgh in 1901. By the turn of the century, almost all public libraries loaned books to children as soon as they could read, and many libraries provided picture books for preschool children.[11]

In 1894 Mary Salome Cutler (later Fairchild) helped to awaken librarians to the need for social work with children:

> It is not enough for us to circulate books, or to circulate good books; we must in some way insure that the children and all those who need individual help get this

help in some way or other. If we as librarians cannot provide it as fully as we wish, we should co-operate with home libraries, with clubs and with various other agencies that can supply this personal element.[12]

At the turn of the century, she and other women library leaders developed the technique of "storytelling" as a dominant feature of work with children. Storytelling was touted as an effective method of Americanizing the foreigner, improving language, softening voices, teaching punctuality, and inculcating courtesy, honesty, neatness, industry, obedience, and gentle manners. It was also, rather incidentally, "the only means by which we can get the children to want the books 'we want them to want.' "[13]

From social reformers like Charles Birtwell, general secretary of the Children's Aid Society in Boston, public librarians borrowed the idea of the "home library," a collection of forty to fifty books for about ten children placed in tenement homes. Many of the early home libraries were located in settlement houses. The home visitor from the library, sometimes a librarian but very often a lady volunteer, went about once a week to meet with the children, not merely to exchange books and to discuss the reading, but to play games or to arrange outings, and just as importantly, to nurture children of low parentage and to spread her elevating influence over the home. The early children's librarians were repeatedly reminded that "it is a higher aim to help the boys and girls to be *good* than to be merely wise." Above all, children would learn from the lady librarian the "higher ideals of manhood and womanhood."[14] She could control, "if she will, their habits of thought, their personal cleanliness, the whole trend of character development."[15]

Birtwell attended the ALA meetings of 1891, 1894, and 1902, and the home-library movement quickly spread to major city libraries in the East and Midwest. In Pittsburgh the home-library supervisor expanded her work to include the formation of boys' clubs for the teen-age gangs in the poorer sections of the city. Even as late as 1924, long past the peak of library involvement with home-library work, the Pittsburgh Public Library still circulated over 3,000 books in home-library sets.[16] The Cleveland Public Library, typically following the example of other cities, established its first home library in 1902 and appointed a supervisor for the work in 1905. By 1911 there were over fifty home sets circulating among the foreign areas of Cleveland, and other sets were placed at the juvenile court, the children's detention homes, and the Boys' Farm outside the city. The children's librarians in Cleveland reported 3,352 home visits in 1913 alone.[17]

Librarians, by 1905, worked directly with social workers, charity agencies, and child-saving organizations in the large cities of the nation. In that year a study of "the public library and other allied agencies" in fourteen cities showed that in Baltimore, Brooklyn, Buffalo, Cleveland, Grand Rapids, New York City, and Pittsburgh close cooperation between children's librarians and social workers was a central feature of the library's service program.[18] In Buffalo, for example, two library branches operated within settlement houses, where 461 assistants sent out 10,500 books in one year. In Grand Rapids, women librarians in the settlement house organized clubs for children and mothers. In Cleveland, where library branches were established in three settlement houses, the librarians were also settlement residents who supervised the reading of recently paroled boys. Cora Stewart, a branch librarian in Boston, wrote in 1909 that in those Maine villages where there was no settlement house "the librarian there needs settlement training, for settlement work she must do, and do it alone."[19] The presidential address to the ALA in 1915 was a proud summation of the social work performed by librarians in almost every city in the nation. Librarians were employed in visiting families, making social and statistical surveys, working with factory girls and juvenile delinquents, and presiding over an amazing array of library-extension programs in their communities.[20] Much of the early library social work was in association with the sponsors of public playgrounds. In Chicago, New York, Hartford, Boston, Cleveland, St. Louis, and scores of other cities, librarians opened reading rooms in field houses and provided storytellers to the playgrounds.[21]

Thus, in order "to fulfill its purpose as a distributor of light and power," the public library eagerly established connections with "other agencies of enlightenment throughout the community."[22] Indeed, librarians feared that if they did not join in settlement-like activity they would be "deprived of popular approval and support."[23] Many public libraries added former kindergarten teachers or social workers to their staffs in order to enrich library service to recreation centers, churches, children's clubs, juvenile courts, parole officers, reform schools, the YMCA and YWCA, mothers' clubs, and businesses that employed large numbers of children.[24] In 1911 a survey revealed that the lives of approximately 1,035,195 children were being directly touched by the work of a woman from the public library, both inside and outside the library building.[25]

By 1914 most large public library systems had greatly expanded their branch stations. Before World War I branches were chiefly built in the poorer sections of the city, where the immigrant population was concentrated. Utilizing every technique of publicity they could envision, librarians sought to attract new readers with storytelling, clubs, contests, exhibits, and home visits. As soon as the branch doors were opened hundreds of children often came flooding in. It was a proud tradition at the Cleveland Broadway branch that after the first day of operation not a single book in the children's room was left on the shelves.[26] At many of the branch libraries children immediately became the largest part of the clientele. In 1913 the ALA estimated that children's books comprised about one-fifth of the nation's library collections and about one-third of the total circulation, but in the branches it was not uncommon for 90 per cent of the work or more to be with children.[27] In the first decade of the new century, service to 300 or even 600 children a day was typical in branch work, especially in the poorer sections of large cities.

With the expansion of children's services, the question of discipline in the library became important. Hordes of children, many of them foreign-born and unaccustomed to handling books or to conforming to middle-class standards of proper decorum, often posed a real problem of control in the children's room. The first mention of discipline in the library literature in 1901 revealed an almost universal use of policemen and janitors to keep order. Sometimes youngsters who violated library rules were arrested. More common was the practice of forbidding the use of the library to those children who stole or abused the books or refused to observe the rules of behavior. Children were commonly forced to wash their face and hands before being given access to the book collection. "Clean hearts, clean hands and clean minds" was the motto of the children's Library League at the Cleveland Public Library. Children's librarians also insisted on a careful collection of the fines, not to provide a source of library income, but to teach moral discipline to the young.[28]

Defense of public morality was maintained through the censorship of children's reading. At first, public librarians applied much the same standard of selection of juvenile books as they had originally used to censor adult literature. Idealistic literary standards persisted longer for children than for their parents, however, chiefly because the necessity to monitor the mind of the child was so generally accepted by the public at large. The first children's books to be derided and removed from library shelves were the popular series by Horatio Alger, Oliver Optic Castleman, and Martha Finley. Later the attack would widen to include the Bobbsey Twins, the Rover Boys, Tom Sawyer, and Huckleberry Finn.[29]

Contrary to what is commonly believed, Progressive critics were not the first to attack the books of Horatio Alger. Algerism was repudiated during the Victorian period itself, and not by the left, but by the genteel elements of the middle class, as is evidenced by the anti-Alger reaction centered in the public library. Librarians responded to the get-ahead gospel by questioning the materialistic values of Alger readers and by favoring the gradual, earned path to success taken by a natural aristocracy of morality, learning, and sobriety. The Alger hero's meteoric rise to fortune through reliance upon luck was criticized as distracting children from this slow, merited process of achievement. Alger readers, it was felt, became unfitted for the practical, hard realities of life; they were always waiting "for some great and unexpected turn of fortune which will place them beyond their present surroundings in some lofty imagined sphere." Librarians objected to any encouragement of the selfish aim to "get rich quick."

> Unless we hold that the attempt to evade a two cent fine for an overdue book is of a piece with the lack of honor which prompts the older person to make all he can at the expense of people less sharp than himself; unless we realize that our children

are absorbing from the very air today the false and debasing idea that "success" means "making money;" . . . we shall not be the nursery of good citizenship we are meant to be.[30]

Public librarians also attacked the Alger books and certain other children's series because the overweening self-reliance of the young heroes and heroines threatened family discipline and social order. S. S. Green feared those juvenile books which left "the impression upon the minds of the young that they can get along by themselves without the support and guidance of parents and friends."[31] Librarians sought stories of "happy, sunny childhood in sheltered homes, of simple country pleasures, or home life in cities where the father and mother rule the household gently but firmly and the children do not decide important questions for themselves."[32] The innocuous stories of Pollyanna and the books of the Elsie Dinsmore series were banned by libraries, for example, because these heroines attempted to "improve adults." No book was to be allowed into the children's library that represented any authority in an unenviable light. Librarians believed that the immigrant child, especially, should be given books in which the paternal figure was sympathetically presented and inevitably obeyed: "We cannot boast of too much reverence or respect for authorities in a modern child . . . for the distance between the foreign-born fathers and their American-born sons is unfortunately growing greater every day."[33]

Just as boys were to be denied fiction that led them to feel discontent with meager salaries or a soberly traditional life-style, so should girls be forbidden books that encouraged them to break away from domesticity. The influential child-study expert George Stanley Hall spoke to the librarians in convention several times and cautioned that the young girl, like her older sisters and mother, should not be given books that caused her to desire more money or to "make excessive and impossible demands" that would "crowd her life with discontent." Girls' books must be "calculated to fit them for domestic life or womanly vocations of any kind," Hall warned.[34] Librarian Caroline Burnite, a pioneer in children's work, denounced the books for girls that fed their "desire for freedom from home restraints." Because this perverse wish led girls to like boarding-school stories, Burnite advised librarians to choose a boarding-school book that had "no warmth of life in the school atmosphere, and in which the heroine gets most fearfully homesick." Children's librarians were early agreed, then, that the basis for judgment of juvenile reading was "first the ethical," secondly the character of the personages portrayed, and only after these the book's literary worth or style.[35]

If one can judge by the crisis atmosphere apparent in the discussion of children's reading at the ALA's annual meetings of children's librarians, it is evident that most parents and children did not share the literary standards applied by the public library. The librarian at the Dayton, Ohio, public library reported in 1914 that her careful investigation had shown that less

than one-third of the schoolchildren in Dayton used the public library and
that the other two-thirds

> wriggled and squirmed and waved their hands in the air in the hotness of their
> desire to tell me how many dozens of books they had read, how many complete
> series they owned, and how much the library missed by not having these same
> series, which were of a "swellness" that beggared description. In fact, they made it
> very clear to me that in the matter of choosing between the "swell" authors and the
> "punk" ones the library often strangely and perversely inclined toward
> "punkness."[36]

This was why the one-third of Dayton children who did use library books supplemented their reading by buying and borrowing forbidden literature, and
"this was why, no doubt, the other two-thirds never came [to the library] at
all."[37]

Faced with such realities, children's librarians were forced to relax their
moral standards. The losing battle fought to control adult reading between
about 1876 and 1910 was repeated with little variation in the field of
children's literature from about 1890 to 1915. First the librarians found it
necessary to cater to the taste for books of new fiction rather than to supply
the nonfiction and the great classics they really preferred children to read.
Next it was decided appropriate to offer "mediocre" fiction as a bait to attract the uncultured and to serve as "stepping stones upward" to a better class
of reading. By 1916 the exhausted (or wiser) defenders of library morality
made no protest when a New Jersey librarian suggested that "after all, the
difficulties are in the high standards of the libraries themselves. . . . I am
told [that] Alger, and some of the others that we read, must be thrown out,
but I don't believe it is fully justified; they are entertaining" and immensely
popular. Two other speakers, perhaps emboldened by his protest, immediately arose and confessed that they, too, stocked Alger and other questionable series, and, heresy of heresies, failed to "really find that they do
much harm."*

The particular twist given to the early child-saving rhetoric in the public
library is best understood not just as an extension of women's homemaking
role into the community but also as an attempt to teach respectable morality
to the newly literate masses. Juvenile literature of a bad sort was seen as a
"fingerpoint looking toward a change in national character from the conservatism of older days to a restlessness and spirit of adventure, a disregard of
the rights of others and the settled relations of life, that are communistic and
revolutionary in their tendency."[38] Mellen Chamberlain admitted it seemed
useless to ask children to be sober moderates when all society seemed to be

---

*In 1910 an Iowa librarian confessed to her mentor at the University of Illinois Library School
that, even though "Miss Lyman [at the library school] would not approve," she had been
handing out "Alger and Ellis and Henty . . . to some very happy and often ragged little
urchins, who had better be reading these than doing nothing downtown." (Alumni Files,
University of Illinois Library School, Urbana, Ill.)

running riot. But "we may hope to change the present aspect of things; and, with this inspiring prospect, that when we have changed the habits of the readers of our public libraries, we shall also have changed the habits of society itself."[39] In his presidential address of 1905, E. C. Richardson told the ALA that "in view of the fact that in the work of assimilating the foreign immigration, we can never hope to make great progress with the adult, but must of necessity rely on beginning work with children, the importance of [children's] work in our national problem of Americanizing our immigrants can hardly be overestimated."[40]

By the turn of the century many public librarians had tired of their highly unsuccessful attempt to direct the reading habits of their adult patrons. Adults, it was generally agreed, were impossibly set in their reading tastes, and were besides notoriously intolerant of any well-meant efforts to raise their literary standards. Children, on the other hand, could be trained to appreciate the "best," and in the children's room there was little protest from the small clients over library censorship of reading.

The responsibilities that librarians had claimed as moral guides were channeled by 1900 almost entirely into the care of the minds of underage Americans. The children's room was

> the one work of the library where we can see results. . . . It is almost the only work that gives us real encouragement to go on with the detail, the everlasting round of duty, maintaining the public library and hoping for its influence on humanity. . . . We have an axiom that we cannot help an adult very much about his reading; but the child, we are certainly forming like clay in the hands of the potter.[41]

What kept the children's librarian laboring "day in and day out with crowds of children trying to see that they put their books back after reading them, that their hands are clean, and that they do not talk" was the knowledge that she was an agent to counteract the "coarsening effect of promiscuous living in crowded tenements, the narrow range of ideas which life in the city creates and the criminal tendencies." Her special mission was to "create an illusory home" for the deprived child.[42]

Yet the librarian, forced to *inhibit* childish activity, could only judge her influence by small outward signs such as improvement in a child's manners or cleanliness. Miss Underhill, of the Brooklyn Public Library, related the wonderful way in which parents could be influenced by their children who had come in contact with the gentle librarian. For example, one Rebecca, after reading several books, had begged her mother to buy a tablecloth. Another child had taken home a cookbook, thus giving a distinct elevation to the family standard of dining. When "the 'Iliad' and the 'Odyssey' fill the mind of Joe Ginsburg . . . when Esther Lichtenstein . . . reads Dickens and Scott, we know that without their realizing it they are getting ideas of chivalry, courtesy and courage that are fitting them to be wholesome units of society."[43] Thus, through the child, the elusive adult could be indirectly influenced — a situation that reforming lady librarians, kindergarten teachers, temperance workers, and settlement residents all recognized at about the same time.

If much of the work with children was overly sentimental and excessively controlling, still the lives of thousands of immigrant children who were introduced to books through the American public library system were enriched by the experience. Many foreign observers have recorded their amazement and admiration concerning the work done in children's rooms during this period. The interest of librarians also had a national influence upon the formation and development of higher literary standards in children's books.[44] It was well known, too, that immigrant parents and working siblings often sent the children of the family to the library to select books for the adults at home.

The work supervised by Anne Moore at the New York Public Library was a model of service to children. Liberal, humanitarian, warmhearted, imaginative, Moore was a dynamic and democratically minded woman who inspired children's librarians and expanded the experiences of many children for whom books became a joyous and vital concern. She loved children without affectation, treated them as equals, and did her utmost to instill ethnic pride into the young immigrants who frequented the New York libraries. Under her direction the children's department developed well-chosen collections and trained assistants, as well as clubs, festivals, exhibits, and story-hours. Appointed as supervisor of children's rooms in 1906, Moore had phenomenal energy and administrative ability that made children's work in New York a specialty famous all over the world.[45]

Any attitude of bemused wonder at the excessive prudery of the lady librarians' child-saving work in the Progressive period must be balanced by a recognition of the beneficial effect of their activity, to which many children, grown to adults, have later gratefully testified. Especially is this true of the Jewish youngsters, whose cultural heritage prepared them to cherish books and learning. More than any other immigrant group they made delighted and serious use of everything the library had to offer, a situation repeatedly remarked upon and lauded by the librarians.[46]

Actually, a reaction against the prim standards of the children's department and the library's concentration on children's service had begun as early as 1905, when criticism of the effects of feminization upon the public library became an issue among some librarians. An article that year in *The Independent* classed the library as a mere "municipal amusement," which served only housewives and children with a taste for the latest fiction and was presided over by fussy women who did not know how to select proper books for male patrons of any age. As a result adult males had deserted the public library, for "the men have come to think there is nothing in the library for them, and . . . they are usually right in thinking so."[47] The debate within the profession over sentimental and female-oriented library service continued for several years.[48]

Certainly the emphasis upon the child was overdone in the first years of the century, as women librarians waxed ecstatic over their newly discovered social mission to the nation's young. Caroline Matthews, a member of the Examining Committee at the Boston Public Library, found the atmosphere in many children's rooms "a horror . . . intellectually, physically, morally." She saw "no corresponding effort made to reach the adult . . . the young mechanic, to draw to the library the parent. I at times wonder whether the librarians . . . are even aware that exaggerated leaning toward one phase of library work must throw out of true the work as a whole."[49] E. L. Pearson, in a widely discussed article, ridiculed the children's librarians whose notion of propriety banished *The Adventures of Tom Sawyer, The Adventures of Huckleberry Finn,* and the works of Rudyard Kipling on the ground that these books "glorified mischief" and were "irreverent toward sacred things and Sunday-schools." He charged that one by one public libraries were "putting up the little dimity curtains of Extreme Respectability" and handing out books to "a set of little goody-goodies."[50]

It was left to John Dana to smite that almost-sacred activity, the story-hour. Storytelling, he said, was "so slight a factor in the education work of a town or city as to make the library's pride over its work seem very ludicrous." In the children's room, Dana believed, "library motherhood" had created "a very perceptible atmosphere of religious devotion, almost of fanaticism."[51] The "altruistic, emotional, dramatic, and irrepressible child-lovers" in the storytelling corps wasted the library's time, money, space, and energy, he argued.[52] At about this same time a new emphasis upon technical service to industry and business began to build among librarians. By World War I library service to children had boiled down to more normal and modern proportions.

Perhaps Clara Hunt in 1913 summed up best the remarkable growth and value of library work with children without ignoring its defects. She admitted that children's librarians had taken many knocks, mostly deserved, from spectators of the sterner sex who were worried about the feminization of the library and who declared that no unmarried woman could possibly understand the needs of young boys. "We know that some women are sentimental. . . . [H]owever, . . . [t]he influence of the children's libraries upon the ideals, the tastes, the occupations, the amusements, the language, the manners, the home standards, the choice of careers, upon the whole life, in fact, of thousands of boys and girls has been beyond all count . . . a civic force in America."[53] With this statement many American children would agree, for they had discovered children's books in all languages and met the staff of solicitous spinsters, who, although they seemed perhaps a little old-fashioned and moralistic, were nonetheless eager to entertain and delight them with books, festivals, parties, and storytelling.

Just as the exhilaration over children's services began to wane, the public library turned its attention to a new social crusade—the Americanization of the adult immigrant. The first response of the *Library Journal* in 1894 had been to deny the validity of providing books in their own language to foreign patrons, on the grounds that this would encourage a "polyglot literature," serve "as a most effective factor in maintaining . . . barriers of race and language," and be "prejudicial to [American] unity of sentiment and tradition."[54] The *Journal's* stance represented a rare misreading of the general mood of the profession. Within a few years it reversed its stand and supported the effort to reach foreigners through books in their own language. Reluctantly begun at first, the advancement of library service to the foreign population was no doubt enhanced by its initial success (it was tentatively tried in the Midwest in the 1890s) in attracting that hard-to-grasp creature, the adult male, to the public library. Although the professed basic mission of the public library movement from its inception had been to provide educational reading to the working class, the library did not in fact attract many male laborers until it began to stock foreign-language materials.

The volume of work done with immigrants varied greatly around the country and was centered, of course, in the largest cities. By 1913 one-tenth of the total holdings of the New York Public Library were printed in twenty-five foreign languages. The circulation department advertised its foreign wares in booklists, circulars, and posters written in foreign languages and distributed them to settlement houses, churches, schools, and business places. The library at Mt. Vernon, New York, typically offered public library service tailored to the needs of the community's specific ethnic groups. It gave lectures on American life in Italian; published an "immigrant's guide" in Italian, Polish, and Yiddish; and provided ethnic musical events in its building to attract readers. For its Italian patrons the library purchased classics in Italian, as well as French, Russian, and English novels in Italian translation. (For those Italians who were judged to be prone to abuse the books, the librarian produced a copy of the immigrants' guide that had been borrowed once and returned in such a bad condition it could not be sent out again and then compared this to a copy of Dante, printed in 1529, which was still white and clean.) The Passaic, New Jersey, library boasted of being the first library in the East to circulate books in eleven languages. The year it put in 500 foreign-language books circulation dramatically increased by 22 per cent. John Dana's library in Newark, New Jersey, chose to concentrate on the provision of foreign newspapers instead of the classics. Numerous libraries in

California, Massachusetts, New Jersey, Pennsylvania, and New York held night classes for instruction in English. In St. Louis in 1919 the immigrant who applied for naturalization papers was given a card of introduction to the public librarian and directed to the nearest branch. An ALA committee on work with the foreign-born was commissioned in 1918 to coordinate information on "desirable methods of assisting in the education of the foreign born in American ideals and customs and the English language." In 1920 a library survey showed that 800 public libraries were extremely active in immigrant work and that 300 more were in the process of expanding their programs.[55]

Still, despite all the recorded activity of the public library in work with adult foreigners it is important to remember that the direct contribution of the public librarian to the reading of adult immigrants was relatively minor. One might conclude that the library's traditional paternalism toward the laboring masses proved as offensive to most foreign adults as it did to native workers. While the public library made an important impact upon many immigrant children, work with immigrant adults was necessarily limited. In fact, few workingmen had either the energy or interest for reading library books — partly because of the long work hours against which labor was protesting.[56]

In library literature of the 1890s there is an unmistakable sense of queasiness about the immigrant adult, as well as an undertone of condescension. Articles appeared which assured librarians that association with foreign-speaking men would cause them to revise their judgments of the immigrant male, while the refining influence of the library would act favorably upon the alien.[57] By 1900, however, the tone of library literature noticeably changed. As Phyllis Dain has pointed out in her study of the New York Public Library, the librarian began to demonstrate more real compassion, understanding, and respect for the struggling immigrant, through daily contact with immigrant life.[58]

Librarians reacted with joy when they discovered that the immigrants possessed a rich culture by way of inheritance. The average native American, as the librarians had learned to their regret, had little interest in the products of high European culture; yet the Italian laborer loved Dante, New York's library circulation of classics was highest on the Jewish East Side, and Russian construction workers knew Gregorian chants by heart! Mary Antin, author of *The Promised Land*, received a standing ovation at the 1913 ALA convention when she pointed out the thoroughly unAmerican respect for classical literature characteristic of so many of the immigrant class.[59] By the mid-1920s, when the library's Americanization attempt reached its peak, the public librarians who were active in urban work with immigrants, like most settlement workers, tended to speak in favor of a rich cultural pluralism in American life, in contrast to those who sought to create a "melting pot" to mold immigrants into a homogenous mass.

The concentration on community social work that had characterized progressive library administration in the first years of the century was overshadowed by the new responsibilities the public library assumed in response to the coming of World War I. Prior to the war, librarian Burton E. Stevenson said, the ALA had been "merely a humdrum professional organization, wrapped round with tradition, settled in its habits of thought. . . . Its members were quiet, inoffensive, well-behaved people, cherishing the same hobby and agreeing upon everything except whether a large circulation was a merit or disgrace."[60] In 1917, however, the ALA was launched into unprecedented activity and a new self-importance.

In league with other service organizations, the ALA took as its task the provision of reading material to American troops. By 1920 the library association had organized a national campaign to raise $5 million and had distributed 10 million books and magazines to American military men at home and overseas. The war effort was organized and managed by the Library War Service of the ALA, formed in October 1917 under the direction of Herbert Putnam, Librarian of Congress.

Library chiefs excitedly awoke to their new mission, anticipating that the value of their war activity would at last bring the public library the recognition it deserved as the capstone of the nation's educational system. In the summer of 1917 the War Service Committee of the ALA summoned librarians to enlist in the new effort: "If we succeed in this emergency in rendering national service, libraries are going to be a national and community force as never before." But, if the libraries failed, the committee warned, they would be "looked on as weak, dreary, go-sit-in-the-corner affairs that are not worth public support."[61]

One reason why librarians greeted war service with such enthusiasm was because they were so delighted to be serving in numbers, at last, the elusive male. The heavy demand by American soldiers for library books seemed to indicate that the tide had turned; that the new male patrons, having formed the reading habit, would continue to use the library on the same scale in the postwar era. It was not until the early 1920s that librarians realized that this hope would prove to be unfounded.

Because the Library War Service was generally directed and created by men, the male library leaders, already sensitive to their position within a feminized profession, especially welcomed the new horde of masculine readers. It seemed that more than the future role of the library was at stake. There was also an expressed hope that greater use of the public library by the male population would in itself serve to increase the prestige and professional status of the librarian.

This present movement is the opportunity for which we have been waiting. It is an opportunity to demonstrate to the MEN of America — both those in military service and those in the higher circles of governmental activities — that library work is a profession; that we librarians are in this work because it offers expression to our ideals. . . . It is an opportunity for all of us to participate in such a way that we can carry ourselves a little straighter and hold our heads a little higher, with the pride that comes from knowing that an increasing number of people believe in us and our work.[62]

True to their heritage as moral guardians, librarians were thrilled to learn that the soldiers' reading habits did not parallel the taste of most public library patrons in the past. The ALA's first list of approved books for libraries in military camps contained 58 per cent fiction. The surprising discovery that the men wished to read more nonfiction — chiefly technical and vocational literature — was happily noted by the national association. The *War Library Bulletin* printed dozens of accounts of librarians who testified not only to the popularity of library books among the soldiers but also to the generally "higher" level of reading among military men.[63]

The American public library's traditional assumption of moral guidance was also revealed by its collaboration in the excessive wartime censorship of this period, a policy held in common with most public institutions of the time. In a widely disseminated 1918 article, librarians were told that the public library was "itself in this war against Germany. To be neutral now is disloyal." Much publicity was given to the advice of the law librarian at Columbia University that under the Espionage Act of 1917 libraries could be prosecuted for sending "treasonable" literature through the mails. Wellington House, the English secret propaganda agency, sent hundreds of books to American public libraries disguised as gifts from British professors. A study of the collections of ten large public libraries revealed that from 1914 to 1918 they held only about 9 per cent of the pro-German propaganda titles cited in Harold D. Lasswell's *Propaganda Technique in the World War*, while they stocked about 47 per cent of the pro-Allied titles. Unlike John Dana, the great majority of American librarians did not risk a stand against wartime propaganda and censorship, for fear of losing public support.[64]

Beginning in the summer of 1918, the War Department issued orders to the ALA that forbade the stocking of certain books in the camp libraries. Despite the military's instructions to the Library War Service not to publicize the list of forbidden books, the War Department action was exposed in several newspapers. Although press reaction was generally favorable to the list of banned books, some newspapers denounced library censorship.

In peacedays our national literature was puritanized and mollycoddled practically out of existence by the Comstockery of the post office department and the public libraries. . . . In an American city one can go across the street and buy or order a book that the public library has refused to furnish. In military camps no such opportunity is open. . . . A man . . . has a right to choose his own reading material.[65]

Among the banned authors were Mary Baker Eddy, Ambrose Bierce, Max Eastman, Alexander Berkman, Leon Trotsky, and David Graham Phillips. In December 1918, shortly after the end of hostilities, the secretary of war rescinded the censorship policy. The ALA Library War Service nevertheless continued to recommend the destruction of doubtful books until as late as April 1919.

Throughout the war years, library literature strongly defended library censorship. Indeed, most public librarians had on their own initiative removed "improper" books from general circulation as soon as war began. This policy of banning certain books of nonfiction was a new development in American library history. Although the public library had long been concerned with the control of fiction, the years of World War I mark the first time in which librarians practiced widespread and serious censorship of nonfiction material.

Another change came out of the war experience. Long an exploited majority within the profession, library women suddenly became more assertive and demanded equality with male librarians. The controversy centered around the exclusion of female librarians from service in the camp libraries in the United States. Beatrice Winser, Dana's assistant and longtime friend at the Newark Public Library, wrote directly to Secretary of War Newton Baker in February 1918. She asked why women worked in camp hospitals and in hostess houses but were not allowed to serve as paid staff members in camp libraries.[66] When Baker passed her letter on to the Library War Service, Herbert Putnam replied to her that women had been barred from camp libraries by the War Department. Actually, there was no such federal directive in force.

Winser accused the Library War Service of "deceitfully" stating that it was the War Department which was responsible for the exclusion of women from camp libraries. She challenged Putnam to produce a document proving that such a regulation existed.

> I gather that . . . you chose to assume that women were not fitted as well for this service and that, as chairman, you ruled women out. . . . The fundamental mistake made by you, Dr. Putnam, . . . seems to have been the usual one of thinking that men are better qualified than women for work in the world. . . . Let us not forget that women form a half of all democracies.[67]

In the summer of 1918, women at the annual ALA convention made speech after speech defending women's abilities and petitioned the ALA's War Service Committee to announce an official policy regarding the presence of women in camp libraries. Putnam professed to welcome "the *manly* expressions" the discussions had provoked.[68] The women's protest brought results. By the next summer, women headed eight camp libraries and held most of the top positions at the headquarters of the Library War Service.[69]

Exhilarated by the war experience, an influential group of library leaders developed an ambitious plan to continue expansion of library service into the postwar era.[70] The proposed Enlarged Program, later retitled Books for Everybody, was designed to extend library service to 6 million rural Americans, to aid in the building of citizenship and patriotism, and to foster general adult education through self-study courses. A major survey of the role of libraries in the educational life of the nation was also envisioned. The Enlarged Program was to be financed by a fund of $2 million, obtained from foundations and general subscriptions. As the "Red scare" swept the country, publicity for the Enlarged Program emphasized the role that the library could play in combatting bolshevism among immigrant groups. The extensive press coverage given to the Enlarged Program in early 1920 did not mention the growing opposition within the ALA to this grandiose dream of library expansion.

A large group within the ALA was not willing to undertake new responsibilities of this magnitude. In November 1920 the ALA Executive Board was forced to terminate the fund drive for lack of support. Despite the intense efforts of important library leaders, only a little over $50,000 had been collected. For the supporters of the Enlarged Program, it was a humiliating defeat. Acute staff shortages, the temporary recession, and postwar weariness contributed to the reluctance of most librarians to commit themselves to the new undertaking. But the repudiation of the Enlarged Program was also an indication that the public library had lost much of its original institutional purpose. In 1920, the American public library was suffering a period of stagnation and uncertainty.

Although the Progressive years marked a peak of socially sensitive librarianship, there is an overlay of failure upon success, decline upon climax, during this period of public library involvement in community service. Between 1900 and 1920 the public library enriched reference service; developed branch library work; greatly expanded library service to children, immigrants, and adults; established facilities for use as social centers; and successfully organized a large-scale distribution of books to military men. The new forms of activity manifested in the Progressive period unquestionably served to democratize both the librarian and the library collection. But these years were also a period of deteriorating pay scales, low morale, and protoprofessionalism for the librarian. By 1920 the public library had assumed much of its modern form. The early vision of the public library as an intellectual center and of the librarian as a major educational figure in the community was unrealized. The public library survived as a peripheral cultural and intellectual institution, chiefly providing light fiction to middle-class women and children, encased in an image of genteel traditionalism, ineffectual males, and shushing spinsters. How can this development best be explained?

Part of the answer lies in the recognition of a prime motivation behind the funding and staffing of public libraries. To a large degree, the founding of public libraries was an urban reform movement of moral uplift, initiated by elements of the middle and upper classes and intended to promote social stability through the weakening of class conflict. The last decades of the nineteenth century were years of social turmoil as Americans experienced far-ranging economic and technological change and were forced to accommodate their traditional institutions and attitudes to fit the new conditions of an urban-industrial nation. Especially during the 1890s, farmer and worker protest—set against a background of economic depression and increased immigration—had shaken the social order. In response to social tensions, library leaders consistently billed their institution as an effective agency to reduce the supposed assault of mass action and economic radicalism upon democratic principles. The use of the public library, it was assumed, would aid in the conquest of crime and poverty through the Americanization of aliens. The reading of library books would increase educational and vocational opportunities for the native workers, as well as for the unassimilated immigrants in the cities. Properly instructed workers and voters, in turn, would be supportive of the existing legal, economic, and political structures.

Through the Progressive years librarians continued to focus upon the political benefits of public library use, promising that access to library books would increase upward economic and social mobility and disseminate middle-class ideals among the uneducated and overexploited. Despite the fact that the public library had never attracted a significant number of working-class males, librarians again and again asserted their faith that the educational opportunities it provided would encourage workers "not to envy millionaires."[71] Once knowledge from the public library was obtained, all classes of patrons could be brought to mutual and harmonious appreciation of each other.

After World War I, supporters of the Enlarged Program once more assured the public that expanded library service would weaken the appeal of socialist doctrines from abroad. The lukewarm response to the plan is an indication of just how much of its raison d'être the public library had lost by 1920. Progressive reforms, the growth of welfare organizations, immigration controls, and long-term material prosperity, as well as government and private repression, had served to quiet class fears and to lessen economic conflict between employers and workers.

The hope that the library would function as a conservative defense in an unsettled era is reflected in the growth and financing of public libraries during the period under consideration. The explosive growth of tax-supported public libraries in towns and cities was almost entirely a result of the efforts of the well-off and educated native citizens in these communities. Many public libraries owed their existence to the organizational work of associations of leisured women. In 1876 there were 188 public libraries in the nation. By 1896 there were 971 public libraries, each holding 1,000 volumes or more. In 1903 the number of public libraries of this size had grown to 2,283; and in 1913 to 3,562.

Much of this growth was dependent upon the support of wealthy donors. During the years from 1880 to 1899, $36 million was contributed to libraries, primarily by manufacturers, merchants, and politicians who had formerly been lawyers.[72] Andrew Carnegie, alone, between 1886 and 1917 gave a total of $41 million to the construction of public libraries in 1,420 towns and cities. By 1917 the growth of public libraries had considerably slowed. In that year the Carnegie Foundation declined to make further grants to nine states because so many communities in those states had failed to give their Carnegie-built libraries the promised tax support. Carnegie completely ended his gifts for library buildings in November 1917 after an investigation showed that lack of interest, rather than lack of money, was the reason for this feeble community support.

The need for the public library to function as a social stabilizer was also weakened because other agencies—the public schools, universities, special libraries, the mass media—assumed many of the educational and recreational services that the public library had sought to perform. The educational revolution of the nineteenth century established a national system of public schooling, modernized the university curriculum, and professionalized teaching. The enrollment in public schools doubled between 1870 and 1900. In 1860 there were about 300 public high schools; by 1900 the number had jumped to almost 6,000. With a highly developed and relatively well financed educational system in existence, the need for the library to serve as "the people's university" was less compelling. The public library was also bypassed by the special-library movement, which mushroomed after 1909 to serve the specialized interests of various groups of businessmen and professionals. Meanwhile, new forms of mass entertainment—especially movies, sports events, and popular magazines—consumed more of people's recreational time. The popularity of library books suffered accordingly.

Stripped of much of its older mission, the public library contracted to its essential core: a generalist collection of books, chiefly fiction, read by middle-class patrons, chiefly female. Appended to this center in the Progressive period, however, was the service to children developed by library women. The juvenile department became a major component of public library work, partly because women dominated librarianship in numbers and partly because library leaders, discouraged by their failure to shape the reading tastes of adults, turned to library service to children as one of the best means of guiding the minds and morals of the future citizenry.

The public library's assumed mission of cultural uplift was long in dying. The nineteenth-century librarian's attempt to counteract the popularity of literary realism—especially as the new mass literature addressed changes in sexual morality and in women's status—was never very successful. In order to attract patrons, the public library was moved to provide whatever bestsellers its readers demanded. As the genteel tradition in literature tottered and collapsed, the conflict between the censorship and the consumership models of the public library was decided: By 1920 the demand of women readers for modern fiction had clearly prevailed.

Still, the historical mission of the public librarian as genteel guardian persisted in its effects upon library use. Although there are other reasons to explain the reluctance of the working-class male to use the library, the conservative middle-class milieu of the library must be given its due. Nevertheless, long after it became clear that the laborer did not thirst for either serious fiction or for technical and scientific information from the public library, the myth continued that he did. Not until well into the twentieth century did public librarians openly admit their inability to attract male readers of any class in significant numbers.

The genteel beginnings of the public library lingered on in the popular image of public librarians as bespectacled, unmarried women intent upon upholding middle-class proprieties and enforcing iron-clad rules—"muffled, muted souls with little of the vital elements of life."[73] The spinster librarian was a well-defined figure in American literature by 1900, usually presented as a comic creature whose anachronistic beliefs seemed strangely unrelated to reality. In this connection it is interesting to note that librarians as a group were perhaps more committed to conventional standards of behavior in the Progressive period than were other groups of professional women. Of a sample of 879 women in *Woman's Who's Who in America, 1914–1915,* the librarian ranked at the bottom of the list among occupational groups of women who favored the equal rights movement at the turn of the century. Only 6 per cent of the listed librarians supported the battle for women's suffrage.[74]

Yet, although the image of the convention-bound librarian persisted in the public mind, the decline and eventual disappearance of the genteel library hostess was already distressingly apparent to many librarians by 1920. This decline was not so much a result of vulgarization of reading materials, as some claimed, or even of feminization, as others thought. The decline of the genteel library hostess was a product of changes taking place outside the library walls—changes that profoundly affected the world of women.

15

The Decline of the
Genteel Library Hostess

By 1900 EMPLOYMENT OPPORTUNITIES for middle-class women had greatly expanded. The college-educated or intellectually inclined women who had
once chosen a career in library service became increasingly reluctant to accept the low wages and prestige accorded to librarians. Librarians, by 1912,
were commonly recognized to receive less pay than teachers and to have
longer working hours.[1] Meanwhile, social work in the cities had become an
idealized mission for ambitious spinsters; women welfare workers trebled in
number between 1910 and 1920.[2] A Minneapolis survey in 1918 revealed that
42.6 per cent of librarians received less than $900 annually, whereas only
29.3 per cent of social workers and 17.2 per cent of teachers did so. Almost
10 per cent of social workers earned over $2,100 per year, in contrast to one
per cent of librarians.* In the 1870s and 1880s, societal prejudices had led
many women to shrink from work in the competitive business world. By 1920
the expanding fields of journalism, clerical work, and sales work offered new
and relatively well paid jobs to middle-class women.[3] In 1917 the graduates
of Pratt Institute Library School who entered library employment received
an annual wage of $845. Those graduates who began business or government
careers could expect to earn an average yearly salary of $1,177.[4] A vicious cy-
cle was thus established by the 1920s. The nature of library work did not attract men, and salaries remained low because they were paid to women.

*Perhaps some of the salary differential can be traced to the difference in rate of feminization.
By 1920 women numbered 88 per cent of librarians, whereas women social workers composed
only 52 per cent of their profession in 1910 and 62 per cent in 1920. Also see Elizabeth Kemper,
Women Professional Workers (New York: Adams, Macmillan Company, 1921), 180–87,
362–64.

In the first decades of the new century the majority of women library workers were employed as assistants. In library literature between 1900 and 1920 there is abundant evidence of the dissatisfaction of head librarians with their staffs. References to assistants are singularly carping in nature. There is frequent mention of the staff's distressing lack of intelligence, accuracy, education, efficiency, motivation, and amiability. Assistants in turn, in their rare appearances in print, seem to be equally resentful of their low prestige, inadequate salary, and monotonous work.

This growing tension in the library field is an important indication of the changing nature of women's opportunities in the working world. As a living wage became available to middle-class women in other fields, the quality of library workers slowly declined. The head librarian was increasingly forced to recruit women assistants with inadequate preliminary education, many of whom were very young or intellectually unsuited to the work. Library employment across the nation became, for most women, temporary work between graduation from the public school and marriage. The *Library Journal* held the dubious distinction of being probably the only professional journal in the country that ran a regular "marriage column."[5]

Because so much of the assistant's work was strictly routine monotony, a constant effort was necessary to incite enthusiasm for the job. Arthur Bostwick claimed that catalogue filing, pasting labels, and addressing postcards had high professional implications. "A label pasted awry may ruin the library's reputation . . . ; a mis-sent card may cause trouble to dozens of one's fellow assistants. Routine work is dull only when one does not understand it[s] purport."[6] The vice-director of Pratt Institute Library School told her students in 1916:

> We won't keep doing monotonous things over and over in a mechanical way because we will find some way to make them interesting and to get benefit or pleasure from them. If mending books be your task you will gain expertness, find out new and better ways of saving the lives of the books and at the same time increase your . . . familiarity with authors and titles, and by seeing what books are the most worn, you can get an impression of the popularity of certain authors and certain subjects.[7]

Much of the romantic rhetoric and messianic fervor of the library literature of this period can be traced to the overwhelming presence of women in librarianship. And much can be attributed to the necessity of inspiring these women to continue altruistic service as technicians performing underpaid tasks, without protest or resentment. Once again, as in the nineteenth century, library workers were assured by their leaders that women were peculiarly fitted by biology for sacrificial devotion to librarianship, regardless of personal discomforts or material needs. Although some librarians, male and female, commented that women were partly to blame for their low pay because they "systematically put a low value on

. . . [their] own services,"[8] a more common response to the salary situation was a plea for library workers to recognize their duty as women. The assistant who could maintain a belief in library missionary work was "well on the road toward the real compensation . . . which can never be measured by salary scales. She knows something of that satisfaction which comes of being needed and used."[9]

Yet oratory designed to raise the performance of assistants by a revival of idealism was only moderately successful. The desk assistant in the first decades of the twentieth century worked, on an average, forty-two to fifty hours a week for a salary of $45 to $50 a month. An anonymous assistant expressed a common attitude in 1902 when she complained that it was "practically absurd" for the librarian to lay so much stress "upon the 'spirit of the work' which he feels should be so ardent and zealous as to rise above all considerations of salaries and hours, and to make the assistant feel that sufficient for her work is the joy of doing it."[10]

Even the college-educated woman librarian was a source of concern to some library leaders. Speaking to the graduating class of women at Simmons College in 1912, Librarian of Congress Herbert Putnam frankly acknowledged the discrimination women librarians would face in professional life. Women would suffer in the library world, he said, because they lacked "the superior traits of men" — specifically, "manliness" and "a sense of proportion." Fortunately women could develop these traits, Putnam believed. The most debilitating of women's faults, in his opinion, was the tendency to "peevishness," to ascribe sinister personal motives to official actions that affected them unfavorably. Moreover, women were hampered in business and the professions because they became too absorbed in small details and lacked initiative. Still, women's special talents — devotion, loyalty, and a disposition to regard "the personal and domestic virtues as of the utmost concern" — were also needed in the working world. And whereas these latter traits "do not lead to promotion, they at least assure preference in the positions which are subordinate," Putnam noted with wholly unconscious irony.* In 1916 Putnam again spoke of women's biologically ordained talent for detailed, repetitive work, asserting that women librarians are "not merely supplementary to . . . men; they are absolutely complementary. . . . The lack in men of the qualities characteristic of women, can never be made good enough except through the auxiliary co-operation of women themselves."[11] Apparently his chiefly female audience, representative of almost 88 per cent of the profession, saw little incongruity in their "auxiliary" relationship to the other 12 per cent.

*Herbert Putnam, "The Prospect," *LJ* 37 (1912), 651–58. Recognition of the "feminine" traits which hampered professional excellence was by no means limited to male librarians. See Louise Connolly, "Women as Employees," *Public Libraries* 19 (May 1914), 196. Simmons College, an outgrowth of the vocational training at the Women's Educational and Industrial Union at Boston, was one of the first schools in the East to concentrate on training for the new women's professions of librarianship and social work.

Nor was much respect given to library workers by the educators at the best women's colleges in the war years. The products of the library school at the University of Illinois were incensed that the Association of Collegiate Alumnae did not grant membership to library school graduates because library science was judged to be technical, rather than academic, training.* A library school instructor at the University of Illinois in 1917 wrote to an ex-student that "many of the women's colleges in the country seem to be classifying training in librarianship along with work in the domestic sciences as some sort of handicraft which has no intellectual features whatever . . . their attitude has been most discouraging so far."[12] By 1918, according to the report of the ALA Committee on Library Training, at least one dean of a women's college refused to allow librarianship to be presented to her students as a possible field of service "on the ground that they could not afford to enter that profession."[13]

Female dissatisfaction with the position of women in the American library was rarely expressed, but discontent did surface briefly between 1917 and 1919, when a movement to unionize librarians flourished in Boston, Philadelphia, New York, and Washington, D.C. The advent of library unionization was influenced by the growth of trade unions during the war years and by the establishment of the American Federation of Teachers in 1917. But the immediate issue that sparked library unionization was the protest of library women against sex discrimination in their profession. It was the union statement of women's grievances, rather than the "unprofessional" agitation for higher salaries, that brought the most angry response from the library press.

The first public library union, the New York Public Library Employees' Union, was dominated by women and was aligned with other women's reform groups — the New York City Federation of Women's Clubs, the Federation of Women's Civil Service Organizations, and the Women's Trade Union League of New York — as well as with the American Federation of Labor. Like the Library Workers' Union of Boston Public Library, the New York library union was organized by low-grade assistants who were frustrated by their low pay and routine work. In contrast, the union at the Washington, D.C., public library was chiefly composed of senior staff members; yet it was also dominated by women. Library unionists demanded not only better salaries and working conditions but also an end to sexual discrimination in hiring and promotion. Antiunionists charged that union members were materialistic and self-serving — were, in fact, unfeminine.[14]

A heated debate between women unionists and opponents of unionization in the library erupted at the ALA convention of 1919. The conflict began in

*The Alumni Files of the University of Illinois Library School, Urbana, before 1920 are filled with complaints regarding this decision. In 1888, of 524 women who were members of the ACA, only 7 were working as librarians or library assistants. (Grace Weld Saper, "The Occupations of Women College Graduates," *Harper's Bazaar* 21 [January 14, 1888], 18.)

the Catalogue and Trustees Joint Session of the convention when Arthur Bostwick compared library unionism to Russian communism. George Bowerman, of the Washington, D.C., library, rose to accuse the library profession of "old class-conscious prejudice" and "anti-union fetishism." Bowerman was supported by Maude Malone, from the New York union, who had been an assistant for nine years but shunned ALA membership. Malone denounced librarianship as an elitist occupation whose members claimed superiority over the laboring class they pretended to serve. She was openly contemptuous of the "caste" of library leaders, who, she said, felt "we are 'professionals,' we will educate the great outside body of people who are not as good as we are."[15] Malone's charge of sexual discrimination in the library was directed against the fact that men generally held the most prestigious and best-paid library positions, while women were restricted to subordinate or monotonous work. In the New York library, she said, "with one exception, and that an unimportant department, all the heads of departments . . . are men, the director is a man, all the members of the boards of trustees are men. Selection of these upper officers is not made on the basis of superiority of intelligence or ability; it is simply made on the basis of sex."[16]

Rebuffed by the Catalogue and Trustees Joint Session at the ALA convention, Malone decided to present a resolution on salaries and sexual inequality to the ALA Committee on Resolutions. This committee agreed to discuss salaries, but not sexual discrimination. Malone then angrily demanded that the New York union's resolution be discussed and voted upon at the general meeting of the ALA. The resolution read, in part:

> WHEREAS, The present low and inadequate salaries paid to librarians . . . are due solely to the fact that all of the rank and file in the work are women, and . . . all the highest salaried positions are given to men by the board of trustees, and . . . the present policy of library boards is to remove women from all positions of responsibility . . . and replace them with men only, and . . . this discrimination is based on sex . . . therefore BE IT RESOLVED, That we are against this system . . . and are in favor of throwing open all positions in library work . . . to men and women equally, and for equal pay.[17]

The abortive outcome of this attempt to arouse female fury and to unionize library employees was no doubt determined by the shocking radicalism of Malone, whose sympathies and origins were too obviously working-class. The resolution was defeated by an audience composed of four-fifths women and by a vote of 121–1. Library leader Alice Tyler rose to formally assure the remaining one-fifth that women "desire the men members of the Association to realize that the women understand the men have no thought of crowding women out of the profession."[18]

Nevertheless, women librarians were voting with their feet, so to speak, for when World War I began there was a startling exodus from libraries all over the nation as women moved into war work or into positions left vacant by men. An urgent need for stenographers, file clerks, and persons trained to use the typewriter during this period of rapid expansion of governmental and business activity drew hundreds of poorly paid librarians into office work.[19] In 1918, for example, 19 per cent of the reference workers and twenty-seven members of the circulation staff at the New York Public Library resigned for better pay. Western Union operators, even during their period of training, received higher pay than the average library assistant could hope to earn. Whereas the subsistence wages paid to library workers had forced most of them to live at home, the new jobs offered in war work allowed young women enough money to move into their own apartment or into a boardinghouse.[20]

The resignations of educated women from library work did not stop wth the armistice, to the surprise of many library leaders. Anne Carroll Moore sensed that the exodus of competent women from the library was the "gravest crisis" ever faced by the profession and would have long-lasting, detrimental effects upon the quality of library workers.[21] Margery Doud, speaking at the ALA conference of 1920, stated her belief that college-educated women were leaving the library not simply for better salaries but for more challenging jobs that were not so bound by strict supervision and rigid routine. As a "friendly critic" she warned head librarians not to "wait too long to provide measures of self-expression" for their "supposedly inarticulate" staff. "Conditions of to-day are forcing self expression . . . [W]ith the lucrative as well as in-teresting positions open to librarians in other fields, even the meekest assis-tant has reached an alarming state of independence."[22]

Much attention was paid to an article by Clara Herbert that told of her distressing experience in recruiting a training class in 1919. Anticipating a surge of women freed from government war work bureaus, she made ready to select fifteen candidates from a group of five hundred interested inquirers. Two hundred and forty-nine took away the application, twelve filed, eight took the exam, and one lone woman qualified for the job. Herbert reported that her interview experience had made her feel like "an unscrupulous employer of child labor being grilled by a social service investi-gator . . . there was a new note of distrust of the value of the work." At about this time an ALA study showed that the national average paid for room and board for one person was $45 a month. "If the library could pay only $55 a month . . . then [it seemed] the work must be of a simple mechanical nature requiring small attainments."[23]

Not until the changes brought by World War I did the question of low pay become a vital topic of discussion among librarians. So long as there had been sufficient numbers of educated women eager to work for any amount, however small, there had been little incentive to rectify the salary situation. After the war librarians were forced to realize that, in contrast to the cir-cumstances existing in the late nineteenth century, library work was no longer attracting enough cultivated women of intellectual capacities. Social workers also experienced a similar, though temporary, crisis during the war years. As one social worker commented, the labor crisis which that profession faced was partly because "the missionary ideal still persist[ed]" among professional women to such an extent that they were unwilling to demand more than subsistence wages.[24] It was high time, Adeline Zachert said in 1918, that women librarians denounced the "general feeling" among them "that 'it is not lady-like to mention salaries.' "[25]

In truth, the genteel lady herself, in her reforming nineteenth century role, had by 1920 largely disappeared from American life, as well as from the American library. Influenced by the currents of their age, professional women of the Progressive period fumbled for a new personal identity. Although the new model contained an element of sexual and secular release from Victorian restraints, it still attempted to overlay feminist ideas upon the old mold of "femininity." The resultant frustration and confusion of educated women is aptly portrayed in Sinclair Lewis's novel *Main Street*, written in 1920 and set in a small midwestern town in the years before World War I.

Significantly, Lewis had his central character, Carol Kennicott, choose librarianship as her "career" in about 1909. Carol in her senior year at college had originally desired to seek "a cell in a settlement house . . . and enormously improve a horde of grateful poor." But on the advice of an English professor she instead decided to attend library school in Chicago. She saw herself "persuading children to read charming fairy tales, helping young men to find books on mechanics . . . the light of the library, an authority on books, invited to dinners with poets and explorers, reading a paper to an association of distinguished scholars." She found library training "easy and not too somniferous." At work in the St. Paul library for three years, she "slowly confessed that she was not visibly affecting lives," but was handing out love stories instead of elevating essays; she began to feel "in dread of life's slipping past." Although Carol was "fond of the other librarians, proud of their aspirations," in college she had been repulsed by the genteel "earnest virgins" she knew who were bent upon lifelong careers—"bulbous-browed and pop-eyed maidens who at class prayer-meetings requested God to 'guide their feet along the paths of greater usefulness.' " She gratefully turned to marriage as soon as the opportunity presented itself in 1912.

Today Carol seems amazingly naive, with her romantic reverie, misguided idealism, optimistic hopes for social regeneration, and concept of "culture." Yet she faithfully reflected the position in which the turn-of-the-century New Woman found herself—"a woman with a working brain and no work," except in the ill-paid spinster's world of the altruistic women's service professions. Carol became a dilettante, stirred by new ideas but unable to integrate them into her own life. No wonder that Carol and so many young college women in real life chose the perhaps equally narrow but at least more approved and secure road to marriage in the years before the war.[26]

The eventual failure of Carol Kennicott to achieve either psychological or economic independence was the failure of feminism to sustain its thrust past 1920.[27] Organized women during the nineteenth century had promoted legal reforms, gained access to higher education, and protested against the various patriarchial imperatives that demeaned the female. Originally demanding a variety of rights in the name of justice and democracy, the growing number of social feminists eventually turned their energies into the pursuit of one goal—suffrage. Once women received the franchise, suffragists promised, they would force through measures of social reform. But by 1925 it had become apparent that the "women's vote" did not exist. Women generally voted as their men did, and reform movements of all sorts, including feminism, suffered in the 1920s.

The death of the women's movement after 1920 can be partially explained by the unfulfilled promise of suffrage and partially by the way in which the Victorian ideals held by most of the older leaders of the women's movement alienated the new "flapper" generation. By the postwar years, youthful attitudes had shifted. The advancement of women's status, moral reform, or personal career goals had little appeal to the burgeoning female college population. Despite the lowering of barriers, the proportion of women engaged in the professions rose a mere .4 per cent between 1920 and 1940. The feminist movement collapsed in a period of postwar conservatism, prosperity, and consumerism. The college woman of the 1920s felt little dedication to anything more overriding than the role of wife and mother.

The coming of the Depression exaggerated the already debased status of women librarians. With growing competition for fewer jobs, employers increasingly denied married women the right to work.* Although the majority of working women labored out of economic necessity, to support themselves or their dependents, the popular belief that most females worked merely for pin-money served to encourage the custom of paying women about 50 to 60 per cent of what men earned. Societal disapproval of working wives, who theoretically kept jobs from men, had its effect upon librarianship. A 1938 survey revealed that out of fifty-seven major libraries polled, five did not employ married women, twelve required resignation upon marriage, and ten, as a matter of policy, did not place married women in responsible positions.[28] Economic conditions in the 1930s also served to draw a slightly larger percentage of men into library work. By 1938 it had become apparent that men were being openly favored over women for the best administrative positions, in recruiting, and in placement by library schools.

The economic tensions created by the Depression led to the first heated discussion of the "woman question" among librarians since the 1890s. The controversy began in 1933 when the *Wilson Library Bulletin* printed a letter

*In almost every state between 1932 and 1940 bills limiting the right of wives to work were introduced. The National Economy Act successfully pushed many married women out of civil service positions between 1932 and 1937.

from an English librarian in which he expressed his regret that women dominated the library profession in the United States, for women, lacking the "natural curiosity" of men, were unfamiliar with good literature and therefore unable to serve as efficient guides to books. In response, the *Wilson Library Bulletin* offered three money prizes for the best reply to the question: "Should the preponderance of women in the American library profession be considered an evil?" The column in which the contest was run frequently sponsored such competitions and was a popular feature in the journal. Because the majority of prizewinners in the past had been women, it was unusual that this particular contest was won by three men, a situation which led the editor to comment that "perhaps the ladies were embarrassed by being put on the offensive." The sole female winner, who tied for third place, based her defense of women in library work upon their preordained feminine role: "Women are more naturally sympathetic and patient interpreters of individual tastes." Another reply completely denied female domination of American librarianship:

Women do most of the minor clerical work [in the library] . . . Men, however, still hold the senior posts in an impressive and almost impregnable array. . . . As long as the American female librarian continues to concern herself with routine problems of circulation, cataloguing and the like, and is content to leave the theorizing in the hands of the male, there is no danger of an emasculated library service [in the United States]. The gentler sex is only carrying on work which is based on the theories of the sterner male.[29]

Provoked by an editorial in the *Library Journal* entitled "The Weaker Sex?", feminine resentment exploded again in 1938.[30] The editorial noted that although 90 per cent of librarians were women, men were invariably hired for any positions that paid over $3,600 a year. Alice Tyler, who had opposed the 1919 union attempt to organize librarians on a women's issue, now claimed that sexual discrimination in the library profession was a recent development and urged library women to "not shrink from being called a feminist." The influential Margaret Mann pleaded for women to use their numerical majority in the ALA to seize power there. Other women commented upon the "increasing tendency at ALA headquarters to ignore women or to keep them subservient" or argued that women had too long "been satisfied to be 'the power behind the throne' as assistants to the man in charge." The editorial, another woman wrote, "at last states in print what has become a bromide among us at meetings." And Marietta Daniels called for a "Lady Pankhurst who will champion the cause of women in the library profession." The angry discussion of 1938 elicited a request from a male librarian that the ladies "should not work up a crusade" to put the good positions on a more equal basis, for to do so would drive out most of the men. "And that," he said, "would keep out more of the best minds than the present system does." Robert Alvarez presented a careful selection of statistics to prove that "women still rule" in the library world. As W. H. Kaiser quickly pointed out, however, Alvarez forgot to mention that although only 8.9 per cent of librarians were males, men headed 60 per cent of the libraries holding over 100,000 volumes.[31]

Still, despite these few protests of the 1930s, the great majority of library women continued to silently suffer sexual discrimination with little dissent. Perhaps, as Katherine Stokes suggested, they were "too disillusioned after years of observation to be interested in a situation which they must long since have accepted as inevitable."[32] But it is more likely that their passivity reflected a voluntary servitude, made agreeable by the entire socialization process.

It was not only in the United States that the socialization of women shaped the development of library systems. Abroad, the integration of women into library work occurred somewhat later than in the United States, was most often resisted by male librarians, and was advanced by the effect of both World Wars. Still, despite these differences, the pattern of the feminization of librarianship is of striking sameness, in countries as different as the western democracies and the Communist states.

In England, the entrance of women into library work came about twenty years later than it did in the United States. The first woman assistant was · hired at Manchester, in 1871. Eight years later, thirty-one women assistants were employed in the Manchester library. In the next ten years, a significant number of women infiltrated the lowliest ranks of library service, numbering 1,250 assistants by 1889. A few women moved into top library positions in the smaller public libraries. About 10 per cent of the 250 rate-supported libraries in England were headed by women librarians by 1890.[33]

Through the 1890s the educated spinsters in England who had begun careers in the library frequently contrasted their lack of opportunity with the greater equality offered women librarians in the United States, where, unlike England, women formed the bulk of the assistants.[34] M. S. R. James, the only woman in the nineteenth century to head a large public library in England, commented in 1900 from the safety of Boston that in the United States "we find in libraries, as in other occupations, the elysium of women."[35] Middle-class Englishwomen were "only gradually making their way" into small library posts, against the strong resistance of male librarians.[36]

Males in England conceded, however, that there was one good reason for hiring female library workers:

> The salary offered to assistants is insufficient to attract educated men of the pro-
> fessional classes; but . . . their sisters are willing to accept the posts . . . [The
> public] secures the help and advice of a cultivated woman at a smaller salary than
> would satisfy a man of the artisan class, much less a man of equal cultivation.[37]

Moreover, women librarians were "less clumsy than the class of men who can be obtained at the same emolument; and much of the work is eminently suited to deft-handed women." Thus, librarian W. L. Selby assured his male colleagues in 1899, it was probably fortunate that educated Englishwomen were content to enter library work as a prelude to marriage, for a male assistant hired at the same price would surely be so incompetent that the library would be stuck with him until he died. By 1900, the male librarians in England had adapted to the presence of educated female overseers in the smallest village libraries, where the pay was either nonexistent or "at the sweating limit."[38]

Between 1900 and the beginning of World War I, women workers came to compose almost one-half of the library assistants in England. This was no doubt a product of the greater economy of hiring women workers as well as a result of the increased educational opportunities for women. As women encroached upon library positions, male librarians became increasingly intolerant of the feminization process. Men charged that since women were incapable of holding the top library posts, females flocked into assistant jobs and thus lowered the prestige and professional status of librarianship. Although British women, like their American sisters, cited inherent female traits as proof of women's suitability for library work, the English males did not often agree. Resistance to the feminization of librarianship in England was so high among male librarians that they would not even concede the argument that women were "naturally" fitted for library work with children.[39] The British debate between outraged males and defensive women was closely followed by amused American librarians. The spate of articles which defined the British conflict was frequently cited in the United States as comic proof of the "complete stagnation of library work in the United Kingdom."[40]

Feminization of English librarianship, well along by 1914, was greatly advanced by the effect of both World Wars. By 1919 women had moved into many of the assistant jobs vacated by men. The increased number of women in the field discouraged the entry of new males. In 1921 an article in *The Library World* noted that library work appealed to few men "of the more able sort. As in America, the best men are not entering the profession."[41] Although feminization of British librarianship has never been as complete as in the United States, male and female membership in the professional association was almost equal by 1937. After World War II a large number of library women continued to work after marriage. Since 1945, the number of women in the librarians' national association has remained at about 60 per cent.[42] The only "crumb of comfort" which men could find in the existence of the feminized profession, one Englishman remarked in 1948, was that women were still confined to the lowest-paid, most menial jobs and were not appointed to top positions in large libraries.[43] This situation is little changed today, although female students numbered 57 per cent of library school enrollment in 1975.[44]

Attempting to draw large generalizations about female entry into library work in the other countries of Western Europe, with their diversity of cultural traditions, is to run the risk of facile oversimplification. Although the library systems in the United States, Britain, and the Communist countries show many common features, the Western European states have traditionally shown less interest in the provision of books to the populace and in the social role of the library. In Western Europe the librarian is generally a scholar first and professional librarian second. Another unique feature of library service in Western Europe is that formal library education is most often organized on a part-time, apprenticeship basis and is rarely centered in academic institutions or supervised by professional associations.[45]

Having noted these dissimilarities and divergences in practice, it still must be said that librarianship in Western Europe also became a refuge for educated femininity. However, the entry of significant numbers of women into library work generally began later than in Britain and never achieved the level reached in the United States. A few educated women were employed as library assistants in Belgium, Sweden, Norway, Denmark, Austria, Germany, and Switzerland by 1900.[46] Germany first opened library schooling to women in 1907.[47] By 1915 an eminent French professor's defense of library work for cultivated women had a familiar ring:

> Young women . . . come to the Universities in greater and greater numbers . . . [T]he administration should endeavor . . . to find channels . . . for this movement, reserving for women those situations most in harmony with the natural aptitudes of their sex. Among these positions there are none perhaps better fitted to women than those offered by the public libraries. An indoor occupation which consists in classifying books carefully, keeping them dusted, preserving order on the shelves, recopying with painstaking accuracy . . . using taste in the binding of books, serving readers with attention and affability. . . . It is work which suits a woman much better than a man. This subordinate role does not suit the natural pride of men. . . . The learned man suffers in being the servant of others. . . . [Women are] naturally more flexible, more teachable, more affable than men, they would accomplish with pleasure and smilingly, without tiring, the modest duties which do not belong to the other sex. . . . That is so true that one may be allowed to wonder why we have not thought earlier of confiding to a feminine staff the public library service.[48]

By the 1970s, Western European women held a majority of library jobs, but, as in the United States and Great Britain, a man generally held the top position and was "twice as likely to reach the highest level of his career as a woman."[49] Interestingly, the evidence indicates that library women in Western Europe today are still moved to justify their presence in library work through reference to their "inherent" feminine qualities. Their rhetoric in their own defense sounds much like the statements made by women librarians in America more than fifty years ago.[50]

Librarians in Britain and in Western Europe often looked to the United

States as a model of library practice, but in Soviet Russia the direct influence of American librarianship was especially pronounced. This was so because Lenin and his wife, Krupskaia, known as "the mother of Soviet libraries," deliberately shaped Russian library service to match the excellence they perceived in the American system. Lenin was mightily impressed by his reading of the 1912 report of the New York Public Library. He marvelled at the American effort to provide books "not only to scholars . . . but to the masses, the crowds, the man in the street"; at the wide circulation of books; at "the speed with which requests for books are satisfied"; and at the number of children enrolled as readers.[51] On the evening of November 9, 1917, Lenin issued orders to his newly appointed people's commissioner of education to convene a meeting of librarians and to establish a library system similar to that of America in Soviet Russia.[52] As in Great Britain and the United States, library service in Russia is extensive and relatively well financed. Considerable emphasis is placed, too, upon the exploitation of the book stock, rather than in its preservation, and upon the social function of the library. The Russian pattern has had a strong influence upon other Eastern European states—particularly Bulgaria, Hungary, Poland, and East Germany.[53]

In Soviet Russia, as in the Western democracies, public library work was sex-typed as an appropriate occupation for women. Furthermore, although over half the professionals and two-thirds of the semiprofessionals in all fields in Russia are women, they, like their Western counterparts, are concentrated in the relatively low paid, sexually segregated occupations. In Russia women dominate in numbers the health, educational, and cultural services.[54] Not surprisingly, a 1961 survey of the Soviet economy reported that "wages for doctors, teachers, librarians, etc., tend to be on a par with, or slightly below, the average annual wage of all Soviet workers and employees."[55]

The pattern of the feminization of librarianship thus shows more similarities than differences in countries as politically and socially diverse as the capitalist and socialist states. As women's educational and employment opportunities increased in the late nineteenth and early twentieth centuries, educated females entered the expanding tertiary sector of the economy. They moved into those areas in which women had traditionally been employed, in service positions, or into the new sex-typed occupations and "professions" of a comparable nature.[56] Educated females in all countries experiencing industrial development defended their right to work by emphasizing their biologically ordained qualities as women. Librarianship was universally acclaimed as a suitable female job when it required only mechanical training, housekeeping skills, cultural interests, and feminine readiness to serve. Even in the United States, the "elysium" of women librarians, those positions that required business talent, political wisdom, and intellectual ability were usually reserved for the male leadership. In the industrializing nations, the myriad of social and economic changes engendered by modern war appreciably speeded the feminization process. As the reserve female labor force was moved into spots left vacant by departing males, the presence of women discouraged male entry into a feminized profession.

In the United States, too, the waging of modern warfare brought with it increased employment opportunities for women. It was World War II which proved to be the catalyst that radically transformed the economic outlook and self-image of American women. During the war years the female labor force increased 50 per cent. More important, the manpower shortage caused rigid employment barriers to be broken in many areas of work once closed to women, and public attitudes toward working wives made a dramatic shift. Despite persistent discrimination and unequal wage scales, female employment, aided by a postwar boom, continued to rise after 1945. In the 1950s the female labor force was increasing at a rate four times faster than that of the male. The greatest postwar gains occurred among married women. In 1900 the young, unmarried, and poor constituted the majority of working women. Fifty years later the female labor force was dominated by the married and middle-aged, with a substantial growth in the numbers of employed middle-class women. By 1970, 60 per cent of all non-farm wives in families with an annual income of over $10,000 were working, and more than half the mothers of children aged six to seventeen years were employed. The extraordinary social change these figures represent set the economic foundations for the revival of feminist ideology in our own time.*

Women's increased economic activity after World War II was a necessary precondition for the rebirth of feminist consciousness. Maternal employment had its impact upon the distribution of domestic responsibilities, the attitudes of men, and the self-image of female children. Social scientists have pointed out that revolutions tend to begin not among the brutally oppressed but in those groups that have been given a taste of emancipation and are experiencing "rising expectations." Historically, women's rights have advanced in times of generalized social reform. Abolitionism, then progressivism, and in the 1960s the civil rights and New Left movements all resulted in generating a demand for equal rights for women. But if so many women had not already departed from their traditional roles during the 1940s and 1950s, it seems doubtful that the feminists' call for further change in the 1960s would have met with the response it did.

In very recent years a new insurgency has shaken the 3″ × 5″ world of the library system. Many library science graduates of the 1960s shared with their college peers a strong conviction that the American political and economic system was in basic ways monumentally and monstrously wrong. In a burst of energy maverick librarians challenged the stultifying content of

*William A. Chafe, *The American Woman: Her Changing Social, Economic, and Political Role, 1920–70* (New York: Oxford University Press, 1972). Contrary to popular belief, only 5 per cent of women war workers joined the American labor force for the first time during World War I. The fact that the earlier war lasted only a year and a half for this country also served to slow the pace of social change in that period.

many library school courses, the image of librarians as "old-made [sic] ladies sipping custom's tea,"[57] the stand-pat library bureaucracy, and even the labelling system of the Library of Congress, which they charged was sexist, racist, and prissy to boot. Although the radicalism expressed at the 1969 Atlantic City Conference, at which the ALA made a quavering commitment to social change, has succumbed to the new mood of the 1970s, still the library system, like all our institutions, has felt the effect of that turbulent preceding decade.

In the mid-1960s the first trickle of what would become a flood of articles on women began to appear in library periodicals. By 1970 the studies of Anita Schiller and others had collected the statistical evidence that convincingly portrayed women as the "disadvantaged majority" in the profession.[58] The September 1971 issue of the *Library Journal* emerged as a sort of feminist manifesto for library women. Women librarians are now expressing dissatisfaction with the public library's feminized world of propriety and respectability. They urge, for example, that librarians live up to their Bill of Rights, which enjoins them to stock material representing all possible viewpoints and to fiercely resist community pressure for censorship of books and ideas. A 1969 article in the *Wilson Library Bulletin* resulted in the placing of thousands of NO SILENCE signs as librarians revolted against the tradition of a shushing woman presiding over decorous and hushed rooms. As a Virginian librarian wrote: "Tombs and . . . libraries are silent places indeed. Perhaps we should ask why."[59] In attempts like this to break with inertia, public librarians are in effect considering a course that would place them in opposition to hallowed conservatism within their communities. Such a radical change in the library tradition would require that the librarian defy the Victorian concept of femininity and assume a new confidence in her right and duty to protect standards of intellectual freedom by bold exercise of intellectual leadership.

The 1970 organization of the ALA Task Force on the Status of Women is symptomatic of the new attitude of women toward their own potential and ability. With the growing consciousness of the effects of sexism on the library profession as a whole has come a formal admission that sexual discrimination "wastes needed professional resources and assaults our sense of human dignity."[60] Because a majority of librarians are members of that group which now feels especially frustrated by traditional ideals—the educated women in America—they desire to fuse personal and professional development within the library system. Not surprisingly, as they denounce passivity in themselves and propriety in the world at large, they extend their criticism to their institution and their profession.

Today, the feminist consciousness expressed by nationally organized and active groups of women librarians far exceeds the militancy demonstrated by any other feminized profession in the United States. So far mostly concentrated among university librarians and library school educators, this new ideology may in time have some effect upon the professional activity of public librarians at large. Kathleen Weibel has recently called for the transition of librarianship from a "feminized" profession to a "feminist" one. Feminist in this sense would mean a commitment of both male and female librarians to the development of role-free human beings and to a transformation of our concept of power: cooperation, compassion, and humanism rather than aggression, dominance, and hierarchy.[61] A feminist library profession would necessarily implement change in library service, challenge reading censorship, and redirect and influence the values and character of those men and women who choose to enter the field. Yet any discussion of librarianship as a feminist profession is still largely theoretical, for the heritage of library history is very heavy.

The feminization of public librarianship did much to shape and stunt the development of an important American cultural institution. Because the first generations of library women did not question their sex-typed roles, the socially designated femininity that library women elected to act out had a major influence upon the formation of the public library's "homey" atmosphere, its patrons, its book collection, and its "helpful" staff.

It is apparent that modern members of the profession are seeking to modify this conventional role of the public librarian. One hope is to establish librarianship on a scientifically oriented, abstract-knowledge base and to train the librarian as the indispensable expert in knowledge retrieval. The communications explosion has decidedly created a need for such a person. As the printed material grows to an unmanageable mass, certainly someone, if not the public librarian, will move in to perform this vital function. Another hope is to reverse library tradition and create a library profession that would zealously guard and promote the concept of intellectual freedom through organized resistance to community forces which threaten that democratic ideal. However, until the librarian deals with the implications of feminization — with its varied inhibitory effects upon intellectual freedom and leadership — progress toward these goals may be limited. So long as sexist attitudes govern our society, the intellectual base that supported the historical development of the public librarian seems unlikely to change.

Appendix

Public Library
Leadership

Homer Bassett (1826-1902). Silas Bronson Library, Waterbury, Conn., 1872-1901. He apparently was inactive in the professional association and made no contributions to library literature.

Mary A. Bean (1840-1893). Boston Athenaeum, 1860-1869; Brookline, Mass., public library, 1871-1893. Active in the national association, Bean pioneered in library work with children.

William Beer (1849-1927). Topeka, Kans., public library, 1890-1891; Howard Memorial Library, New Orleans, 1892-1927. Born in Plymouth, England, Beer was a mining engineer in the American West during the 1880s.

William Howard Brett (1846-1918). Cleveland Public Library, 1884-1918; president, American Library Association, 1896-1897. Brett was concerned throughout his career with a careful selection of books for readers. He is best known for his defense of open shelves and his militant library work in World War I.

Eliza Gordon Browning (1856-1927). Indianapolis Public Library, 1880-1927. The great-granddaughter of the first woman doctor in Indiana, Browning was a caustic and strong-minded woman.

Edward Capen (1821-1901). Boston Public Library, 1852-1874; Haverhill, Mass., public library, 1874-1899. Capen was inactive within the national association.

Henry James Carr (1849-1929). Grand Rapids, Mo., public library, 1886-1890; St. Joseph, Mo., public library, 1890-1891; Scranton, Pa., public library, 1891-1913; president, American Library Association, 1900. Carr seemed best known among librarians for his hearty friendliness. He was a faithful attender of the annual conferences.

242

Mellen Chamberlain (1821–1900). Boston Public Library, 1878–1890. Noted as a jurist and historian, Chamberlain entered a library career late in life, after working as a lawyer, state legislator, and educator.

John Vance Cheney (1848–1922). San Francisco Public Library, 1887–1894; Newberry Library, Chicago, 1894–1909. To Cheney, a quiet, urbane poet, the library profession was a secondary interest in his life. He was a literary conservative and a religious liberal. See Cheney, *That Dome in Air* (Chicago: A. C. McClurg & Company, 1895).

Frederick Morgan Crunden (1847–1911). St. Louis Public School and Public Library, 1877–1909; president, American Library Association, 1889–1890. Crunden was a leading spokesman for a liberal provision of fiction in public libraries and for a close relationship with the public schools. In the mid-1890s he wrote and spoke in favor of Henry George and the single tax.

Charles Ammi Cutter (1837–1903). Boston Athenaeum, 1869–1893; Forbes Library, Northampton, Mass., 1894–1903; editor, *Library Journal*, 1882–1893; president, American Library Association, 1887–1889. With William Frederick Poole and Justin Winsor, he was one of the most influential librarians in 1876. An accomplished writer, Cutter was also known for his classification system.

John Cotton Dana (1865–1929). Denver Public Library, 1889–1897; Springfield, Mass., public library, 1898–1902; Newark Public Library, 1902–1929; president, American Library Association, 1895–1896. Along with Melvil Dewey, Dana was one of the most controversial and radical innovators among library leaders. He effectively challenged paternalism and the leadership of the New Englanders. The conservatism of his last years may have been simply the result of a compulsion to oppose whatever was popular.

Melvil Dewey (1851–1931). Amherst Library, 1874–1877. Columbia College Library, 1883–1889. New York State Library, 1889–1906. Dewey was the major organizer of the American Library Association, the creator of the decimal system of classification, and the originator of schools for training librarians.

Theresa West Elmendorf (1855–1932). Young Men's Association Library, Milwaukee, 1892–1896; Buffalo Public Library, 1906–1926; president, American Library Association, 1911. Elmendorf replaced the disgraced president of the American Library Association, K. A. Linderfelt, when he was tried for graft in 1892 in Milwaukee. After her husband's death in 1906 she became the chief librarian in Buffalo.

Mary Salome Cutler Fairchild (1855–1921). Columbia University Library and the New York State Library School, 1889–1905.

William I. Fletcher (1844–1917). Amherst College, 1883–1911; president, American Library Association, 1891–1892. Fletcher's political and social conservatism often led him to side with Justin Winsor and William Frederick Poole in opposition to Melvil Dewey.

William Eaton Foster (1851–1930). Hyde Park, Mass., public library, 1873–1876; Providence, R.I., public library, 1878–1930. A very active member of the American Library Association, Foster was one of the first librarians to institute an information desk, reference service, art and music department, industrial department, and foreign languages department in the public library. Along with Samuel Green he was a pioneer in the coordination of the library with the public school system.

Samuel Swett Green (1837–1918). Free Public Library, Worcester, Mass., 1871–1909; president, American Library Association, 1891. One of the most dedicated supporters of the American Library Association, Green, a born Brahmin, was a pioneer in encouraging the use of library books in the public schools. He was an earnest popularizer of some of the earliest library innovations, such as Sunday openings, technical service to laborers, and approval of "sensational" fiction for the masses.

Caroline M. Hewins (1846–1926). Boston Athenaeum, 1866–1867; Hartford, Conn., public library, 1875–1926. An active member of the American Library Association, Hewins was considered a pioneer in the development of library work for children.

Frederick Hild (1858–1914). Chicago Public Library, 1875–1909. After a bitter contest that involved political considerations, he replaced Poole as chief librarian in 1887.

James Kendall Hosmer (1834–1927). Minneapolis Public Library, 1892–1904. A well-known author and teacher. Hosmer's life in the library was secondary to his other literary and intellectual interests.

Hannah Packard James (1835–1903). Newton, Mass., free library, 1870–1887; Osterhout Free Library, Wilkes-Barre, Pa., 1887–1903. James was active in library work with the schools and led a crusade to improve children's reading.

Josephus Nelson Larned (1836–1913). Buffalo Public Library, 1877–1897; president, American Library Association, 1893–1894. Larned was very active in civic life in Buffalo. He was the first to organize a whole library by the Dewey Decimal System.

Stephen Butterick Noyes (1833–1885). Mercantile Library Association, Brooklyn, 1858–1885, except for three years at the Library of Congress. He apparently led a quiet and relatively inactive life.

Frederick Beecher Perkins (1828–1899). Boston Public Library, 1874–1879; San Francisco Public Library, 1880–1887. A grandson of Lyman Beecher and father of Charlotte Perkins Gilman, he was best known for his crusade against "unclean fiction." He resigned as a librarian in 1887, partly because his uncompromising morality and quick temper had alienated his employers.

Mary Wright Plummer (1856–1916). St. Louis Public Library, 1888–1890; Pratt Institute Free Library, 1890–1894; director, Pratt Institute Library School, 1895–1911; director, Library School of the New York Public Library, 1911–1916; president, American Library Association, 1915–1916. A Quaker and poet, Plummer was considered a learned woman by her peers. She was very active in library school training.

William Frederick Poole (1821–1894). Boston Mercantile Institute, 1852–1856; Boston Athenaeum, 1856–1869; Cincinnati Public Library, 1869–1873; Chicago Public Library, 1873–1887; Newberry Library, 1887–1894; president, American Historical Association, 1888; president, American Library Association, 1885–1887. One of the deans of American librarians in 1876, Poole was a well-known scholar. He was generally considered by younger librarians to exert a conservative force upon the profession.

George Herbert Putnam (1861-1955). Minneapolis Public Library, 1884-1891; Boston Public Library, 1893-1899; Librarian of Congress, 1899-1939; president, American Library Association, 1898 and 1904. An unusually efficient organizer, Putnam was one of the first to institute open shelves, a borrower's card, a children's department, and library branches in the public library system.

William Rice (1821-1897). Springfield, Mass., public library, 1861-1895. Rice, inactive in the American Library Association, had been an abolitionist.

Minerva A. Sanders (1837-1912). Pawtucket, R.I., public library, 1876-1895. Sanders was one of the first proponents of open stacks and service to children under fourteen.

Lloyd Pearsall Smith (1822-1886). Philadelphia Company Library, 1849-1886. "Nestor Number Two" to William Poole, Smith was a Quaker, classicist, and library conservative.

Bernard Christian Steiner (1867-1926). Enoch Pratt Library, Baltimore, 1892-1926. A strong Presbyterian, he was not in favor of moral censorship in the library and gave important support to John Dana and the liberal element.

Henry Munson Utley (1836-1917). Detroit Public Library, 1885-1913. President, American Library Association, 1895. For many years a city editor, he entered librarianship at age forty-nine.

Albert W. Whelply (1831-1900). Cincinnati Public Library, 1886-1900. Whelply worked as a stereotyper and book salesman before entering library work at age fifty-five.

James Lyman Whitney (1835-1910). Boston Public Library, 1869-1910. Not enthusiastic about missionary work, he spent a quiet life as a cataloguer and indexer.

Justin Winsor (1831-1897). Boston Public Library, 1868-1877; Harvard University Library, 1877-1897; president, American Library Association, 1876-1885, 1897. Although Winsor was not a public librarian after 1877, his influence upon public library development is significant. Thus I have included an analysis of his social ideals as a part of the attitudinal study of public librarians (Chapter 2).

Notes and Sources

Manuscript Collections Consulted

Alumni Files, Library School, University of Illinois, Urbana
American Library Association Archives, University of Illinois, Urbana
Boston Athenaeum Archives, Boston, Mass.
R. R. Bowker Papers, New York Public Library, New York City
Nicholas Murray Butler Papers, Columbia University Library, New
    York City
Mellen Chamberlain Papers, Boston Public Library, Boston, Mass.
John Cotton Dana Papers, Newark Public Library, Newark, N.J.
Melvil Dewey Papers, Columbia University Library, New York City
Mary Wright Plummer Papers, New York Public Library, New York City
Fremont Rider Papers, Godfrey Memorial Library, Middletown, Conn.
Justin Winsor Papers, Harvard University, Cambridge, Mass.

Interviews

Godfrey Dewey, son of Melvil Dewey
Bill Quigley, employee of Lake Placid Club
Julia Sabine, librarian under John Cotton Dana, Newark Public Library

Introduction

1. A lively debate began in the early 1970s regarding the nature of early public library development, partly in response to my dissertation, "Cultural Missionaries: A Study of American Public Library Leaders, 1876-1910" (Ph.D. dissertation, University of California, 1973), of which this book is a much revised and expanded version; to John Colson's "The Public Library Movement in Wisconsin, 1836-1900" (Ph.D. dissertation, University of Chicago, 1973); and to Michael H. Harris's *The Purpose of the American Public Library in Historical Perspective: A Revisionist Interpretation* (ERIC Reports, ED 071 668, L1004063 [Washington, D.C.: ERIC Clearinghouse on Library and Information Sciences, 1972]) and "The Purpose of the American Public Library: A Revisionist Interpretation" (*Library Journal* 98 [1973], 2509-14). Also see Harris, "Portrait in Paradox: Commitment and Ambivalence in American Librarianship, 1876-1976," *Libri* 26 (1976), 281-301, and Harris with Gerard Spiegler, "Everett, Ticknor and the Common Man: The Fear of Societal Instability as the Motivation for the Founding of the Boston Public Library," *Libri* 24 (1974) 249-75.

   Phyllis Dain wrote a carefully reasoned corrective to "revisionist" library history in "Ambivalence and Paradox: The Social Bonds of the Public Library," *Library Journal* 100 (1975), 261-66. Also see, in this vein, Richard Harwell and Roger Michener, "As Public as the Town Pump," *Library Journal* 99(1974), 959-63; Jesse H. Shera, "Failure and Success: Assessing a Century," *Library Journal* 100 (1976), 281-88; and Edward G. Holley, "The Past as Prologue: The Work of the Library Historian," *Journal of Library History* 12 (1977), 110-127.

   Evelyn Geller deals with the question of censorship in "Intellectual Freedom: Eternal Principle or Unanticipated Consequence?" (*Library Journal* 99 [1974], 1364-67) and "The Librarian as Censor" (*Ibid.,* 101 [1976], 1255-58).

   Elaine Fain, in "Manners and Morals in the Public Library: A Glance at Some New History" (*Journal of Library History* 10 [1975], 99-105) is critical of Harris's interpretation and of my analysis of feminization in my "Tender Technicians: The Feminization of Public Librarianship, 1876-1905" (*Journal of Social History* 6 [1973], 131-59). See the responses: Harris's "Externalist or Internalist Frameworks for the Interpretation of American Library History—The Continuing Debate" (*Journal of Library History* 10, 106-10) and my "Rejoinder" (*Ibid.,* 111-16). For defense of my analysis see also Anne E. Brugh and Benjamin R. Beede, "American Librarianship," *Signs* 1 (1976), 943-56; Jody Newmyer, "The Image Problem of the Librarian: Femininity and Social Control," *Journal of Library History* 11 (1976), 44-67; and James W. Milden, "Woman, Public Libraries, and Library Unions: The Formative Years," *Ibid.* (1977), 150-58.

   A special issue of *Library Trends* 25 (July 1976), devoted to library history and edited by Howard Winger, contains some useful articles. John Colson concludes in the historiographical lead essay, "The Writing of American Library History, 1876-1976" (7-21), that "as for the conservative purpose behind the promotion of public libraries, the weight of evidence seems to be amassing on the side of Harris and Garrison" (16).

2. Sidney Ditzion, *Arsenals of a Democratic Culture: A Social History of the American Public Library Movement in New England and the Middle Atlantic States from 1850 to 1900* (Chicago: American Library Association, 1947), and

Jesse H. Shera, *Foundations of the Public Library: The Origins of the Public Library Movement in New England, 1629–1855* (Chicago: University of Chicago Press, 1949).

3. "To What Extent Should the Library Become a Social Center?" *Proceedings, Pacific Northwest Library Association* (1913), 56.

4. Ann Douglas, *The Feminization of American Culture* (New York: Alfred A. Knopf, 1977), 11.

Chapter 1. The Genteel Setting

1. Cited in C. Seymour Thompson, *Evolution of the American Public Library, 1653–1876* (Washington, D.C.: The Scarecrow Press, 1952), 215. Also see Edward G. Holley, *Raking the Historic Coals: The American Library Association Scrapbook of 1876* (Urbana: University of Illinois Press, 1967).

2. *American Library Journal* 1 (1876), 143 (later renamed the *Library Journal* and hereafter cited as *LJ*).

3. "Call for a Library Conference," reprinted in Holley, 54.

4. Cited in Thompson. Justin Winsor, William Poole, and Charles Cutter acknowledged that it was Dewey's enthusiasm and organization that made the 1876 conference possible. See Winsor, "The President's Address," *LJ* 2 (1877), 6; Poole, "Address of the President," *LJ* 11 (1886), 201; and Cutter, "Cooperation Committee," *LJ* 4 (1879), 287.

5. Charles Cutter, "Notes," *Nation* 25 (October 11, 1877), 228. Also see U. S. Bureau of Education, *Public Libraries in the United States of America: Their History, Condition and Management,* Special Report, pt.1 (Washington D.C.: U.S. Government Printing Office, 1876). Arthur P. Young's "Reception of the 1876 Report on Public Libraries" (*Journal of Library History* 12 [1977], 50–56) is a careful study of the welcome given the *1876 Report* by the genteel establishment. See also Francis Miksa, "The Making of the 1876 Special Report on Public Libraries," *Journal of Library History* 9 (1973), 30–40.

6. For a thorough survey and bibliography of the process and history of professionalization see Samuel Haber, "The Professions and Higher Education in America: A Historical View," in Margaret S. Gordon, ed., *Higher Education and the Labor Market* (New York: McGraw-Hill Book Company, 1974), 237–80. Also see Morris L. Cogan, "Toward a Definition of Professionalism," *Harvard Educational Review* 23 (1953), 33–50.

7. Cited in Barbara Gutmann Rosenkrantz, "Cart Before Horse: Theory, Practice, and Professional Image in American Public Health, 1870–1920," *Journal of the History of Medicine and Allied Sciences* 29 (January 1974), 60. Also see Burton J. Bledstein, *The Culture of Professionalism: The Middle Class and the Development of Higher Education in America* (New York: W. W. Norton & Company, 1976).

8. William R. Johnson, "Professions in Process: Doctors and Teachers in American Culture," *History of Education Quarterly* 15 (1975), 185–201. Also see Wilbert E.

Moore, *The Professions: Roles and Rules* (New York: Russell Sage Foundation, 1970); Howard M. Vollmer and Donald L. Mills, eds., *Professionalization* (Englewood Cliffs, N. J.: Prentice-Hall, 1966); Philip Elliott, *The Sociology of the Professions* (New York: Herder and Herder, 1972); Kenneth Lynn, ed., *The Professions in America* (Boston: Beacon Press, 1967); Talcott Parsons, "The Professions and Social Structure," *Social Forces* 47 (May 1939), 457-67; William J. Goode, "Community Within a Community: The Professions," *American Sociological Review* 22 (April 1957), 194-200; entire issue of *American Behavioral Scientist* 14 (March/April 1971); Eliot Freidson, comp., *The Professions & Their Prospects* (Beverly Hills: Sage Publications, 1973); Harold L. Wilensky, "The Professionalization of Everyone?", *American Journal of Sociology* 70 (September 1964), 137-58; Ronald M. Pavalko, *Sociology of Occupations and Professions* (Itasca, Ill.: F. E. Peacock Publishers, 1971); Laurence Veysey, "Who's a Professional? Who Cares?", *Reviews in American History* 3 (December 1975), 419-23; C. Wright Mills, *White Collar* (New York: Oxford University Press, 1951).

9. Louis Galambos, *The Public Image of Big Business in America, 1880-1940* (Baltimore: Johns Hopkins University Press, 1975), and Galambos, "The Emerging Organizational Syntheses in Modern American History," *Business History Review* 44 (Autumn 1970), 279-90. For a discussion of the organizational society, see Kenneth E. Boulding, *The Organizational Revolution: A Study in the Ethics of Economic Organization* (New York: Harper & Bros., 1953), and Jerry Israel, ed., *Building the Organization Society: Essays on Associational Activities in Modern America* (New York: The Free Press, 1972), especially Samuel P. Hays, "Introduction: The New Organizational Society," 1-16. Rowland Berthoff's "The American Social Order: A Conservative Hypothesis," *American Historical Review* 65 (April 1960), 495-514, discusses the disintegration and lack of order in nineteenth century American society.

10. Robert Wiebe, *The Search for Order, 1877-1920* (New York: Hill and Wang, 1967).

11. Samuel P. Hays, "The Politics of Reform in Municipal Government in the Progressive Era," *Pacific Northwest Quarterly* 55 (October 1964), 157-69. Also see Michael Katz, *The Irony of Early School Reform: Educational Innovation in Mid-Nineteenth-Century Massachusetts* (Cambridge: Harvard University Press, 1968); Katz, *Class, Bureaucracy, and the Schools: The Illusion of Educational Change in America* (New York: Praeger Publishers, 1971); Gabriel Kolko, *The Triumph of Conservatism, A Re-Interpretation of American History* (New York: The Free Press of Glencoe, 1963); James Weinstein, *The Corporate Ideal in the Liberal State, 1900-1918* (Boston: Beacon Press, 1968); David Rothman, *The Discovery of the Asylum: Social Order and Disorder in the New Republic* (Boston: Little, Brown and Company 1971); Arnold M. Paul, *Conservative Crisis and the Rule of Law: Attitudes of Bench and Bar, 1887-1895* (Ithaca: Cornell University Press, 1960); John C. Burnham, "Medical Specialists and Movements Toward Social Control in the Progressive Era: Three Examples" in Jerry Israel, 19-30; Marvin E. Gettleman, "Philanthropy as Social Control in the Late 19th Century: Some Hypotheses and Data on the Rise of Social Work," *Societas* 5 (Winter 1975), 45-59. For an analysis of the revisionist school in the history of education, see Marvin Lazerson, "Revisionism and American Educational History," *Harvard Educational Review* 43 (1973), 269-83.

12. Examples of this approach are Gerald N. Grob, *Mental Institutions in America: Social Policy to 1875* (New York: The Free Press, 1973); Grob, "Class, Ethnicity and Race in American Mental Hospitals, 1830-75," *Journal of the History of Medicine and Allied Sciences* 28 (July 1973), 207-29; Roy Lubove, *The Professional Altruist: The Emergence of Social Work as a Career, 1880-1930* (Cambridge: Harvard University Press, 1965); Allen F. Davis, *Spearheads for Reform: The Social Settlements and the Progressive Movement, 1890-1914* (New York: Oxford University Press, 1967); Ray Merritt, *Engineering in American Society 1850-75* (Lexington: University of Kentucky Press, 1969); Diane Ravitch, *The Great School Wars: New York City, 1805-1973* (New York: Basic Books, 1974); Monte A. Calvert, *The Mechanical Engineers in America, 1830-1910: Professional Cultures in Conflict* (Baltimore: Johns Hopkins University Press, 1967); David P. Thelen, "Social Tensions and the Origins of Progressivism," *Journal of American History* 61 (September 1969), 323-41; Otis A. Pease, "Urban Reformers in the Progressive Era, A Reassessment," *Pacific Northwest Quarterly* 62 (April 1971), 49-58; and Edwin T. Layton, *The Revolt of the Engineers: Social Responsibility and the American Engineering Profession* (Cleveland: Case Western Reserve University Press, 1971).

13. Wiebe, *The Search for Order*, 44

14. Stow Persons, *The Decline of American Gentility* (New York: Columbia University Press, 1973), 8. For the history of the gentry also see Edwin Cady, *The Gentleman in America: A Literary Study in American Culture* (Syracuse: Syracuse University Press, 1949); John Tomsich, *A Genteel Endeavor: American Culture & Politics in the Gilded Age* (Stanford: Stanford University Press, 1971); Gordon Milne, *George William Curtis and the Genteel Tradition* (Bloomington: University of Indiana Press, 1961); Kermit Vanderbilt, *Charles Eliot Norton, Apostle of Culture in a Democracy* (Cambridge: Harvard University Press, 1959); Howard Mumford Jones, "The Genteel Tradition," *Harvard Library Bulletin* 18 (1970), 5-20; Martin Green, *The Problem of Boston: Some Readings in Cultural History* (New York: W. W. Norton & Company, 1966); and D. H. Meyer, *The Instructed Conscience: The Shaping of the American National Ethic* (Philadelphia: University of Pennsylvania Press, 1972). The classic discussion of the peripheral position of the gentry in the late nineteenth century is Henry Adams, *The Education of Henry Adams* (Boston: Houghton Mifflin Company, 1918).

Besides the sources already mentioned, books helpful in understanding the genteel elite are Daniel Howe, *The Unitarian Conscience* (Cambridge: Harvard University Press, 1970); Arthur Mann, *Yankee Reformers in the Urban Age: Social Reform in Boston, 1880-1900* (New York: Harper & Row, 1966); Barbara M. Solomon, *Ancestors and Immigrants: A Changing New England Tradition* (Cambridge: Harvard University Press, 1956), chaps. 1-3; E. Digby Baltzell, *The Protestant Establishment: Aristocracy and Caste in America* (New York: Random House, 1964); and Geoffrey Blodgett, *Gentle Reformers: Massachusetts Democrats in the Cleveland Era* (Cambridge: Harvard University Press, 1960). Brenda K. Shelton's *Reformers in Search of Yesterday: Buffalo in the 1890s* (Albany: State University of New York Press, 1976) is a careful local study of the gentry. Gerald W. McFarland's *Mugwumps, Morals and Politics, 1884-1920* (Amherst: University of Massachusetts Press, 1975) describes the gentry's "hybrid type of genteel progressivism." Gentry politics are discussed in John Sproat, *"The Best Men": Liberal Reformers in the Gilded Age* (New York: Oxford University Press, 1969).

Also important are Richard Hofstadter, *The Age of Reform* (New York: Random House, 1955); William R. Hutchinson, "Cultural Strain and Protestant Liberalism," *American Historical Review* 76 (April 1971), 386-411; Henry May, *The End of American Innocence* (New York: Alfred A. Knopf, 1959); and Paul Goodman, "Ethics and Enterprise: The Values of a Boston Elite, 1800-1860," *American Quarterly* 18 (Fall 1966), 437-51.

For other views of the postbellum gentry, see James McLachlan, *American Boarding Schools* (New York: Charles Scribner's Sons, 1970); Daniel Horowitz, "Genteel Observers, New England Economic Writers and Industrialization," *New England Quarterly* 48 (March 1975), 65-83; and Richard A. Gerber, "The Liberal Republicans of 1872," *Journal of American History* 62 (June 1975), 40-73.

15. Van Wyck Brooks remarked that the term "genteel tradition" has "been stretched in so many directions it is as useless as old elastic." Nevertheless, genteel is a term commonly understood to describe a complex of ideas that were influential, especially in literature, in the Gilded Age. Some attempts at a precise definition of the genteel tradition are Robert Falk, *The Victorian Mode in American Fiction, 1865-1885* (East Lansing: Michigan State University Press, 1965), 3-10; Grant C. Knight, *James Lane Allen and the Genteel Tradition* (Chapel Hill: University of North Carolina Press, 1935); Clifton Joseph Furness, ed., *The Genteel Female* (New York: Alfred A. Knopf, 1931); William Wasserstrom, "The Genteel Tradition and the Antipodes of Love," *Journal of English Literary History* 23 (1956), 299-316; Frederick I. Carpenter, "The Genteel Tradition: A Reinterpretation," *New England Quarterly* 15 (1942), 427-43; Malcolm Cowley, *After the Genteel Tradition* (New York: W. W. Norton & Company, 1937); and G. A. Santangelo, "Toward a Definition of Victorianism," *Dalhousie Review* 45 (1965), 256-67.

For two important efforts to define Victorian culture see the lead essay by Daniel Howe, "Victorian Culture in America," in Daniel Howe, ed., *Victorian America* (Philadelphia: University of Pennsylvania Press, 1976), 3-28, and Herbert G. Gutman, "Work, Culture and Society in Industrializing America," *American Historical Review* 78 (June 1973), 531-88. Paul Faler's "Cultural Aspects of the Industrial Revolution" (*Labor History* 15 [Summer 1974], 367-94) shows how the workers adapted Victorian culture. Ruth Miller Elson's *Guardians of Tradition: American Schoolbooks in the Nineteenth Century* (Lincoln: University of Nebraska Press, 1964) is a good summation of Victorian values. The impact of gentility upon children's literature is the subject of R. Gordon Kelly's *Mother Was A Lady: Self and Society in Selected American Children's Periodicals, 1865-1890* (Westport, Conn.: Greenwood Press, 1974).

16. Shelton, *Reformers in Search of Yesterday*, 195.

17. Howe, *The Unitarian Conscience*, 140. Tomsich (*A Genteel Endeavor*, 193-95) also discusses the gentry elite's attempt to substitute culture for religion. George Frederickson's *The Inner Civil War* (New York: Harper & Row, 1965, p. 29) speaks of this "secularization" in New England. Frederick Cople Jahr's "The Boston Brahmins in the Age of Industrial Capitalism" (in Jaher et al., *The Age of Industrialism in America: Essays in Social Structure and Cultural Values* [New York: The Free Press, 1968, pp. 188-262]) discusses the Brahmin response to the

new age. See also Jaher, "Nineteenth Century Elites in Boston and New York," *Journal of Social History* 6 (1972), 32–77. The decline of the professions is discussed in Daniel Calhoun, *Professional Lives in America, 1750–1850* (Cambridge: Harvard University Press, 1965).

18. Donald L. Wilson, ed., The Genteel Tradition: Nine Essays by George Santayana (Cambridge: Harvard University Press, 1967), 39–40.

19. Daniel Howe, "The Genteel Tradition," *Reviews in American History* 2 (June 1974), 246.

20. Martin Green, *"The Problem of Boston: Some Readings in Cultural History* (New York: W. W. Norton & Company, 1966), 197. The reasons why the genteel tradition collapsed are eloquently explored in this book.

21. Frederickson, *The Inner Civil War*, 29.

22. Paul S. Boyer's *Purity in Print: The Vice Society Movement and Book Censorship in America* (New York: Charles Scribner's Sons, 1968) is a study of literary censorship and the collapse of the genteel code. Boyer errs, I think, in his conclusion that the library profession as a whole was still maintaining genteel standards in the 1920s.

Chapter 2. Profile of the Library Elite

1. H. E. Green, "Library Experts; Their Rights and Duties," *LJ* 15 (1890), 18. Also see, in the same vein, Justin Winsor, "Presidential Address," *LJ* 4 (1879), 223–25; Charles Cutter, presidential address, "Common Sense in Libraries," *LJ* 14 (1889), 148–154, and "Librarians," *LJ* 17 (1892), 103; Melvil Dewey, "The Profession," *LJ* 1 (1876), 5–6; U.S. Bureau of Education, *Report to the Commissioner of Education, 1883* (Washington, D.C.: U.S. Government Printing Office, 1883), ccii.

2. Henry Carr, in a letter to F. J. Taggart, complained that Whitney's correspondence was not indicative of real literacy and observed "the evident lack of intelligence displayed" by Whitney. Whitney was sixty-four at this time. (Carr to Taggart, Henry Carr Collection, 1898–1900, File T, American Library Association Archives, University of Illinois, Urbana, Ill.; hereafter cited as ALA Archives.)

3. Dewey once described him as "the greatest old maid of the A.L.A." (Dewey to Mary Ahern, June 24, 1925, Melvil Dewey Papers, Columbia University Library, New York City; hereafter cited as MDP.)

4. For the sake of accuracy, women librarians are not included in the analysis of the librarians' fall or rise from fathers' occupations. It is uncertain whether librarianship was a fall in status for a woman. In my opinion, it is safe to assume the relatively low status of librarianship for males, even within the general category of white-collar, middle-class occupations. Librarianship at this time was a new field that did not require special skills and was comparatively low in pay.

5. Cited in Joseph A. Borome, "The Life and Letters of Justin Winsor" (Ph.D. dissertation, Columbia University, 1950), 7.

6. Edward Channing, "Justin Winsor," *American Historical Review* 3 (January 1898), 201.

7. Mrs. Thomas Bailey Aldrich, *Crowding Memories* (Boston: Houghton Mifflin Company, 1920), 91–95.

8. Walter Muir Whitehill, *Boston Public Library: A Centennial History* (Cambridge: Harvard University Press, 1956), 78. See also Horace G. Wadlin, *The Public Library of the City of Boston: A History* (Boston: The Trustees, 1911).

9. Boston Public Library, *Report to the Trustees,* (Boston, 1877), 41.

10. Hugh O'Brien, cited in Whitehill, *Boston Public Library,* 107.

11. See the annual reports of the Harvard Library, 1877–1897, and Kenneth J. Brough, *Scholar's Workshop: Evolving Conceptions of Library Service* (Urbana: University of Illinois Press, 1953), for a comparison of the Chicago, Columbia, Yale, and Harvard libraries from 1876 to 1946. Also see *The Library of Harvard University, Descriptive and Historical Notes* (Cambridge: Harvard University Press, 1934).

12. Channing, "Justin Winsor," 200.

13. David D. Van Tassel, *Recording America's Past* (Chicago: University of Chicago Press, 1960), 170. Albert B. Hart's "The Historical Opportunity in America" (*American Historical Review* 4 [October 1898], 13) discusses Winsor's work.

14. For an index of Winsor's prolific writings, see William F. Yust, "A Bibliography of Justin Winsor," *Bibliographical Contributions* (Cambridge: Harvard University Library, 1902).

15. Winsor to Dewey, February 20, 1885, MDP.

16. Winsor addressed library matters only once after 1890, in a dedication speech at the Northwestern University Library, in 1894.

17. From comments apparently written to accompany a slide-show given at the ALA convention ("ALA Presidents Folder," MDP); see also Josephine Rathbone, "Pioneers of the Library Profession," *Wilson Library Bulletin* 23, (1949), 778.

18. John Higham with Leonard Krieger and Felix Gilbert, *History: The Development of Historical Studies in the United States* (Englewood Cliffs, N.J.: Prentice-Hall, 1965), 89.

19. For analysis of the ASSA, see the interpretations in Luther Lee Bernard and Jessie Barnard, *Origins of American Sociology: The Social Movement in the United States* (New York: Thomas Y. Crowell Company, 1943); Mary O. Furner, *Advocacy and Objectivity: A Crisis in the Professionalization of American Social Science, 1865–1905* (Lexington: University Press of Kentucky, 1975); and Thomas Longdon Haskell, "Safe Havens for Sound Opinion: The American Social Science Association and the Professionalization of Social Thought in the United States, 1865–1909" (Ph.D. dissertation, Stanford University, 1973). Also see the organ of the ASSA, *Journal of Social Science,* from 1869 to 1901. Leading librarians who spoke before the ASSA include Winsor, J. N. Larned, Samuel Swett Green, Melvil Dewey, and Mellen Chamberlain. Also see Gladys Bryson, "The Emergence of the Social Sciences from Moral Philosophy," *International Journal of Ethics* 42 (April 1932), 304–23; Robert L. Church, "Economists as Experts: The Rise of an Academic Profession in the United States, 1870–1920," in Lawrence Stone, ed., *The University in Society* (Princeton, N.J.: Princeton University Press, 1974), 571–609.

20. Higham et al., *Historical Studies,* 95, 6–25; J. F. Jameson, "The American Historical Association: 1884–1909," *American Historical Review* 15 (1909), 1–21;

and Jameson, "Early Days of the American Historical Association, 1884-1895," *Ibid.* 40 (1934), 1-5.

21. The modern historians who attend the yearly AHA convention primarily for its value as a social event probably do not realize the debt owed to Mrs. Winsor, who as hostess in her Boston home in 1887 initiated the annual conviviality.

22. Elizabeth Donnan and Leo F. Stock, eds., *An Historian's World: Selections from the Correspondence of John Franklin Jameson* (Philadelphia: The American Philosophical Society, 1956), 47. See also Winsor, "The Perils of Historical Narrative," *Atlantic Monthly* 66 (1890), 297; Michael Kraus, *The Writing of American History* (Norman: University of Oklahoma Press, 1953), 227-29.

23. Ronald Story's "Class and Culture in Boston: The Athenaeum, 1807-1860" *American Quarterly* 27 [May 1975], 178-99 discusses the elite nature of the institution. Also see Josiah Quincy, *History of the Boston Athenaeum* (Cambridge: Metcalf and Company, 1851) and Neil Harris, "The Gilded Age Revisited: Boston and the Museum Movement," *American Quarterly* 14 (Winter 1962), 545-66.

24. William Landram Williamson, *William Frederick Poole and the Modern Library Movement* (New York: Columbia University Press, 1963), 82-84.

25. Paul Finkelman, "Class and Culture in Late Nineteenth-century Chicago: The Founding of the Newberry Library," *American Studies* 16 (Spring 1975), 8, 16. See also William Warner Bishop, "Some Chicago Librarians of the Nineties: Fragments of Autobiography," *Library Quarterly* 14 (1943-1944), 339-48.

26. Cited in Williamson, 153.

27. William Poole, "The Construction of Library Buildings," *LJ* 6 (1881), 73. See also Poole, "Small Library Buildings," *LJ* 10 (1885), 250-56, "Process of Library Architecture," *LJ* 7 (1882), 130-36.

28. Williamson, 65-92, 118-29. See also William I. Fletcher, "William Frederick Poole, LLD—A Tribute," *LJ* 19 (1894), 81-83; Carl B. Roden, "The Boston Years of Dr. W. L. Poole," in William Warner Bishop and Andrew Keogh, eds., *Essays Offered to Herbert Putnam* (New Haven: Yale University Press, 1929), 388-94; Sidney H. Kessler, "William Frederick Poole, Librarian-Historian," *Wilson Library Bulletin* 28 (May 1954), 788-90; *Memorial Sketch of Dr. William Frederick Poole* (Chicago: The Newberry Library, 1895); Gladys Spencer, *The Chicago Public Library: Origins and Background* (Chicago: University of Chicago Press, 1943); Jim Ranz, *The Printed Book Catalogue in American Libraries 1723-1900* (Chicago: American Library Association, 1964); and Ruth French Strout, ed., *Library Catalogs: Changing Dimensions* (Chicago: University of Chicago Press, 1964)—especially "The Changing Character of the Catalog in America" by David Weber, 20-33.

29. Williamson, 94-95.

30. Poole to Winsor, May 22, 1892. Cited in Thomison, "The History and Development of the American Library Association," Ph.D. dissertation, University of Southern California, Library School, 1973, 83-84.

31. Frank P. Hill to Dewey, May 22, 1892, MDP. Also see Dewey to members of ALA Exposition Committee, June 22, 1892, MDP.

32. F. M. Crunden to Dewey, June 17, 1892, MDP.

33. Dewey to J. Y. W. McAllister, n.d., MDP.

34. Edith E. Clarke to Dewey, July 5, 1893, MDP.

35. Legend has it that only accidental circumstances prevented Cutter rather than Winsor from being offered the chief job at the Harvard Library in 1868. (Clarence Ralph Morse, "A Biographical, Bibliographical Study of Charles Ammi Cutter, Librarian" [master's thesis, University of Washington, 1961], 23.)

36. Quincy, *History of the Boston Athenaeum;* Charles K. Bolton, ed., *The Influence and History of the Boston Athenaeum* (Boston: Boston Athenaeum, 1907).

37. *LJ* 18 (1893), 35.

38. The best study of Cutter's life is Francis Miksa's "Charles Cutter: 19th Century Systemizer of American Public Libraries," Ph.D. dissertation, University of Chicago, 1974. My interpretation of Cutter slightly differs from that of Miksa (pp. 633–34), who sees Cutter as somewhere in between the Winsor-Poole social stance and the Dewey position. Also see William Parker Cutter, *Charles Ammi Cutter* (Chicago: American Library Association, 1931); William E. Foster, "Charles Ammi Cutter," *LJ* 28 (1903), 697–704; and Foster, "5 Men of '76," *ALA Bulletin* 20 (October 1926), 316–317; W. T. Solberg, "Some Memories of Charles Ammi Cutter," *LJ* 28 (1903), 769–70. Cutter was not happy at the Forbes. He sarcastically noted his first day's circulation of one hundred books in Cutter to Miss Browne, September 17, 1859, James I. Wyer Autograph Collection, ALA Archives, and noted his desire to leave Forbes in Cutter to Mrs. Carr, July 28, 1903, *Ibid.*

39. *Bulletin Bibliography* 8 (1914), 59–60. Dewey may have been thinking of Cutter's brief use of Dewey's "simplified spelling" in the pages of the *Library Journal*. See Cutter's "Review of *Bas-Bleus*" *(The Nation* 26 [May 2, 1878], 293) for his liberal view of women's rights.

40. Daniel Walker Howe, *The Unitarian Conscience: Harvard Moral Philosophy, 1805–1861* (Cambridge: Harvard University Press, 1970), 12.

41. Charles Cutter, "The Buffalo Public Library in 1983: An Excursion in the Land of Dreams," *LJ* 8 (1883), 211–17.

42. Charles Cutter, "Should Libraries Buy Only the Best Books or the Best Books That People Will Read?", *LJ* 26 (1901), 70, 71, 72; Cutter, presidential address, "Common Sense in Libraries," *LJ* 14 (1889), 150.

43. Cutter, "The Public Library and Its Choice of Books," *LJ* 3 (1878), 73.

44. Charles Cutter, "The Boston Public Library Catalogue of English Prose Fiction," *Nation* 30 (April 19, 1877), 235.

45. Charles Cutter, "Pernicious Reading in Our Public Libraries," *Nation* 33 (November 10, 1881), 371.

46. *Ibid.*

Chapter 3. The Social Ideals of Early Library Leaders

1. A movement that John Higham, *From Boundlessness to Consolidation* (Ann Arbor, Mich.: William L. Clements Library, 1969, p. 15) argues actually began as early as the 1850s.

2. James Howard Wellard's *Book Selection: Its Principles and Practices* (London: Grafton and Co., 1937) is an excellent comparative study of the social objectives of the public library in the United States and England. Sidney Ditzion's "Social Reform, Education and the Library, 1850-1900" *(Library Quarterly* 9 [1939], 156-84) provides a summation of reformative thought. The best general history of the ALA is Dennis V. Thomison, "The History and Development of the American Library Association," Ph.D. dissertation, University of Southern California, Library School, 1973. Also helpful are Lucy Jane Maddox, "Trends and Issues in American Librarianship as Reflected in the Papers and Proceedings of the American Library Association, 1876-1885" (Ph.D. dissertation, University of Michigan, Library School, 1958), and Francis G. Collier, "A History of the American Public Library Movement Through 1880" (Ph.D. dissertation, University of Chicago, Library School, 1973). For a more detailed documentation of the enunciation of the educational and social ideals of library leaders, see Dee Garrison, "Cultural Missionaries: A Study of American Public Library Leaders, 1876-1910" (Ph.D. dissertation, University of California, 1973).

3. J. P. Quincy, "Free Libraries," U.S. Bureau of Education, *Public Libraries in the United States of America: Their History, Condition, and Management,* Special Report, pt. 1 (Washington, D.C.: U.S. Government Printing Office, 1876), 399-400.

4. Charles Cutter, "Proposed Library Convention," *Nation* 23 (July 27, 1876), 60.

5. J. N. Larned, "Presidential Address," *LJ* 19 (1894), 1.

6. Justin Winsor, "Presidential Address," *LJ* 4 (1879), 223.

7. "Editorial," *LJ* 6 (1881), 39.

8. Mary Imogen Crandall, "The Art Element in Library Work," *LJ* 13 (1888), 365.

9. J. G. Holland, *Every-day Topics: A Book of Briefs* (New York: Charles Scribner's Sons, 1886), 2, 3. This little-known book is an interesting contemporary account of genteel concerns.

10. Paul A. Carter's *The Spiritual Crisis of the Gilded Age* (De Kalb: Northern Illinois University Press, 1971) explores how the general withering of faith extended downward into the populace. Also see D. H. Meyer, "American Intellecutals and the Victorian Crisis of Faith," in Daniel W. Howe, ed., *Victorian America* (Philadelphia: University of Pennsylvania Press, 1976), 59-81. Librarian Mellen Chamberlain recorded his inner battle with religious doubts in his "Journal," Mellen Chamberlain Papers, Boston Public Library.

11. Raymond M. Merritt, *Engineering in American Society* (Lexington: University Press of Kentucky, 1969), 9. In this study of the professionalization of engineering, the author notes how engineers, too, compared themselves to doctors, lawyers, and the clergy. Robert W. Doherty's "Status Anxiety and American Reform: Some Alternatives" *(American Quarterly* 19 [Summer 1967], 329-37) discusses weaknesses in the status anxiety theory and suggests the use of role playing and reference group concepts as intervening variables between status and behavior.

12. Cited in Grosvenor Dawe, *Melvil Dewey: Seer: Inspirer: Doer 1851-1931* (Lake Placid, N.Y.: Lake Placid Club, 1932), 12. J. N. Larned, "Presidential Address," *LJ* 19 (1894), 3; M. Merrington, "Public Libraries and Public Schools," *LJ* 12 (1887), 158; Justin Winsor, "Free Libraries and Readers," *LJ* 1 (1876), 65.

13. Melvil Dewey, "The Profession," *LJ* 1 (1876), 6.

14. James Whitney, "Selecting and Training Library Assistants," *LJ* 7 (1882), 137-38.

15. Lloyd P. Smith, "The Qualifications of a Librarian," *LJ* 1 (1876), 73. Dewey told the story of visiting Smith at the Philadelphia Company Library, where he was shocked to see only three or four patrons in the library. Smith reportedly told Dewey with pride, "There is scarcely a day that *somebody* doesn't come into this library." (Melvil Dewey, "Our Next Half-Century," *ALA Bulletin* 20 [1926], 309.)

16. Samuel Green, "Discussion," *LJ* 7 (1882), 201.

17. Samuel Green, "Personal Relations between Librarians and Readers," *LJ* 1 (1876), 80.

18. *Ibid.*

19. Charles Cutter, "The Public Library and Its Choice of Books," *LJ* 3 (1878), 73.

20. "Letters to the Editor," *LJ* 16 (1891), 201. For an example of the column, see *LJ* 14 (1889), 330.

21. Frederick Perkins, "Public Libraries and the Public with Special Reference to the San Francisco Free Public Library," *LJ* 10 (1885), 228.

22. James M. Hubbard, "How to Use a Public Library," *LJ* 9 (1884), 28.

23. Mary Jane Regan, *Echoes from the Past* (Boston: Boston Athenaeum, 1927), 43-44.

24. William Foster, "Address," *LJ* 22 (1897), 116-17. An amusing interchange between Henry Carr and a novelty company illustrates the genteel librarian's cautious attention to manners. Carr, in exasperation, finally wrote the man who sought to sell him a convention name-badge, "In fact I believe the majority of [ALA] members would rather be found dead, than wearing the usual convention badge." (Carr to Baltimore Badge and Novelty Co., February 17, 1900, Carr Correspondence, ALA Archives.)

25. Cutter, "Public Library Choice of Books," 73.

26. "Library Cranks," *LJ* 12 (1887), 228.

27. Charles Cutter, "The Buffalo Public Library in 1983," "*LJ* 8 (1883), 213; Cutter, "Unwelcome Library Visitors," *LJ* 8 (1883), 73-75.

28. William L. Williamson, *William Frederick Poole and the Modern Library Movement* (New York: Columbia University Press, 1963), 51.

29. *LJ*, 7 (1882), 235.

30. "Report of Bridgeport, Connecticut, Public Library," *LJ* 7 (1882), 233-34.

31. John L. Thomas, "Romantic Reform in America, 1815-1865,"*American Quarterly* 18 (Winter 1965), 656-81; Henry J. Perkinson, *The Imperfect Panacea: American Faith in Education, 1865-1965* (New York: Random House, 1968); Robert Wiebe, "The Social Functions of Public Education," *American Quarterly* 21 (Summer 1969), 147-65.

32. *LJ* 1 (1877), 395.

33. A. M. Pendleton, "Notions Wise and Otherwise," *LJ* 5 (1880), 4.

34. "The New York Free Circulating Library," *LJ* 11 (1886), 80-81.

35. "Report of Levi Parsons Library, Gloversville, New York," *LJ* 12 (1887), 528.

36. A. L. Peck, "Workingmen's Clubs and the Public Library," *LJ* 23 (1898), 612.

37. John Sproat, *"The Best Men": Liberal Reformers in the Gilded Age* (New

York: Oxford University Press, 1969), 238–42. Larned's position as a gentry reformer and his alliance with the elite of Buffalo is further confirmed in a careful local study of the elite reformers in the 1890s in Brenda K. Shelton's *Reformers in Search of Yesterday* (Albany: State University of New York Press, 1976).

38. J. N. Larned, "Presidential Address," *LJ* 19 (1894), 2, 3, 4; Larned, "Retrospect and Prospect in the Last Years of the Century," *LJ* 21 (1896), 12.

39. *Ibid.*

40. William Brett, "The Present Problem," *LJ* 19 (1894), 5, 7, 8.

41. J. N. Larned, "An Experiment in University Extension," *LJ* 13 (1888), 76. Also Larned to Dewey, July 6, 1889, MDP.

42. William Brett, "The Public Library Made Useful," *Independent* 49 (November 18, 1897), 3.

43. J. N. Larned, *Talks About Labor* (New York: D. Appleton and Company, 1876).

44. *Ibid.*, 45.

45. *Ibid.*, 82.

46. *Ibid.*, 96.

47. *Ibid.*, 124.

48. *Ibid.*, 127.

49. *Ibid.*, 129.

50. J. N. Larned, "A Criticism of Two-Party Politics," *Atlantic Monthly* 107 (1911), 291.

51. J. N. Larned, "The Flaw in Our Democracy," *Atlantic Monthly* 84 (1899), 530.

52. J. N. Larned, "Prepare for Socialism," *Atlantic Monthly* 107 (1911), 577–80. Also see Larned, "Our Money Problems," *Ibid.* 25 (1870), 615–26; "A Practicable Organization of Democracy," *Ibid.* 112 (1913), 610–616; Sidney Ditzion, "The Social Ideals of a Library Pioneer, Josephus Nelson Larned, 1863–1913," *Library Quarterly* 13 (1943), 113–31.

53. William Foster, *The Civil Service Reform Movement* (Boston: George H. Ellis, 1882), 46. Also see Foster to Chamberlain, October 18, 1889, Mellen Chamberlain Papers.

54. Bernard Poll, "Working People and Their Relationship to the American Public Library: History and Analysis," master's thesis, School of Librarianship, University of Washington, 1950; Dorothy Kuhn Oko and Bernard F. Downey, *Library Service to Labor* (New York: The Scarecrow Press, 1963). Samuel Gompers, commenting on a proposed Carnegie Library, wrote to a local labor leader: "After all is said and done, he [Carnegie] might put his money to a much worse act. Yes, accept his library, organize the workers to secure better conditions and particularly, reduction of hours of labor and then workers will have some chance and leisure in which to read books." (Cited in George S. Bobinski, *Carnegie Libraries: Their History and Impact on American Public Library Development* [Chicago: American Library Association, 1969, p. 104].) In 1895 a library survey showed that about 20 per cent of the population used the public library; almost all of these were professionals, women, and children. ("Proceedings," *LJ* [1900], 125.) Also see J. F. Olle, "Andrew Carnegie, the 'Unloved Benefactor' " (*Library World* 70 [1969], 255–62) and David McLeod, *Carnegie Libraries in Wisconsin* (Madison: State Historical Society, 1968).

55. Cited in Bobinski, *Carnegie Libraries*, 103.

56. Lutie E. Stearns, "An Innovation in Library Meetings," *LJ* 31 (1906), 55-57. Library elitism toward labor is illustrated in Philip A. Kalisch, *The Enoch Pratt Free Library: A Social History* (Metuchen, N.J.: The Scarecrow Press, 1969), 84.

57. On the question of Sunday openings, the interested reader can consult "The New Sunday," *Atlantic Monthly* 47 (1881), 526-37; Mary S. Cutler, "Sunday Openings of Libraries" and "Statistics of Sunday Openings" in *U.S. Bureau of Education, 1893 Report* (Washington, D.C.: U.S. Government Printing Office, 1893), 771-95; and *LJ*, for 1889, 176-90, 279-81, and for 1907, 103-07, 112-13, and for 1916, 336-38. Sidney Ditzion's study of the Sunday question as it developed in Boston is in "Opening the People's Library on the Lord's Day," *School and Society* 70 (July 23, 1949), 49-53. On the open-shelf question, see Thomas Wentworth Higginson, "Access to the Shelves," *Harper's Bazaar* (May 24, 1890), and *LJ* 15 (1890), 229-31; *LJ* 23 (1898), 40-42; *LJ* 24 (1899), 136-42; *LJ* 25 (1900), 113-15; and *LJ* 26 (1901), 65-70.

58. The literature on the history of education is voluminous. I found most helpful as a general survey David Tyack's *The One Best System: A History of American Urban Education* (Cambridge: Harvard University Press, 1974). Also see Robert Church, "Educational Psychology and Social Reform in the Progressive Era," *History of Education Quarterly* 11 (Winter 1971), 390-405; Marvin Lazerman, *Origins of the Urban School: Public Education in Massachusetts, 1870-1915* (Cambridge: Harvard University Press, 1971); Laurence R. Veysey, *The Emergence of the American University* (Chicago: University of Chicago Press, 1965); Samuel Bowles and Herbert Gintis, *Schooling in Capitalist America: Educational Reform and the Contradictions of Economic Life* (New York: Basic Books, 1976).

   Lawrence Cremin has traced the Progressive movement in American education which began in the 1870s and has connected it with the larger movement of American progressivism" which gained political power before World War I in *The Transformation of the School: Progressivism in American Education, 1876-1957* (New York: Alfred A. Knopf, 1961). For other views of the diverse strains of Progressive reform in education, see Robert Beck, "Progressive Education and American Progressivism," *Teacher's College Record* 60 (1958-59), 77-89; Louis Filler, "Main Currents in Progressivist Education," *History of Education Journal* 8 (1957), 33-57; and David Tyack, "Education and Social Unrest, 1873-78," *Harvard Educational Review* 31 (1961), 194-212. Timothy Smith's "Progressivism in American Education, 1880-1900" (*Harvard Educational Review* 31 [1961], 168-193) neglects the contribution of the public librarian but presents an argument that educational reform in this period was often imposed by laymen. Smith argues that the reform of education was the first phase of the Progressive movement and that it originated among laymen, in the cities.

59. Herbert Spencer, *Education* (New York: Hurst and Company, 1867), 107.

60. William James, *Talks to Teachers in Psychology* (New York: W. W. Norton & Company, 1958); Dorothy Ross, *G. Stanley Hall: The Psychologist as Prophet* (Chicago: University of Chicago Press, 1972).

61. Lewis F. Anderson, *Pestalozzi* (New York: McGraw-Hill Book Company, 1931); Mary R. Walch, *Pestalozzi and the Pestalozzian Theory of Education* (Washington, D.C.: Catholic University of America Press, 1952).

62. Harold B. Dunkel, *Herbart and Herbartianism: An Educational Ghost Story*

(Chicago: University of Chicago Press, 1970); "Herbartianism Come to America," *History of Education Quarterly* 9 (Spring 1969), 202-34; *ibid.* (Fall 1969), 376-91. A discussion of the culture epochs theory used by Herbartians is in Charles E. Strickland, "The Child, the Community and Clio: The Uses of Cultural History in Elementary School Experiments of the Eighteen-Nineties," *History of Education Quarterly* 7 (Winter 1967), 474-92.

63. As Sidney Ditzion points out in *Arsenals of a Democratic Culture: A Social History of the American Public Library Movement in New England and the Middle Atlantic States from 1850 to 1900* (Chicago: American Library Association, 1947, pp. 91-96), Barnard's influential *Journal of Education*, along with other educational journals, pays relatively little attention to early library-school cooperation. Yet Barnard's attendance at the formative library conventions of 1853 and 1876, as well as his involvement with Dewey, indicates his interest in the movement.

64. See Bureau of Education, *1876 Report*, especially p. 48, and Carelton Joeckel, *The Government of the American Public Library* (Chicago: University of Chicago Press 1939), 8-14.

65. Charles William Eliot, *Educational Reform* (New York Century Co., 1909), 185. The study of short selections was probably borrowed from the older method of study of the Latin and Greek classics, which was designed as an exercise for the grammarian. Criticism of the piecemeal approach to literature began among educators in the 1880s and became widespread by the late 1890s.

66. Phillip Hollis, *The Oswego Normal School* (Boston: D. C. Heath & Company 1898); Ned Dearborn, *The Oswego Movement in American Education* (New York: Bureau of Publications, Teacher's College, Columbia University, 1925).

67. Charles F. Adams, "Address to the Teachers of Quincy," Massachusetts, May 19, 1876, reprinted in S. S. Green, *Libraries and Schools* (New York: F. Leypoldt, 1883), 10. See also Adams, "Scientific Common School Education," *Harper's New Monthly Magazine* 61 (October 1880), 935-40; Adams, "The Development of the Superintendency," *Journal of Proceedings and Addresses of the National Educational Association* (hereafter cited as "NEA"; Chicago, 1880), 68, 74; and Edward Chase Kirkland, *Charles Francis Adams, Jr.* (Cambridge: Harvard University Press, 1965), 147, 150-52. Adams attended several conventions of the ALA. Also see Michael Katz, "The 'New Departure' in Quincy, 1873-81: The Nature of Nineteenth-Century Educational Reform," *New England Quarterly* 40 (March 1967), 3-20.

68. Charles Cutter, cited in "The Public Library and the Public Schools," *LJ* 1 (1876), 437.

69. F. M. Crunden, "The School and the Library—The Value of Literature in Early Education," NEA (1901), 108. For the most representative and comprehensive discussions of what ends librarians believed library materials in the schools would achieve, see Mellen Chamberlain, "Public Library and Public School," *LJ* 5 (1880), 299-302; Minerva Sanders, "The Relation of the Public Library to the School," *LJ* 14 (1889), 79-83; Linda Eastman, "The Child, the School and the Library," *LJ* 21 (1896), 34-39; Caroline M. Hewins, "The Relation of the Hartford Public Library to the Public Schools," *LJ* 19 (1894), 292-95; Ellen M. Coe, "The Relation of Libraries to Public Schools," *LJ* 17 (1892), 193-94; William Brett, "The Relations of the Public Library to the Public Schools," NEA (1892),

692. For examples of the slight esteem given to teachers as a group by early librarians, see Crunden, "Reading by School-Children and College Students," *LJ* 13 (1888), 89, and "Meeting of the New York Library Club," *LJ* 12 (1887), 77.

70. Robert Kendall Shaw, *Samuel Swett Green* (Chicago: American Library Association, 1926).

71. Green, *Libraries and Schools*, 231. See also Green, *The Public Library Movement in the United States, 1853-1893* (Boston: The Boston Book Company, 1913), 304-05, and Green, "Sensational Fiction in Public Libraries," *LJ* 4 (1879), 345-55. Green was apparently known for his deadly verbosity. Henry Carr wrote to Charles Cutter in 1900 that if Green were asked to give a paper at the next conference, "I suspect it will be essential to limit Green strictly as to time . . . for you know he is apt to be prolix." Cutter replied: "Hesitate to ask Mr. G. He has no time-sense. Shall try others." (Henry Carr Correspondence, ALA Archives.)

72. Green, *Libraries and Schools*, 51. See also Green, "The Public Libraries and the Schools in Worcester: Some New Experiments and Their Results," *LJ* 12 (1887), 119-21.

73. William E. Foster, "The Relation of the Libraries to the School System," *LJ* 5 (1880), 99-104; "The School and the Library, Their Mutual Relation," *LJ* 4 (1879), 319-25; "A Plan of Systematic Training in Reading at School," *LJ* 8 (1883), 24-26; "Developing a Taste for Good Literature," *LJ* 22 (1897), 245-51; *Libraries and Readers* (New York: F. Leypoldt, 1883). See also Joseph L. Wheeler, "Providence Pioneer: William E. Foster," *Wilson Library Bulletin* 40 (1965), 275-78, and C. E. Sherman, "William E. Foster, 1851-1930: Liberal Librarian," *Ibid.* 30 (1956), 449-53, 467.

74. Cited in Green, *Libraries and Schools*, 74. See also R. C. Metcalf, "Reading in the Public Schools," *LJ* 4 (1879), 343-45.

75. Green, *Libraries and Schools*, 86. See NEA (1881), 104-17, for further evidence of early beliefs in the mechanization of reading pleasure.

76. William T. Harris, "The Function of the Library and the School in Education," *LJ* 15 (1890), 28, 29.

77. William Brett, "Discussion," *LJ* 17 (1892), 61.

78. Clement Young, "The Public Library and the Public Schools," *LJ* 21 (1896), 143.

79. NEA (1897), 1140. In 1920 the NEA formed a joint committee with the ALA. The only other such alliances of the NEA are with the American Medical Association, the American Legion, and the American Teacher's Association.

80. See Joseph Gusfield, *Symbolic Crusade: Status Politics and the American Temperance Movement* (Urbana: University of Illinois Press, 1963), for a statement of the theory of status politics.

81. Clifford Geertz, "Ideology as a Cultural System," in *The Interpretation of Cultures* (London: Hutchinson and Company, 1975), 193-233.

82. Paul S. Boyer, *Purity in Print: The Vice Society Movement and Book Censorship in America* (New York: Charles Scribner's Sons, 1968), 20.

83. Joseph Gusfield, "Moral Passage: The Symbolic Process in Public Designation of Deviance," *Social Problems* 15 (1967), 187. A defense of popular culture, and a refutation and analysis of its critics, are well argued in Herbert Gans, *Popular Culture and High Culture* (New York: Basic Books, 1974).

Chapter 4. Immoral Fiction in the Late Victorian Library

1. U.S. Bureau of Education, *Public Libraries in the United States of America: Their History, Condition, and Management,* Special Report, pt. 1 (Washington, D.C.: U.S. Government Printing Office, 1876), 393.

2. Esther Jane Carrier's *Fiction in Public Libraries, 1876–1900* (New York: The Scarecrow Press, 1965) is a summation of library literature on the "fiction question."

3. For typical comments addressed to the masses by literary conservatives, see Noah Porter, *Books and Reading or What Books Shall I Read and How Shall I Read Them?* (New York: Charles Scribner's Sons, 1891); Charles F. Richardson, *The Choice of Books* (New York: Useful Knowledge Publishing Company, 1882); J. N. Larned, *A Talk About Books* (Buffalo: The Peter Paul University Press, 1921); William Atkinson, *On the Right Use of Books* (Boston: Roberts Brothers, 1880); and Lyman Abbott, ed., *Hints for Home Reading* (New York: G. P. Putnam's Sons, 1892). For bibliographical aids to the library guides most often recommended by librarians, see William E. Foster, "Books and Articles on Reading," in *Libraries and Readers* (New York: G. P. Putnam's Sons, 1887); Frederick B. Perkins, ed., *The Best Reading* (New York: G. P. Putnam's Sons, 1877); Augusta H. Leypoldt and George Iles, eds., *List of Books for Girls and Women and Their Clubs* (Boston: American Library Association, 1895).

   Richard Altick's *The English Common Reader, A Social History of the Mass Reading Public, 1800–1900* (Chicago: University of Chicago Press, 1957, p. 139) notes the same development occurring in England, where "literally thousands of chatty homilies" were printed between 1850 and 1900. See also J. N. Larned, *A Primer of Right and Wrong for Young People in Schools and Families* (Boston: Houghton Mifflin Company, 1902); Larned, *Books, Culture and Character* (Boston: Houghton Mifflin Company, 1906); Larned, "Public Libraries and Public Education," address to the American Social Science Association, reprinted in *LJ* 9 (1884), 6–12; Larned, "The Mission and the Missionaries of the Book," address before the 1896 Convocation of New York educators, *Regents' Report, New York, 1896,* 90–103;

   The best summaries of earlier reactions to mass reading are G. Harrison Orians, "Censure of Fiction in American Romances and Magazines, 1789–1810," *Publications of the Modern Language Society* 52 (1937), 195–215; W. F. Galloway, "The Conservative Attitude Toward Fiction, 1770–1830," *Ibid.* 55 (1940), 1041–1059; John T. Taylor, *Early Opposition to the English Novel* (New York: King Crown's Press, 1943); and sections of Frank Luther Mott, *Golden Multitudes: The Story of Best Sellers in the United States* (New York: The Macmillan Company, 1947), and James Hart, *The Popular Book* (New York: Oxford University Press, 1950). For similar Victorian attitudes in England see Louis James, *Fiction for the Working Man, 1830–1850* (London: Oxford University Press, 1963), and Altick, *English Common Reader.*

4. Josiah P. Quincy, "The Abuse of Reading," in *The Protection of Majorities* (Boston: Roberts Brothers, 1876), 116.

5. Porter, *Books and Reading,* 16; Frederick Harrison, "The Choice of Books," *Littell's Living Age* 141 (1879), 262.

6. Richardson, *Choice of Books*, 10.

7. Cited in Abbott, *Hints for Home Reading*, 23. Also see Harry Lyman Koopman, *The Mastery of Books* (New York: American Book Company, 1882), 21.

8. Harrison, "Choice of Books," 262.

9. Bureau of Education, *1876 Report*, 236,

10. Fred Lewis Pattee, *The Feminine Fifties* (New York: Appleton-Century, 1940); C. J. Furness, ed., *The Genteel Female* (New York: Alfred A. Knopf, 1931); Herbert Ross Brown, *The Sentimental Novel in America, 1789–1860* (Durham, N.C.: Duke University Press, 1940).

11. Elaine Showalter, *A Literature of Their Own: British Women Novelists from Brontë to Lessing* (Princeton: Princeton University Press, 1977); Ann Douglas, "Why Women Wrote," *American Quarterly* 23 (Spring 1971), 3–24; and Douglas, "Heaven Our Home," *Ibid.* 26 (December 1974), 296–315.

12. Mary L. Beecher, "The Practical Value in Life of a Taste for Good Literature," *Addresses and Proceedings of the National Educational Association* (1888), 83.

13. Abbott, *Hints for Home Reading*, 12, 13. Also see Mary Alice Caller, *Literary Guide for Home and School* (New York: Charles E. Merrill, 1892), 24–25; Lucy Soulsby, *Stray Thoughts on Reading* (New York: Longmans, Green and Company, 1897), 47–54. John Ruskin's *Sesame and Lilies* (New York: Belford, Clarke and Company, 1889, pp. 72–101) is a reprint of a lecture delivered in England in 1864. Both Kate Millet's *Sexual Politics* (New York: Doubleday & Company, 1970, pp. 89–108) and Walter Houghton's *The Victorian Frame of Mind* (New Haven: Yale University Press, 1957, p. 343) consider this essay to be the central document which best represents the idealization of women in Victorian thought and comment upon the lack of attention it has received from scholars.

14. Charles Dudley Warner, "Modern Fiction," in Thomas Lounsbury, ed., *The Complete Writings of Charles Dudley Warner* (Hartford: The American Publishing Company, 1894), 167.

15. William Wasserstrom's *Heiress of all the Ages: Sex and Sentiment in the Genteel Tradition* (Minneapolis: University of Minnesota Press, 1959, pp. 3–38) concentrates upon high literature of the post–Civil War era and finds traces of the New Woman heroine as early as the 1850s. Wasserstrom states that the genteel tradition developed between 1790 and 1830 as conservative opposition to social, political, and theological liberalism, exaggerated by a kind of horror at the revolution in France. Shortly before the Civil War, he believes, the genteel code was challenged, "first in the popular literature of the times"; then, after the war, "serious literature, too, more and more openly reasserted half-forgotten values" (p. 21). Wasserstrom does not elaborate further on the way in which popular literature moved away from the genteel code. His study is of the representation of the American woman in serious literature, from about 1860 to 1914, as artists came to make a more realistic assessment of her sexual and social needs.

16. Fred Weinstein and Gerald M. Platt's *The Wish to Be Free: Society, Psyche and Value Change* (Los Angeles: University of California Press, 1969) revises Weber's concept with an argument that the traits of the "Protestant ethic" have recurred "in circumstances where Protestantism could have had at best only a peripheral and external influence—in, for example, the French and Russian revolutions" (p.

11). They assert that the cultural traits in question typify any society which is withdrawing from traditional authority on institutional levels, Protestantism being but one such occasion. However, their analysis begins to flounder when they equate modernization with an increase in personal autonomy and ever-widening levels of democratization for all classes in society and at the same time require modernization to be characterized by sensual constraint and rational discipline. See Herbert Marcuse, *Eros and Civilization* (Boston: The Beacon Press, 1955) for an anti-Freudian argument that modernization is not dependent upon instinctual repression.

17. Porter, *Books and Reading*, 236.

18. For additional evidence of this attitude, see James Baldwin, *The Book Lover: A Guide to the Best Reading* (Chicago: A. C. McClurg and Company, 1892); Mark Pattison, "Books and Critics," *Littell's Living Age* 135 (1877), 771–83; Edmund Kempus Broadus, *Books and Ideals* (New York: Oxford University Press, 1921); J. A. McLellan, "The Ethical Element in Literature," NEA (1894), 71–84; and H. Morse Stephens *et al.*, *Counsel Upon the Reading of Books* (Boston: Houghton Mifflin Company, 1900). Houghton's *Victorian Frame of Mind* also marks the 1870s as the time in England when more modern ideas began to severely shake faith in traditional morality and religion. See especially his chapter "Character of the Age," pp. 1–23.

19. Porter, *Books and Reading*, 39. See also Alexander Ireland, *The Book-Lover's Enchiridion* (London: Simpkin, Marshall and Company, 1883), 375. See also Earl of Iddesleigh, "On the Pleasures, the Dangers, and the Uses of Desultory Reading," *Littell's Living Age* 169 (1886), 131–40; Larned, *Primer of Right and Wrong*, 152–53; and Foster, *Libraries and Readers* for discussions of reading as a serious moral and intellectual endeavor.

20. Cited in Porter, *Books and Reading*, 72–73.

21. Caller, *Literary Guide*, 90.

22. Warner, *Complete Writings*, 162, 165.

23. Raymond Williams's *Culture and Society, 1780–1950* (London: Chatto & Windus, 1958, pp. 134–39) discusses Ruskin's, Carlyle's and Arnold's concepts of the "good" in an artist.

24. ALA Cooperation Committee, "Report on Exclusion," *LJ* 7 (1882), 28.

25. Arthur Lovejoy, *Great Chain of Being: A Study of the History of an Idea* (Cambridge: Harvard University Press, 1936), 20.

26. David Madden, "The Necessity for an Aesthetics of Popular Culture," *Journal of Popular Culture* 7 (Summer 1973), 2. For another approach to fantasy as an indicator of value changes, see Neil J. Smelser, *Social Change in the Industrial Revolution* (Chicago: University of Chicago Press, 1959), and Edward J. Tiryakian, "A Model of Societal Change and Its Lead Indicators," in Samuel Z. Klausner, ed., *The Study of Total Societies* (New York: Praeger Publishers, 1967), 69–98.

27. Actually, a total of twenty-eight questionable authors were listed; but nine of these will be excluded from consideration in this study because they wrote primarily for children. Three other authors—Edmund Yates, E. L. Bulwer, and Wilkie Collins—also will not be considered because the reaction to the published

list revealed that most librarians did not concur with the committee's inclusion of these men among the objectionable.

28. There has been little serious study of these sixteen authors. Most commentators, however, have seen the domestic and sensational popular fiction of this time as basically conservative. Representative of this view are Mott, *Golden Multitudes;* Hart, *The Popular Book;* Pattee, *Feminine Fifties;* Furness, *Genteel Female;* and Brown, *Sentimental Novel in America.* A few writers have emphasized the revolt against male supremacy: Beatrice Hofstadter, "Popular Culture and the Romantic Heroine," *American Scholar* 30 (Winter 1960-1961), 98-116; and Helen Waite Papashvily, *All the Happy Endings* (New York: Harper & Bros., 1956). Also see Elaine Showalter's unpublished paper presented at the Victorian Studies Conference, 1975: "Family Secrets: Domestic Subversion in the Novels of the 1860's." Robert Reigel's *American Feminists* (Lawrence: University of Kansas Press, 1963) comments that these domestic novelists would not have openly admitted their revolt. It seems to me that anyone reading these novels could not help but see that the heroine triumphs again and again.

29. Mrs. Forrester (Mrs. Colonel Bridges), *Fair Women* (New York: Worthington, 1881), 77.

30. Helen B. Mathers (Mrs. Helen B. Reeves), *Coming Thro' the Rye* (New York: The Macmillan Company, 1898), 209. The first edition was published in 1875.

31. See Ronald V. Sampson, *The Psychology of Power* (New York: Pantheon Books, 1966), 92-102.

32. Rhoda Broughton, *Belinda* (London: Bently, 1883), vol. 2, pp. 63, 76. There is a story that the author's father, a minister, had strictly forbidden her to read her own novels.

33. *Ibid.,* 109.

34. *Ibid.,* 114.

35. *Ibid.,* 141.

36. Jessie Fothergill, *The First Violin* (New York: Grosset & Dunlap, n.d.), 29; first published in 1878.

37. *Ibid.,* 153.

38. *Ibid.,* 171.

39. *Ibid.,* 360.

40. Augusta Jane Wilson, *St. Elmo* (New York; Carlton, 1866), 235. Within four months after publication the book had been read by one million people. Total sales place it securely as one of the ten most popular books ever published in America. Even in 1949 there were four editions printed. For further discussion of the author and her work, see William Perry Fidler, *Augusta Evans Wilson, 1835-1909* (Birmingham: University of Alabama Press, 1951); Ernest Elmo Calkins, "St. Elmo, or Named for a Best Seller," *Saturday Review of Literature* 21 (1939), 3-4; Hofstadter, "Popular Culture"; Papashvily, *All the Happy Endings;* Mott, *Golden Multitudes;* Hart, *The Popular Book;* and Brown, *Sentimental Novel in America.*

41. Wilson, *St. Elmo,* 120.

42. See the author's many asides on the subject, as when Edna, speaking of her readers, muses, "If there should accidentally be an allusion to classical or scientific literature, which they do not understand at the first, hasty, novel-reading glance, will they inform themselves, and . . . then thank me for the hint . . . ?" (p. 519).

43. *Ibid.*, 314.

44. Her earliest memories center upon her hatred of her cruel and domineering father. Donald Meyers's *The Positive Thinkers* (New York: Doubleday & Company, 1965) has noted the hostility toward Father in many popular novels of the day; often he is dead.

45. Mathers, *Coming Thro' the Rye*, 51.

46. *Ibid.*, 258.

47. *Ibid.*, 158.

48. Florence Marryat (Mrs. Florence [Marryat] Church Lean), *Woman Against Woman* (New York: Scribner, Welford, 1869), 164.

49. *Ibid.*, 301.

50. *Ibid.*, 254.

51. Forrester, *Fair Women*, 60.

52. *Ibid.*, 123.

53. See, for example, the portrayal of runaway wives in the characters of Adelaide, May's sister, in Fothergill's *The First Violin;* Mrs. Craven in Marryat's *Woman Against Woman;* Rebecca in G. A. Lawrence's *Guy Livingstone;* and Mrs. Leicester in Stephens's *Fashion and Famine.*

54. See Papashvily, *All the Happy Endings;* Rhoda Ellison, "Mrs. Hentz and the Green-Eyed Monster," *American Literature* 22 (1950), 345-50; Madeline B. Stern, "Ann S. Stephens, Author of the First Beadle Novel, 1860," *New York Public Library: Bulletin 64* (1960), 302-22; Regis Louise Boyle, *Mrs. E. D. E. N. Southworth, Novelist* (Washington, D.C.: Catholic University of America Press, 1939).

55. Caroline Lee Hentz, *Linda, or the Young Pilot of the Belle Creole: A Tale of Southern Life* (Philadelphia: A. Hart, 1854).

56. Mary Jane Holmes, *Edith Lyle* (New York: Carleton, 1876), 75.

57. *Ibid.*, 76.

58. Mrs E. D. E. N. Southworth, *The Hidden Hand* (Chicago: Donahue, n.d.), 122. The book was first published in the *New York Ledger* in 1859. Mott's *Golden Multitudes* estimates that *The Hidden Hand* and *Ishmael* sold over 2 million copies apiece.

59. Southworth, *Ishmael* (New York: Fenne, 1904), 219; first published in 1863.

60. *Ibid.*, 471.

61. See Ann Stephens, *Fashion and Famine* (New York: Bruce and Bros., 1854), for an example of this setting.

62. Cited in Papashvily, *All the Happy Endings*, 144.

63. The term "sensation novel" was first given to a certain class of popular novels by literary critics in the 1860s. It was applied to those novels which contained

something abnormal and unnatural, inserted into the story for its own sake to extract the greatest possible thrill. Often this thrill was intended to shock morality and custom.

64. Keith Hollingsworth, *The Newgate Novel, 1830–1847* (Detroit: Wayne University Press, 1963); Margaret Dalziel, *Popular Fiction 100 Years Ago* (London: Cohen and West, 1957); S. M. Ellis, *William Harrison Ainsworth and His Friends* (London: n.p., 1911); Malcom Elwin, *Victorian Wallflowers* (London: Jonathan Cape, 1934); and Louis James, *Fiction for the Working Man, 1830–1850* (London: Oxford University Press, 1963).

65. William Ainsworth, *Jack Sheppard* (New York: Colyer, 1839); George W. M. Reynolds, *Robert McNaire in England* (London: Willoughby, n.d.). Possible sadism and pornography in fiction seem to be a perennial problem, being even now the chief concern of those who seek to protect public morality.

66. Reynolds, *Robert McNaire*, 38.

67. When his indignation with social injustice grew too great, Reynolds would include in his novels dietary tables to show the deficiencies of workhouse meals or diagrams to show the excesses of wealthy men.

68. In 1879 Frederick Perkins, the librarian of the San Francisco Public Library, removed *Jack Sheppard* and a set of the works of Reynolds from circulation on moral grounds. When attacked in 1885 by a liberal-minded reporter for his action, Perkins insisted that it "is no more right that this library should circulate dirty books than that the Lincoln School . . . should instruct in criminal practices, . . . obscene language and vulgar habits." (Frederick Perkins, "Free Libraries and Unclean Books," *LJ* 10 [1885], 397.)

69. Mary Braddon, *Lady Audley's Secret* (Leipzig: Tauchnitz, 1862); Mrs. Henry Wood, *East Lynne* (London: Bently, 1863). In 1900 Mrs. Wood's sales were advertised as over 2.5 million copies. *East Lynne* was produced as a movie in 1931. Hart lists *Lady Audley's Secret* as the book most widely read in America in 1862; Mott estimates sales as at least 300,000 between 1862 and 1869.

70. G. A. Lawrence, *Guy Livingstone* (New York: Stokes, 1928), 24; first published in 1857 in London. See Gordon H. Fleming, *George Alfred Lawrence and the Victorian Sensational Novel* (Tucson: University of Arizona Press, 1952).

71. Lawrence, *Guy Livingstone* 94.

72. *Ibid.*, 353.

73. Elwin, *Victorian Wallflowers*, 298. See also Eileen Bigland, *Ouida: The Passionate Victorian* (London: Jarrolds, 1950); and Monica Stirling, *The Fine and the Wicked: The Life and Times of Ouida* (London: Victor Gollancz, 1958).

74. Ouida (Louise de la Ramée), *Under Two Flags* (New York: Stein and Day, 1956), 314. Mott believes Ouida was more widely read in the United States than either Braddon or Wood.

75. *Ibid.*, 182.

76. Cited in David Kennedy, *Birth Control in America: The Career of Margaret Sanger* (New Haven: Yale University Press, 1970), 68. See his excellent chapter "The Nineteenth-Century Heritage" for a summary of value shifts in the late nineteenth century.

Chapter 5. The Shift in Attitudes Toward Popular Fiction

1. Agnes Hill, "The Public Library and the People," *LJ* 27 (1902), 13.

2. Emma L. Adams, "Ways of Making a Library Useful," *LJ* 28 (1903), 287, 289.

3. Edwin Gaillard, "A University Education in Two Weeks," *Ibid.*, 8.

4. Charles K. Bolton, "Free Public Libraries as Promoters of Subscription Libraries," *Public Libraries* 12 (1907), 175.

5. The best study of Ticknor and his social ideals is David Tyack, *George Ticknor and the Boston Brahmins* (Cambridge: Harvard University Press, 1967).

6. Boston Public Library, *Report of the Trustees* (Boston, 1852). Reprinted in Shera, *Foundations of the Public Library: The Origins of the Public Library Movement in New England, 1625–1855* (Chicago: University of Chicago Press, 1949), Appendix 5.

7. Shera, *Foundations of the Public Library*, 19.

8. Justin Winsor, "Reading in Popular Libraries," U.S. Bureau of Education, *Public Libraries in the United States of America: Their History, Condition, and Management*, Special Report, pt. 1 (Washington, D.C.: U.S. Government Printing Office, 1876), 433.

9. William Fletcher, "Public Libraries in Manufacturing Communities," *Ibid.*, 410–11.

10. William Poole, "Some Popular Objections to Public Libraries," *LJ* 1 (1876), 44–51; Samuel Green, "Class Adaptation in the Selection of Books," *LJ* 5 (1880), 141–42; George Watson Cole, "Fiction in Libraries: A Plea for the Masses," *LJ* 19 (1894), 18–21; Jacob Schwartz, "Business Methods in Libraries," *LJ* 13 (1888), 334; "Fiction in Libraries," symposium, *LJ* 15 (1890), 261–64.

11. William Kite, librarian in Germantown, Pennsylvania, was the best-known librarian who advocated complete exclusion of fiction. See his "Fiction in Public Libraries," *LJ* 1 (1877), 277–79. In the early 1880s James Hubbard, employed at the Boston Public Library, excited attention because of his protest against "immoral" fiction there. (James Hubbard, "Fiction and Public Libraries," *International Review* 10 [1881], 168–78.)

12. "Novel Reading," *LJ* 1 (1876), 101.

13. "Sixth Session," *LJ* 24 (1899), 136–42; "Access to Shelves," *LJ* 15 (1890), 229–31; Isabel Ely Lord, "Open Shelves and Public Morals," *LJ* 26 (1901), 65–70.

14. E. A. Birge, "The Effect of the Two-Book System on Circulation," *LJ* 23 (1898), 93–101; C. K. Bolton, "Bettering Circulation in Small Libraries: The 'Two-Book System,' " *LJ* 14 (1894), 161–62.

15. Ellen Coe, "Fiction," *LJ* 18 (1893), 251.

16. Frank Hill, "Fiction in Libraries," *LJ* 15 (1890), 325. A survey of sixty large libraries in 1893 revealed that only ten held to the old belief that fiction reading would lead to the reading of more serious works.

17. *LJ* 19 (1894), 14–24.

18. *Ibid.*, 20–21.

19. Mellen Chamberlain, "Report on Fiction in Public Libraries," *LJ* 8 (1883), 210.

20. "Editorial," *LJ* 9 (1884), 207–08.

21. J. N. Larned, "Public Libraries and Public Education," *LJ* 9 (1884), 10.

22. Tessa Kelso, "Some Economic Features of Public Libraries," *Arena* 7 (1893), 711.

23. *LJ* 21 (1896), 107, 141–46, 416.

24. "Notes for an Autobiography," John Cotton Dana Papers, Newark Public Library, Newark, New Jersey, hereafter cited as JCDP. For evidence of the intellectual and emotional turmoil Dana experienced in these years, see John Swinton to Dana, March 11, 1884, and two manuscripts by Dana, "Ignorance" and "Individualism" (JCDP). My understanding of Dana's personality was aided by an interview with Julia Sabine at Utica, New York, in October 1976. Dr. Sabine came to work at the Newark Public Library in 1927. Also see Frank Kingdon, *John Cotton Dana* (Newark: The Public Library and Museum, 1940); Hazel A. Johnson, "John Cotton Dana," *Library Quarterly* 7 (1937), 50–98; Chalmers Hadley, *John Cotton Dana: A Sketch* (Chicago: American Library Association, 1943); and Julia Sabine, "John Cotton Dana in Newark: I Remember, I Remember," *Antiquarian Bookman* (June 1968), 2124, 2126.

25. John Parsons, "First Children's Room," *LJ* 34 (1909), 552. Also see Joseph Franklin Daniels to Miss Sheppard, January 7, 1902, JCDP.

26. Cited in Samuel S. Green, *The Public Library Movement in the United States* (Boston: The Boston Book Company, 1913), 223.

27. *John Cotton Dana: The Centennial Convocation, Addresses by Arthur T. Vanderbilt and L. Quincy Mumford, with a Preparatory Note by James E. Bryan* (New Brunswick, N.J.: Rutgers University Press, 1957), 15–16.

28. Kingdon, *John Cotton Dana*, 86. Also see, for Dana's attitude toward women, Dana, "Woman," undated manuscript, probably from late 1880s, and Dana, "Progress and Woman," *Chicago Current*, June 27, 1885 (both in JCDP).

29. Kingdon, 28, 92. For Dana's opposition to war, see especially "What Next?" in Dana, *Libraries, Addresses and Essays* (New York: H. W. Wilson, 1916), 281–93; Dana to Bowker, January 15, 1896, R. R. Bowker Papers, New York Public Library; "Social Betterment Through Education," undated manuscript, JCDP.

30. Arthur Bostwick, *A Life with Men and Books* (New York: H. W. Wilson, 1939), 211–12.

31. Dana, *Suggestions* (Boston: F. W. Faxon Company, 1921), 24.

32. *Ibid.*, 38.

33. Dana, "What State and Local Associations Can Do for Library Interests," *LJ* 30 (1905), 17–21.

34. Dana, "Letter to Editor," *LJ* 24 (1899), 660.

35. Dana, "A Helpful State of Mind," *Public Libraries* 10 (1905), 179.

36. Dana, "Hear the Other Side," *LJ* 21 (1896), 1–5.

37. Dana, "Public Librarians as Censors," *Bookman* 44 (1919), 147–52.

38. Dana, "Three Factors in Civilization," *Public Libraries* 14 (1909), 44.

39. Dana to Rebecca Rankin, October 13, 1924, JCDP.

40. "Notes for an Autobiography," JCDP. See also, Bowker to Dana, n.d., R. R. Bowker Papers; and Dana to Dr. F. P. Keppel, January 29, 1926, JCDP.

41. Dana, "All Progress Is Change," *LJ* 51 (1926), 327.

42. "Eighth Session," *LJ* 19 (1894), 159.

43. *LJ* 32 (1907), 269. Dana's candidate, Arthur Bostwick, was elected president, the only one of the "radical slate" to win office. Bostwick became edgy over the criticism he received from Dana's forces because they felt he proved to be a compromiser who did not do enough to effect change.

44. Frederick M. Crunden, "Report of the St. Louis Public Library," *LJ* 14 (1889), 97. Also see Crunden, "The Henry George Idea," *Reedy's Mirror*, February 16, 1905, copy received from the St. Louis Public Library.

    When Oscar Wilde was arrested, Crunden insisted that Wilde's books remain on the library shelf, despite the opposition to Wilde in the press. See *LJ* 20 (1895), 198, and Arthur E. Bostwick, ed., *Frederick Morgan Crunden: A Memorial Bibliography* (St. Louis Public Library, 1924).

45. F. M. Crunden, "What of the Future?" *LJ* 21 (1896), 6.

46. *Ibid.*, 7.

47. Melvil Dewey, "Advice to a Librarian," *Public Libraries* 2 (1897), 267. See also "Mr. Dewey on the Choice of Books," *New York Times*, April 27, 1901, 298.

48. Lindsay Swift, "Paternalism in Public Libraries," *LJ* 24 (1899), 609, 610, 615. For a similar view see John Cheney, *That Dome in Air* (Chicago: A. C. McClurg and Company, 1895, pp. 11-43), and James Hosmer, "Libraries from the Reader's Point of View" (*LJ* 14 [1893], 216-17). John Harbourne's "The Guileless West on 'Weeding Out' " (*LJ* 22 [1897], 251-52) is a humorous belittling of a controversy going on at the time in Boston about immoral books.

49. Swift, "Paternalism," 615.

50. *Ibid.*, 615-16.

51. John Ashurst, "On Taking Ourselves Too Seriously," *LJ* 26 (1901), 266.

52. Carolyn Wells, "The Problem," *LJ* 29 (1899), 618.

53. R. G. Thwaites to Henry Carr, April 15, 1901, Carr Correspondence, ALA Archives, University of Illinois, Urbana.

54. George Iles, "The Trusteeship of Literature," *LJ* 26 (1901), 16-22.

55. Richard Ely, "The Trusteeship of Literature," *LJ* 26 (1901), 22-24.

56. Josephine Rathbone, "The Classification of Fiction," *LJ* 27 (1902), 121-24.

57. "The Novel and the Library," *Dial* 33 (1902), 73-75.

58. "Editorial," *LJ* 27 (1902), 119.

59. "Editorial," *LJ* 28 (1903), 755.

60. "Report of the Committee on Prose Fiction," *LJ* 31 (1906), 207. See also "Restriction of Purchases in Current Fiction," *LJ* 29 (1904), 72-74; Anna Garland Rockwell, "Fiction Again: Where Shall We Draw the Line of Exclusion?", *Public Libraries* 8 (1903), 307-13. See also the series of articles in *LJ* (1903) on how to encourage serious reading, and the discussion of these papers at the annual convention.

61. James K. Hosmer, "Some Things That Are Uppermost," *LJ* 28 (1903), 3-8.

62. William Foster, "Where Ought the Emphasis to Be Placed in Library Purchases?", *LJ* 29 (1904), 236-37.

63. "What Shall Libraries Do About Bad Books?" *LJ* 33 (1908), 349-56, and "Editorial," 347.

64. Arthur Bostwick, "The Librarian as Censor," presidential address, *LJ* 33 (1908), 259, 269, 264.

65. James I. Wyer, "Outside the Walls," *LJ* 36 (April 1911), 172-78; Mary Plummer, "The Public Library and the Pursuit of Truth," presidential address, *LJ* 41 (1916), 537-41.

66. "Questionable Books in Public Libraries," I and II, *LJ* 47 (1922), 856-61, 907-12; Mary U. Rothrock, "Censorship of Fiction in the Public Library," *LJ* 48 (1923), 454-56. Evelyn Geller, in "Intellectual Freedom: Eternal Principle or Unanticipated Consequence?" (*LJ* 99 [1974]), 1364-67, correctly argues that the ALA's stand for intellectual freedom in 1939 was a reversal, not a continuation, of the major tradition.

Chapter 6. Formation of a Savior

1. Marie Gallup Rider to Dee Garrison, February 20, 1974.

2. Georgia Benedict, cited in Grosvenor Dawe, *Melvil Dewey: Seer: Inspirer: Doer 1851-1931* (Lake Placid, N.Y.: Lake Placid Club, 1932), 104-5.

3. "Editorial," *LJ* 96 (September 1, 1971), 2567.

4. Fremont Rider, *Melvil Dewey* (Chicago: American Library Association, 1944).

5. Fremont Rider Papers, Godfrey Memorial Library, Middletown, Conn. See correspondence with Frank Walter, James Wyer, and Emily Danton.

6. Paul Adams's *Obsessive Children: A Socio-Psychiatric Study* (New York: Brunner/Mazel, 1973) gives a good review of the various schools of psychology in relation to the obsessive-compulsive, as well as a thorough bibliography. See especially Leon Salzman, *The Obsessive Personality* (New York: Science House, 1968); David Shapiro, *Neurotic Styles* (New York: Basic Books, 1965); T. Braganza and Bingham Dai, "Culture as a Factor in Obsessive-Compulsive Neurosis," *North Carolina Medical Journal* 20 (1959), 142-45. Erwin W. Straus has written on the obsessive fascination with time in "An Existentialist Approach to Time" (*Annals of the New York Academy of Sciences* 138 [1966-1967], 759-66) and *On Obsession: A Clinical and Methodological Study* (New York: Nervous and Mental Disease Monographs [#73], 1948). Sudkir Kakar's *Frederick Taylor: A Study in Personality and Innovation* (Cambridge: Massachusetts Institute of Technology, 1970) is an interesting study of an obsessive personality.

There is enough essential agreement between the camps of psychology to formulate certain generalizations about the formation of the obsessive personality. Paul Adams has grouped these into four: (1) attempts toward overenculturation by the parents (demands for strict conformity); (2) parental lack of empathy (an inability to take up in imagination the role of the child); (3) parental disapproval of spontaneous behavior in the child (caused by strictness and overconformity to traditional ideologies); and (4) the masking of hate for the child, by one or both parents, with a hypocritical loving exterior. There is considerable evidence to indicate that Dewey's home environment manifests the first three preconditions, and perhaps the fourth — Dewey felt that as an infant he had been virtually abandoned emotionally by his mother.

Many persons make use of obsessional techniques in daily living. Some of them are so much a part of our society that we take them for granted; indeed, our work-oriented culture rewards obsessional behavior in many instances. A respect for routine, order, precision, and reason increases one's efficiency and effectiveness and assists in keeping polarities in balance and furthering the pursuit of knowledge. A wide spectrum of obsessional behavior will thus be found, ranging from the "normal" to that of the ritual-bound compulsive whose anxieties seriously impede his capacity for productive living. It is common to find obsessional personalities operating efficiently, often in positions of power and prestige, in settings in which both their dedicated perversity and use of obsessional defenses are evident to all. It is the all-pervasive quality of compulsive behavior that marks the obsessive personality. For these persons any relaxation of tense, deliberative, purposeful activity provokes anxiety, and any temporary abandonment to whim, impulse, or personal desire is experienced as improper, unsafe, or worse.

7. Eliza Dewey to Melvil Dewey, cited in Dawe, *Melvil Dewey*, 28.

8. Melvil Dewey, "Notes for an Autobiography." *Melvil Dewey Papers*, Columbia University Library, New York City; hereafter referred to as MDP.

9. Diary, April 11, 1872, MDP.

10. *Ibid.*, August 30, 1872, MDP.

11. *Ibid.*

12. Dewey to M. J. Dewey, November 1, 1874, MDP.

13. Dewey, "Notes for an Autobiography," MDP.

14. *Ibid.*

15. Diary, December 9, 1869, MDP.

16. Dewey, composition of 1867, MDP.

17. Asa O. Gallup to Dewey, March 4, 1898, MDP.

18. Diary, September 11, 1867, MDP.

19. Cited in Dawe, *Melvil Dewey*, 47.

20. Cited in *Ibid.*, 110.

21. Diary, July 8, 1870, MDP.

22. Diary, February 11, 1870, MDP.

23. Diary, July 13, 1870, MDP.

24. See Dewey to Alumni Association, 1901, MDP. It was Dewey's place, he felt, to formally protest the use of tobacco by his peers at the reunion banquets.

25. Statements of Guy Hinsdale and John Bates Clark, cited in Dawe, 104, 54.

26. Cited in *Ibid.*, 54.

27. *Ibid.*, 55.

28. Diary, July 13, 1870, MDP: "Whichever way I turn I see something that sadly needs improvement and [if] this is so with myself it is also true with the rest of the world and its people. I am altogether happiest when I am engaged in earnest labor of some kind."

29. Diary, September 28, 1867; July 21, 1869; August 9, 1869; August 20, 1869; June 18, 1870; July 8, 1870; July 13, 1870, MDP.

30. Dewey, "Notes for an Autobiography," MDP.

31. Diary, July 21, 1869, MDP.

32. "The Value of Time," April 27, 1869, MDP.

33. Diary, November 15, 1869, MDP.

34. Diary, December 9, 1869, MDP, written on his eighteenth birthday.

35. "Life," June 8, 1870, MDP.

36. Cited in Dawe, *Melvil Dewey,* 57-58.

37. *Ibid.,* 165.

38. *Ibid.* Kurt F. Leidecker's "The Debt of Melvil Dewey to William Torrey Harris" (*Library Quarterly* 15 [1945], 139-42) makes an argument that Dewey borrowed much of his idea from Harris's scheme of classification at the St. Louis Public School Library.

39. Diary, December 10, 1872, MDP. Dewey began his free instruction of Amherst students in Tackigraphy, a shorthand system, in January 1875. (Dewey to W. S. Biscoe, January 29, 1875, James I. Wyer Autograph Collection, ALA Archives, University of Illinois, Urbana.) Dewey was paid $900 a year at Amherst. (Dewey to Biscoe, January 5, 1875, *Ibid.*)

40. Diary, March 29, 1875, MDP. For a description of his accommodations with Pratt, see Dewey to "my dear fellow" (probably Biscoe), May 1, 1875, James I. Wyer Autograph Collection, ALA Archives.

41. Diary, December 1875, MDP.

42. Diary, April 9, 1876, MDP.

43. An explanation of the origins of the Economy Company, probably written in late 1879, for it is marked as having been compiled for the use of his lawyer and shown to Cutter, MDP.

44. Copy of contract between Frederick Jackson and Dewey, May 8, 1879, MDP.

45. R. R. Bowker to Dewey, February 11, 1892, MDP.

46. Diary, May 2, 1876, MDP.

47. Diary, May 2, 1876, MDP.

48. E. McLung Fleming, *R. R. Bowker, Militant Liberal* (Norman: University of Oklahoma Press, 1952), 38-67; J. W. Beswick, *The Work of Frederick Leypoldt: Bibliographer and Publisher* (New York: R. R. Bowker, 1942).

49. Contract between Leypoldt and Dewey, May 18, 1876, MDP. Dewey also loaned Leypoldt $4,000 of the Pratt money, charging him 10 per cent interest, giving Mrs. Pratt the legal limit of 7 per cent, and keeping 3 per cent for himself as a fee for negotiating the loan. It is possible that Dewey paid the entire 10 per cent to Mrs. Pratt. Dewey stated that the arrangement was designed to avoid the usury laws. Bowker wrote that his "remembrances of the complexity of the Pratt contract are gloomy in the extreme." See Bowker to Dewey, February 14, 1895, and Mary Ahern to Nina Browne, October 13, 1905, MDP.

50. Mrs. Leypoldt to Bowker, September 18, 1880, R. R. Bowker Papers, New York Public Library, New York City.

51. Contract between Dewey and Leypoldt, January 1, 1877, MDP.

52. A close friend of Ellen Richards, Annie was one of the founders of the American Home Economics Association. The first organizers met at Lake Placid in

September 1899. See Emma S. Weigley, "It Might Have Been Euthenics: The Lake Placid Conference and The Home Economics Movement," *American Quarterly* 26 (March 1974), 79-98.

53. Annie Godfrey, correspondence with Phillip Reyholdt, 1878-1884, MDP.

54. Box 19, MDP.

55. Dewey to "Brooks," Transcribed Letters, 1876-1884, MDP.

56. Bowker to the ALA, 1880, R. R. Bowker Papers.

57. Contract between Leypoldt and Dewey, January 24, 1878, MDP.

58. The *Journal* resumed publication with the issue of July-August 1880.

59. "Bulletin," probably printed in 1882 or 1883, MDP.

60. Identified as a "Mrs. Godfrey," possibly Annie's mother. (Business agreement, Dewey and Jackson, Box 81, MDP.)

61. Box 61, MDP, contains a copy of the minutes of the stockholders' meetings and other documents relating to the reorganization of the company in 1880-1881.

62. *Ibid.*

63. Edward Wigglesworth, M.D., was a member of an old and prominent family in New England. He graduated from Harvard in 1865 and was one of the first dermatologists in Boston. See Dewey to "my business and educational friends," October 11, 1880, J. I. Wyer Autograph Collection, ALA Archives.

64. Box 61, MDP.

65. *Ibid.*

66. Dewey hotly denied as "madness" any idea of committing suicide. (Dewey to Wigglesworth, November 30, 1880, MDP.)

67. Dewey to Barnard, October 25, 1880; Dewey to Jackson, October 19, 1880, MDP.

68. Dewey to Wigglesworth, October 21, 1880, MDP.

69. Dewey to Economy Company, November 1, 1880, MDP.

70. Dewey to Wigglesworth, November 16 and 30 and December 8, 1880, MDP.

71. Dewey to Winsor, December 18, 1880, MDP.

72. Dewey asked Bowker if at this time he would advise Dewey to go into the publishing business or even to think of reading for a career in law. (Dewey to Bowker, January 1, 1881, R. R. Bowker Papers.)

Chapter 7. Columbia College, 1883–1888

1. John W. Burgess, *Reminiscences of an American Scholar* (New York: Columbia University Press, 1934), 175. Dewey was a member of the Amherst class of 1873 that elected to give up a part of its vacation time in order to extend the class hours of Burgess's course in modern political history. See also Bernard E. Brown, *American Conservatives: The Political Thought of Frances Lieber and John W. Burgess* (New York: Columbia University Press, 1951).

2. Barnard to Seth Low, December 15, 1888, MDP. The only opposition to a new library came from Librarian Betts, who argued that the old library was not used enough to justify a new one.

3. The original copies of these letters are in the Columbia College Folders, MDP.

4. Barnard to Dewey, May 4, 1883, MDP.

5. Frederick Poole to Dewey, April 23, 1883, MDP.

6. Nicholas Murray Butler, *Across the Busy Years: Recollections and Reflections* (New York: Charles Scribner's Sons, 1934), 76.

7. The development of the Columbia library school and library has been discussed in Ray Trautman, *A History of the School of Library Service, Columbia University* (New York: Columbia University Press, 1954); Ernest J. Reece, ed., *School of Library Economy of Columbia College, 1887–1889: Documents for a History* (Columbia University School of Library Service, 1937): Henry Watson Kent, "Reminiscences of Early Days," *LJ* 62 (February 1, 1937), 146–48; W. Boyd Rayward, "Melvil Dewey and Education for Librarianship," *Journal of Library History* 3 (1968), 297–313. Also see Winifred Linderman, "History of the Columbia University Libraries," Ph.D. dissertation, Columbia University, 1959; School of Library Economy, *Circular of Information*, 1884 through 1887; *Library Notes*; and Melvil Dewey, "Librarianship as a Profession for College-Bred Women," address to the Association of Collegiate Alumnae, March 13, 1886, MDP.

8. Columbia College, *Annual Report of the President* (New York, 1884), 84–114.

9. Barnard to Seth Low, December 15, 1888, MDP.

10. See Boxes 61 and 64 for the documents regarding the Library Bureau, MDP.

11. See especially Davidson to Dewey, August 22, September 7 and 15, October 25 and 27, 1883, MDP.

12. Dewey to Attorney Elder, January 1, 1883, MDP.

13. Unidentified newspaper clipping, April 13, 1888, Box 64, MDP.

14. Bowker to Dewey, May 8, 1888, MDP.

15. The 1888 loan was probably from M. J. Dewey, his older brother, who had bought a rubber factory in New Jersey in 1884 for $12,000—when he sold it a little over five years later he made a profit of $52,000.

16. W. E. Parker to Dewey, September 9, 1898, MDP.

17. Cited in Fremont Rider, *Melvil Dewey* (Chicago: American Library Association, 1944), 45.

18. *Ibid.*, 49.

19. Reece, *School of Library Economy of Columbia College*, 235.

20. William Foster to Dewey, September 19, 1905, MDP.

21. *Library Notes* 2 (March 1887), 274. Francis Miksa ("Charles Cutter: 19th Century Systemizer of American Public Libraries," Ph.D. dissertation, University of Chicago, 1974) believes that the competiton from *Library Notes* led Cutter to change the format of the *Library Journal* so as to be of more service to small libraries.

22. Melvil Dewey, "Women in Libraries: How They Are Handicapped," *Library Notes* 2 (October 1886), 89–90.

23. Columbia College, *Annual Report* (1882), 85.

24. *Ibid.*, 1883, 85.

25. Cited in Alice Duer Miller and Susan Meyers, *Barnard College: The First Fifty Years* (New York: Columbia University Press, 1939), 9.

26. Burgess, *Reminiscences*, 241–42.

27. Annie Nathan Meyer, *Barnard Beginnings* (Boston: Houghton Mifflin Company, 1935), 3. She married Dr. Alfred Meyer on December 15, 1887.

28. *Ibid.*, 30.

29. Mary Mapes Dodge was editor of the genteel children's magazine *St. Nicholas.*

30. Meyer, *Barnard Beginnings*, 145.

31. *Ibid.*

32. Linderman, "History of Columbia University Libraries," gives the fullest account of Dewey's problems at Columbia.

33. Cited in Rider, *Melvil Dewey*, 46.

34. Columbia College, *Minutes of the Trustees* (New York, December 3, 1883).

35. W. T. Peoples to George W. Cole, January 18, 1889, Cole Correspondence, 1885-1889, ALA Archives, University of Illinois, Urbana. Also see Frank C. Patten to Cole, January 14, 1889, *Ibid.*

Chapter 8. Albany, 1888–1905

1. "Libraries as Related to the Educational Work of the State," *Report of the Board of Regents of New York State* (Albany, 1888), 111–27.

2. *Messages from the Governors of the State of New York*, vol. 8, Charles Z. Lincoln, ed. (Albany: J. B. Lyon Company, 1909), 170.

3. Frank C. Abbott, *Government Policy and Higher Education: A Study of the Regents of the University of the State of New York, 1784–1949* (Ithaca: Cornell University Press, 1958), 1–57.

4. Copies of the replies are in the Dewey Papers at Columbia. This was the same strategy Dewey had used before, on his move from Boston to Columbia.

5. Dewey to Whitelaw Reid, November 25, 1888, MDP.

6. Dewey was told by Chancellor H. R. Pierson that he would receive $6,000 when the treasurer of the Albany State Normal School retired and probably another $1,000 the year after. Pierson's death negated the agreement and Dewey's salary remained at $5,000, except in 1891-1892, until his raise in 1900. (Statement of Bishop William Croswell Doane and Daniel Beech, n.d., probably 1906.) Also see Dewey to Howard J. Rogers, December 13, 1905, MDP.

7. Columbia College, *Minutes of the Trustees* (New York, February 4, 1889).

8. Cited in Grosvenor Dawe, *Melvil Dewey: Seer: Inspirer: Doer 1851–1931* (Lake Placid, N.Y.: Lake Placid Club, 1932), 199.

9. There is a trace of evidence which indicates that some feared his complete emotional breakdown in his last months at Albany. (See Frank K. Walter to Fremont Rider, 1943, and Emily Danton to Fremont Rider, August 30, 1943, Fremont Rider Papers, Godfrey Memorial Library, Middletown, Conn.)

10. Cited in Dawe, 123. Regent Sexton quoted another regent who said that "about the only duties we have since Mr. Dewey came here [are] to sit on his coattails." "Proceedings," *LJ* 15 (1890), 132.

11. "Convocation Proceedings," *Report of the Regents* (1891), 420.

12. *Ibid.* (1892).

13. *Report of the Regents* (1893).

14. "Dewey and the Albany Library School," *LJ* 53 (1928), 665.

15. *Report of the Regents* (1890-1891), R-35.

16. *Ibid.* (1889-1897); Helen Vloebergh, "A History of the New York State Library," unpublished master's thesis, Catholic University of America, 1957; Cecil R. Roseberry, *The New York State Library* (Albany: New York State Library, 1970).

17. See the copy of the "Report of the Subcommittee of the Joint Committee of the Senate and Assembly to Investigate the State Departments, 1895," and accompanying documents, in MDP.

18. Dewey to Regents, August 17, 1895, MDP.

19. The theater was completed in 1923. See Lake Placid Folders; John Willy, "Impressions of Lake Placid Club," *Hotel Monthly,* October 1923; F. C. Kelly, "Novel Ways of Saving Your Time, Labor and Money," *American Magazine* 98 (1924), 34-35; A. Gray, "That Darned Literary Fellow Across the Lake," *Ibid.* 103 (1927), 56-59, all in MDP.

20. Frank K. Walter to Fremont Rider, n.d., probably 1943, Fremont Rider Papers.

21. Report to Directors, September 1922. See Dewey to R. R. Bowker, June 23, 1898, MDP; there Dewey said the "majority of ALA members would never be invited to join."

22. Morris Longstreth, *The Adirondacks* (New York: The Century Company, 1922), 247.

23. Lake Placid Club circular, probably printed in 1902, Box 52, MDP.

24. William Frederick Poole, "Presidential Address," *LJ* 11 (1886), 202.

25. William Fletcher, "Close Classification and Bibliography," *LJ* 11 (1886), 211.

26. "Proceedings," *LJ* 11 (1886), 351, and 12 (1887), 423.

27. *Ibid.,* 14 (1889), 277.

28. *Ibid.,* 284-85.

29. *Ibid.*

30. Dewey to William Harper, January 23, 1892, MDP.

31. "Proceedings," *LJ* 18 (1893), 56.

32. Dewey to H. L. Elmendorf, September 12, 1895. See also Dewey to Theresa West, September 17, 1895, MDP. Thorwald Solberg's "A Chapter in the Unwritten History of the Library of Congress from January 17 to April 5, 1899" (*Library Quarterly* 9 [July 1939], 285-99) reports that President McKinley considered offering Dewey the job of Librarian of Congress in 1897.

33. Henry Carr to William C. Lane, January 14, 1899, ALA Archives, University of Illinois, Urbana.

34. W. E. Parker to Dewey, September 9, 1898, MDP.

35. Ronald Maberry Johnson, "Captain of Education: An Intellectual Biography of Andrew S. Draper," Ph.D. dissertation, University of Illinois, Urbana, 1970; Harlan H. Horner, *The Life and Work of Andrew Sloan Draper* (Urbana: University of Illinois Press, 1934).

36. Dewey to Whitelaw Reid, June 23, 1899; Dewey to Theodore Roosevelt, 1900, MDP; New York State Assembly, "Report on the Commission on Educational Unification," *Assembly Documents,* no. 17 (Albany, 1900).

37. Abbott, *Government Policy and Higher Education,* 84–88.

38. New York State Department of Education, "Libraries and Home Education," *Second Annual Report of the Department of Education* (Albany, 1904–1905), 416–22.

39. Dewey to Professor J. Laughlin, March 10, 1896, MDP.

40. "Asks Regents to Depose State Librarian Dewey," *New York Times,* January 21, 1905.

41. *Ibid.*

42. "Do Not Use Position to Boom Club-Dewey," *New York Times,* January 24, 1905, p. 5. His papers reveal a great deal of correspondence during his tenure at Albany that is related, at least peripherally, to his Lake Placid interests. It is probable, though, that he had cut down on the bulk of this type of mail before the convening of the investigation committee of 1895.

43. Taylor to Gallup, November 28, 1904; Dewey to Taylor, December 7, 1904, MDP.

44. Dewey to Draper, January 18, 1905, MDP.

45. Sulzberger to Dewey, February 13, 1905, MDP.

46. Copy of minutes of the meeting, MDP.

47. *Ibid.*; "Say Dewey Offered to Quit Club Office," *New York Times,* February 3, 1905.

48. Collection of press clippings, MDP.

49. "State Librarian Dewey is Rebuked by Regents," unidentified newspaper clipping, February 16, 1905. MDP.

50. *Harper's Weekly,* February 4, 1905.

51. "State Librarian Dewey is Rebuked." See also *Annual Report of the Department of Education* (1904–1905), 480–84.

52. The pamphlet had clearly been begun by February 22 because Dewey then invited Mary Ahern to send supportive material. Dewey to Ahern, February 22, 1905, MDP. See also Louis Marshall to Regent Edward Lauterbach, June 17, 1905, and Canfield to Dewey, July 8, 1905, MDP. Also see Gallup to Dewey, June 28, 1905, and the correspondence between Henry Weinstock and Dewey of March and April 1905 (Boxes 69 and 70, MDP) which clearly reveals the rigidity of Dewey's prejudiced views.

53. *Annual Report of the Department of Education* (1904–1905), 419.

54. New York State Library Association, Advisory Committee, *Report* (Albany, June 1905), MDP.

55. Woodworth to Annie Dewey, September 17, 1905. From another angle Dewey was assailed by an old opponent, Bowker, in the *Library Journal*; Bowker's editorial implied that Dewey was not spending enough time at Albany. It was a little rough to have "my own old *Library Journal*" repeat this rumor, Dewey scolded Bowker. (Dewey to Bowker, June 24, 1905, MDP.)

56. Dewey to Pliny T. Sexton, September 18 and 19, 1905, MDP. Dewey seemed to have considered founding a graduate school of library science in the New York, Washington, or Chicago area. (See Charles W. Needham [president, George Washington University] to Dewey, December 30, 1905, and Dewey to Needham, January 1906, MDP.)

57. Dewey to Regent Smith, September 16, 1905, MDP; Annual Report of New York State Educational Department, 1905–1906, 392.

58. Dewey to Chancellor Day, October 16, 1905, MDP.

59. Dewey to Anderson, February 2, 1906; see also Dewey to Anderson, December 19, 1905, MDP.

60. Seymour to Nicholas Murray Butler, February 3, 1906. See also Seymour to Anderson, February 15, 1906; Draper to Seymour, February 16, 1906; Agreement between Dewey and Seymour, May 1, 1906, all in MDP. Seymour believed Anderson's most important reason for firing her was because he wanted to hire a man to take her place. She agreed to work for Dewey at Lake Placid for room and board and half the net receipts from the seventh revision of the Decimal System and any other editions she might produce.

61. Anderson to Dewey, February 27, 1906, MDP.

62. Reminiscence of Dorcas Fellows to Grosvenor Dawe, MDP.

63. William Mason to Dewey, July 11, 1906. Also see Dewey to Sexton, March 17, 1903, MDP.

64. Seymour to Dewey, July 2, 1906, MDP.

65. Cited in Seymour to Dewey, July 2, 1906, MDP. Ahern wrote to Dewey's second wife, Emily, on February 27, 1932, that during the Alaska trip she "nailed my flag permanently to the mast of the fleet bearing the Dewey flag." Dewey apparently did not feel so kindly toward her. He remarked to H. E. Davidson that he had once heard Ahern address a minister who was a Yale graduate "in [a] way that a fishwife" would talk to sailors on a dock. (Dewey to Davidson, November 1903, MDP.)

66. Woodworth to Dewey, n.d., MDP. Woodworth remained at work in Albany for some years and then retired in Europe. On December 9, 1906, she wrote Annie Dewey that she could not come to Placid "for . . . reasons, which I need not discuss." It seemed better, she said, if she did not visit Placid "for a year or two at least . . . I cannot do you any good and perhaps only harm." When Emily Dewey asked Woodworth to reminisce about her years with Dewey, Woodworth answered coyly: "Stupid and strange . . . as it may seem, I cannot recall any incident of those days . . . to relate. I feel sure, dear Emily, that you will not misunderstand me!" (Woodworth to Emily Dewey [from Paris], April 21, 1932, MDP.) Also see Dewey to Canfield, June 12, 1906, and Dewey to Henry Carr, June 28, 1906, MDP.

67. Annie Dewey to Isabel Lord, June 15, 1906.

68. Annie Dewey to Edwin Fairchild, June 19, 1906.

69. Fairchild to Annie Dewey, June 23, 1906.

70. Fairchild to Woodworth, June 27, 1906.

71. Canfield to Annie Dewey, June 25, 1906.

72. Annie Dewey to Canfield, June 27, 1906.

73. Dewey to Canfield, June 29, 1906.

74. Walter to Rider, Fremont Rider Papers. Also see "The True Library Spirit," *Public Libraries* 11 (1906), 441. In 1913 a group of Albany students petitioned the faculty to allow Dewey to speak to them; the petition was denied. (See correspondence between Dorcas Fellows and Mr. Rue, March 1932, MDP.)

75. Sharp to Mr. and Mrs. Dewey, July 1906.

76. See the correspondence between Dewey and Adeline Zachert in September 1920, and between Tessa Kelso, John Lowe (president of the New York Library Association), and Godfrey Dewey in April and May 1924. Kelso charged Dewey "with obscene and criminal attacks" upon women in the library profession. After a thorough investigation, Lowe concluded that Kelso's charges had no basis. In 1930, when he was seventy-nine years old, Dewey was sued by a much younger woman who accused him of overly familiar behavior with her. On the advice of his lawyer Dewey settled out of court for $2,145.66. (See Harvey Ferris to Dewey, February 11, 1930, MDP.)

77. Dewey to Bowker, November 11, 1905; Bowker to Dewey, November 1905 (n.d.); MDP. Also see the American Library Institute Collection in the ALA Archives. See especially *The ALI*, a pamphlet of 1917, and the *ALI Handbook* of 1938; Sister Tressa Piper, "The American Library Institute, 1905-1951, An Historical Study and Analysis of Goals," paper for Specialist Certificate in Librarianship, Library School, University of Wisconsin, 1975.

78. Carr to Dewey, April 4, 1906; Dewey to Bowker, May 11, 1906.

79. Tressa Piper presents different figures. Her sources evidently indicate thirty-eight replies, with twenty-seven in favor of continuation and eleven opposed.

80. Dewey to American Library Institute Board, January 16, 1908.

81. Anonymous, "To the American Library Institute," *LJ* 37 (1912), 197. In 1911, only fourteen out of the fifty-six members were women.

82. Mary Ahern, "A Review of the First Twenty-five Years' Activity of the American Library Institute," *Libraries* 36 (1931), 311. "The idea of the ALI has always seemed to be undemocratic," E. H. Anderson wrote to F. C. Richardson in 1916. Anderson felt many believed it to be a "snobbish segregation" of librarians. (Anderson to Richardson, February 23, 1916, ALA Archives.)

Chapter 9. Final Diversions, 1906–1931

1. "Editorial," *LJ* 37 (1912), 585.

2. In 1918 Dewey offered $1 rooms, a 50¢ reduction in meals, and the free use of the boats and recreation facilities at the Lake Placid Club to all "hardworking librarians." (*LJ* 43 [1918], 434.)

3. "Library Efficiency," 1911, MDP.

4. "What the American Library Association Was Intended to Do," *Wisconsin Library Bulletin* 13 (1917), 42.

5. Interview with Godfrey Dewey, Melvil Dewey's son, Lake Placid, N.Y.

6. Melvil Dewey, "Speech at Political Rally," 1912, MDP.

7. Dewey to Republican County Committee, October 8, 1912; and undated statement by Melvil Dewey. (MDP.) In his seventy-sixth birthday letter to friends, Dewey noted that, while in Albany, "the more I saw of politicians, the better I liked dogs." (January 1, 1927, James I. Wyer Autograph Collection, ALA Archives, University of Illinois, Urbana.)

8. Dewey to Directors, June 6, 1923, MDP.

9. Undated plan for profit sharing, Box 38, MDP. Although he did not institute it at Lake Placid, Dewey once worked out a plan for dividing the surplus left after wages, salaries, expenses, and a 6 per cent dividend had been paid. Under this plan one-fifth of the surplus went to workers, whose individual share was prorated according to salary, and the remaining four-fifths was divided between owners, management, and a reserve fund.

10. Samuel Haber, *Efficiency and Uplift: Scientific Management in the Progressive Era, 1890–1920.* (Chicago: University of Chicago Press, 1964), 52. Arthur Bostwick discusses Taylorism in the library in "Two Tendencies of American Library Work," *LJ* 36 (1911), 275–78. Also see Samuel P. Hays, *Conservation and the Gospel of Efficiency* (Cambridge: Harvard University Press, 1959); Raymond E. Callahan, *Education and the Cult of Efficiency* (Chicago: University of Chicago Press, 1962); and Sudhir Kakar, *Frederick Taylor: A Study in Personality and Innovation* (Cambridge: Massachusetts Institute of Technology Press, 1970); Frank Barkley Copley, *Frederick Winslow Taylor: Father of Scientific Management* (New York: Harper & Bros., 1923).

11. Melvil Dewey, "Office Efficiency," reprint from *The Business of Insurance* (New York: The Ronald Press Company, 1912), pp. 1, 3, 29, 7; MDP.

12. *Ibid.,* 3, 6.

13. *Ibid.,* 2. See also Efficiency Folders, MDP. Also see Annie Dewey, "Manpower, Organization and Rewards," *Journal of Home Economics* 5 (December 1913), 387–98. Annie, a chief leader of the home economics movement, urged the mechanization and systematization of the home, partly in order to free women for work in the world outside. See also "Melvil Dewey: Apostle of Simplification," *Journal of Calendar Reform* (March 1932), 18, MDP.

14. Dewey to Harold T. Pulsifer, December 5, 1924, March 26, 1925; Pulsifer to Dewey, April 6, 1925; Dewey to F. R. Bellamy, August 6, 1928.

15. Annie had been blind for several years when she died at age seventy-three. Left unfinished in her typewriter was a poem she had begun to her husband. (Cited in Grosvenor Dawe, *Melvil Dewey* [Lake Placid, N.Y.: Lake Placid Club, 1932, p. 74].) Annie had been active in the eugenics movement and social-purity organizations. She was on the central committee of the National Conference on Race Betterment held at Battle Creek, Mich., in 1914. In 1916 Melvil Dewey was a member of the American Social Hygiene Association, which supported sex education, suppression of prostitution, and birth control. (See "Race, Purity and Manpower," speech by Annie Dewey, undated, MDP.)

16. Lake Placid Folder, 1931, MDP.

17. Statement by Melvil Dewey, July 31, 1927, MDP.

18. Dictated by Dewey, February 3, 1927, MDP.

19. *Ibid.*

20. Written after Dewey's eightieth birthday, 1931. (Cited in Dawe, 107.)

Chapter 10. From Missionary to Professional

1. William Warner Bishop, "The American Library Association: Fragments of Autobiography," *Library Quarterly* 19 (January 1949), 38.

Chapter 11. Feminization: Symbol and Reality

1. Cited in Robert W. Smuts, *Women and Work in America* (New York: Columbia University Press, 1959), 110.

2. "The English Conference: Official Report of Proceedings," *LJ* 2 (1878), 280.

3. Joseph Adna Hill, *Women in Gainful Occupations, 1870–1920,* Census Monograph no. 9 (Washington, D.C.: U.S. Government Printing Office, 1929), 42. Librarianship has been termed a "profession" by the U.S. Census and is used in that sense here. Hill cites 43 women library workers in 1870; 3,122 in 1900; and 8,621 in 1910. See Sharon B. Wells, "The Feminization of the American Library Profession, 1876-1923" (unpublished master's thesis, Library School, University of Chicago, 1967) for statistics on the number of women employed in all American libraries, including public libraries, and the number of women enrolled in library schools. Wells counts 191 men and 18 women managing collections of over 10,000 volumes in 1875.

4. Cynthia F. Epstein, *Woman's Place: Options and Limits in Professional Careers* (Berkeley: University of California Press, 1971), 7.

5. Melvil Dewey, "The Ideal Librarian," *LJ* 24 (1899), 14.

6. U.S. Bureau of Education, *Public Libraries in the United States of America: Their History, Condition and Management,* Special Report, pt. 1 (Washington, D.C.: U.S. Government Printing Office, 1876), 111.

7. Carl M. White, *The Origins of the American Library School* (New York: The Scarecrow Press, 1961), 14.

8. R. R. Bowker, "Libraries and the Century in America: Retrospect and Prospect," *LJ* 26 (1901), 5.

9. Cited in Virginia Penny, *Employments of Women* (Boston: Walker, Wise and Company, 1863), 20. Penny claimed to have written the first book of this kind. She concludes that women librarians could expect one-third to one-half as much pay as men. The seven ladies at Boston earned $7 a week for an eight-to-ten-hour day. Women librarians in Philadelphia earned about $380 a year. Penny's little-known book is a meticulously prepared source for data on women's work. Amy Srebnik discovered that Penny's years of work were never adequately rewarded. Penny sold the copyright to her manuscript for only $100; it was later printed in book form. (See Srebnik, unpublished manuscript, "True Womanhood and Hard Times: Women and Early New York Industrialization, 1840-60," 43-44.)

10. "The English Conference," 280.

11. Peter Filene, *Him/Her/Self: Sex Relations in Modern America* (New York: Harcourt, Brace, Jovanovich, 1974).

12. *Ibid.*, 23–28.

13. *Ibid.*

14. William Poole, "Being a Librarian," *LJ* 15 (1890), 202. See also Anna Garland Spencer, "The Day of the Spinster," *Forum* 48 (1912), 194–210.

15. Alumni Files, University of Illinois Library School, Urbana. I was given access to these files on condition that I not reveal the identities of the persons quoted. Permission to obtain this information may be requested from the director of the Library School, University of Illinois, Urbana, Ill.

16. *Ibid.* See also Laurel Ann Grotzinger, *The Power and the Dignity: Librarianship and Katherine Sharp* (Metuchen, N.J.: The Scarecrow Press, 1966). Sharp fell ill and retired from library work in 1907. She lived for the rest of her life with the Deweys at Lake Placid, where she was killed in an automobile accident in 1914. Also see Grotzinger, "The Proto-Feminist Librarian at the Turn of the Century: Two Studies," *Journal of Library History* 10 (1975), 195–213.

17. Hill, *Women in Gainful Occupations*, 42.

18. Mabel Newcomer's *A Century of Higher Education for Women* (New York: Harper & Bros., 1959) offers a good overview of the employment opportunities open to educated women in the late nineteenth century. The economic causes she cites for the predominance of women teachers can also be applied to the feminization of librarianship. In 1870 three-fifths of all teachers were women. Also see Robert E. Riegel, *American Women: A Story of Social Change* (Cranbury, N.J.: Associated University Presses, 1970), 132–200.

19. Aileen S. Kraditor, ed., *Up from the Pedestal* (Chicago: Quadrangle Books, 1968); William L. O'Neill, *Everyone Was Brave* (Chicago: Quadrangle Books, 1969); Jill Conway, "Women Reformers and American Culture, 1870–1930," *Journal of Social History* 5 (Winter 1971–1972), 164–77.

20. Richard le Gallienne, quoted in M. S. R. James, "Women Librarians," *LJ* 18 (1893), 148.

21. Linda A. Eastman, "Aims and Personal Attitude in Library Work," *LJ* 22 (1897), 80.

22. "Library Employment vs. the Library Profession," *Library Notes* 1 (June 1886), 50.

23. *Ibid.*, 51.

24. Melvil Dewey, "Libraries as Related to the Educational Work of the State," *Library Notes* 3 (June 1888), 346.

25. Melvil Dewey, "The Attractions and Opportunities of Librarianship," *Library Notes* 1 (June 1886), 52. See also Melvil Dewey, "Address Before the Association of Collegiate Alumnae," March 13, 1886, in *Librarianship as a Profession for College-Bred Women* (Boston: Library Bureau, 1886).

26. Virginia Graeff, "The Gentle Librarian: A Transcript from Experience," *LJ* 30 (1905), 922.

27. Lilian Denio, "How to Make the Most of a Small Library," *Library Notes* 3 (March 1889), 470.

28. Theresa H. West, "The Usefulness of Libraries in Small Towns," *LJ* 8 (1883), 229.

29. Mary Salome Cutler Fairchild, "Women in American Libraries," *LJ* 29 (1904), 162.

30. *Ibid.*

31. Herbert Putnam, "The Woman in the Library," *LJ* 41 (1916), 880; See also Celia A. Hayward, "Woman as Cataloger," *Public Libraries* 3 (April 1898), 121-23; "Female Library Assistants," *LJ* 14 (1889), 128-29; John Dana, "Women in Library Work," *Independent* 71 (August 3, 1911), 244.

32. Robert Wiebe's *The Search for Order: 1877-1920* (New York: Hill and Wang, 1967, pp. 122-23) discusses how sexual roles were expressed in this period by women social workers, lawyers, and doctors in their service to children.

33. *LJ* 25 (1900), 123.

34. *Ibid.*

35. Minerva Sanders, "Report on Reading for the Young," *LJ*, 15 (1890), 59.

36. Annie Carroll Moore, "Special Training for Children's Librarians," *LJ* 23 (1898), 80.

37. E. M. Fairchild, "Methods of Children's Library Work as Determined by the Needs of the Children," *LJ* 22 (1897), 26.

38. Sophie H. Powell's *The Children's Library: A Dynamic Factor in Education* (New York: H. W. Wilson Company, 1917, pp. 1-7, 191-96, 255-71) is a careful study of the limited educational function of the children's section of the library. For a history of the development of library service to children see Harriet G. Long, *Public Library Service to Children: Foundation and Development* (Metuchen, N.J.: The Scarecrow Press, 1969) and Effie L. Power, *Work with Children in Public Libraries* (Chicago: American Library Association, 1943).

39. For examples of women's mild tone see Mary S. Cutler, "What a Woman Librarian Earns," *LJ* 17 (1892), 89-91; Mary E. Ahern, "The Business Side of a Woman's Career as a Librarian," *LJ* 24 (1899), 60-62; Martha B. Earle, "Women Librarians," *Independent* 64 (February 18, 1897), 30. In the Detroit *Tribune*, September 6, 1901, a Dr. Henri Leonard, a Library Commission member, was reported to have said, "The additional four ounces of brain in the male cranium indicates their superiority for executive work. No female head connected with the library has enough executive ability to take charge of the branches." (Cited in Frank B. Woodford, *Parnassus on Main Street: A History of the Detroit Public Library* [Detroit: Wayne State University Press, 1965, p. 279].)

40. "Woman's Meeting," *LJ* 17 (1892), 89-94.

41. Dewey to G. P. Putnam, January 18, 1898, MDP. This letter refers to a controversy arising in 1897 when Rutherford Hayes, first vice-president of the ALA, claimed his right to succession when Justin Winsor died. Hannah James, who joined the majority of the executive board in a vote for Putnam to replace Winsor, told Dewey that "when Mr. Winsor died my first thought in regard to his succession was one of gratitude that I had not rec'd the most votes for VP and I intended making the occurrence the text for a homily against putting women librarians in such a position." (James to Dewey, December 6, 1897, MDP.)

42. Also see Anita Schiller, "Women in Librarianship," in Melvin J. Voigt, ed., *Advances in Librarianship* (New York: Academic Press, 1974); Raymond L. Carpenter and Susan Akerstrom, *Carolina Libraries* 31 (Fall 1973), 22-32; Raymond

L. Carpenter and Kenneth D. Schearer, "Sex and Salary Update," *LJ* 99 (1974), 101-7; Margaret Ann Corwin, "An Investigation of Female Leadership in Regional, State and Local Library Associations, 1876-1923," *Library Quarterly* 44 (April 1974), 133-44.

43. "Proceedings," *LJ* 1 (1876), 90.

44. Caroline M. Hewins, "Library Work for Women," *LJ* 16 (1891), 273-74.

45. Cutler, "What a Woman Librarian Earns," *LJ*, 17 (August, 1892), 90.

46. *Ibid.*, 91.

47. Tessa L. Kelso, "Woman's Section of the A.L.A.," *LJ* 17 (1892), 444.

48. Ahern, "The Business Side of a Woman's Career as a Librarian," *LJ* 24 (1899), 60-62; Frances Hawley, "Some Non-Technical Qualifications for Library Work," *LJ* 29 (1904), 362. Also see Annie Dewey, "Women in Librarianship," address at the 1893 World's Congress of Representative Women (MDP), in which she praises the library profession for granting recognition to women.

49. M.S.C. Fairchild, "Women in American Libraries," 153-62.

50. *Ibid.*, 162.

51. Epstein, *Woman's Place*, 2.

52. See, for example, William Goode, "The Theoretical Importance of Love," *American Sociological Review* 24 (1959), 38-47. The best discussion of occupational segregation is Martha Baxall and Barbara Reagan, eds., *Women and the Workplace: The Implications of Occupational Segregation* (Chicago: University of Chicago Press, 1976).

53. David Pivar, *Purity Crusade: Sexual Morality and Social Control, 1868-1900* (Westport, Conn.: Greenwood Press, 1973).

Chapter 12. The Effect on Professionalization

1. Melvil Dewey, "The Profession," *LJ* 1 (1876), 5-6; Ernest C. Richardson, "Being a Librarian," *LJ* 15 (1890), 201-2. As a result of Charles C. Williamson's critical survey of library schools in 1923, the curriculum standards in library education were revised and a national system of accreditation was established. See Charles C. Williamson, *Training for Library Service: A Report Prepared for the Carnegie Corporation of New York* (Boston: The Merrymount Press, 1923); Sarah K. Vann, *The Williamson Reports: A Study* (Metuchen, N.J.: The Scarecrow Press, 1971); C. Edward Carroll, *The Professionalization of Education for Librarianship* (Metuchen, N.J.: The Scarecrow Press, 1970). For discussions of library professionalization, see Phillip H. Ennis, ed., *Seven Questions About the Profession of Librarianship* (Chicago: University of Chicago Press, 1961); Pierce Butler, "Librarianship as a Profession," *Library Quarterly* 21 (1951), 235-47; Robert D. Leigh, *The Public Library in the United States* (New York: Columbia University Press, 1969); Robert B. Downs, ed., *The Status of American College and University Librarians*, ACRL Monograph no. 22 (Chicago: American Library Association, 1958); William J. Goode, "The Theoretical Limits of Professionalization," in Amitai Etzioni, ed., *The Semi-Professions and Their Organization: Teachers, Nurses, Social Workers* (New York: The Free Press, 1969), 266-313.

2. Carl M. White, *The Origins of the American Library School* (Metuchen, N.J.: The Scarecrow Press, 1961), *passim*.

3. Ennis, *Seven Questions*, 83.

4. See, especially, A. M. Carr-Saunders, *The Professions* (Oxford: The Clarendon Press, 1933); T. A. Caplow, *The Sociology of Work* (Minneapolis: University of Minnesota Press, 1954); Ernest Greenwood, "The Attributes of a Profession," *Social Work* 2 (1957), 139-40; Howard M. Vollmer and Donald Mills, eds., *Professionalization* (Englewood Cliffs, N.J.: Prentice-Hall, 1966); Ronald M. Pavalko, *Sociology of Occupations and Professions* (Itasca, Ill.: F. E. Peacock Publishers, 1971); Raymond M. Merritt, *Engineering in American Society* (Lexington: University Press of Kentucky, 1969); Daniel H. Calhoun, *Professional Lives in America* (Cambridge: Harvard University Press, 1965); Kenneth S. Lynn, ed., *The Professions in America* (Boston: Houghton Mifflin Company, 1965).

5. William F. Poole, "Buffalo Conference Proceedings," *LJ* 8 (1883), 281. See also William H. Brett, "The Present Problem," *LJ* 19 (1894), 5-9; S. S. Green, *Libraries and Schools* (New York: F. Leypoldt, 1883), 56-74; Max Cohen, "The Librarian as an Educator and Not a Cheap-John," *LJ* 13 (1888), 366-67; Melvil Dewey, "Public Libraries as Public Educators," *LJ* 11 (1886), 165.

6. Robert W. Smuts, *Women and Work in America* (New York: Columbia University Press, 1959), 36.

7. For a thorough documentation of characteristic behavior of women workers see Richard L. and Ida Harper Simpson, "Women and Bureaucracy in the Semi-Professions," in Etzioni, *Semi-Professions*, 196-265. The nineteenth-century woman would demonstrate even more strongly the traits the Simpsons outline.

8. Ennis, *Seven Questions*, 7, 9; Marjorie Fiske, *Book Selection and Censorship* (Los Angeles: University of California Press, 1959), 100-12.

9. Sociologist Talcott Parsons has also noted the "tendency for women to gravitate into 'supportive' types of occupational roles, where functions of 'helpfulness' to the incumbent of more assertive and ultimately, in the social function sense, more responsible roles is a major keynote." Parsons points to sex composition as "both a symptom and a partial determinant" of the pattern of "the 'quietness,' the rather passive character of the attributes of librarians as a group, wishing as it were to be unobtrusively 'helpful' but avoiding assertiveness." (Talcott Parsons, "Implications of the Study," in J. Periam Danton, ed., *The Climate of Book Selection* [Berkeley: University of California Press, 1959, pp. 94-95].)

10. William E. Goode, "The Librarian: From Occupation to Profession?", in Ennis, 13.

11. White, *Origins of American Library School*, 32-33.

12. "Report of the Committee on The School of Library Economy," *LJ* 12 (1887), 427; "Report on the Library School," *LJ* 15 (1890), 93; "Report of the Committee on Library Schools," *LJ* 25 (1900), 83-85; "American Library Association," *LJ* 37 (1912), 440; Adelaide R. Hasse, "Women in Libraries," *Journal of the Association of Collegiate Alumnae*, cited in *LJ* 43 (1918), 141-42; Ernest J. Reece, *The Curriculum in Library Schools* (New York: Columbia University Press, 1936); Tse-Chien Tai, *Professional Education for Librarianship* (New York: H. W. Wilson Company, 1925); Donald G. Davis, *The Association of American Library Schools,*

1915–1968 (Metuchen, N.J.: The Scarecrow Press, 1974); Jesse Shera, *The Foundations of Education for Librarianship* (New York: Becker and Hays, 1972); Rachael K. Schenk, "The Dread and the Terror, Curriculum of 1910," *Journal of Education for Librarianship* 1 (Fall 1960), 75–80; Mary W. Plummer, "The Beginnings of a Library School," *LJ* 37 (1912), 14–16. Abraham Flexner, in 1930, cited the Graduate School of Library Science at the University of Chicago as an example of all that was worst in higher learning in *Universities: American, English, German* (New York: Oxford University Press, 1930), 171–73. That library training is still facing the same problems is evident in Margit Kraft's "What Would You Do with Brighter People?", *Journal of Education for Librarianship* 7 (Summer 1966), 21–28.

13. "Library Work of New York Library Association," *LJ* 28 (1903), 721; Melvil Dewey to B. I. Wheeler, August 1905, MDP.

14. See, for example, *Library World* 4 (1901), 245–48, 286–88, 319–22; Chalmers Hadley, "What Library Schools Can Do for the Profession," *ALA Bulletin* 6 (1912), 147–51.

15. Williamson, *Training for Library Service*, 149, 107, 52. Between 1910 and 1920 the proportion of female librarians increased from 79 to 88 per cent of the total (table cited in Cynthia Epstein, *Woman's Place* [Los Angeles: University of California Press, 1971, p. 7].)

16. "Proceedings," *LJ* 30 (1905), 174. Jody Newmyer's "The Image Problem of the Librarian: Femininity and Social Control" (*Journal of Library History* 11 [January 1976], 44–67) is a good discussion of the faults of a "masculine-feminine" personality test but does not discuss the informal personality testing in use in some of the first library schools.

17. Williamson, 49, 40.

18. Cited in Sarah Vann, *Training for Librarianship before 1923* (Chicago: American Library Association, 1961), 105.

19. U.S. Department of Commerce and Labor, Bureau of the Census, *Statistics of Women at Work* (Washington, D.C.: U.S. Government Printing Office, 1907), 33.

20. Normal schools were faced with similar problems during this period. A predominantly bureaucratic control is evident in schoolteaching and librarianship. See Simpson and Simpson in Etzioni, *Semi-Professions*, 196–221.

21. Dawe, *Melvil Dewey* (Lake Placid, N.Y.: Lake Placid Club, 1932), 91–92

22. "Report of the Committee on the Proposed School of Library Economy," *LJ* 10 (1885), 293.

23. Lutie E. Stearns, "The Question of Library Training," *LJ* 30 (1905), 68, 70.

24. "Fifth Session," *LJ* 30 (1905), 167–68.

25. *Ibid.*

26. *Ibid.*, 164–76.

27. Simpson and Simpson, 260–65. For current feminist protest, see Anita R. Schiller, "The Widening Sex Gap," *LJ* 94 (1969), 1098–1100; Janet Freedman, "The Liberated Librarian," *LJ* 95 (1970), 1709–1711; Anita R. Schiller, "The Disadvantaged Majority: Women Employed in Libraries," *American Libraries* 4

(April 1970), 345–49. See also Athena Theodore, ed., *The Professional Woman* (Cambridge: Schenkman Publishing Company, 1971).

28. "Editorial," *LJ* 17 (1892), 371. For discussions of the old and new librarian, see "The New Librarians," *LJ* 15 (1890), 338; R.R. Bowker, "The Work of the Nineteenth-Century Librarian for the Librarian of the Twentieth," *LJ* 8 (1883), 247–50.

29. William H. Form, "Popular Images of Librarians," *LJ* 71 (1946), 851–55; Robert Leigh and Kathryn W. Sewny, "The Popular Image of the Library and of Librarians," *LJ* 85 (1960), 2089–2091.

30. Ennis, *Seven Questions*, 74.

31. Howard Mumford Jones, "Reflections in a Library," *Saturday Review* 43 (April 9, 1960), 34.

Chapter 13. Librarianship, Charity Work, and the Settlement Movement

1. David J. Pivar, *Purity Crusade: Sexual Morality and Social Control, 1868–1900* (Westport, Conn.: Greenwood Press, 1973); Joseph Gusfield, *Symbolic Crusade: Status Politics and the American Temperance Movement* (Urbana: University of Illinois Press, 1963); Anthony Platt, *The Child Savers: The Invention of Delinquency* (Chicago: University of Chicago Press, 1969). See also Phillida Bunkle, "Sentimental Womanhood and Domesticity," *History of Education Quarterly* 14 (1974), 13–31, and Roberta Wein, "Women's Colleges and Domesticity, 1875–1918," *Ibid.*, 31–49.

2. Aileen Kraditor, *The Ideas of the Woman Suffrage Movement, 1890–1920* (New York: Columbia University Press, 1965).

3. Anna Edith Updegraff Hilles, "Woman in Society Today," *Arena* 16 (July 1896), 163–75. Two other especially interesting accounts illustrating the unsettling as well as the conservative aspects of women's new mission are: Ella Wheeler Wilcox, "The Restlessness of the Modern Woman," *Cosmopolitan* 31 (1901), 314–17; Kate Gannett Wells, "The Transitional American Woman," *Atlantic Monthly* 46 (December 1880), 817–823.

4. Governor J. Bagley, "Presidential Address," *Proceedings of the National Conference of Charities and Corrections* (1875), 13. Hereafter cited as PNCCC.

    I found most helpful as studies of philanthropy: Walter I. Trattner, *From Poor Law to Welfare State: A History of Social Welfare in America* (New York: The Free Press, 1974); Nathan Huggins, *Protestants Against Poverty: Boston's Charities* (Westport, Conn.: Greenwood Publishing Co., 1971); Alfred J. Kahn, *Issues in American Social Work* (New York: Columbia University Press, 1959); Robert Bremner, *From the Depths: The Discovery of Poverty in the United States* (New York: New York University Press, 1956); Gary A. Lloyd, *Charities, Settlements and Social Work: An Inquiry into Philosophy and Method, 1890–1915* (New Orleans: Tulane University School of Social Welfare, 1971); Frank D. Watson, *The Charity Organization Movement in the United States* (New York: The Macmillan Company, 1922); Frank J. Bruno, *Trends in Social Work,*

1874–1946 (New York: Columbia University Press, 1948); Roy Lubove, *The Professional Altruist: The Emergence of Social Work as a Career, 1880–1930* (Cambridge: Harvard University Press, 1965).

Also see Joanna Colcord and Ruth Mann, eds., *The Long View: Papers and Addresses by Mary E. Richmond* (New York: Russell Sage Foundation, 1930); Margaret Rich, *Josephine Shaw Lowell* (New York: Family Service Association of America, 1954); Mary E. Richmond, *Friendly Visiting Among the Poor* (New York: The Macmillan Company, 1899); and Kathleen Woodroofe, *From Charity to Social Work in England and America* (Toronto: University of Toronto Press, 1962). An interesting study of English social work is Ronald G. Walton, *Women in Social Work* (London: Routledge & Kegan Paul, 1975). Also see Dorothy G. Becker, "The Visitor to the New York City Poor, 1843-1920," *Social Service Review* 35 (December 1961), 382-96; Becker, "Exit Lady Bountiful: The Volunteer and the Professional Social Worker," *Social Service Review* 38 (March 1964), 57-72; and Becker, "Social Welfare Leaders as Spokesmen for the Poor," *Social Casework* 49 (February 1968), 82-89; Marvin E. Gettleman, "Charity and Social Classes in the United States, 1874-1900," *American Journal of Economics and Sociology* 22 (April 1963), 313-30; *Ibid.*, 22 (July 1963), 417-26; Gettleman, "Philanthropy as Social Control in Late Nineteenth Century America: Some Hypotheses and Data on the Rise of Social Work," *Societas* 5 (Winter 1975), 49-59.

Also see Milton Speizman, "Poverty, Pauperism, and Their Causes: Some Charity Organization Views," *Social Casework* 46 (March 1965), 142-49; Muriel Pumphrey, "The 'First Step' — Mary Richmond's Earliest Professional Reading, 1889-91," *Social Service Review* 31 (June 1957), 144-63; Margaret Rich, "Mary Richmond, Social Worker, 1861-1928," *Social Casework* 33 (October 1952), 363-70; Clarke A. Chambers, "Social Service and Social Reform: A Historical Essay," *Social Service Review* 37 (March 1963), 76-90; Ralph and Muriel Pumphrey, eds., *The Heritage of American Social Work* (New York: Columbia University Press, 1961); and David and Sheila Rothman, eds., *On Their Own: The Poor in Modern America* (Reading, Mass.: Addison-Wesley Publishing Company, 1972); Clarke A. Chambers, *Seedtime of Reform: American Social Service and Social Action, 1918–1933* (Minneapolis: University of Minnesota Press, 1963). For pre-Civil War philanthropy, see Benjamin J. Klebaner, *Public Poor Relief in America, 1790–1860* (New York: Arno Press, 1976).

5. Mary Richmond, "The Friendly Visitor," in Colcord and Mann, *The Long View*, 40. In "Social Welfare Leaders" (p. 86), Becker composed a socioeconomic profile of the thirty-seven men and twenty women of this period listed in the 1965 edition of the *Encyclopedia of Social Work*. She found the males to be generally native-born, white, Protestant, the sons of professional men, college graduates, previous teachers or ministers, married and of urban background. The women were native, white, Protestant, and middle-class, college graduates, daughters of professional men or of men holding high political office, reared in small towns, unmarried, and had mothers who were active in the suffrage movement. The women volunteers tended to be wealthier but from the same general background. Also see Clarke A. Chambers and Andrea Hinding, "Charity Workers, the Settlements and the Poor," *Social Casework* 49 (1968), 96-101; Dorothy Becker, "Early Adventures in Social Casework: The Charity Agent, 1880-1910," *Ibid.* 45 (1963), 255-65.

6. See Mary Richmond, "The Need of a Training School in Applied Philanthropy," *PNCCC* (1897), 181–86. Richmond was the first to propose a training school for charity workers; she compared the paucity of such schools with the existing library schools. In 1904 Simmons College and Harvard University cooperated in founding the Boston School of Social Work. The affiliation of the private Chicago school with the University of Chicago in 1907 marked the first real university sponsorship of a school of social work. In 1919 the Association of Training Schools for Professional Social Work was formed with seventeen charter members.

7. "Organization of Charities," *PNCCC* (1897), 154. See *Ibid.*, pp. 123–63, for the first general discussion of Friendly Visiting at the national association meeting. See also Mrs. W. P. Lynde, "Prevention in Some of Its Aspects," *PNCCC* (1879), 167.

8. Lynde, 170.

9. "Organization of Charities," *PNCCC* (1887), 152, 149.

10. Becker, "Exit Lady Bountiful."

11. See especially the sections on Charity Organization in *PNCCC*, 1884, 1887, 1888, 1892, 1893, for information on the increasing difficulty with Friendly Visiting.

12. Mrs. Anne B. Richardson, "The Co-operation of Women in Philanthropy," *PNCCC* (1892), 216–22. See also Virginia T. Smith, "The Co-operation of Women in Philanthropic and Reformatory Work," *PNCCC* (1891), 230–42, and Lucy M. Sickels, "Women's Influence in Juvenile Reformatories," *PNCCC* (1894), 164–67.

13. John Lovejoy Elliott, "After Twenty Years in the Tenement Houses of New York," in Lorene M. Pacey, ed., *Readings in the Development of Settlement Work* (New York: Books for Libraries Press, 1971), 115.

14. Woodroofe, *From Charity to Social Work*, 22.

15. Watson, *The Charity Organization Movement*, 218.

16. Mary Richmond, "The Friendly Visitor," 40.

17. Thorstein Veblen, *The Theory of the Leisure Class* (New York: New American Library, 1953), 197.

18. See *Lend-A-Hand, Charities Review, Charities,* and *PNCCC.*

19. Robert Paine, "Presidential Address," *PNCCC* (1895).

20. E. T. Devine, "Economic Aspects of Material Relief," *Charities* (1903), 541.

21. Jane Addams, "Charity and Social Justice," *PNCCC* (1910), 1. In this connection it is interesting to note Jacob J. Abt's "The Settlement and Education" (*PNCCC* [1896], 117–123). Abt mentions that the poor were afraid to enter the Chicago Public Library in 1896 because they were ashamed to admit that they could not use the card catalogue. Abt instituted a system whereby the settlement worker took them to the library, taught them to use the catalogue, and then signed as an endorser on the certificate which the library required from its patrons. Also see James G. Schonfarber, "Charities from the Standpoint of Knights of Labor," *PNCCC* (1890), 58–59.

22. Allen Davis, *Spearheads for Reform: The Social Settlements and the Progressive Movement, 1890–1914* (New York: Oxford University Press, 1967); John P.

Rousmaniere, "Cultural Hybrid in the Slums: The College Woman and the Settlement House, 1889-1894," *American Quarterly* 22 (Spring 1970), 45-66.

By the early twentieth century the settlement and organized-charity movements had merged into the profession of "social work." In the first decades of the century, advocates of preventive social reform, most of them settlement residents, dominated the councils of the national association. In 1912, that year which seemed to promise so much to Progressive leaders, the national association's Committee on Standards of Living and Labor drafted a program for social reform that became a part of the Progressive party's presidential platform. During and after the war, when the tide of social action receded, professional social workers (mainly caseworkers) gained control of the national conference, but casework— the central methodology of the new profession—had been enriched by the attention that the settlement movement had focused on the environment.

Settlement workers were keenly aware of the need to acquire knowledge in areas like economics, sociology, and political science in order to understand the social forces creating poverty. The settlement workers' emphasis upon scientific research and the importance of social theory influenced social work educators to place heavy emphasis upon theory and general knowledge in professional training. This is in sharp contrast to the early development of the schools of library science, where practice was emphasized to the near exclusion of theory. A curriculum pattern emerged that was common to all schools of social work: a substantial number of courses in theory and some training in research, plus experience in field work.

With the publication of Mary Richmond's *Social Diagnosis* (New York: Russell Sage Foundation, 1917), the techniques of social casework were enunciated as a systematic method, and the practice of social work was established as an occupation that required special training and theoretical knowledge. If public recognition of a specialized worker as an "expert" is assumed as a criterion for measuring professionalization, then the profession of social work had moved farther along the scale than librarianship by 1920, chiefly because the settlement movement had emphasized the value of research and broader social knowledge as a means of dealing with poverty. (See Esther L. Brown, *Social Work as a Profession* [New York: Russell Sage Foundation, 1935]; Ernest Greenwood, "Attributes of a Profession," *Social Work* 2 [July 1957], 45-55; Ernest Hollis and Alice Taylor, *Social Work Education in the United States* [New York: Columbia University Press, 1951]; Abraham Flexner, "Is Social Work a Profession?", *PNCCC* [1915], 576-90.)

After World War I, social work swung away from socioeconomic determinism to psychological determinism. Until the era of the New Deal, social workers were preoccupied with psychiatric social work and the emphasis shifted once again to individual frailty as the source of poverty. In a sense, the "undeserving" poor now became the "emotionally disturbed" poor. Like librarians, social workers in the 1920s embraced method to such an extent and with such a singleness of purpose that they veered toward becoming technicians. During the 1920s some social workers, of course, remained reformers; most, however, did not. The professional organizations and schools generally embodied a distinctly conservative spirit during the 1920s.

Chapter 14. Maid Militant: The Progressive Years and World War I

1. Arthur Bostwick, "The Future of Library Work," *ALA Bulletin* 12 (1918), 51, 53.

2. See, for example, "Branch Library Uses," *Survey*, 25 (1911), 1038–1039; "The Library as a Social Centre," *Public Libraries* 21 (1916), 315–16; Mary Frances Isom, "The Library a Civic Center," *Ibid.* 19 (1914), 93–96.

3. Arthur Bostwick, "The Public Library, the Public School and the Social Center Movement," *Proceedings and Addresses of the National Educational Association* (1912), 240–46.

4. See "Library Extension Work," *LJ* 39 (1914), 404; "Library Reading Clubs for Young People," *LJ* 37 (1912), 547–50; "Relation of the Public Library to Social Betterment," *Iowa Library Quarterly* 7 (1913), 1–9; "Some Phases of Library Extension," *ALA Bulletin* 1 (1907), 96–100; Nannie W. Jayne, "Work Outside the Library Walls," *Public Libraries* 20 (1915), 197–200.

5. Hiller C. Wellman's "Presidential Address" (*LJ* 40 [1915], 467–71) is a good summation of the effect of settlement-like activity on the development of the public library. Also see address of Jane Addams to the Drexel Institute library personnel, reported in *LJ* 37 (1912), 36; address of Florence Lattimore, Department of Child-Helping, Russell Sage Foundation, to librarians of Pennsylvania and New Jersey, reported in *LJ* 36 (1911), 191; F. W. Jenkins, "The Social Worker and the Library," *Ibid.*, 499–500; Clara Herbert, "Establishing Relations Between the Children's Library and Other Civic Agencies," *LJ* 34 (1909), 195–96; Arthur Bostwick, "The Social Work of the St. Louis Public Library," *LJ* 36 (1911), 461–63; Cora Stewart, "Libraries in Relation to Settlement Work," *LJ* 31 (1906), 82–85; "Social Activities of the Library," *LJ* 39 (1914), 441–43. The National Child Conference for Research and Welfare, held in 1909 at Clark University, presented librarians who gave papers on storytelling. Graham Taylor, the founder of the Chicago Commons Social Settlement, spoke to the ALA in 1908. Also see "The Story of Irishtown," *PNCCC* (1914), 397–400; Henry S. Curtis, "The Playground," *PNCCC* (1907), 278–86: "The Library as a Civic and Social Center," *Public Libraries* 17 (1912), 362; "County Social Service Work," *LJ* 39 (1914), 872. D. W. Davies, in *Public Libraries as Culture and Social Centers: The Origin of the Concept* (Metuchen, N.J.: The Scarecrow Press, 1974), argues that extension activities originated in the early nineteenth century in England in an effort to attract the masses to the library.

6. Stewart, "Libraries in Relation to Settlement Work," 83.

7. *Ibid.*

8. Mary Bean, "The Evil of Unlimited Freedom in the Use of Juvenile Literature," *LJ* 4 (1879), 341.

9. "Papers on Fiction and the Reading of School Children," *Ibid.*, 319–66.

10. "The Pawtucket Free Library and the Dime Novel," *LJ* 10 (1885), 105; Joseph Peacock, "Mawtucket of Pawtucket," *LJ* 40 (1915), 792–94; reports of the Free Public Library, Pawtucket, Rhode Island, 1885–1910, xeroxed copies in possession of author. Minerva Sanders's report on reading for the young (*LJ* 15 [1890],

59-64), read before the ALA, started a new flurry over children's literature. Interest peaked again at the 1897 conference.

11. Harriet G. Long, *Public Library Service for Children: Foundation and Development* (Metuchen, N.J.: The Scarecrow Press, 1969); Alice Hazeltine, ed., *Library Work with Children: Reprints of Papers and Addresses* (New York: H. W. Wilson Company, 1917).

12. Mary S. Cutler, "Home Libraries," *LJ* 19 (1894), 13-14. See also Charles Birtwell, "Home Libraries," *Ibid.*, 9-13.

13. Harriot Hassler, "Common-Sense and the Story Hour," *LJ* 30 (1905), 78. Also see Elizabeth P. Clarke, "Story-telling, Reading Aloud and Other Special Features of Work in Children's Rooms," *LJ* 27 (1902), 189-90. An attempt to judge the practical results of storytelling was made by the Children's Librarian's Section (see *ALA Bulletin* 3 [1909], 408-27). See Frances C. Sayers, *Anne Carroll Moore* (New York: Atheneum, 1972) for a description of the influence of Marie Shedlock upon the development of storytelling in American libraries.

14. Clara M. Hunt, "Some Means by Which Children May Be Led to Read Better Books," *LJ* 24 (1899), 149.

15. Arthur Bostwick, "The Social Work of the St. Louis Public Library," *LJ* 36 (1911), 463.

16. Long, *Public Library Service for Children*, 135-53.

17. *Ibid.*

18. "The Public Library and Allied Agencies," *LJ* 30 (1905), 459-72.

19. Stewart, "Libraries in Relation to Settlement Work," *LJ* 31 (1906), 85.

20. Wellman, "Presidential Address," *LJ* 40 (1915), 467-71.

21. "Work Outside the Library Walls," *Public Libraries* 20 (1915).

22. "The Public Library and Allied Agencies," 459-72.

23. "The Library and Social Movements," *Wisconsin Library Bulletin* 7 (1911), 6.

24. Wellman, "Presidential Address," *LJ* 40 (1915).

25. "Children's Librarian's Section," *ALA Bulletin* 5 (1911), 245.

26. Long, *Public Library Service for Children*, 140. Also see "Branch Library Uses," *LJ* 36 (1911), 299-300.

27. "Volume of Children's Work in the United States," *ALA Bulletin* 7 (1913), 287-91.

28. Lutie Stearns, "The Question of Discipline," in Hazeltine, *Library Work with Children*, 223-29.

29. For a full discussion, see Dee Garrison, "Cultural Custodians in the Gilded Age: The Public Librarian and Horatio Alger," *Journal of Library History* 6 (October 1971), 327-36.

30. Clara M. Hunt, "The Children's Library: A Moral Force," *LJ* 31 (1906), 100.

31. S. S. Green, "Sensational Fiction in Public Libraries," *LJ* 4 (1879), 349.

32. C. M. Hewins, "Children's Books," *LJ* 22 (1897), 108-09. Hewins, a leading pioneer in work with children, lived in North Street settlement house in Hartford for twelve years and created a library branch there.

33. Aniela Poray, "The Foreign Child and the Book," *LJ* 40 (1915), 237.

34. G. Stanley Hall, "What Children Do Read and What They Ought to Read," *Public Libraries* 10 (1905), 391, 392, and "Children's Reading as a Factor in Their Education," *LJ* 33 (1908), 123-28.

35. Caroline Burnite, "Good and Poor Books for Boys and Girls," *Public Libraries* 11 (1906), 361-62. Also see E. M. Fairchild, "Methods of Children's Library Work as Determined by the Needs of the Children," *LJ* 22 (1887), 19-28; Electra Collins Doren, "Action Upon Bad Books," *LJ* 28 (1903), 167-69; Frances Jenkins Olcott, "Rational Library Work with Children and the Preparation for It," *LJ* 30 (1905), 71-75; Ada Jones, "The Library as an Educator," *Library Notes* 3 (1892), 367-79; Gertrude Andrus, "How the Library Is Meeting the Changing Conditions of Child Life," *ALA Bulletin* 7 (1913), 188-92.

36. Mary Ely, "Our Present Problem," *ALA Bulletin* 8 (1914), 220.

37. *Ibid.*

38. "Fit Reading for Boys and Girls," *Springfield Republican*, April 1, 1879, cited in *LJ* 4 (1879), 171.

39. "Papers on Fiction and the Reading of Schoolchildren," *LJ* 3 (1879), 365.

40. E. C. Richardson, "Presidential Address," *LJ* 30 (1905), 8.

41. "Children's Section," *LJ* 31 (1906), 246.

42. Ethel P. Underhill, "Crumbs of Comfort to the Children's Librarian," *LJ* 35 (1910), 155, 157.

43. Elizabeth White, "Reaching Parents Through the Children," *LJ* 42 (1917), 522-23. Also see Marvin Lazerson, "Urban Reform and the Schools: Kindergartens in Massachusetts, 1870-1915," *History of Education Quarterly* 1 (1971), 115-37.

44. Richard Darling, *The Rise of Children's Book Reviewing in America, 1865-1881* (New York: R. R. Bowker Company, 1968).

45. Phyllis Dain, *The New York Public Library: A History of Its Founding and Early Years* (New York: The New York Public Library, 1972), 299-306; Anne Carroll Moore, *My Roads to Childhood: Views and Reviews of Children's Books* (Boston: The Horn Book, Inc., 1961); Moore, "What the Community Is Asking of the Department of Children's Work in the Public Library," *LJ* 38 (1913), 595-600.

46. Timothy Smith's "Immigrant Social Aspirations and American Education, 1880-1930" (*American Quarterly* 21 [1969], 523-43) discusses how immigrants from southern and eastern Europe eagerly sought education for their children.

47. "Libraries for Men," *Independent*, June 15, 1901, reprinted in *LJ* 30 (1905), 408-9.

48. "Editorial," *LJ* 33 (1908), 122.

49. Caroline Matthews, "The Growing Tendency to Over-Emphasize the Children's Side," in Hazeltine, *Library Work with Children*, 91-99. Also see "Fear of Feminization in School and Home," *World's Work* 16 (May 1908), 10242-10243, and "The Woman Problem in American Education," *Educational Review* 47 (February 1914), 115.

50. E. L. Pearson, "The Children's Library *Versus* Huckleberry Finn: A Brief for the Defense," *LJ* 32 (1907), 312-14.

51. John Dana, "What the Library Is Doing," n.d., JCDP.

52. Dana, "Story-Telling in Libraries," *Public Libraries* 13 (1908), 350.

53. Clara Hunt, "Values in Library Work with Children," *ALA Bulletin* 7 (1913), 276. See also Arthur Bostwick, "Library Work with Children," *Ibid.* 10 (1916), 209-10.

54. "Editorial," *LJ* 19 (1894), 328.

55. See the series on library work with the foreign-born. *LJ* 49 (1924), 964-81.

56. John Carr, "What the Library Can Do for the Foreign Born," *LJ* 38 (1913), 566-68. See also J. Maud Campbell, "What the Foreigner Has Done for One Library," *Ibid.*, 610-15; "Americanization Through Foreign Print," *LJ* 43 (1918), 884-85; Josephine Gratiaa, "Making Americans," *LJ* 44 (1919), 729; Josepha Kudlicka, "Library Work with Foreigners," *Public Libraries* 15 (1910), 375-76; H. H. Wheaton, "An Americanization Program for Libraries," *ALA Bulletin* 10 (1916), 265-69; "Books for the Foreign Population," *LJ* 31 (1906), 65-72; Jasmine Britton, "The Library's Share in Americanization," *LJ* 43 (1918), 723-27; Carol Ackerman, "The Book-Worms of New York: How the Public Libraries Satisfy the Immigrant's Thirst for Knowledge," *Independent,* 74 (1913), 199-201.

57. Dorothy Kuhn Oko and Bernard F. Downey, compilers, *Library Service to Labor* (New York: The Scarecrow Press, 1963), 49-71. Edward Hartmann, *The Movement to Americanize the Immigrant* (New York: Columbia University Press, 1948); Robert Carlson, "Americanization as an Early Twentieth-Century Adult Education Movement," *History of Education Quarterly* 10 (1970), 440-64.

58. Dain, *The New York Public Library,* 288-310.

59. Mary Antin, "The Immigrant in the Library," *ALA Bulletin* 7 (1913), 145-50.

60. Cited in Arthur Price Young, "The American Library Association and World War I" (Ph.D. dissertation, Library Science, University of Illinois, Urbana, Ill., 1976), 33.

61. *Ibid.*, 60. Also see Theodore W. Koch, *Books in the War: The Romance of Library War Service* (Boston: Houghton Mifflin Company, 1919).

62. "Personal Note from a Library," *War Library Bulletin,* September 1917, p. 5. ALA Archives, University of Illinois, Urbana.

63. See collection of *War Library Bulletin* issues, ALA Archives.

64. Young, 26-29.

65. "Censorship Puts Grip on Camp Libraries," *Detroit News,* March 31, 1918; War Services Committee, clippings, 1917-20, ALA Archives; Young, 133; Ralph T. Esterquest, "War Attitudes and Activities of American Libraries, 1914-18," *Wilson Library Bulletin* 15 (April 1941), 621-23.

66. Winser to Newton D. Baker, February 20, 1918, War Service Correspondence, ALA Archives.

67. Winser to Putnam, March 28, 1918, *Ibid.*

68. *ALA Bulletin* 12 (1918), 286-87.

69. Young, 91.

70. See also Peggy Sullivan, *Carl Milam and the American Library Association* (New York: H. W. Wilson Company, 1976), 88–98.

71. "Why Do We Need a Public Library? Material for a Library Campaign," *Library Tracts* (Boston: Houghton Mifflin Company, 1910), 31.

72. Sidney Ditzion, *Arsenals of a Democratic Culture: A Social History of the American Public Library Movement in New England and the Middle Atlantic States from 1850 to 1900* (Chicago: American Library Association, 1947), 139.

73. Margaret Ann Nation's "The Librarian in the Short Story" (ACRL micro-card [Rochester, N.Y., 1956, p. 45]) is a study of the development of the librarian in fiction written between 1900 and 1915. See also C. H. Compton, "The Librarian and the Novelist," *South Atlantic Quarterly* 26 (October 1927), 392–403; Bernard Berelson, *The Library's Public* (New York: Columbia University Press, 1949).

74. Richard Jensen, "Family, Career and Reform Women Leaders of the Progressive Era," in Michael Gordon, ed., *The American Family in Social-Historical Perspective* (New York: St. Martin's Press, 1973), 267–80.

Chapter 15. The Decline of the Genteel Library Hostess

1. "Editorial," *LJ* 37 (1912), 2; Agnes A. Perkins, ed., *Vocations for Trained Women: Opportunities Other Than Teaching* (New York: Longmans, Green & Company, 1910).

2. U.S. Department of Labor, Women's Bureau, Bulletin no. 27 *The Occupational Progress of Women,* (Washington, D.C.: U.S. Government Printing Office, 1922).

3. Joseph A. Hill, *Women in Gainful Occupations, 1870–1920,* Census Monograph no. 9 (Washington, D.C.: U.S. Government Printing Office, 1929). Between 1870 and 1930, women's share of clerical employment grew from 2.45 per cent to 52.4 per cent.

4. Mrs. J. T. Jennings, "Statistics of Women in Library Work," *LJ* 43 (October 1918), 737. See also Josephine Rathbone, "Salaries of Library School Graduates," *LJ* 39 (March 1914), 188–90; Charles H. Compton, "Comparison of Qualifications, Training, Demand, and Remuneration of the Library Profession with Social Work," *Public Libraries* 30 (March 1925), 115–21.

5. Wilhelm Munthe, *American Librarianship from an European Angle: An Evaluation of Policies and Activities* (Chicago: American Library Association, 1939), 165. Cynthia F. Epstein, *Woman's Place: Options and Limits in Professional Careers* (Berkeley: University of California Press, 1971), 71.

6. Arthur Bostwick, "System in the Library," *LJ* 34 (November 1909), 477. Also see his "Labor and Rewards in the Library" (*Public Libraries* 15 [January 1910], 1–5) for a discussion of why women were paid less than men.

7. Josephine Rathbone, "Some Aspects of Our Personal Life," *Public Libraries* 21 (February 1916), 54; also see Ida A. Kidder, "The Creative Impulse in the Library," *Public Libraries* 24 (May 1919), 156–57.

8. Bostwick, "Labor and Rewards in the Library," *Public Libraries* 15 (January 1910), 4.

9. Jennie M. Flexner, "The Loan Desk from Both Sides," *LJ* 49 (1924), 412. See also the series by R. R. Bowker, "Women in the Library Profession," *LJ* (1920); and Theresa Hitchler, "The Successful Loan-Desk Assistant," *LJ* 32 (December 1907), 554-59. For protest see "Editorial" (*Public Libraries* 15 [July 1910], 284-85) and Mabel South-Clife, "A Protest — "Subordinates' vs. 'Assistants,' " *LJ* 39 (1914), 198.

10. "The Case of the Desk Assistant," *LJ* 27 (1902), 877. Also see "Library Assistants: Shortcomings and Desirable Qualifications," *Ibid.* 29 (1904), 349-59; "A Few Brickbats from a Layman," *Public Libraries* 18 (July 1913), 277-79; "The Desk Assistant: An Imaginary Conversation," *LJ* 27 (1902), 251-54; Margery Doud, "The Inarticulate Library Assistant," *Ibid.* 45 (1920), 540-43; Mary Macmillan, "The Relation of Librarian and Assistants," *LJ* 28 (1903), 717-18.

11. Herbert Putnam, "The Woman in the Library," *LJ* 41 (1916), 879.

12. Letter from instructor to graduate, October 19, 1927. Alumni Files. Identities withheld.

13. "Report of Committee on Library Training," *ALA Bulletin* 12 (1918), 260.

14. James W. Milden, "Women, Public Libraries, and Library Unions: The Formative Years," *Journal of Library History* 2 (Spring 1977), 150-58. Richard Hall's "Professionalization and Bureaucratization" (American Sociological Review 33 [February 1968], 92-104) is a careful study which argues that if an occupation is badly paid, the level of dedication to work often rises. This is especially true, according to Hall, for teachers, nurses, and social workers.

15. *ALA Bulletin* 44 (1919), 380.

16. Cited in Milden, 151.

17. *ALA Bulletin* 44 (1919), 359.

18. *Ibid.*

19. "Stenographers and Typewriters Wanted," *LJ* 43 (1918), 334.

20. Marie Newberry, "What Should Be the Standards of Admission to the Training Class?", *LJ* 44 (1919), 284-87; Frank W. Walter, "The War and Library Training," *LJ* 43 (1918), 728-32.

21. "Discussion," *ALA Bulletin,* 43 (1918), 285.

22. Doud, "The Inarticulate Library Assistant," *LJ* 45 (1920), 543.

23. Clara M. Herbert, "Recruiting a Training Class," *LJ* 44 (1919), 108. See comments by William Henry, "Living Salaries for Good Service," *Ibid.* 44 (1919), 282-84.

24. Edith Shatto King, "Wanted: Social Workers," *Survey* 40 (May 1918), 126.

25. "Professional Training Section," *ALA Bulletin* 43 (1918), 304-5.

26. Sinclair Lewis, *Main Street* (New York: Harcourt, Brace, 1920), 3, 7-8, 9, 10, 11.

27. William A. Chafe, *The American Woman: Her Changing Social, Economic and Political Role, 1920-70* (New York: Oxford University Press, 1972), 48-132; J. Stanley Lemons, *The Woman Citizen: Social Feminism in the 1920s* (Chicago: University of Illinois Press, 1973); William O'Neill, *Everyone Was*

Brave: The Rise and Fall of Feminism in America (Chicago: Quadrangle Books, 1969).

28. "Status of Married Women," *ALA Bulletin* 32 (1938), 402.

29. "Problems," *Wilson Library Bulletin* 8 (1933), 409; for other quotes above, see *Ibid.*, 230-31, 403-8.

30. See *LJ* 63 (1938), 232, 294-96, 342-43, 438, 569.

31. Robert S. Alvarez, "Women's Place in Librarianship," *Wilson Library Bulletin* 13 (1938), 175-78; W. H. Kaiser, *Ibid.* 14 (1939), 336.

32. Katherine Stokes, "Warning—Soft Shoulders," *Ibid.* 14 (1939), 470-71; See also Josephine Rathbone, "Library School Graduates and the Depression," *LJ* 60 (1935), 240-41.

33. Ethel Gerard, "Librarianship from a Woman Assistant's Point of View," *Library Assistant* 9 (September 1912), 164-71; B. L. Dyer and Joseph Lloyd, "Women Librarians in England," *Ibid.* 1 (June 1899), 219-22.

34. M. S. R. James, "American Women as Librarians," *The Library* 5 (1893), 270-74; G. E. Wire, "Library Assistants in the United States," *Library Assistant* 1 (June 1899), 214-17.

35. M. S. R. James, "Women Librarians and Their Future Prospects," *Library Association Record* 2 (June 1900), 295.

36. Miss Richardson, "Librarianship as a Profession for Women," *The Library* 6 (1894), 137-42.

37. W. L. Selby, "Women as Librarians in Bristol," *Library Assistant* 1 (June 1899), 217.

38. Edmund Verney, "Village Libraries," *The Library* 10 (1898), 24-28. See also *Library Assistant* 2 (October 1899), 45.

39. *Library Assistant* 7 (1910), 217-18; Mizpah Gilbert, "The Education of the Library Assistant," *Ibid.* 6 (1908), 52-55; Douglass Hartham, "Lonely Women in the Library," *Library World* 9 (1907), 360-63; Frank E. Chennell, "Lady Assistants in Public Libraries," *Library World* 4 (1902), 245-48; Ethel S. Fegan, "Women Librarians," *Library Association Record* 12 (1910), 224-26.

40. "Women Librarians and Assistants," *Library World* 4 (1902), 7.

41. Cited in *Library Assistant* 15 (1921), 206. See also Margaret Reed, "Women Assistants," *Librarian* 7 (1915), 254-55; see series by Reed in *The Librarian and the Book World* 3 (1912), especially May 1912 issue, pp. 388-89, and Reed, "Women and Librarians in the New Age," *Ibid.* 9 (1919), 133; Gwendolen Rees, "Symposium on Public Libraries After the War," *Library Association Record* 19 (1917), 230-33; "The Position of Women in Library Work Today," *Ibid.* 17 (1915), 131-32; "Women as Librarians and Library Assistants," *Library Assistant* 16 (1922), 52-53; Mizpah Gilbert, "The Position of Women in Public Libraries," *Library World* 18 (October 1915), 100-105.

42. P. Layzell Ward, *Women in Librarianship* (London: Library Association Press, 1966).

43. A. G. S. Enser, "Shall the Misses Be Masters," *Library Association Record* 15 (1948), 124-25. See also "Figures and Facts," *Ibid.* 18 (1951), 14-15; H. A. Tillie, "Women in Librarianship," *Library World* 31 (1928), 144-45; Rena Cowper, "Not in Our Stars," *Library Association Record* 7 (1940), 166-67.

44. P. Layzell Ward, "Women and Librarianship in 1975," *Library Association Record* 77 (1975), 82-83.

45. The best discussion of differences is Donald Davidson, "Trends in Library Education—Europe," in Melvin J. Voigt and Michael H. Harris, eds., *Advances in Librarianship*, vol. 6 (New York: Academic Press, 1976), 217-52.

46. M. S. R. James, "Women Librarians and Their Future Prospects," *Library Association Record* 2 (June 1900), 291-304.

47. Max A. R. Brinner, "The Library as a Place for Women," *Library World* 10 (1907), 137-39; "Library Notes from Germany," *Public Libraries* 12 (1907), 394-95.

48. "Women as Librarians—A French Viewpoint," *LJ* 40 (1915), 657-58. See also Jean Hassenforder, "Development of the Public Libraries in France, the United Kingdom and the United States," *UNESCO Bulletin for Libraries* 22 (1968), 13-19.

49. Genevieve Boisard, "Do Women Hold the Reins of Power in French Libraries," *UNESCO Bulletin for Libraries* 29 (1975), 312. Also see Arne Keldal, "American Influence on European Librarianship," *Library Quarterly* 8 (1937), 196-211; Margaret Chaplan, "American Ideas in the German Public Libraries: Three Periods," *Ibid.* 41 (1971), 35-53.

50. Boisard, 303-14. The universality of women's suppression in the library is illustrated in K. C. Harrison, *Libraries in Scandinavia* (London: Andre Deutsch, 1961); M. W. Shilling, "Women in Librarianship," *South African Library* 5 (1938), 186-90; "Women in Professional Library Work," *New Zealand Libraries* 32 (1969), 4-15; F. B. M. Cass, "W(H)ither a Female Profession?", *Australian Library Journal* 22 (1973), 49-55; Anne Smart, "Women—The Four-Fifths Minority," *Canadian Library Journal* 32 (1975), 14-17.

51. Simsova Fla, ed., *Lenin, Krupskaia and Libraries* (London: Clive Bingley, 1968). See also Lenin, "What Can Be Done for Public Education," *Ibid.*, 15; Melville J. Ruggles, *Soviet Libraries and Librarianship* (Chicago: American Library Association Press, 1962), a report on the visit of American librarians to the USSR in 1962; and Paul J. Horecky, *Libraries and Bibliographical Centers in the Soviet Union* (Bloomington: University of Indiana Press, 1959).

52. G. Fonotov, "The Libraries of the USSR During the Last 50 Years," *UNESCO Bulletin for Libraries* 21 (1967), 240.

53. Davidson, "Trends in Library Education" in Voigt and Harris, *Advances in Librarianship*; Magda Jobórú "Women Librarians and Documentalists in Hungary," *UNESCO Bulletin for Libraries* 29 (1975), 315-18.

54. Michael Paul Sachs, *Women's Work in Soviet Russia: Continuity in the Midst of Change* (New York: Praeger Publishers, 1976); G. M. Serebrennikov, *The Position of Women in the USSR* (Freeport, N.Y.: Books for Libraries Press, 1970); Norton T. Dodge, *Women in the Soviet Economy: Their Role in Economic, Scientific and Technical Development* (Baltimore: Johns Hopkins University Press, 1966).

55. Nicholas DeWitt, *Education and Professional Employment in the USSR* (Washington, D.C.: National Science Foundation, 1961), 529, 543, and 490-95.

56. Joan Acker, "Women and Social Stratification, A Case of Intellectual Sexism," *American Journal of Sociology* 78 (1973), 936-45; Harry Braverman, *Labor and*

Monopoly Capital (New York: Monthly Review Press, 1974), 392-94, 385-86; Martin Oppenheimer, "Women Office Workers: Petty-Bourgeoisie or New Proletarians?", *Social Scientist,* monthly journal of The Indian School of Social Sciences, Trivandrum, Kerala, nos. 40-41 (November-December 1975), 55-75; and Martha Blaxall and Barbara Reagan, eds., *Women and the Workplace: The Implications of Occupational Segregation* (Chicago: University of Chicago Press, 1976).

57. Richard B. Moses, "a library pome," in Celeste West and Elizabeth Katz, eds., *Revolting Librarians* (San Francisco: The Bootlegger Press, 1972).

58. Anita Schiller, "The Disadvantaged Majority: Women Employed in Libraries," *American Libraries* 1 (April 1970), 345-49.

59. Art Plotnik, "Sweet Library Lips," in West and Katz, *Revolting Librarians,* 10.

60. Pat Schuman, "Task Force Meets in Detroit," *LJ* 95 (1970), 2635.

61. Kathleen Weibel, "Toward a Feminist Profession," in Patricia G. Schuman, *Social Responsibilities and Libraries* (New York: R. R. Bowker, 1976), 85-95.

Selected Bibliography

Books

Abbott, Lyman, ed. *Hints for Home Reading*. New York: G. P. Putnam's Sons, 1892.

Atkinson, William. *On the Right Use of Books*. Boston: Roberts Brothers, 1880.

Baltzell, E. Digby. *The Protestant Establishment: Aristocracy and Caste in America*. New York: Random House, 1964.

Baxall, Martha, and Reagan, Barbara, eds. *Women and the Workplace: The Implications of Occupational Segregation*. Chicago: University of Chicago Press, 1976.

Berelson, Bernard. *The Library's Public*. New York: Columbia University Press, 1949.

Bledstein, Burton J. *The Culture of Professionalism: The Middle Class and the Development of Higher Education in America*. New York: W. W. Norton & Company, 1976.

Blodgett, Geoffrey. *Gentle Reformers: Massachusetts Democrats in Cleveland Era*. Cambridge, Mass.: Harvard University Press, 1960.

Bobinski, George S. *Carnegie Libraries: Their History and Impact on American Public Library Development*. Chicago: American Library Association, 1969.

Bolton, Charles K., ed. *The Influence and History of the Boston Athenaeum*. Boston: The Boston Athenaeum, 1907.

The Boston Athenaeum. *The Athenaeum Centenary*. Boston, 1907.

Bostwick, Arthur. *A Life with Men and Books*. New York: H. W. Wilson, 1939.

Boyer, Paul S. *Purity in Print: The Vice Society Movement and Book Censorship in America*. New York: Charles Scribner's Sons, 1968.

Bremner, Robert. *From the Depths: The Discovery of Poverty in the United States*. New York: New York University Press, 1956.

Brough, Kenneth J. *Scholar's Workshop: Evolving Conceptions of Library Service.* Urbana: University of Illinois Press, 1953.

Cady, Edwin. *The Gentleman in America: A Literary Study in American Culture.* Syracuse, N. Y.: Syracuse University Press, 1949.

Calhoun, Daniel. *Professional Lives in America, 1750–1850.* Cambridge, Mass.: Harvard University Press, 1965.

Calvert, Monte A. *The Mechanical Engineers in America, 1830–1910: Professional Cultures in Conflict.* Baltimore, Md.: Johns Hopkins University Press, 1967.

Carrier, Esther Jane. *Fiction in Public Libraries, 1876–1900.* New York: The Scarecrow Press, 1965.

Carroll, C. Edward. *The Professionalization of Education for Librarianship.* Metuchen, N. J.: The Scarecrow Press, 1970.

Carter, Paul A. *The Spiritual Crisis of the Gilded Age.* DeKalb: Northern Illinois University Press, 1971.

Chafe, William A. *The American Woman: Her Changing Social, Economic and Political Role, 1920–1970.* New York: Oxford University Press, 1972.

Chambers, Clarke A. *Seedtime of Reform: American Social Service and Social Action, 1918–1933.* Minneapolis: University of Minnesota Press, 1963.

Cremin, Lawrence. *The Transformation of the School: Progressivism in American Education, 1876–1957.* New York: Alfred A. Knopf, 1961.

Cutter, William Parker. *Charles Ammi Cutter.* Chicago: American Library Association, 1931.

Dain, Phyllis. *The New York Public Library: A History of Its Founding and Early Years.* New York: The New York Public Library, 1972.

Dana, John Cotton. *Libraries, Addresses and Essays.* New York: H. W. Wilson, 1916.

——. *Suggestions.* Boston: F. W. Faxon Company, 1921.

Danton, J. Perriam, ed. *The Climate of Book Selection.* Berkeley: University of California Press, 1959.

Davies, D. W. *Public Libraries as Culture and Social Centers: The Origin of the Concept.* Metuchen, N. J.: The Scarecrow Press, 1974.

Davis, Allen. *The American Heroine: The Life and Legend of Jane Addams.* New York: Oxford University Press, 1973.

Davis, Allen F. *Spearheads for Reform: The Social Settlements and the Progressive Movement, 1890–1914.* New York: Oxford University Press, 1967.

Dawe, Grosvenor. *Melvil Dewey: Seer, Inspirer, Doer 1851–1931.* Lake Placid, N. Y.: Lake Placid Club, 1932.

Ditzion, Sidney. *Arsenals of a Democratic Culture: A Social History of the American Public Library Movement in New England and the Middle Atlantic States from 1850 to 1900.* Chicago: American Library Association, 1947.

Douglas, Ann. *The Feminization of American Culture.* New York: Alfred A. Knopf, 1977.

Eliot, Charles William. *Educational Reform.* New York: The Century Company, 1909.

Elliott, Philip. *The Sociology of the Professions.* New York: Herder and Herder, 1972.

Etzioni, Amitai, ed. *The Semi-Professions and Their Organization: Teachers, Nurses, Social Workers*. New York: The Free Press, 1969.

Falk, Robert. *The Victorian Mode in American Fiction, 1865–1885*. East Lansing: Michigan State University Press, 1965.

Foster, William E. *The Civil Service Reform Movement*. Boston: George H. Ellis, 1882.

———. *Libraries and Readers*. New York: F. Leypoldt, 1883.

Frederickson, George. *The Inner Civil War*. New York: Harper and Row, 1965.

Furner, Mary O. *Advocacy and Objectivity: A Crisis in the Professionalization of American Social Science, 1865–1905*. Lexington: University Press of Kentucky, 1975.

Furness, Clifton Joseph, ed. *The Genteel Female*. New York: Alfred A. Knopf, 1931.

Galambos, Louis. *The Public Image of Big Business in America, 1880–1940*. Baltimore, Md.: Johns Hopkins University Press, 1975.

Gans, Herbert. *Popular Culture and High Culture*. New York: Basic Books, 1974.

Garceau, Oliver. *The Public Library in the Political Process*. New York: Columbia University Press, 1949.

Geertz, Clifford. "Ideology as a Cultural System." In *The Interpretation of Cultures*. London: Hutchinson and Company, 1975.

Green, Martin. *The Problem of Boston: Some Readings in Cultural History*. New York: W. W. Norton & Company, 1966.

Green, S. S. *Libraries and Schools*. New York: F. Leypoldt, 1883.

Green, Samuel S. *The Public Library Movement in the United States, 1852–1893*. Boston: The Boston Book Company, 1913.

Grotzinger, Laurel Ann. *The Power and the Dignity: Librarianship and Katherine Sharp*. Metuchen, N.J.: The Scarecrow Press, 1966.

Gusfield, Joseph. *Symbolic Crusade: Status Politics and the American Temperance Movement*. Urbana: University of Illinois Press, 1963.

Haber, Samuel. *Efficiency and Uplift: Scientific Management in the Progressive Era, 1890–1920*. Chicago: University of Chicago Press, 1964.

———. "The Professions and Higher Education in America: A Historical View." In Margaret S. Gordon, ed., *Higher Education and the Labor Market*. New York: McGraw-Hill, 1974.

Hart, James. *The Popular Book*. New York: Oxford University Press, 1950.

Hazeltine, Alice, ed. *Library Work with Children: Reprints of Papers and Addresses*. New York: H. W. Wilson, 1917.

Hill, Joseph A. *Women in Gainful Occupations 1870–1920*. Census Monograph 9. Washington, D. C.: Government Printing Office, 1929.

Holley, Edward G. *Raking the Historic Coals: The American Library Assocation Scrapbook of 1876*. Urbana: University of Illinois Press, 1967.

Howe, Daniel. *The Unitarian Conscience*. Cambridge, Mass.: Harvard University Press, 1970.

———. "Victorian Culture in America." In Daniel Howe, ed., *Victorian America*. Philadelphia: University of Pennsylvania Press, 1976.

Israel, Jerry, ed. *Building the Organization Society: Essays on Associational Activities in Modern America.* New York: The Free Press, 1972.

Jaher, Frederick Cople. "The Boston Brahmins in the Age of Industrial Capitalism." In Frederick Cople Jaher, ed., *The Age of Industrialism in America: Essays in Social Structure and Cultural Values.* New York: The Free Press, 1968.

Joeckel, Carleton. *The Government of the American Public Library.* Chicago: University of Chicago Press, 1939.

Kalisch, Philip A. *The Enoch Pratt Free Library: A Social History.* Metuchen, N.J.: The Scarecrow Press, 1969.

Katz, Michael. *The Irony of Early School Reform: Educational Innovation in Mid-Nineteenth Century Massachusetts.* Cambridge, Mass.: Harvard University Press, 1968.

Kelly, R. Gordon. *Mother Was a Lady: Self and Society in Selected American Children's Periodicals, 1865–1890.* Westport, Conn.: Greenwood Press, 1974.

Kett, Joseph F. *The Formation of the American Medical Profession: The Role of Institutions, 1780–1860.* New Haven, Conn.: Yale University Press, 1968.

Kingdon, Frank. *John Cotton Dana.* Newark, N. J.: The Public Library and Museum, 1940.

Koch, Theodore W. *Books in the War: The Romance of Library War Service.* Boston: Houghton Mifflin, 1919.

Kolko, Gabriel. *The Triumph of Conservatism: A Re-Interpretation of American History.* New York: The Free Press, 1963.

Larned, J. N. *Books, Culture and Character.* Boston: Houghton Mifflin, 1906.

——. *A Primer of Right and Wrong for Young People in Schools and Families.* Boston: Houghton Mifflin, 1902.

——. *A Talk About Books.* Buffalo, N. Y.: The Peter Paul University Press, 1921.

——. *Talks About Labor.* New York: D. Appleton and Company, 1876.

Layton, Edward T. *The Revolt of the Engineers: Social Responsibility and the American Engineering Profession.* Cleveland, Ohio: Case Western Reserve University Press, 1971.

Leigh, Robert D. *The Public Library in the United States.* New York: Columbia University Press, 1969.

Lemons, J. Stanley. *The Woman Citizen: Social Feminism in the 1920's.* Chicago: University of Illinois Press, 1973.

Long, Harriet G. *Public Library Service to Children: Foundation and Development.* Metuchen, N. J.: The Scarecrow Press, 1969.

Lubove, Roy. *The Professional Altruist: The Emergence of Social Work as a Career, 1880–1930.* Cambridge, Mass.: Harvard University Press, 1965.

Lynn, Kenneth S., ed. *The Professions in America.* Boston: Houghton Mifflin, 1965.

McFarland, Gerald W. *Mugwumps, Morals and Politics, 1884–1920.* Amherst: University of Massachusetts Press, 1975.

McLeod, David. *Carnegie Libraries in Wisconsin.* Madison, Wisc.: State Historical Society, 1968.

Mann, Arthur. *Yankee Reformers in the Urban Age: Social Reform in Boston, 1880–1900.* New York: Harper and Row, 1966.

May, Henry. *The End of American Innocence.* New York: Alfred A. Knopf, 1959.

Merritt, Ray. *Engineering in American Society, 1850–1875.* Lexington: University of Kentucky Press, 1969.

Meyer, D. H. "American Intellectuals and the Victorian Crisis of Faith." In Daniel Howe, ed., *Victorian America.* Philadelphia: University of Pennsylvania Press, 1976.

——. *The Instructed Conscience: The Shaping of the American National Ethic.* Philadelphia: University of Pennsylvania Press, 1972.

Mills, C. Wright. *White Collar.* New York: Oxford University Press, 1951.

Moore, Wilbert E. *The Professions: Roles and Rules.* New York: Russell Sage Foundation, 1970.

Mott, Frank Luther. *Golden Multitudes: The Story of Best Sellers in the United States.* New York: Macmillan and Company, 1947.

Oko, Dorothy Kuhn, and Downey, Bernard F. *Library Service to Labor.* New York: The Scarecrow Press, 1963.

O'Neill, William L. *Everyone Was Brave: The Rise and Fall of Feminism in America.* Chicago: Quadrangle Books, 1969.

Papashvily, Helen Waite. *All the Happy Endings.* New York: Harper and Row, 1956.

Pavalko, Ronald M. *Sociology of Occupations and Professions.* Itasca, Ill.: F. E. Peacock Publishers, 1971.

Perkins, Frederick B., ed. *The Best Reading.* New York: G. P. Putnam's Sons, 1887.

Persons, Stow. *The Decline of American Gentility.* New York: Columbia University Press, 1973.

Pivar, David. *Purity Crusade: Sexual Morality and Social Control, 1868–1890.* Westport, Conn.: Greenwood Press, 1973.

Porter, Noah. *Books and Reading: Or What Shall I Read and How Shall I Read It?* New York: Charles Scribner's Sons, 1882.

Power, Effie L. *Work with Children in Public Libraries.* Chicago: American Library Association, 1943.

Prentice, Ann E. *The Public Library Trustee.* Metuchen, N. J.: The Scarecrow Press, 1949.

Quincy, Josiah. *History of the Boston Athenaeum.* Cambridge, Mass.: Metcalf and Company, 1851.

Ranz, Jim. *The Printed Book Catalogue in American Libraries 1723–1900.* Chicago: American Library Association, 1964.

Reece, Ernest J. *The Curriculum in Library Schools.* New York: Columbia University Press, 1936.

Regan, Mary Jane. *Echoes From the Past.* Boston: Boston Athenaeum, 1927.

Richardson, Charles F. *The Choice of Books.* New York: Useful Knowledge Publishing Company, 1882.

Rider, Fremont. *Melvil Dewey.* Chicago: American Library Association, 1944.

Roseberry, Cecil R. *The New York State Library.* Albany: The New York State Library, 1970.

Sayers, Frances C. *Anne Carroll Moore.* New York: Atheneum, 1972.

Shaw, Robert Kendall. *Samuel Swett Green*. Chicago: American Library Association, 1926.

Shelton, Brenda K. *Reformers in Search of Yesterday: Buffalo in the 1890's*. Albany: State University of New York Press, 1976.

Shera, Jesse. *The Foundations of Education for Librarianship*. New York: Becker and Hayes, 1972.

——. *Foundations of the Public Library: The Origins of the Public Library Movement in New England, 1629–1855*. Chicago: University of Chicago Press, 1949.

Showalter, Elaine. A Literature of Their Own: British Women Novelists from Bronte to Lessing. Princeton, N. J.: Princeton University Press, 1977.

Solomon, Barbara M. *Ancestors and Immigrants: A Changing New England Tradition*. Cambridge, Mass.: Harvard University Press, 1956.

Spencer, Gladys. *The Chicago Public Library: Origins and Background*. Chicago: University of Chicago Press, 1943.

Sproat, John. *"The Best Men:" Liberal Reformers in the Gilded Age*. New York: Oxford University Press, 1969.

Tai, Tse-chien. *Professional Education for Librarianship*. New York: H. W. Wilson Company, 1925.

Theodore, Athena, ed. *The Professional Woman*. Cambridge, Mass.: Schenkman Publishing Company, 1971.

Thompson, C. Seymour. *Evolution of the American Public Library, 1653–1876*. Washington, D. C.: The Scarecrow Press, 1952.

Tomsich, John. *A Genteel Endeavor: American Culture and Politics in the Gilded Age*. Palo Alto, Cal.: Stanford University Press, 1971.

Trautman, Ray. *A History of the School of Library Service, Columbia University*. New York: Columbia University Press, 1954.

Tyack, David. *George Ticknor and the Boston Brahmins*. Cambridge, Mass.: Harvard University Press, 1967.

——. *The One Best System: A History of American Urban Education*. Cambridge, Mass.: Harvard University Press, 1974.

United States Bureau of Education. *Public Libraries in the United States of America: Their History, Condition and Management*. Special Report, Pt. 1. Washington, D.C.: U. S. Government Printing Office, 1876.

Vann, Sarah K. *The Williamson Reports: A Study*. Metuchen, N. J.: The Scarecrow Press, 1971.

Vollmer, Howard M., and Mills, Donald L., eds. *Professionalization*. Englewood Cliffs, N. J.: Prentice-Hall, 1966.

Wasserstrom, William. *Heiress of All the Ages: Sex and Sentiment in the Genteel Tradition*. Minneapolis: University of Minnesota Press, 1959.

Weinstein, James. *The Corporate Ideal in the Liberal State, 1900–1918*. Boston: Beacon Press, 1968.

Wellard, James Howard. *Book Selection: Its Principles and Practices*. London: Grafton and Company, 1937.

White, Carl M. *The Origins of the American Library School*. New York: The Scarecrow Press, 1961.

Whitehill, Walter Muir. *Boston Public Library: A Centennial History.* Cambridge, Mass.: Harvard University Press, 1956.

Wiebe, Robert. *The Search for Order, 1877–1920.* New York: Hill and Wang, 1967.

Williamson, Charles C. *Training for Library Service: A Report Prepared for the Carnegie Corporation of New York.* Boston: The Merrymount Press, 1923.

Williamson, William Landram. *William Frederick Poole and the Modern Library Movement.* New York: Columbia University Press, 1963.

Woodford, Frank B. *Parnassus on Main Street: A History of the Detroit Public Library.* Detroit: Mich.: Wayne State University Press, 1965.

Articles

Ahern, Mary E. "The Business Side of a Woman's Career as a Librarian." *Library Journal* 24 (1899): 60–62.

Ashurst, John. "On Taking Ourselves Too Seriously." *Library Journal* 26 (1901): 265–68.

Bean, Mary. "The Evil of Unlimited Freedom in the Use of Juvenile Literature." *Library Journal* 4 (1879): 341–43.

Becker, Howard S., and Vesey, Laurence. "The Development of Identification with an Occupation." *American Journal of Sociology* 61 (January 1956): 289–98.

Bostwick, Arthur. "The Public Library, the Public School and the Social Center Movement." *Proceedings and Addresses of the National Educational Association* (1912): 240–46.

Brett, William H. "The Present Problem." *Library Journal* 19 (1894): 5–9.

——. "The Relations of the Public Library to the Public Schools." *Proceedings of the National Education Association* (1892): 692.

Britton, Jasmine. "The Library's Share in Americanization." *Library Journal* 43 (1918): 723–27.

Brugh, Anne E., and Beede, Benjamin R. "American Librarianship." *Signs* 1 (1976): 943–56.

Bryson, Gladys. "The Emergence of The Social Sciences from Moral Philosophy." *International Journal of Ethics* 42 (April 1932): 304–23.

Carpenter, Frederick I. "The Genteel Tradition: A Reinterpretation." *New England Quarterly* 15 (1942): 427–43.

Chamberlain, Mellen. "Public Library and Public School." *Library Journal* 5 (1880): 299–302.

——. "Report on Fiction in Public Libraries." *Library Journal* 8 (1883): 208–10.

Cole, George Watson. "Fiction in Libraries: A Plea for the Masses." *Library Journal* 19 (1894): 18–21.

Conway, Jill. "Women Reformers and American Culture, 1870–1930." *Journal of Social History* 5 (Winter 1971–72): 164–77.

Corwin, Margaret Ann. "An Investigation of Female Leadership in Regional, State and Local Library Associations, 1876-1923." *Library Quarterly* 44 (April 1974): 133-44.

Crunden, F. M. "What of the Future?" *Library Journal* 21 (1896): 5-11.

Cutler, Mary S. "Home Libraries." *Library Journal* 19 (1894): 13-14.

———. "What a Woman Librarian Earns." *Library Journal* 18 (August 1892): 89-91.

Cutter, Charles. "The Buffalo Public Library in 1983: An Excursion in the Land of Dreams." *Library Journal* 8 (1883): 211-17.

———. "Common Sense in Libraries." *Library Journal* 14 (1889): 141-54.

———. "Pernicious Reading in Our Public Libraries." *Nation* 33 (November 10, 1881): 371.

———. "The Public Library and Its Choice of Books." *Library Journal* 3 (1878): 73.

———. "Should Libraries Buy Only the Best Books or the Best Books That People Will Read?" *Library Journal* 26 (1901): 70-72.

Dain, Phyllis. "Ambivalence and Paradox: The Social Bonds of the Public Library." *Library Journal* 100 (1975): 261-66.

Dana, John Cotton. "Hear the Other Side." *Library Journal* 21 (1896): 1-15.

———. "Public Libraries as Censors." *Bookman* 44 (1919): 147-52.

———. "Women in Library Work." *Independent* 71 (August 3, 1911): 244-50.

Dewey, Melvil. "The Ideal Librarian." *Library Journal* 24 (1899): 14.

———. "Librarianship as a Profession for College-Bred Women." Address before the Association of Collegiate Alumnae, March 13, 1886.

———. "The Profession." *Library Journal* 1 (1876): 5-6.

Ditzion, Sidney. "The Social Ideals of a Library Pioneer, Josephus Nelson Larned, 1863-1913." *Library Quarterly* 13 (1943): 113-31.

Eastman, Linda A. "Aims and Personal Attitude in Library Work." *Library Journal* 22 (1897): 80-81.

Ely, Mary. "Our Present Problem." *American Library Association Bulletin* 8 (1914): 219-23.

Esterquest, Ralph T. "War Attitudes of American Libraries, 1914-1918." *Wilson Library Bulletin* 15 (April 1941): 621-23.

Fain, Elaine. "Manners and Morals in the Public Library: A Glance at Some New History." *Journal of Library History* 10 (1975): 99-105.

Fairchild, Mary Salome Cutler. "Women in American Libraries." *Library Journal* 29 (December 1904): 157-62.

"Fiction in Libraries." *Library Journal* 15 (1890): 261-64.

Finkelman, Paul. "Class and Culture in Late Nineteenth-Century Chicago: The Founding of the Newberry Library." *American Studies* 16 (Spring 1975): 1-16.

Form, William H. "Popular Images of Librarians." *Library Journal* 71 (June 15, 1946): 851-55.

Foster, William E. "The School and the Library, Their Mutual Relation." *Library Journal* 4 (1879): 319-25.

———. "Where Ought the Emphasis to Be Placed in Library Purchases?" *Library Journal* 29 (1904): 229-37.

Garrison, Dee. "Cultural Custodians in the Gilded Age: The Public Librarian and Horatio Alger." *Journal of Library History* 6 (October 1971): 327-36.

——. "Rejoinder." *Journal of Library History* 10 (1973): 111-16.

Geller, Evelyn. "Intellectual Freedom: Eternal Principle or Unanticipated Consequence?" *Library Journal* 99 (1974): 1364-1367.

——. "The Librarian as Censor." *Library Journal* 101 (1976): 1255-1258.

Goodman, Paul. "Ethics and Enterprise: The Values of a Boston Elite, 1800-1860." *American Quarterly* 18 (Fall 1966): 437-51.

Graeff, Virginia. "The Gentle Librarian: A Transcript from Experience." *Library Journal* 30 (1905): 922-23.

Green, Samuel S. "Personal Relations Between Librarians and Readers." *Library Journal* 1 (1876): 74-81.

——. "Sensational Fiction in Public Libraries." *Library Journal* 4 (1879): 344-55.

Grotzinger, Laurel Ann. "The Proto-Feminist Librarian at the Turn of the Century: Two Studies." *Journal of Library History* 10 (1975): 195-213.

Gusfield, Joseph. "Moral Passage: The Symbolic Process in Public Designation of Deviance." *Social Problems* 15 (1967): 187.

Hall, G. Stanley. "What Children Do Read and What They Ought to Read." *Public Libraries* 10 (1905): 391-93.

Harbourne, John. "The Guileless West on 'Weeding Out.' " *Library Journal* 22 (1897): 251-52.

Harris, Michael H. "Externalist or Internalist Frameworks for the Interpretation of American Library History—The Continuing Choice." *Journal of Library History* 10 (1973): 106-10.

——. "Portrait in Paradox: Commitment and Ambivalence in American Librarianship, 1876-1976." *Libri* 26 (1976): 281-301.

——. "The Purpose of the American Public Library: A Revisionist Interpretation." *Library Journal* 98 (1973): 2509-2514.

Harris, Michael H., and Spiegler, Gerard. "Everett, Ticknor and the Common Man: The Fear of Societal Instability as the Motivation for the Founding of the Boston Public Library." *Libri* 24 (1974): 249-75.

Harris, Neil. "The Gilded Age Revisited: Boston and the Museum Movement." *American Quarterly* 14 (Winter 1962): 545-66.

Harris, William T. "The Function of the Library and the School in Education." *Library Journal* 15 (1890): 27-33.

Hasse, Adelaide, R. "Women in Libraries." *Journal of the Association of Collegiate Alumnae.* Cited in *Library Journal* 43 (1918): 141-42.

Hayward, Celia A. "Woman as Cataloguer." *Public Libraries* 3 (1898): 121-23.

Hewins, Caroline M. "Library Work for Women." *Library Journal* 16 (1891): 273-74.

Hofstadter, Beatrice. "Popular Culture and the Romantic Heroine." *American Scholar* 30 (Winter 1960-61): 98-116.

Holley, Edward G. "The Past as Prologue: The Work of the Library Historian." *Journal of Library History* 12 (1977): 110-27.

Hosmer, James K. "Some Things That Are Uppermost." *Library Journal* 28 (1903): 1-8.

Isom, Mary Frances. "The Library a Civic Center." *Public Libraries* 19 (1914): 93-96.

Jaher, Frederick Cople. "Nineteenth Century Elites in Boston and New York." *Journal of Social History* 6 (1972): 32-77.

James, M. S. R. "American Women as Librarians." *The Library* 5 (1893): 270-74.

Jenkins, F. W. "The Social Worker and the Library." *Library Journal* 36 (1911): 499-500.

Katz, Michael. "The 'New Departure' in Quincy, 1873-1881: The Nature of Nineteenth-Century Educational Reform." *New England Quarterly* 40 (March 1967): 3-20.

Kelso, Tessa. "Some Economic Features of Public Libraries." *Arena* 7 (1893): 711.

Larned, J. N. "The Mission and the Missionaries of the Book." Address before the 1896 Convocation of New York educators. In *Regent's Report* (1896): 90-103.

———. "Public Libraries and Public Education." *Library Journal* 9 (1884): 6-12.

Leigh, Robert, and Sewny, Kathryn W. "The Popular Image of the Library and of Librarians." *Library Journal* 85 (1960): 2089-2091.

"The Library as a Social Centre." *Public Libraries* (1916): 315-16.

Lord, Isabel Ely. "Open Shelves and Public Morals." *Library Journal* 26 (1901): 65-70.

Macmillan, Mary. "The Relation of Librarian and Assistants." *Library Journal* 28 (1903): 717-18.

Miksa, Francis. "The Making of the 1876 Special Report on Public Libraries." *Journal of Library History* 9 (1973): 30-40.

Milden, James W. "Woman, Public Libraries, and Library Unions: The Formative Years." *Journal of Library History* 12 (1977): 150-58.

Newmeyer, Judy. "The Image Problem of the Librarian: Femininty and Social Control." *Journal of Library History* 11 (1976): 44-67.

Olle, J. F. "Andrew Carnegie, the 'Unbeloved Benefactor.' " *Library World* 70 (1969): 255-62.

Plummer, Mary W. "The Public Library and the Pursuit of Truth." *Library Journal* 41 (1916): 537-41.

Poole, William. "Being a Librarian." *Library Journal* 15 (July 1890): 202.

———. "Some Popular Objections to Public Libraries." *Library Journal* 1 (1876): 47-51.

Putnam, Herbert. "Per Contra." *Library Journal* 40 (1915): 471-76.

———. "The Prospect." *Library Journal* 37 (1912): 651-58.

———. "The Woman in the Library." *Library Journal* 41 (1916): 879-80.

Rockwell, Anna Garland. "Fiction Again: Where Shall We Draw the Line of Exclusion?" *Public Libraries* 8 (1903): 307-13.

Rousmaniere, John P. "Cultural Hybrid in the Slums: The College Woman and the Settlement House, 1889-1894." *American Quarterly* 22 (Spring 1970): 45-66.

Sanders, Minerva. "Report on Reading for the Young." *Library Journal* 15 (1890): 58-64.

Santangelo, G. A. "Toward a Definition of Victorianism." *Dalhousie Review* 45 (1965): 256-67).

Schiller, Anita R. "The Disadvantaged Majority: Women Employed in Libraries." *American Libraries* 4 (April 1970): 345-49.

Smith, Lloyd P. "The Qualifications for a Librarian." *Library Journal* 1 (1876): 69-74.

Stewart, Cora. "Libraries in Relation to Settlement Work." *Library Journal* 31 (1906): 82-85.

Story, Ronald. "Class and Culture in Boston: The Athenaeum, 1807-1860." *American Quarterly* 27 (May 1975): 178-99.

Swift, Lindsay. "Paternalism in Public Libraries." *Library Journal* 24 (1899): 609-18.

Underhill, Ethel P. "Crumbs of Comfort to the Children's Librarian." *Library Journal* 35 (1910): 155-57.

Walter, Frank W. "The War and Library Training." *Library Journal* 43 (1918): 728-32.

Wasserstrom, William. "The Genteel Tradition and the Antipodes of Love." *Journal of English Literary History* 23 (1956): 299-316.

Weigley, Emma S. "It Might Have Been Euthenics: The Lake Placid Conference and the Home Economics Movement." *American Quarterly* 26 (March 1974): 79-98.

Wein, Roberta. "Women's Colleges and Domesticity, 1875-1918." *History of Education Quarterly* 14 (1974): 31-49.

Wellman, Hiller C. "Presidential Address." *Library Journal* 40 (1915): 467-71.

White, Elizabeth. "Reaching Parents Through the Children." *Library Journal* 42 (1917): 522-23.

Wiebe, Robert. "The Social Functions of Public Education." *American Quarterly* 21 (Summer 1969): 147-65.

Wyer, James I. "Outside the Walls." *Library Journal* 36 (1911): 172-78.

Young, Arthur P. "Reception of the 1876 Report on Public Libraries." *Journal of Library History* 12 (1977): 50-56.

Index

J. M. HODGES LEARNING CENTER
WHARTON COUNTY JUNIOR COLLEGE
WHARTON, TEXAS 77488

59541